# Complicity

We live in a morally flawed world. Our lives are complicated by what other people do, and by the harms that flow from our social, economic, and political institutions. Our relations as individuals to these collective harms constitute the domain of complicity. This book examines the relationship between collective action and individual accountability. It presents a rigorous philosophical account of the nature of our relations to the social groups in which we participate, and uses that account in a discussion of contemporary moral and legal theory.

Christopher Kutz shows that the two dominant theories of moral philosophy, Kantianism and consequentialism, both have difficulties resolving problems of complicity. He then argues for a richer theory of accountability in which any real understanding of collective action not only allows but demands individual responsibility.

Grounded in philosophical analysis and examples from literature, history, and law, this book provides an ethics of collective action that reattaches individuals to their collective deeds, while accommodating differences in choice, power, and psychology. It should be of interest to students of philosophy, political theory, and law, especially those interested in the problem of retaining accountability in times of social consolidation.

Christopher Kutz is Assistant Professor of Law in the Jurisprudence and Social Policy Program, Boalt Hall School of Law, University of California at Berkeley.

# Cambridge Studies in Philosophy and Law

*Other books in the series:*

# Complicity

## Ethics and Law for a Collective Age

CHRISTOPHER KUTZ

*University of California at Berkeley*

PUBLISHED BY THE PRESS SYNDICATE OF THE UNIVERSITY OF CAMBRIDGE
The Pitt Building, Trumpington Street, Cambridge, United Kingdom

CAMBRIDGE UNIVERSITY PRESS
The Edinburgh Building, Cambridge CB2 2RU, UK   http://www.cup.cam.ac.uk
40 West 20th Street, New York, NY 10011-4211, USA   http://www.cup.org
10 Stamford Road, Oakleigh, Melbourne 3166, Australia
Ruiz de Alarcón 13, 28014 Madrid, Spain

First published 2000

Printed in the United States of America

*Typeface* Palatino 10/13 pt.     *System* MagnaType™ [AG]

*A catalog record for this book is available from the British Library.*

Library of Congress Cataloging in Publication Data
Kutz, Christopher.
Complicity : ethics and law for a collective age / Christopher Kutz.
p.   cm. – (Cambridge studies in philosophy and law)
Originally presented as the author's thesis (doctoral) – University of California,
Berkeley.
Includes bibliographical references.
ISBN 0-521-59452-9 (hb)
1. Law and ethics. 2. Guilt (Law) 3. Responsibility. 4. Collectivism. I. Title. II. Series.
K247.6.K88 2000
340'.112 – dc21        99-057892

ISBN 0 521 59452 9 hardback

*For my mother*

# Contents

# Contents

# Acknowledgments

This book began its life as a doctoral dissertation, and so is itself a project both individual and collective. I am grateful to the members of my graduate advisory committee, Samuel Scheffler, Bernard Williams, Kwong-loi Shun, and Jeremy Waldron, for their keen and generous guidance. Sam Scheffler was an ideal advisor and model of a professional philosopher, unstinting in patience, constructive criticism, and inspiration.

The Department of Philosophy at Berkeley provided an extremely happy environment during my graduate education, both institutionally and personally. Steve Arkonovich, Donald Davidson, Stephen Neale, and John Searle all read and commented upon parts of this book. I am especially grateful to Michael Green, who read most of the manuscript, for his insight and encouragement. My teachers at Yale Law School were kind in harboring a student whose interests ran more to theory than doctrine. I especially thank Jules Coleman and Owen Fiss for offering me their wisdom and mentorship.

I am wealthy in philosophically minded colleagues at Boalt Hall in general, and in the Jurisprudence and Social Policy Program in particular. I have drawn deeply on their counsel, friendship, and criticism. I thank Robert Cooter, Meir Dan-Cohen, Lauren Edelman, Andrew Guzmán, Sanford Kadish, David Lieberman, and Eric Rakowski, who have saved my discussion from many errors, doctrinal, practical, and philosophical. Michael Bratman and Derek Parfit have set another model for me, both in their own work and in the generosity they displayed toward an unknown student who applied to them for their responses. Peter Levine's thoughtful comments have improved Chapter 2. I am also grateful to David Franklin, Mark

Kingwell, Martin Putnam, Seana Shiffrin, and Kevin Stack for many important discussions. Anonymous referees for Cambridge University Press and *Philosophy and Phenomenological Research* provided exemplary readings, both probing and constructive. Mark Antaki provided crucial help with the index and proofs.

Ruth Kutz has been constantly generous in her support and encouragement, as have Robert Kutz, Daniel Greenberg, Pat Salt, Myra Jehlen, and Carl Riskin. Jessica Riskin has been my most uncompromising critic, felicitous editor, and inspiring interlocutor.

The Charlotte W. Newcombe Foundation provided crucial support during the writing of the dissertation as did the University of California Regents.

Christopher Kutz
Berkeley, California

Material from the following previously published article is incorporated within: Christopher Kutz. "Acting Together," *Philosophy and Phenomenological Research* (July 2000).

# Chapter 1

# Introduction

## 1.1

We live in a morally flawed world, one full of regrets and reproaches. Some of the things we regret, or for which we are reproached, we bring about intentionally and on our own. But our lives are increasingly complicated by regrettable things brought about through our associations with other people or with the social, economic, and political institutions in which we live our lives and make our livings. Try as we might to live well, we find ourselves connected to harms and wrongs, albeit by relations that fall outside the paradigm of individual, intentional wrongdoing. Here are some examples: buying a table made of tropical wood that comes from a defoliated rain forest, or owning stock in a company that does business in a country that jails political dissenters; being a citizen of a nation that bombs another country's factories in a reckless attack on terrorists, or inhabiting a region seized long ago from its aboriginal occupants; helping to design an automobile the manufacturer knowingly sells with a dangerously defective fuel system, or administering a national health care bureaucracy that carelessly allows the distribution of HIV-contaminated blood. Although in each of these cases we stand outside the shadow of evil, we still do not find the full light of the good. Even individual acts of violence are characterized by a whole spectrum of relations between agents and harms, doers and deeds. Consider the burglar whose partner violates the understanding that there will be no violence during a robbery, or the members of a military firing squad, each eased in his conscience by the knowledge

1

that one of them – it could be any – has been distributed a blank cartridge.

It is an undeniable feature of our social life that people have a host of morally significant reactions when they stand in such mediated relations to harms – reactions ranging from discomfort to regret to guilt – and that they are judged by victims and onlookers. They are also often punished or compelled to make restitution and repair. These cultural and legal practices, surrounding relations of an agent to a harm that are mediated by other agents, comprise the domain of *complicity.*

Moral philosophers have tended to avoid the problem of collective wrongdoing, a tendency reflected in the origins of philosophical ethics. Aristotle, for example, when discussing the concept of the "voluntary," gave the example of someone ordered by a tyrant to do something shameful, lest harm come to his family.[1] On its face, this is a case of forced collaboration, in which an essential feature is that the plan to do wrong originates with one person, and is completed by another. But Aristotle ignores this relational feature, in effect reducing the problem of shared responsibility to the purely individualistic question of whether the threat was grave enough to defeat any element of choice. If the threats were more than human fabric can bear (at least relative to the badness of the crime demanded) then we cannot say the agent has acted voluntarily; and so, on Aristotle's account, there is no question of imputing shame to the person.[2] Responsibility appears wholly a function of individual choice.

Immanuel Kant likewise reduced cases of apparently collective responsibility to questions of individual choice and action. Kant infamously claimed that it would be wrong even to lie to a murderer who asks whether your friend has taken refuge in your house.[3] Kant transforms the example into a case of complicity when he argues that if, intending to deceive the murderer, you said your friend "was not at home when he had really gone out without your knowing it, and if the murderer had then met him as he went away and murdered him, you might justly be accused as the cause of his death." By contrast, "if you have held rigorously to the truth, public justice can lay no hand on you, whatever the unforeseen consequences may be."[4] His reason for this surprising conclusion is that by lying, but not by telling the truth, you make the murderer into an instrument of your will, and so assume responsibility for the harms arising from that instrument. Now Kant may well have mistaken the implications of his own theory;[5] but the essential point for our purposes is to notice that, like Aristotle, Kant answers the question of responsibility purely in terms of facts about you, in this case what you intended and what you caused, and without regard to the aims and acts of the murderer. A virtuous will, in Kant's view, seems to insulate from responsibility, while only a vicious will implicates. What Primo Levi called "the gray zone" of collaboration with evil is artificially transformed into the sharp light of duty and the darkness of its violation.[6]

1.2

Recognizing complicity and its uncertain terrain poses problems not just for those who are (as Aristotle said in another context) "maintaining a thesis at all costs."[7] The responses called for by complicitous relations to harm and wrong also seem to conflict with a set of principles of commonsense morality and moral psychology that limn our common, nonphilosophical understanding of individual accountability. Call these the *Individual Difference, Control,* and *Autonomy Principles.* The Individual Difference Principle holds that I am only accountable for a harm if something I did made a difference to its occurrence.[8] If substantially the same harm would have occurred regardless of what I have done, I cannot be accountable for it. The Control Principle holds that I am only accountable for events over which I have control, and whose occurrence I could have prevented.[9] Finally, the Autonomy Principle holds that I am not accountable for the harm another agent causes, unless I have induced or coerced that agent into performing an act.[10] At work implicitly in our norms and practices of inculpation, these principles reveal themselves most openly in our pleas for excuse. We may repeat mischievous gossip with the thought that it's going around anyway, or dissociate ourselves emotionally from the policies of our institutions when we do not occupy administrative positions, or regard a customer's informed, voluntary purchase of a dangerous product as exculpating the seller from untoward consequences. These principles may or may not be well applied in such instances; but they are a standard, regulative element of our ethical practices of allocating responsibility.

Together, these principles of accountability define an individualistic conception of moral agency. This conception of accountability is individualistic in three respects: its *subject* is an individual moral agent; the *object* of accountability, or the harm or wrong for which the subject is reproached, is ascribable to that subject alone; and the *basis* of accountability, or the grounds for holding the subject accountable, consists primarily in facts about that subject, such as the subject's causal contributions or the content of the subject's intentions. Paradigmatically, individual moral agents are reproached, or reproach themselves, for harms ascribable to them and them alone, on the basis of their intentional actions and causal contributions.

The individualism of this understanding of the subject of accountability is deeply rooted in modern consciousness. It owes much, clearly, to Protestant theologies and Kantian moral theories, but it is not the product of a moral theory or doctrinal theology. Rather, this conception is an expression of the social and economic transformations that have made the conviction, in Emerson's words, "that imitation is suicide; that [each] must take himself for better, for worse, as his portion," a primary element in our cultural self-understanding.[11] The Autonomy Principle expresses the primacy of the individual subject.[12]

The other two aspects of this conception of moral agency, the individualistic object and basis of accountability, reflect a commitment to what I call *evaluative solipsism*.[13] This evaluative solipsism has two elements, *relational* and *causal*. Evaluation is relationally solipsistic in the sense that questions of accountability are resolved without reference to the nature of the agent's relations to particular others, whether fellow actors, victims, or bystanders. Rather, individuals are evaluated exclusively according to the content and effects of their wills, and the relation of that content and those effects to highly general normative standards. Considerations of what others do, or of how they may be warranted in responding to what the agent does, play no role in the evaluation. Kant's discussion of lying to the murderer was solipsistic in this sense: The special relation of trust between you and your friend, and of opportunism between the murderer and you, made no difference to the permissibility of your lie. Such a conception of accountability is essentially retributivist or desert-based: its primary question is what treatment the agent deserves in virtue of what that agent has done, rather than how others ought to respond to the agent's actions.[14]

The causally solipsistic element consists in the presumption that the object of evaluation is solely what an individual has caused or meant to cause, as captured by the Individual Difference Principle.[15] States of affairs to which an individual has made no significant contribution lie outside the bounds of assessment.[16] Thus, causal relations that depend upon sets of individual acts, but upon no particular individual act, fall outside the bounds of individual normative evaluation as well. This aspect of the individualistic conception is strongly supported phenomenologically: our sense of ourselves as agents emerges from the experience of making changes in our environment.[17] The distinctive contribution of causal solipsism is to translate this point about the experience of action into the sole basis of normative evaluation.

It should be clear how the relational and causal solipsism of the individualistic conception tends to preclude moral accountability based upon complicity. As I said, this is a problem for moral philosophers, whose theories of moral evaluation make little conceptual room for the socially pervasive claims of complicitous participation in wrong. But this theoretical problem also carries with it a set of practical problems. Practices of accountability comprise a system for protecting and maintaining social interests, and these underlying interests are routinely violated so long as the accountability system remains solipsistic. These violations are frequently the products of what can be called *I-We problems*, in which I participate in a harm caused by something we do, but am not personally accountable for that harm, because of the insignificance of my contribution. The individualistic conception drives a wedge between me and us, between private and public. Since individuals are only accountable for local effects, responses aimed at individuals are inappropriate. But since there is also no legitimate moral subject corresponding to the *we*, responses to collective harms find no proper target.

We face two general sorts of I-We problems in modern life. The first concerns the accountability of persons within structured groups, such as business groups, government bureaucracies, political organizations, and criminal conspiracies. Individual members of such groups often do bad things on behalf of their groups, and members with special responsibilities are sometimes called to account for what they have done. Sometimes the group or organization as a whole is also held accountable: Corporations are fined, governments make reparations, and so on. The trouble is that these forms of collective or ministerial accountability fail to provide the kind of individual motivational considerations necessary to prevent such harms from occurring in the first place. Particular culpable agents who regard a group as primarily accountable for what they do and who inhabit a microculture of covert support consider being held accountable as an incidental cost attached to their institutional role, rather than as a warranted response addressed to them personally.[18] Moreover, these willing scapegoats displace the individual ethical concerns of the other members of the group, each of whom can now regard responsibility as discharged collectively. The burden of constraining individual actors from doing wrong is thus shifted from the ordinary (and crucially effective) basis of social and moral norms applicable to all, to the coercive threats of civil liability and criminal punishment applicable to only a few, threats whose marginal costs rational agents must discount by the extreme improbability of their realization. Nor can this problem be solved simply by aggravating the severity of legal sanctions, for very severe individual punishments for collective harms are often thought unfair just because they are inconsistent with individualistic principles of accountability.

The second form of I-We problem concerns unstructured collectives: relations among large and uncoordinated sets of individuals. This is the familiar class of "public goods" (and "public bads") problems. Grave harms occur because of what large numbers of people do or fail to do. Say that the use of some widely available and cheap refrigerant causes a hole to develop in the ozone layer, and this hole causes increases in skin cancer among northern Australians. People individually do little to foster this outcome and can do nothing to prevent it. But people collectively bring it about and could have averted it. If what I do doesn't make a difference (or makes no perceptible difference) to what we bring about together, then I can't be accountable for what we have done, and so I have no reason to attempt repair or prevention.

Thus, the problem with relational and causal solipsism is that they make the individual's role in collective agency disappear. It is true

6

that from the first-personal perspective of the individual agent these restrictions on accountability are compelling, inasmuch as individuals identify with what they alone bring about. From the agent's perspective, there is no *we*, but only aggregates of *I's*. However, from the perspective of those affected by a harm, the harm itself is salient, and a collective agency made up of individual members often easily identifiable. If a system of accountability is to afford us some protection from the serious harms we can so easily bring about together, it must therefore move beyond the first-personal perspective implicit in the individualistic conception, in order to accommodate the perspectives of all the parties to the harm. The problem of how to combine these perspectives, and not merely to suppress some, is the task of this book.

### 1.3

So I-We problems are soluble – but not within the terms of the individualistic conception. A possible route to a solution would be to seek to overcome the individual subject of accountability, to substitute a *we* for the *I*; this is the path of communitarianism. But, quite apart from the difficulties (and dangers) of trying to forge a strong sense of social unity in modern circumstances of limited cooperation among radically differing individuals, a conceptual divergence between we and I is inevitable at the level of agency. Because individuals are the ultimate loci of normative motivation and deliberation, only forms of accountability aimed at and sensitive to what individuals do can succeed in controlling the emergence of collective harms. The oughts of morality and politics must apply to *me*. The trick lies, then, not in modifying the fundamental bearer of accountability, but in expanding the scope of individual accountability by including an assessment of what an individual does with others.

How to include such an assessment? The two most prominent theoretical elaborations of accountability, Kantian and consequentialist, help little in comprehending the terrain of complicity. For the Kantian, causal solipsism, which also characterizes the deliberative framework of the Categorical Imperative (CI) test procedure, poses an immediate problem. Kantians' central question is whether they might successfully act on their maxims in a world in which everyone does likewise. But cases of overdetermination of a harm, or marginal contribution to it – in other words, the possible insignificance of an individual's participation – generate notorious difficulties for the procedure. The CI test works when an individual's maxim can be realized only when it is exceptional, not when it, on the contrary, owes its success to the fact that others act in precisely the same way.[19] Relational solipsism also poses a problem for Kantians: their exclusive focus on the content of the will as the object of moral evaluation creates problems when agents' maxims link them to the projects of other agents, so expanding the scope of their wills. How are Kantians to include such interpersonal projects without presupposing a collective agent whose unified maxims are subjected to the CI test?

Consequentialism, meanwhile, permits any form of accountability that maximizes aggregate welfare, including individual accountability for collective harm. But such flexibility is a dubious advantage, since it means that accountability for collective harms, like all forms of accountability under consequentialism, is conceived of purely instrumentally, in relation to maximal welfare. This instrumental conception fails to make sense of the special nature of associative wrongdoing. In order for moral agents to be genuinely motivated by responses of accountability, they must understand and acknowledge the basis of those responses. This demand can only be satisfied by a response of accountability that is grounded in an explanation of the wrongness of participating in a collectively harmful act. A purely contingent, instrumental basis for reproach will always be, in a deep sense, alien to a moral agent's self-understanding.

Thus, solving the I-We problems requires more than simply tailoring our received stock of moral precepts or moral theories to the particular case of collective action. Rather, we must dig deeper, in order to understand and then to change the underlying conception of agency that structures our accountability system. Such a project is potentially caught between the perils of utopianism, on the one hand, and conservatism, on the other. It risks utopianism by erecting an idealized self whose concern for the group is not anchored by a sense of its own distinctive identity within that group.[20] This is a recipe for inaction, not collective action. Meanwhile, it risks conservatism, because the conception of individual agency it reveals is inevitably already informed by our normative sensibilities, and so may offer us a starting point too close to the conclusions we seek to avoid. Given the already narrow space in moral and political philosophy between truism and absurdity, our argumentative path is tightly constrained.

Despite these constraints, there is reason for hope. The possibility of success is warranted not by the cleverness of theory but by the very tangle and intricacy of our normative practices and our social lives. Both our normative practices and our routinely exercised capacities for collective action contain material sufficiently critical to ground an expanded conception of the object of accountability. Samuel Scheffler has recently written that, in a world of essentially supra-individual processes and harms, the moral philosopher's task is to provide a theory with "a set of clear, action-guiding, and psychologically feasible principles which would enable individuals to orient themselves in relation to the larger processes, and general conformity to which would serve to regulate those processes and their effects in a morally satisfactory way."[21] Similarly, Gerald Postema has argued that moral theory in general and consequentialism in particular must reorient themselves around what he calls a "plural deliberative perspective."[22] Such a perspective would, among other things, allow us to see that something's being a collective responsibility does not entail that it is *not* an individual responsibility, but that it is therefore an individual responsibility, at least of the individuals who compose the collective.[23] This book's task is to develop such a perspective and to give it a philosophical foundation. I want to make our individualistic ethical concepts at home in a collective world.

To do this, I will try to show how conceptions of collective action and of individual responsibility both rely on a common notion of *participation*. My strategy accordingly has two components. First, I will try to expose the structural and substantive complexity of our practices of individual accountability. Both moral theorists and common sense often miss this complexity, generalizing the simple, retributivist picture of the agent who scrutinizes in his conscience the motives underlying his act. But an accurate picture of the social practices of accountability cannot be drawn from one perspective. Rather, an accurate picture must register the views of all participants in transactions surrounding a harm. The meaning and consequences of what someone did and the response thereby warranted are a function of the perspective (or position) of the respondent and of the relations between the parties. In particular, the saliency of intention, consequence, and character vary with the parties' relations and positions, although in no direct way. It is not always the case, for example, that victims care about consequences while actors care about intentions. I call this conception of accountability a "relational and positional" conception; and I take this portion of my argument to be primarily descriptive, not revisionary, although it does call for revision to traditional conceptions of accountability. I believe it forces us to discard a picture of accountability that sees judgments of accountability as external outputs, or verdicts, of a process of moral evaluation, which are then used as premises in a separate process of justifying liability. Rather, judgments of accountability (and the further responses, attitudes, and demands they support) are elements of a unified, dynamic system of social life, themselves constitutive of the goods and relations they protect.

The differences between the individualistic conception and a relational and positional conception are subtle but important. First, we can use them to understand the nuanced responses that reveal themselves when we attend to complicated cases, responses that include elements of accountability without necessarily being simple responses of guilt, anger, or shame. Take, for example, the sense of moral uneasiness many feel when by mere luck of birthright they find themselves occupying privileged positions in unjust political or economic orders. This sense is inchoate, and the specific responses agents think it entails will often be poorly defined. But it is a real form of accountability, generating sentiments and motives that resonate throughout one's social and political relations. Since such attenuated relations to harm and wrong characterize much of the terrain of complicity, it should be obvious why we need a nuanced account of the nature of accountability.

Tying accountability conceptually to warranted responses has some further virtues. Put roughly, on the one hand, the community may be better protected against the individual. On the other, the individual may be better protected against the community. By shifting from the agent's perspective to the respondents', harmful collective relations among individual agents can assume a normative significance otherwise lost from view. Since desert, individually conceived, is no longer a necessary element in the justification of others' responses, restrictions on accountability imposed by desert no longer obtain. Thus, the harms to the community in which individual agents play systemic roles become salient features to which the individual must respond, prospectively and retrospectively. However, because individual desert is also no longer sufficient to warrant responses, individuals are also protected from the community they affect. An individual may deserve a nasty fate without any respondent being warranted in bringing that fate about.

But a conception of accountability is not just a set of responses to wrongful intentions, harmful consequences, and dangerous dispositions. It also includes a theory of agency that rationally relates those elements to one another, so that, for example, consequences can be seen as the product of intention and thus ascribable to an agent, or as otherwise reflecting underlying behavioral dispositions. Thus, the second crucial step in my argument is providing a theory of agency that explains our capacity for collective action, both in its weakly coordinated and fully cooperative forms. Philosophers studying collective action have tended to focus only on the fully cooperative form, the string quartet paradigm. Such examples inevitably generate a conception of collective action thick with mutual obligations and egalitarian dispositions: an account unsuited to the depersonalized, hierarchic, bureaucratic, but nonetheless collective institutions that characterize modern life. I offer instead a minimalist analysis of collective action, weak enough to cover cases ranging from scenes of coordination at a traffic intersection to the carefully planned group bank robbery, but deep enough to reveal the structure of individual intentions that make such collective action possible. This I call the *participatory conception* of collective action, for its centerpiece is a distinctive, individual, instrumental intention to play one's part in a joint act. The act's content therefore makes ineliminable reference to the concept of collective action.

Taken together, a nuanced conception of accountability and a theory of collective action provide what we need to understand how coordination and cooperation give rise to complicitous accountability: individual, intentional participation in a collective act warrants individual accountability for the consequences of that act. The specific form of accountability warranted – when grief or repair, when

11

resentment or forgiveness – will, of course, be a function of the particular social, causal, and intentional relations between individuals and harms; but some response will be warranted. This conclusion is grounded descriptively, in both an interpretation of moral practice and in an account of intentional participation. Nonetheless, it requires rethinking the commonsense principles of accountability. The difference I make fades when viewed against the difference we make; the primary force of the Control Principle, likewise, bears now on our collective plans and capacities. And the Autonomy Principle, which makes me not my brother's keeper, simply fails to hold in contexts of cooperation. When revised, these principles make room for a conception of accountability robust enough to treat the problems of modern consolidation, yet sensitive enough to individual circumstance to remain psychologically feasible. The second half of this book is devoted to showing how a participatory conception of accountability provides a basis for allocating responsibility in exemplary moral and legal contexts of cooperation: through market exchange, such as when dangerous goods are sold; through bureaucratic or corporate organization; through criminal enterprise; and even in the most difficult case, of unstructured, parallel individual action. In this last instance I suggest that we can see these parallel individual acts as occurring within a social context that must itself be understood as cooperative. Thus, my participatory account can be extended to unstructured harms.

### 1.4

Let me offer an explicit word about my method. My argument belongs to no specific philosophical tradition, although it has affinities with all the major traditions. It is both roughly consequentialist in its instrumental focus on protecting and promoting antecedent interests, and roughly Kantian in its focus on what individuals mean about their conceptions of themselves and others as moral agents, shown by how they act and what they do, jointly and severally. And my attention to questions of character and disposition, and the expressive dimension of ethical life, has obvious Aristotelian overtones. Mainly, however, my argument proceeds not from a general theory to particulars, but rather from an interpretation of our actual social, ethical, and legal practices to a philosophical conception that explains, justifies, and criticizes those practices. Thus I will frequently make claims about what people say, feel, or do in specific circumstances. Sometimes I will substantiate my claims by drawing upon fiction and memoir. The epistemological authority of writers may be no greater than that of professional philosophers; but, as Bernard Williams has remarked, the result of substituting the philosopher's imagined examples for those drawn from literature "will not be life, but bad literature."[24] It is true that the attempt to draw argumentative support from literature comes up hard against the resistance of imaginative writing to the extraction of a single thesis or interpretation. But the very refractory nature of literature makes it well suited to ethical study. For the problem of extracting interpretation from literature is similar to the problem of assigning moral or legal responsibility in life. Both seek to reduce particularity to a procrustean set of categories of meaning and motive.

Interpretive, or "practice-based" normative theories have become increasingly prominent in the philosophical literature, though they harken back to Aristotle.[25] Such approaches raise familiar but important concerns. I referred already to the worry that the aim of eliciting a conception of agency presupposed by our practices is inherently too conservative for a project with revisionary ambitions. Apart from the worry about conservatism, interpretivism might also be thought to imply ethical relativism, understood as the thesis that the truth of normative judgments depends entirely upon culturally circumscribed beliefs and practices. Clearly, the social norms that license and limit the range of warranted responses vary with cultural differences.

Although I do not wish to take sides on the question of the merits of relativism, I think worries about relativism are in any event misguided at this purely methodological level for a number of reasons. In the first place, any plausible denial of moral relativism must be consistent with defensible, pluralistic variation in social and ethical practices. Second, I describe what I take to be structural features of complex normative systems, invariant over different systems. Third, objective moral assessment of cultural practices is obviously wholly compatible with the fact of conventional variance. It may well be that our present practices of blame and forgiveness are inhumane by some objective standard of decency. It is likely some of our practices of punishment are. And fourth, nothing in the interpretive approach precludes the possibility that many substantive elements in our practices are, in fact, universal, for example functions of basic human needs and wants for security and community.[26] Indeed, the heart of my argument is the analysis I offer of the intentional structure of collective action, an analysis I take to apply unrestrictedly to all instances. It is unclear to me, in short, how any other approach could offer a superior bundle of objectivity, feasibility, and criticism. The test is in the details of the argument.

The second interpretive aspect of this account is that it seeks to illuminate the practices, beliefs, and institutions that comprise our accountability system by reference to their social functions. These render both possible and valuable the exercise of our capacity for sociability. I interpret the elements of the accountability system, and particularly judgments that one is responsible, in terms of those judgments' role in constituting and fostering the relations with others that make our lives good, materially, emotionally, and psychically.

This weak kind of instrumentalism stands opposed to a conception of accountability that sees judgments of responsibility as merely reflections or realizations of independent moral facts, which I take as the metaphysical hard core of retributivism. I think little sense can be made of the idea that we are simply accountable for wrongs, rather than that we are due particular kinds of responses from particular others. If any generic content can be attributed to an inherently fragmented concept like accountability, that content comes by reference to the function of the network of social practices and commitments in which judgments of accountability find their point. But weak instrumentalist also stands opposed to naturalistic reductions of moral values and practices to such nonmoral bases as the maximization of reproductive success or facilitation of coordination, where the reduction leaves no room for the distinctive and constitutive roles played in our relations by concepts and attitudes like dignity and respect, outrage and reproach, mercy and redemption. Our ethical beliefs, attitudes, and practices, like our scientific and mathematical beliefs and practices, do have a practical point and are grounded in mental capacities that clearly confer competitive advantages upon those who have them. But just as our scientific and mathematical beliefs and practices demand justification by reference to their internal standards of evidence and proof, not just in the crassly pragmatic terms of "what works," so our ethical practices include demands for justification in specifically ethical terms. Thus, a genuine elucidation of our ethical practices must respect (rather than reduce) the internal demand for coherence and justification.

## 1.5

Here is a road map of this book's path. Chapter 2 explores the structure of individual accountability for individual harms. That is, it examines the relational and positional conception of accountability in light of our practices and of some of the philosophical theories that have been offered to explain them. Along the way, I consider the critique of the accountability system suggested by Nietzsche: the attitudes and practices of blame and liability do not, in fact, foster good relations as my optimistic story would have it, but rather conceal darker motives of subversion and revenge. Finally, I consider the character of the special responsive position occupied by the state when it inflicts legal sanctions.

The framework for understanding accountability presented in Chapter 2 prepares the ground for the difficult issues of collective accountability as an individual problem – how individuals can and should make normative sense of their relations to harms they bring about together. Chapter 3 begins the discussion of structured harms through an examination of the fundamental notions of cooperation and joint action. It argues that cooperative action can be made sense of in individualistic but nonreductive terms, through the primitive notion of a "participatory intention" to do one's part in a collective act. I then explain how actions and events can be ascribed to individuals as members of jointly acting groups. Chapter 4 introduces the notion of individual moral accountability for collective harms, and argues that participatory intentions serve as the basis for legitimate claims of complicity in many contexts. Chapter 5 amplifies and complicates this argument, by examining the radical differences that the particular positions of moral respondents make to the evaluation of collective harms.

Chapter 6 then extends the prior discussion of moral accountability to the problems of collective but unstructured wrongdoing, and to the question of the legitimacy of taking collectives as subjects of accountability. And Chapter 7 takes up the issues of criminal and civil liability as applied to members of groups, corporate and conspiratorial. After presenting a philosophical reconstruction of complicity doctrine, I argue that the criminal liability of accomplices and co-conspirators for their confederates' acts is normatively defensible, so long as differences in individual culpability are taken into account in ways they currently are not. I turn then to consider the limitation of civil liability for corporate shareholders, a rule at odds with the presumption in tort law that participants share personal liability for collective acts. I argue that, as a matter of prima facie justice, limited shareholder liability for corporate torts is indefensible when corporate assets have been exhausted. The current rule should be replaced by personal liability for corporate torts, apportioned to the degree of ownership. While there may be overriding practical considerations that dictate retaining the limited liability rule, the rule lacks independent ethical justification.

# Chapter 2

# The Deep Structure of Individual Accountability

## 2.1 INTRODUCTION

My aim in this chapter is to define a conception of individual accountability for individual harms that overcomes the limitations of the individualistic conception I discussed in Chapter 1, particularly the way it excluded the significance of the accountable subject's relations to others. I called this exclusive focus on the subject a kind of ethical solipsism, and suggested that it was radically mistaken. Instead, as I argue here, our practices of accountability are both *positional* and *relational*. The responses that agents warrant because of their connection to a harm depend upon both prior moral and social relations among the parties, and the particular perspective of the respondent. The relational and positional conception of individual accountability for individual harms that I define and employ in this chapter will serve later as a basis for understanding individual accountability for collective harms. But I will not address problems of collective harms here. Instead I focus upon what I have called the retributive or desert-based model of individual accountability, which is relationally and causally solipsistic. I will analyze the shortcomings of this model by comparing it with our actual practices and will then suggest a nonretributive alternative conception of responsibility that better fits those practices.

In the sense in which I want to use it, *accountability* is somewhat narrower in meaning than *responsibility*. Although sometimes used synonymously with accountability, responsibility bears two distinct senses, an internal and an external sense. Given a certain relation of an agent to a harm, the first sense of responsibility refers to a set of internal psychological competencies a person must have in order to be answerable for the harm. The second sense of responsibility refers instead to a set of normative, external affiliations, the duties of the agent to other surrounding agents. In the first, internal sense, responsibility is nonrelational. The second sense of responsibility, by contrast, is fundamentally relational, and it is this sense I want to segregate for specialized use, and to call by the name *accountability*. Agents are accountable to others for a harm as a function of their relations to others, as well as of everyone's relation to the harm or wrong.[1] Accountability and responsibility in this sense are deeply related but not synonymous: Responsible agents are candidates for accountability, but may not necessarily be accountable for what they have done. (The bank teller who, at gunpoint, empties the cash drawer is paradigmatically responsible but not accountable.)

According to a retributivist, or desert-based, model the judgments, expressions, and practices characteristic of accountability – resentment, gratitude, demands for compensation, punishment, reward – are owed to individual agents because of the rights and wrongs they have done. What agents have done is a function of their wills, where *will* stands for the complex of practical motivations, including desires, intentions, and reasons, that culminate in actions. Facts about agents' wills – what they have intended, what motivated them, the reasons for which they acted – determine the responses they deserve. Although this model does not exclude associative forms of accountability, it does disfavor such forms, because associative accountability typically depends more on the social or structural relations agents bear to one another than on facts about their wills. Associative accountability, the concern of later chapters, is not principally at issue here. However, this chapter is centrally concerned with the feature of the retributive model that makes it disfavor associative accountability: its solipsism.

Retributive models of accountability are solipsistic in the sense that responses are warranted exclusively by the agent's desert, without regard to the position of the respondent in relation to the agent. Robert Nozick's model of retributivism exemplifies this solipsistic tendency. According to Nozick, the treatment an agent deserves is mapped by the formula "$r \times H$," where "$r$" stands for an agent's degree of responsibility for a harm and "$H$" for the magnitude of the harm.[2] An agent's desert is a function exclusively of that agent's capacities and (actual or potential) causal influence. The agent's relations to others, notably victims, do enter into the determination that an act was wrongful and the description of the wrong. But the crucial relationship for judgments of *accountability* as opposed to judgments of *wrongfulness* is the relationship between agent and respondent. As I will show, all might agree that the agent acted wrongly, but what response the agent merits depends on the expectations between the agent and the evaluator. This relationship plays no role in retributivist judgments of accountability. So, by describing retributivist conceptions of accountability as solipsistic, I mean they fail to take into account the relation between the respondent and the agent.

To restate this with different emphasis, the solipsism I attribute to retributivist conceptions means they are nonpositional. They fail to take into account the multiplicity and particularity of the positions from which respondents respond. Because retributivists conflate the judgment of wrongfulness with the judgment of accountability, they require that responses to agents be univocal.[3] Accordingly, all evaluators, including the agents themselves, owe the same judgment or expression of blame in response to a harm.[4] This assumption that any act deserves a uniquely determined response is at odds with one of the most striking features of our practices of accountability: the dependence of any response upon the perspective of the respondent. Guilt, for example, is not merely self-directed blame; and a spectator's indignation differs not just in form but also in content from a victim's resentment.

The conception of accountability I propose is, in contrast with the retributivist conception, relational and positional. In arguing for a relational conception of accountability, I separate the fact of wrongdoing from the responses warranted by it, and base the decision about what responses are warranted upon the relationship of the respondent to the agent. In arguing for a positional conception of accountability, I emphasize the importance of recognizing that for any given harm there is no single, uniquely determined response warranted.

In the next section I will offer an examination of the pretheoretical form of social accountability in order to make clear the complexly perspectival character any adequate conception must have in order to conform with social practices deeply rooted in common sense. In section 2.3, the heart of this chapter, I identify the three bases of moral accountability, an agent's conduct, the consequences of that conduct, and the agent's character, and show how these are best supported by a relational conception of accountability. I stress also the dynamic nature of accountability in Section 2.4: how our responses reshape the relations they define. Section 2.5 shows how the important notion of degrees of moral accountability depends not only upon properties of the individual agent, but also upon the character of warranted response by others. Section 2.6 distinguishes the functionalism of my conception of accountability – the emphasis on its function in maintaining social, moral, and political relationships – from consequentialism. Section 2.7 attempts to allay fears about the hidden nature of our responses raised by Nietzsche. And Section 2.8 shows how the special character of legal responses depends upon the relationship between the agent and the state as respondent.

## 2.2 SOCIAL ACCOUNTABILITY AS AN EXAMPLE OF THE FUNDAMENTALLY RELATIONAL NATURE OF ACCOUNTABILITY

Social accountability is accountability for harms whose primary standards of assessment are nonmoral. Standards of etiquette and confidence among intimates represent the domain of social accountability.[5] Our practices of social accountability maintain and restore harmony by relating agents to one another and the harms they cause. They prevent and repair breaches in social trust and cooperation. As a normative concept, accountability consists in a *warrant* for certain kinds of typically interpersonal responses – attitudes, sanctions, and claims – that serve this social function. A response is warranted if it is permitted or required by the governing moral or social norms. If I am accountable for a harm, then other people are warranted in responding to my relation to that harm in certain ways. To be held (properly) accountable is to be subjected to such warranted responses, and to hold oneself accountable is to subject oneself to them. The central point I want to emphasize is that actual or idealized responses to an agent by other persons give the concept of accountability its distinctive shape and its content.

Social, moral, and legal forms of accountability overlap. Breaking a promise is generally rude, often wrong, and sometimes legally actionable. Also, social and moral accountability share a common set of psychological responses, notably resentment, indignation, shame, and guilt. Legal institutions of punishment and enforcement may be regarded as, in significant part, externalized or "universalized" versions of these responses, although it would, of course, be a mistake to see them as only expressive.[6] Because of this commonality in forms of response, it is not surprising that all three kinds of accountability share certain deep structural features, namely relationality and positional dependence.

Although moral and legal accountability are my central focus, in this section I draw upon an example of social accountability. Examples of social accountability, perhaps more clearly than moral or legal accountability, illustrate the fragmentation and variability of warranted responses. If I carelessly break a neighbor's vase at a party while dancing on his grand piano, my neighbor is warranted in resenting my carelessness and asking for an apology, though not in, say, smashing my glasses. Reciprocally, an apology or restitution is warranted on my part (and perhaps even obligatory). But my accountability does not end with a simple interaction between my neighbor and myself. There are countless other positions from which other agents may respond to my act. For example, other guests at the party may also feel indignant at having their pleasant evening disrupted by my loutish behavior, and they may expect a public display of contrition for their sake, though they could not appropriately feel personally aggrieved in the same way as my neighbor. Perhaps some of the guests are relatives of my neighbor, however, and they may take the event more personally than friends and acquaintances present. Different responses are probably warranted by those who were in the room when the mishap took place, and those who were not. Perhaps the friend who had given the vase to my neighbor is present, and warranted in responding differently from all other guests at the party. Perhaps another guest is a collector of rare vases, and feels a special sense of proprietorship toward the museum-quality specimen I broke. I may also be accountable to my own family for the harm, since they will now be embarrassed before the neighbor. I may owe them a promise to take more care in the future. Finally, to and from the public at large only very constrained responses are warranted. While anyone who heard about my accident could consider me a fool, and say so, a more direct response to me personally would be thought self-righteous and nosy; and it would be self-abasing of me to confess my shame to a random person I met in the street.

This essential and obvious fact of accountability, its positional dependence, is unexplained by the retributive, desert-based model. The retributivists' exclusive focus upon an agent's intentional state and actions dictates that all warranted responses flow from a single constant value: what the agent deserves. The response warranted by desert is thus univocal, dependent upon facts about the agent rather than the agent's relations to others. One could object that the variability of warranted responses can be made consistent with the retributive model: An agent "deserves" multiple and varied responses from different people. But this use of *desert* is no longer consistent with the retributive sense, because it defines desert according to warranted responses from others, rather than vice versa.

The retributivist notion of desert fails to explain not only the variability of warranted responses, but the character and justification of any single warranted response. Retributivists often claim that desert maintains an equilibrium in rightful benefits and burdens: What I gain through acting wrongfully is paid back through a proportionate deprivation.[7] In this sense my "gain" in breaking the vase was the taking of an undue liberty with regard to the possessions of another, and I must compensate for this liberty by being constrained to apologize and make restitution. But the inadequacy of this idealized notion of corrective balancing is immediately obvious, first of all in the radically different nature of the response warranted from the ill-gotten gain. If my wrong was an undue liberty with another's property, it is hard to see how anything other than either purely economic compensation, or a similar liberty by others with my own possessions, could effect an equilibrium. The impermissibility of such an answering liberty is inexplicable, as are the crucially important social responses of resentment, accusation, apology, and contrition. Here I mean something slightly different from the familiar criticism, voiced by Hart, that retributivism makes two ordinarily impermissible acts amount to justice by a "mysterious piece of moral alchemy."[8] The problem I want to indicate is that responses generally do not mirror harms and, in any case, the notion of "mirroring," other than in the context of the most concrete version of *lex talionis*, is too indeterminate to explain any particular response.[9] This leaves open the question of what relation a response *does* properly bear to a harm.

In order to understand what particular responses are the appropriate ones through which to "repay" my undue liberty in the social case of the broken vase, we need more than an abstract notion of balance. We need to understand the particular nature of the social and moral relations being maintained. For example, for my neighbor, forgiving me for breaking the vase is one appropriate response. This would not, however, be an appropriate response from bystanders. Instead, they might respond by sympathizing with me, or alternatively, with my neighbor, or even with both. This panoply of different responses from different agents can only be accounted for by the nature of the relationships from which they flow. First of all, the harm itself creates a host of different relationships: victim, witness, interested parties of various sorts. These new relationships overlay preexisting ones. My host and I, as people who come into routine contact, have probably developed a relationship based upon reciprocity, and so forgiveness is warranted. In contrast, my relationship with other partygoers may be more attenuated, and consists in a mutual desire to appear decently mannered.

I want to put aside two immediate worries about this highly contextualized look at social accountability. Clearly, the social norms that license and limit the range of warranted responses vary with cultural, class, and social differences, indeed to the point of idiosyncrasy. By contrast, substantive moral norms, such as "You should clean up the messes you make," appear to have more uniform content, although they may also reflect significant cultural differences. Questions arise then whether, first, conclusions derived from the model of social accountability generalize interestingly to moral accountability and, second, whether given the variety of individually warranted responses, there is simply no fact of the matter, even in the social case, about what responses are warranted. In other words, does positional dependence imply perspectival subjectivism, the claim that the warrant for a normative judgment or response depends entirely upon the preferences or beliefs of the individual respondent?

Let me take up the second concern first. Positional dependence as I have characterized it only holds that the standards governing warranted response depend upon the structure of relationships between respondents and agents. But respondents in different positions may be variously correct or mistaken about what those standards warrant without there being one correct response, just as differently placed listeners might be variously correct or mistaken about the pitch of a moving train whistle without there being one pitch all listeners ought to report.[10] In ethics, as in acoustics, the subjective and objective perspectives are not contraries but complements. The objective perspective is what gives the subjective its normative character, transforming attitudes into claims, and preferences into warrants.

More concretely, my host's demand that I apologize and make repair may be peculiar to him, but it is objectively his right to make that demand, because the social norms that govern our relations will be endorsed as authoritative by all members of the relevant normative community. I mean to leave open the ultimate explanation of the normative authority of his claims. Contenders include the possibility that I and the other members of the community simply accept the norms as authoritative (perhaps out of natural predisposition), or that their authority is derived from the demands of practical reason, or that they represent conventions we reflectively endorse.[11] Whatever its source, the authority of these norms is objective, notwithstanding the limited domain of their application. I do not mean to rest anything on this assertion of objectivity. If the claims I make about the warrant for various responses are plausible (or not) to you, that will probably be due to their consonance with your sensibility, not your acceptance (or rejection) of a metaphysical claim. My general argument depends only on the metaphysically weak presupposition that our moral practices display some form of systematic ordering.

The other worry was that the kind of positional variation characteristic of social relations and responses simply does not generalize to the moral realm. One might think, for example, the norms governing social relations are functions of highly specific roles – such as host, guest, neighbor – while moral norms are functions of very

24

thinly described general roles – such as member of the Kingdom of Ends. Indeed, the movement of modern morality has been from specificity to generality, from the morality of aristocrats and Christians to the morality of rational agents as such. But two points allay the concern. First, it would be a mistake to move from moral generalities to the conclusion that our moral relations with others are wholly expressed in the pure terms of moral agency. This is a point I will return to shortly. But for now my argument is simply that the moral relations that make up the everyday troubles of life are, essentially, relations between well-defined roles and characters: colleagues, buyers and sellers, supervisors and subordinates, parents and children. Moral disturbances in these relations – disagreements, betrayals, self-dealing – can only be thought through, and responded to, by reference to the grainy texture of those very relations. The ethereal realm of abstract morality plays little role. Variation in the moral sphere mimics, if it does not simply supervene upon, variation in the social.[12] The second point is that the positionality I describe in both the moral and social spheres falls into three main types: that of agents, victims, and onlookers. Even if there is more variety within these types in the social case, there should be little question that moral accountability at least reflects these principal divisions. (Otherwise, to pick an obvious example, the asymmetries between proper self- and other forgiveness would be inexplicable.)

In the next several sections, I draw from the model of social accountability lessons for understanding moral accountability as well. I show how the three principal bases upon which agents hold themselves and are held accountable, conduct, consequence, and character, function in terms of the particular relations among agents and their respondents. Because respondents bear different normative and epistemic relations to these bases of accountability, they respond in very different ways to agents and harms.

## 2.3 THE RELATIONAL BASES OF MORAL ACCOUNTABILITY: CONDUCT, CONSEQUENCES, AND CHARACTER

I have argued that no single basis such as the agent's desert can explain the several and varied nature of the responses we make to harms. Instead, accountability must be understood in terms of a multiplicity of relations among agents. In this section I extend the argument to the case of moral accountability, or accountability for the infringement of morally protected interests. By "morally protected interests," I mean the interests of agents in autonomy, substantial well-being, integrity of property and person, and fair consideration. These are interests that the standards of common sense, Western, secular morality protect and promote.

Agents are held morally accountable for intentionally threatening or acting indifferently towards morally protected interests, inadvertently causing those interests harm, or symbolically impugning the significance of those interests through their statements, convictions, and associations. The three principal bases of accountability, consisting in how agents act, what they cause, and who they are, I call reasons of conduct, reasons of consequence, and reasons of character. Here I discuss the ways in which variously placed respondents take account of these reasons. I argue that the special and differential significance of each basis of accountability can only be understood in terms of the particular character of the relations between agent and respondent. The discussion of reasons of conduct takes up the bulk of this section, because of the special significance of such reasons in our relations with others. Whether or not we are affected causally by others, or whether we are in a position to make judgments about their characters, we are nearly always in the process of evaluating others' attitudes towards us.

### 2.3.1 *Accountability Warranted by Reasons of Conduct*

The intuitive idea behind reasons of conduct is commonplace. We are sometimes morally accountable for the manner in which we act towards other people – generously, malevolently, carelessly – independently of the consequences of our actions. Though the kind of conduct we find morally objectionable is often linked to a risk of harm, it is our conduct that is faulty, whether or not it actually results in harm. And, indeed, some forms of obnoxious conduct, such as condescending or contemptuous behavior, can be most objectionable even when they accompany consequences that might otherwise be positively beneficial, as when we scorn the help of those who scorn us. The paradigmatic first-person response to faulty conduct is guilt. But guilt is by no means the only first-person response possible. We can often be ashamed of our conduct, for example for having been spineless, stupid, or imprudent, when we feel no guilt. Second-person responses to faulty conduct cover the spectrum of blame and resentment, from forgiveness to indignation to oaths of vengeance. Onlookers, depending upon their sympathies for agent or victim, impute fault, feel righteous indignation (or, alternatively, *Schadenfreude*), or offer excuse. When conduct is good rather than faulty, the first-person response is often pride, the second-person response, gratitude, and the third-person response, admiration.

What about our relations to others provokes these responses? One group of theories, labeled "Quality of Will" theories by T.M. Scanlon, explains the reasons why wrongful conduct provokes responses of resentment, blame, and guilt in the context of specific interpersonal relations. Quality of Will theories divide into two sorts. The first, *expressivist* theories, focus on the way responses convey attitudes and sentiments between agents. The second, *cognitivist* theories, emphasize instead the content of judgments of wrongful conduct, and the role this content plays in agents' understanding of the character of their relations to others. Since our reactions to others clearly have both attitudinal and judgmental components, I will draw on both expressivist and cognitivist approaches in exploring accountability for conduct. But I depart from traditional expressivism and cognitivism by using these theories to show the dependence of particular responses upon the nature of the moral relationship between agent and respondent.

Peter Strawson's famous lecture, "Freedom and Resentment," contains the best purely expressivist account of the role of blame and resentment, and the way those reactions depend upon concrete forms of interpersonal relations.[13] According to Strawson, our practices of accountability are made up of natural patterns of emotional reaction, or "reactive attitudes," to the welcome and unwelcome attitudes of others manifested in their conduct towards us.[14] The object of our welcome or censure is the attitude or "quality of will" the agent expresses. When I blame you for slapping me on the back of the neck, I am venting my resentment at the hostility implicit in your act. When I am grateful to you for courteously holding the door for me, I am expressing my delight at the good will you demonstrate. My responses to your actions flow principally from my assumptions about the sentiments expressed by your conduct, not the consequences produced by it. Thus, when I discover that the attitude to which I am reacting is absent or different than I had supposed, my reaction naturally transforms. If I discover that you slapped my neck in order to swat away a bee, then I will no longer resent the action as an attack upon me. Or if I discover that you have been merely careless in swinging your hand around, I may revise my resentment to focus upon your disregard rather than your hostility. My reactions similarly shift when the attitude is present, but has a suspect etiology – perhaps an effect of your paranoid delusions. Now I do not resent your hostility, but try to understand it, because it no longer expresses your considered sentiments, but only the state of your mental health.

The crucial point, not made explicitly by Strawson, is that our disinclination to express reactive attitudes to partly or wholly non-responsible agents is explained not merely by the quality of their wills, but by the nature of our relationship with them. Though children and the insane do indeed manifest attitudes of hostility and good will, we tend to take what Strawson calls an "objective" rather than a "participant's" view of their attitudes. Strawson emphasizes how our awareness of cognitive and affective limitations in non-responsible agents naturally precludes them from participating in the relationships characteristic of adult society.[15] I would add to this description that our attribution of an incompetent will to such agents is just the projection of ourselves into a certain type of relationship with them. We see them not as accountable subjects but as the objects of understanding, treatment, or education.

In fact, it is very difficult to say precisely what features of responsible agents' wills support "ordinary inter-personal relations," for we often hold one another accountable for unconsidered judgments, errant moods, and flights of fancy. But when such judgments and mood swings can be understood as minor deviations against a background pattern of normal interaction, they become features of an ongoing relationship to which affective response is appropriate. If the deviation from the norm is very great, as when an ordinarily trustworthy friend in the midst of protracted unemployment be-

comes suddenly unreliable, our response modulates between participant and objective perspectives.[16]

Thus, Scanlon's characterization of Strawson's theory as a "Quality of Will" theory is misleading in an important sense. This characterization implies that Strawson's understanding of accountability
rests exclusively upon the internal will, rather than on the external
affiliations, of the moral agent. But it should now be clear that the
attitudes and expressions of agents only warrant response given a
certain understanding of the nature of the relationship between
agent and respondent. In Strawson's very rough terms, the relationship must be either participatory or potentially participatory: The
agent to whom we respond must be someone with whom we will or
could cooperate in social life. Agents' attitudes and expressions both
indicate and constitute the nature of a participatory relationship. In
general, we care about our relationships with others in virtue of the
ways they make our lives good, both as good things in themselves,
and as vehicles for promoting our interests. So the responses characteristic of accountability are warranted by the point and demands of
the relationship. This allows, as Strawson acknowledges, a necessary
variability in warranted responses depending upon the nature of the
relationship in question. What might constitute callous indifference
between friends or lovers is simply good manners between commercial transactors.[17]

Strawson's account works best where the form of background
participatory relationship that grounds and warrants response is
most conspicuous, that is, in the domain that I have called social
accountability. His account is less helpful in explaining the special
character of our moral responses to agents with whom we share no
particular set of relationships – for example, my reaction upon reading in the paper that an employer has exploited its immigrant
workers. Here I am outraged, towards the employer and on behalf of
the immigrant workers, although I cannot in any deep sense identify
myself with either of their positions. Strawson says the relationship
among moral respondents in such cases is simply a "generalized"
form of the claim to goodwill made by members of participatory
social relationships. He does so in order to explain what he calls the
"vicarious" nature of moral reactions. Responses like moral indignation are "essentially capable" of being directed at others' attitudes

towards others as well as at attitudes directed towards ourselves.[18] Strawson says these vicarious reactions are "humanly connected" with participant reactions, although he does not explain the nature of this connection.[19] Strawson is surely right to suggest that it is a deeply rooted fact that humans – or at least members of minimally cohesive societies – have a propensity to pass judgment generally on others' compliance with social norms.[20] Indeed, it is hard to imagine how a society could maintain its normative structure if its members were not disposed to monitor and censure each other for non-compliance.[21]

Such a general tendency to react vicariously to others might seem to undermine my claim that accountability is fundamentally relational, for we seem to have a broad domain of responses despite the absence of any well-defined relationships among the parties. Here the cognitivist theories of morality and moral accountability, of which Kant's and Scanlon's are exemplary, may be helpful, both in explaining the nature of the background relationship that informs these moral responses, and in explaining our wont to react to the wrongs of unknown others. According to cognitivist theories, my conduct is subject to warranted response, not primarily because of the sentiment or attitude it manifests, but because of its conformity with moral standards of behavior.[22] Although the source of these standards is in principle left open, cognitive theorists have tended to construct them in a general, universal vein, by considering what suitably disposed agents might reasonably agree to as a basis for a scheme of social cooperation among equals.[23]

I want to suggest that the standards generated by such cognitivist criteria, albeit very general, can be interpreted not merely as guides to conduct, but as constitutive of a particular form of relationship, just as the standards of intimacy and confidence are constitutive of close friendship. These very general moral standards define what might be thought of as a default relationship between any two members of the moral community, a relationship typically structured by a principle of equal respect and possibly equal concern. I bear such a relationship to any other person by virtue of our common humanity, a commonality that makes possible, however unlikely, our having significant relations with one another. I do not want here to defend any particular form of this default moral relationship or the structure of claims it justifies, but only to establish that moral standards are defined by their role in structuring moral relationships.[24] In most contexts, this background relationship grounds only minimally acceptable standards, which are then overlaid by those standards constitutive of the more particular relationships that any two persons are likely to share and to which they attribute significance, e.g., common citizenship, class membership, or religious affiliation. For example, someone considering how to react upon discovering the dangerous carelessness of a co-worker might first consider what general responsibilities to take care an agent has towards others, and then to rethink these responsibilities in the context in which the parties are colleagues. Depending upon the nature of the risks co-workers routinely impose upon one another, the warranted response to carelessness might be either more or less severe than those appropriate to any noncollegial potential victim.

A further advantage of seeing our moral responses as manifesting compound abstract and concrete relations is that we get a far more realistic picture of the complex effects of moral criticism, real and imagined. The special force, or sting, of moral criticism (as opposed to mere description of our conduct) varies with the importance we accord to the relationships from which the relevant norms are derived. From what is surely the varied importance people attribute to the contractualist ideal of dealing with others on a rationally justifiable basis, we have an explanation of both the motivational fragility of much moral criticism, as well as of the appeal of the idea that the immoral and unreasonable are tightly linked. And from the central and distinctive roles played in our lives by more concrete affiliations, we can understand why, say, the special venom carried for strike-breaking scabs does not translate into a general outrage at infidelity.[25]

Once these very general moral standards are seen as flowing from, and being justified by, a particular conception of a relationship and not merely a generalization of self-directed concern, we have a basis for understanding why moral agents are inclined towards blame and indignation even when their own interests are unaffected. Through conceiving of myself as a potential participant in a more determinate relationship with any given agent, I attribute significance to the minimal moral standards that govern our respective conduct towards one another. Because our courses of conduct do not in fact conflict, and so my interests are not directly threatened, it would be unwarranted for me to muster the rage or resentment that accompanies more direct interaction. But the wrongful acts of another, even when I am not the victim, still symbolically affront the standards I value, and the interests those standards protect. And so I react with more than a neutral observation of the wrongfulness of the other's conduct. I react with what might be called righteous indignation, at the mere fact that another has acted wrongfully.[26]

Cognitivist accounts of moral relationships and warranted response still omit the positionality of moral response. This omission in cognitivist theories stems from their tendency, as with retributivist theories, to confuse the univocal judgment of moral wrongness with the multivocal character of moral response. On Kant's and Scanlon's accounts, if an agent acted wrongly, then that fact should be affirmed from any perspective.[27] But it does not follow from the fact that all must agree an agent acted wrongly, that the responses from all must also be identical. The very fact of a harm creates asymmetries in the positions of respondents. The variance in warranted moral response is less extreme than in the social case. But victims, for example, clearly have a special moral relation to a harm that others lack, simply in virtue of having suffered. Only victims can forgive or demand compensation, and thereby determine the consequent response warranted by the agent.[28] On any satisfactory theory, then, being a victim, agent, or onlooker of immoral behavior must give rise to special kinds of response (and so too must differences within those categories).

Nathaniel Hawthorne displayed the full range of possible moral responses – or better, the limits of that range – in his novel about guilt, shame, and expiation, *The Scarlet Letter*. A good novel derives its interest from the unwarranted, rather than warranted, nature of its characters' responses to one another, dramatizing the difference between the two in the nature of the characters' moral relationships. Chillingworth, Hester's cuckolded husband, responds to Hester's and Dimmesdale's adultery by taking on a false identity in order to torture Dimmesdale psychologically. Clearly, Chillingworth's response is so inappropriate as to be unjustified even by Dimmesdale's own inappropriate response, the concealment of his own identity as

Hester's lover and the father of her child. It is the concealment of their moral relationships with Hester, and their attempts to respond to the harm from outside those relationships, that makes both Chillingworth's and Dimmesdale's responses inappropriate, no matter how genuinely Chillingworth has been wronged, or how earnestly Dimmesdale punishes himself. Meanwhile the most striking response in the novel, the townspeople's sentencing of Hester to wear the scarlet "A," is an allegory of how a moral response is defined by the moral relationship between the respondent and the agent, and how the response changes as the relationship changes. The Bostonians' punishing symbol is initially intended to label Hester an adulteress and express her expulsion from the moral community. But Hester instead becomes the Bostonians' moral guardian, thereby transforming the meaning of their retributive gesture. The "A" comes to stand for "Able," then for "Angel" and "Apostle," remaining on Hester's dress, but eventually carrying the opposite meaning from that originally intended. The point to note is not just the exaggeratedly self-referential character of Puritanical responses to sexual transgression. Rather, the novel's realistic psychology is manifested in the ways the response of each party – victim, confederate, and bystanders – reflect the particular desires and frustrations of the given respondent, as well as the nature of their relationship to Hester.

The dependence of moral responses upon moral relationships is also nicely illustrated by Herman Melville's *Billy Budd*. Captain Vere must choose between two irreconcilable perspectives, or relationships to Billy, the "handsome sailor" falsely accused by the evil Claggart of conspiring to mutiny. As a representative of naval authority, Vere regards Billy's assault on Claggart as a capital offense within the meaning of the Mutiny Act, liable to immediate punishment. As a fellow sailor (and fellow Christian), Vere regards Billy's act as provoked and at least excusable, if not justified as well. Peter Winch and David Wiggins have described Captain Vere's dilemma as an expression of the indeterminacy of moral judgment. There is no single answer to the question "How should one respond to Billy's act?"[29] But I think Vere's dilemma is better understood not as a representation of indeterminate standards given a single moral perspective, but rather as a conflict between perspectives, each with its own norms of wrongfulness and warranted response. From a captain, speedy and rigid justice was required, while from a fellow sailor, the quality of mercy might have been preferred unstrained.

From the perspective of common humanity, intent is salient. The perspective demands a narrative of motive, choice, and outcome in order to make full sense of the participants' relations to one another. From this perspective, Billy responds to Claggart's treachery with righteous anger. His intended act is not wrongful aggression but justified response, the only kind of response to insult he can offer because of his stutter. The tragedy of the narrative from this perspective is that the act's consequences far exceed its intent and Claggart is killed.[30] But the unintended consequence does not change the moral. Vere's exclamation, "It is the divine judgment on Ananias," the biblical liar rebuked by Peter, neatly captures this perspective and its endorsement of righteous anger.[31]

This version of the story rests also upon an understanding of the relevant relations: the deceitful but fluent Claggart has an advantage over the honest but stuttering Billy. Consider the story, again from the perspective of common humanity, but with different relations in mind. Claggart is weak and obsessed with Billy's handsomeness. Billy is strong and impervious to the resentments that cripple Claggart. Billy strikes Claggart not because he cannot speak but because the strong naturally express themselves through violence. Billy has acted in keeping with his nature, but his nature is not Christian innocence but rather barely repressed power. The form of social relations Billy seeks through his blow is not equal respect, but rather dominance of the strong. Now common humanity does demand a severe response to Billy, for a central function of the accountability system is to impose normative equality in order to compensate for unequal endowments of power. Evidence for this interpretation can be found in Vere's subsequent exclamation, "Struck dead by an angel of God! Yet the angel must hang!"[32] One possible meaning is this: Angels, too, act according to their natures, but their natures are incompatible with the ways of humans. The human order and the divine do not mesh.

The perspective of a superior in the military hierarchy yields the same result for very different reasons. Intent no longer matters and consequence is all. Hierarchical relations are best sustained by external signs, not internal dispositions, because the ambiguities of intention undermine the possibility of decisive moral judgment. Now any form of blame or forgiveness incorporates a forgetting as much as a remembering; every response of accountability entails a reduction of the complexity of circumstance and motive to suit the governing norms. But the reductiveness of the martial perspective is extreme: the Mutiny Act, as "War's child . . . . looks but to the frontage, the appearance . . . . Budd's intent or non-intent is nothing to [its] purpose." Billy's blow becomes a cipher, a meaningless explosion of violence that can only be treated in terms of its effects.[33] All that matters is that it is an affront to naval order. The norms governing response are similarly constrained. Within the utilitarian logic of the military, there is no moral space for the individual instance – the space demanded by mercy – but only for the instrumental relation between the rules of discipline and the end of unified power.[34] The thinnest description of Billy's act, his intentional striking of a superior officer, governs the judgment of wrongfulness and the collective goal of discipline governs the permissible response. Once Vere decides that adherence to the strict rules of the Act is demanded, he is left, as a fellow sailor, with the manifestly inadequate comfort that "did [Billy] know our hearts . . . he would feel even for us."

In *Billy Budd*, Melville portrays the fracturing of the responsive position into a multiplicity of positions, each of whose demands the respondent tries to satisfy. Vere stands as a witness both to Budd's innocent character and to his violent act. Further, he takes on the special onlooker position of judge, a position itself caught between the demands of "natural justice" and of the martial ends served by the positive law of the Mutiny Act. Indeed, Vere's judicial position itself is further compromised, because not only does Vere as judge embody the law as means, but as captain he embodies its ends. Thus he stands also as a victim of Budd's assault on military discipline. No wonder Vere seems feverish in his deliberations as he paces his cabin, caught amid so many positions. This is the stuff of every day moral indecision, even when there is no hanging to concentrate the mind: parents caught between positions as moral educator and source of comfort, and victims caught between vengeful claims grounded in anger and irenic impulses grounded in a desire to put the past behind.

I have written thus far only of the varied responses of victims and onlookers to conduct. But the most complicated perspective from which to respond to a harm is that of the agent, because the structure of relationships from which that response flows is the most intricate. The resentment of victims and indignation of onlookers are warranted by the judgment that an agent's behavior fails to conform to standards constitutive of a valued relationship. An agent's response to resentment and indignation, whether these are actual or merely imagined, takes the form of shame and guilt. Agents' self-reflexive responses are reactions to the attitudes of others toward the agents' own attitudes, and so, when fully spelled out, may involve as many as four distinct figures: the agent as actor, as respondent, as onlooker, and the actual victim.[35] The victim's response need not play an important psychological role, as when I feel shame at the way my shoddy treatment of another has engendered contempt in others, but do not feel ashamed before my victim. But the respondent, internal or actual, always provides the prism through which an agent's behavior is refracted back, its unseemly, cruel, or wrongful elements revealed. And because agents may be in an especially good position to know the real character of that behavior or its underlying intentions, their responses may be far harsher than those occupying less epistemically privileged positions. This is not to exclude the common possibility that agents will be particularly obtuse about their motivations, whether through ordinary thoughtlessness or through the familiar psychoanalytic mechanisms of repression and displacement. When this is so, first-person responses will again vary, perhaps driven more by internal drama than by the actual wrong.

Kant claimed that "[a]ll [respect] for a person is properly only [respect] for the law . . . of which that person gives us an example."[36] This suggestion, that proper guilt relates the agent only superficially to other persons, and essentially only to the moral law, is a serious distortion of the self-reflexive responses of accountability, which are fundamentally relational. The responses of guilt and shame emerge from an agent's relationships with a victim and with the agent as internal respondent.[37] Furthermore, guilt and shame are usually acknowledgments of the warranted nature of the evaluator's response. Guilty or ashamed agents see their emotions as responses to warranted resentment. This component of warrant is, of course, not essential to an instance of the response – a former believer may sensibly regard the guilt felt at breaking away from orthodox religious standards as an unwarranted response to unwarranted reproach – but it is an essential component in the general, matured capacity for the response of guilt.

Thus self-reflexive responses such as guilt are especially inflected by the particular moral and social relationships among agent, victim, and onlooker. Guilt can move an agent to feel an obligation to offer repair and compensation. Gestures of repair, whether in the concrete form of compensation or the abstract form of apology, are warranted by the standards of mutual respect and concern internal to the particular moral and social relationship between agent and victim. The abstract and idealized terms of the background moral relationship only inform responses between total strangers, and then only motivate the least personal forms of apology or compensation. The actual responses guilt engenders are rather a function of how the agent understands his or her thicker, social and moral relationships to the aggrieved. If, for example, there is special trust between two family members, then the agent may warrantably feel that more serious repair is required, something beyond cash payment or a quick apology.[38]

Actual moral psychology can differ from the normative ideal of repair, and differently reflect social relations. Guilt, and the accompanying feeling of obligation, can engender resentment toward a victim.[39] If the agent sees the victim as an equal, the agent will probably be motivated to respond by repairing the wrong. But if the agent sees the victim as a social or moral superior or inferior, then the agent's response to guilt may be resentment or intensified anguish, either because the victim's superiority has been reinforced by the bond of obligation, or because the previously inferior victim has been made a superior by that bond.[40] Here the cognitive content of the response of guilt is recognized, but it supports a perverted practical inference of resentment rather than repair. Hester's loyalty and devotion to Dimmesdale, despite his abandonment of her, exacerbates his guilt to the point of distraction, because it confirms his moral inferiority. Similarly, what Dostoevsky's Raskolnikov regrets about his murder of the (to him) contemptible old woman, before his final repentance, is not its wrongfulness, but rather the guilt he feels for it. He resents this guilt for demonstrating to him that he is not an "extraordinary individual," but rather, that he is inescapably a party to minimal moral relationships, in particular the one which joins him to the old woman.

### 2.3.2   Accountability Warranted by Reasons of Consequence

Sometimes responses to agents are not motivated by the attitudes those agents manifest, nor by their failure to conform their conduct to appropriate norms. Sometimes an agent's mere causal linkage with a harm may warrant a response from others. In this section, I argue that the responses characteristic of accountability for consequences can also only be understood in terms of the moral and social relationships among the parties, and their different positions with respect to the harm. In particular, the striking asymmetry in accountability for consequences between the responses of agents, on the one hand, and victims and onlookers, on the other, has not been fully appreciated. Agents can reproach themselves for faultless conduct that causes a harm, when neither their victims nor onlookers reproach them. This asymmetry, or extreme positional dependence, of responses to consequences reflects the deep role that causal relations have for agents in structuring their understanding of themselves. Those affected by the agent, in contrast, care less about causal relations in the absence of faulty conduct.

While conduct-based responses are warranted by the way that agents' behavior manifests attitudes of respect, contempt, or indifference regardless of whether that conduct causes harm, consequence-based responses are warranted by the fact of a harm regardless of whether the conduct was faulty. Causality, in isolation from conduct, indicates nothing about how agents have previously viewed their relations with others. The ready-to-hand example of the significance of causality is Oedipus. The characters' reactions in *Oedipus Rex* can be intelligible to modern readers who do not share Sophocles' magical beliefs in fatalism and pollution, in terms of reasons of consequence. "Incest" describes a situation, not a content of will or an attitude. Oedipus has, by his own actions, brought on this situation, and this contingent, causal connection grounds his horror and self-reproach.[41]

Oedipus' response to the fact of his causal role is what Bernard Williams calls "agent-regret": regret that a state of affairs exists whose occurrence involved one's own agency.[42] Agent-regret rests on no sense of wrongdoing, and is compatible with impeccable conduct, even conduct so recognized by the agent.[43] However, it seems a mistake to distinguish agent-regret fully from guilt, for although an awareness of wrongful acting is a typical part of guilt, awareness of having done something awful, even if unwittingly, can suffice.[44] Oedipus' response was partly shame at his incestuous disgrace. But his horrible self-mutilation can only be explained by something else, something we can recognize as a form of guilt: a gesture at repaying a wrong he has done. The causal relation need not be entirely direct to trigger guilt. If, while I am tending a friend's cat, it slips outdoors despite my protections and gets hit by a car, I will feel not merely sorry for my friend but guilty toward her. Although the death is not my fault, I have provided for its occasion, and so my relations to her differ from those of any other sympathetic friend. Indeed, because of the friend's trust in me, I am likely to feel even worse than the driver who, also let us assume faultlessly, actually killed the cat.[45]

These examples bring out a striking feature of consequential accountability: Where conduct is not at issue, there is a radical asymmetry in response among the various positions the harm creates. My friend is unlikely to resent me, even though I feel guilty. More precisely, if the accident is not my fault, then my friend would be unwarranted in resenting my role, since I will not have acted badly, while my feelings will be warranted by my causal role and our prior relationship.[46] Likewise, Oedipus' compatriots more pity than despise him for his crime. The principal reason for this asymmetry is that agents' causal relations necessarily inform their conceptions of themselves. This gives causal relations to a harm a salience to the agent that they do not have to the victim or to onlookers.

The relation between agents and their effects is one of identity. What agents have caused is an important part of their histories and lives, as important as what they have intentionally done, believed, and hoped for. Regret signals the fundamental unluckiness of the causal connection between agents and consequences. Because regret for faultless accidents maps agents' actual (as opposed to idealized) course through the world, the general absence of such regret is found primarily among children and extreme Kantians, for whom the fantasy or ideal world is more salient than the real. As H.L.A. Hart and Tony Honoré have suggested, it is through claims of causal authorship that "[i]ndividuals come to understand themselves as distinct persons, to whatever extent they do, and to acquire a sense of self-respect. . . ."[47] It is important to note, however, that "what I have done" does not name a naturally limited universe of events: Agents are causally related to infinitely many events, under infinitely many descriptions, and only some of those events, under some descriptions, will be salient. The understanding of what an agent has done is itself given by our social relations and practices of accountability. Beyond bodily movements the extension of an agent's field of causal influence is given by a complex and deeply rooted normative conception.[48]

The shape of that conception – what causal relations are picked out as warranting a response – is the subject of an enormous literature.[49] A person's act is typically one item among enormously many causally relevant events and conditions that are jointly sufficient for an event's occurrence. As many philosophers have argued, whether that act is highlighted as noteworthy ("*the* cause") by the agent or another depends in part upon its relation to stable background conditions, its role in durable structures of events, and its susceptibility to intervention or control.[50] The relevance of the agent's intervention in the cat and Oedipal cases is obvious. But I want to suggest that, in more difficult cases, agents' social and moral relations to others are especially important to agents' seeing their acts as causally connected to harms. This is particularly true of omissions, as when my failure to bring a sick child promptly to the doctor results in suffering: Whether I am counted the cause depends upon my relation to the child. My seeing myself as the positive cause of another's misery also depends upon my understanding of the structure of our mutual relations. If we are competitors in business and my low prices unintentionally drive you into bankruptcy, I may see your failure to meet my prices, rather than my own act, as the cause of your demise.[51] In contrast, if we are friends and my unintentional act results in your suffering, I am likely to reproach myself for my causal role and do what I can to make amends.

My gesture of repair as an agent is, in these cases, more complicated than just reaffirming or reestablishing a relationship between agent and victim. When I see myself as accountable for a harm I merely cause, and when repair is possible in part, my gesture of repair is directed at myself as well as at my victim. It is directed at the victim insofar as it attempts to compensate for a burden I have imposed. And it is directed at myself insofar as it provides a way for me to transform my trajectory through the world, eliminating what is unfortunate about what I have done. Here we see a further asymmetry in the responsive positions of agent and victim, in cases of faultless wrongdoing: While my victim may be indifferent to the source of compensation, I may feel that it must, in symbolic part at least, come from me.[52] And even if neither I nor my victim feels it necessary that I provide compensation, an apology or other gesture of repair may also be called for, and that can come only from me.

This account of causation as a source of reasons warranting a response of accountability may seem circular. If merely singling out a causally relevant factor as *the* cause depends upon a prior conception of appropriate relations between the parties, then the notion of causation is doing no independent normative work.[53] The notion of cause and warranted response are indeed interdependent and so, in a sense, circular, but the circularity is not vicious. We make our causal contributions in social as well as physical space. The norms and interests that define that social space inevitably play a role in delineating the causal relations we perceive. Once we have identified a given act as the cause of a harm, on the basis of background expectations of appropriate behavior, then we are led to modify our conception of that background, and so alter our future perceptions of what is a cause and what a mere condition. My friend forgives me this time for letting the cat out; either the driver or the cat itself may be regarded as the cause of its death. But if several more cats die while in my care, my friend's perceptions of my causal role will undoubtedly change, as will her responses to me.

Causation, too, is positional as well as relational, its significance varying as much as the conditions of its attribution. The position of victims, and the responses warranted by their relations to the harm, differ dramatically from the agents' own responses, particularly in cases of faultless causation. These responses also depend upon the way victims view their relations to agents and onlookers. For agents, their causal relation to a harm warrants feelings of self-reproach. But because the agents manifested no ill conduct or will, victims' resentment on that basis is unwarranted. No prior moral or social relationship has been devalued by the harm, but only a distribution of goods distorted. As a result, the victim's response is more likely to be a demand for compensation unaccompanied by reproach. Whether this claim for compensation is seen as having normative force by victim or agent, it is a product of the relationships among the parties and society at large. "It wasn't my fault," when true, is a perfect excuse from accountability for conduct, but it bears no direct relationship to the question of compensation. Given a certain understanding of social and moral relationships, "that you caused it" can sufficiently warrant a claim for compensation.

The positive and normative force of the claim from the victim for compensation depends, among other things, upon patterns of wealth distribution, whether exposure to risky behavior is mutual, and the availability of third-party mechanisms of compensation.[54] Strikingly, what is today considered the natural view, that compensation in law for accidents is morally owed only when there has been wrongful conduct, probably dates back only to late nineteenth-century jurists.[55] Presumably this natural view was not shared by those who suffered from faultless industrial accidents. If distributions of wealth are fair, exposure to risk is reciprocal, and compensation readily available elsewhere, victims may be unlikely to demand compensation from agents, or even to demand compensation at all. In contrast, if the state of a victim's well-being is highly vulnerable to accidents and risk is not reciprocal, then even faultless causation may give rise to demands for compensation.[56] Even when a victim's demand for compensation by the agent is warranted, however, the significance of compensation from the victim's point of view lies primarily in its role in reestablishing a distribution of goods, and not in its role in restoring good moral relations.

### 2.3.3   *Accountability Warranted by Reasons of Character*

Reasons of character are significant aspects of agents' identities, such as motivations, dispositions, commitments, and affiliations, on the basis of which they may be held accountable in relation to a harm or wrong. Unlike reasons of conduct or consequence, which rely upon direct causal or attitudinal links between agent, victim, and harm, reasons of character can warrant response in the absence of any such link. When an evaluator holds an agent accountable for a harm for reasons of character, it means that the evaluator associates the harm with the agent because the harm manifests or symbolizes an enduring trait of the agent. Reasons of character are also invoked negatively, to deny accountability. If an agent behaves badly, in a way that is "out of character," evaluators might be moved to find extenuating reasons for the behavior, in order to excuse it.

For many retributivist philosophers, accountability independent of causality or conduct – vicarious accountability, in other words – is either inexplicable or inexcusable.[57] In this section, I will defend accountability on the basis of character alone. I will argue that reasons of character function primarily subjunctively, or counterfactually. The agent did not cause the harm, consciously or otherwise. But a response may be warranted to the agent if there is reason for the respondent to think that this agent might have caused or endorsed it in the right circumstances. The counterfactuals involved in reasons of character make these reasons, like reasons of consequence, function very differently for diversely positioned parties, notably for agents as opposed to victims or onlookers. But an even more important consideration for demonstrating the relationality of accountability is that because what agents identify or affiliate with is an aspect of their character, reasons of character directly express the significance of their relationships to others. Accountability for character is therefore perhaps the most clearly relational of the three forms of accountability discussed here.

The central distinguishing feature of reasons of character is that the relation between agent and harm need not be mediated by either causality or intentional conduct. Harms may be symbolic, standing for elements of character in agents other than those who brought them about. Thus, reasons of character can allow for associative forms of accountability that reasons of conduct and consequence cannot. Indeed, only reasons of character can make sense of the powerful phenomena of purely vicarious guilt and shame. These vicarious feelings are extremely stable, not fading under reflection. Although institutions enforcing such associative forms of accountability have all but disappeared in the modern world, with the important exceptions of the law of vicarious commercial and conspiratorial liability, the feelings of taint and complicity generated by social membership and association persist.

A combination of basic shame and identification, or imaginative projection, can handle some of the simple cases of associative accountability. If a relative or associate of mine is humiliated or acts badly, I may feel ashamed. The most obvious reason for this is that I may be disgraced by association, depending upon the society I inhabit. It is still, although decreasingly, the case that to have a family member in disgrace is to be disgraced oneself. Similarly, if while in a restaurant in a foreign country, I hear another tourist speaking loudly and abrasively, I hide my guidebook in shame, not for the other tourist, but for myself as someone in whom the same shameful characteristics are likely to be expected by association with the category "tourist." My own, rather than others', inclusion of myself in the objectionable category may also be a basis for shame. If I think of myself under the description "tourist," I will cringe when another member of that category warrants disdain. My identity as a co-national provides a ground – albeit a weak epistemic one – for the inference that I too share the objectionable trait. I may draw the inference myself, or simply fear that others will. So my shame need not be a function of sympathy with the other, but only identification with the other's role in the transaction. I simply imagine myself as the one acting shamefully.

A related form of identification can also give rise to the phenomenon of partial accountability: an urge to repair harms unaccompanied by self-reproach. Because of my identification with a group, whether voluntary or involuntary, I bear a special reparative relationship to a harm committed by a member of that group, though I do not imagine myself to be a wrongdoer or feel disgraced by the wrong.[58] Contemporary Germans, for example, often claim that they accept collective responsibility without collective guilt, by which they mean all Germans, in virtue of their citizenship, owe duties of commemoration and reparation to the victims and survivors of the Holocaust regardless of any actual complicity.[59]

Sometimes, however, association can deliver the full stinging force of guilt, a feeling that cannot be explained by the simple identification model, but which involves an awareness of one's own character as compared with that of the actual wrongdoer. The response of shame relies on the belief that one's inadequacies have been exposed. If those inadequacies are provided only by identification, in which the agent simply imagines himself or herself to be the wrongdoer, then the feeling of shame is likely to be ephemeral, lasting no longer than the imaginative projection. In contrast, the enduring self-hatred of veterans of the My Lai period and the sardonic introspections of Gunther Grass can only be explained by what I will call *counterfactual guilt:* guilt at the suspicion one might oneself have acted wrongly, even monstrously.[60] Here awareness of one's actual character traits warrants the responses ordinarily directed only to actual wrongdoers. Dostoevsky delivered a complex anatomy of counterfactual guilt in *The Brothers Karamazov,* a novel constructed around the idea that action is only a trivial element in the economy of wrongdoing and responsibility. All the brothers are guilty of their father's death although only one has killed him, because each recognizes he might have done so instead. In this sense, and contra Gabriele Taylor and Joel Feinberg, guilt as well as shame can be vicarious. I can feel guilt at the actions of another, holding myself counterfactually accountable for them by reasons of character – or, in these cases, inferences to character traits supported by shared affiliation.[61]

Instances of counterfactual wrongdoing need not be so spectacular as parricide. The problem of the origins of benefits, for example, provides a commonplace example of counterfactual wrongdoing. Benefit accountability is at issue when someone accepts or receives a benefit with whose origins a wrongdoing is associated. If, for example, I learn that a fellowship I have been awarded was endowed by a notorious imperialist who earned his fortune through theft and exploitation, I am likely to keep it but feel guilty, on the principle that it is wrong to benefit from the wrongs of others. But just what sort of wrongness is it that can explain how, although I did not bring about and could not have prevented the harm, I become complicit in it through accepting benefits from it?

Some have suggested that the feeling of complicity manifests itself as an essentially magical belief, for example, that a benefit can bear a moral taint that transfers to its recipient.[62] Reasons of character provide a better, nonmagical explanation of counterfactual guilt. Accepting a benefit from a tainted source manifests a certain trait: willingness to be associated with moral compromises. Or, put slightly differently, acceptance transforms the agent's identity by creating an affiliation with the harm. Enjoying a tainted benefit puts one in an ongoing relationship with a wrongful act; it forces the realization that one might have been willing *ex ante* to trade principles for benefits since one has done so *ex post*. Doubtless, too great a concern about compromised sources amounts to criticizable piety or self-righteousness. But there is room for a concern for the character implications of one's commitments that lies between amoralism and self-indulgence.[63] Self-reflexive responses to reasons of character can play a special role in sustaining and strengthening commitments. Feelings of complicity on the basis of character force agents to study their own associations, to decide whether or not these associations reflect the character they want. In Charles Taylor's phrase, reasons of character provoke "strong evaluation" – second-order reflection on the value of what the agent values.[64]

## 2.4   A COMPLICATION: THE DYNAMICS OF ACCOUNTABILITY

I have so far treated responses of accountability in one important respect as the retributivist model does: as exogenous events, interventions which channel the relations among the participants, but which remain external to those relations. This feature of retributivist conceptions is seen most starkly in the support they offer to institutions of punishment. The relation of pain and domination essential to even legitimate punishment stands sharply opposed to the ideal relation between state and citizen, which is conformity, and the relation among citizens, which is equal respect. Even with "Quality of Will" approaches, which emphasize the extent to which the affects and judgments of accountability constitute the material of our interpersonal relations, the process of holding another accountable plays the essentially static role of expressing underlying concerns and attitudes. In Strawson's account, for example, the projection of interpersonal rather than objective attitudes has the aspect of a choice by the respondent, who might have opted otherwise had he or she not craved intimacy. The complication I have omitted is that responses of accountability also function dynamically, as transformative points of inflection in our relationships whereby new norms and expectations come to be warranted.

The transformative aspect of accountability is, of course, central to the parent-child relation, perhaps so central its general character is concealed. Through external punishment and admonition the child internalizes the relevant norms and becomes responsible, a change that makes for movement towards a new familial equilibrium.[65] But this dynamic function of accountability responses is not specific to parents and children. Again, let us consider a literary example, here Jane Austen's *Emma*. Emma is proud, rich, and clever, used to manipulating others to fulfill her various (essentially benevolent) designs. Mr. Knightley, a family friend, has an apparently avuncular relationship to her. Not knowing her own heart, she projects her romantic desires onto others until an event at a group picnic. Emma cruelly mocks the sweet if dull spinster Miss Bates, and Knightley later takes her to task for it. "How could you be so unfeeling to Miss Bates?," he asks. "How could you be so insolent in your wit to a woman of her character, age, and situation?" Emma is stunned, and Knightley takes her silence as further arrogance. But he is wrong:

He had misinterpreted the feelings which had kept her face averted and her tongue motionless. They were combined only of anger against herself, mortification, and deep concern. . . . Never had she felt so agitated, so mortified, grieved, at any circumstance in her life. She was most forcibly struck. The truth of his representation there was no denying. She felt it at her heart. How could she have exposed herself to such ill opinion in any one she valued![66]

Emma's crime is expressed in the idiom of a violation of class norms – she has acted beneath herself in mocking an inferior – but that idiom expresses what is for Austen a deeper flaw, arrogance to the point of solipsism. Emma has acted as though other people existed only to suit her taste for arrangement, and her machinations cause them pain. This being a novel of manners, Knightley's chastisement has great effect: not only does Emma repair the insult to Ms. Bates and become gentler in her ways, but she also comes to see Knightley in a new light, because of his hard words. In short, she recognizes the possibility of love. In the very harshness of his scolding she sees that she has attained adulthood in his eyes – she is expected to know the demands of her station – and in his words' shaming effect she discovers her vulnerability to his opinion. The scolding transforms Emma's understanding of her place in the world, her relations to others, and leads directly to that perfection of social relations in Austen's world, marriage.

How we respond to affronts, and how we meet the responses of those who criticize us, shapes the trajectory of our future dealings with them. It determines the character of the respect (or enmity) we show. Insisting upon an acknowledgment of what has been done is an essential part of the practice of autonomy, and it is in making such claims that we come to regard ourselves as members of a common enterprise. The accountability system makes possible a world of significant relations with others by continually remaking us into the kinds of people who can enjoy those relations in their varied courses through our lives. I stress this point about the dynamism of the accountability system because it will figure centrally in my argument that even weak relations of complicity can foster structure in circumstances of social dispersion. Virtuous circularity results when mutual responses of accountability strengthen social cohesion, which in turns lends motivational efficacy to those responses. This is what underlies the possibility of noncoercive control of collective harms.

These sections have proposed that responses of accountability may be warranted by three distinct grounds, or sets of reasons: those stemming from agents' intentional conduct, the possibly unintended effects of that conduct, and the content of their characters. The forms of response supported by these different bases will invariably reflect both the position of the respondent and the background moral and social relations between the agent, victim, and respondents. In the ensuing chapters, I will put these bases of accountability to work, in exploring the nature of moral and legal responses to complicitous participation in the harmful or wrongful acts of others. Before moving on to that substantive ethical discussion, however, I want to explore further the nature of the theory of accountability that I am presenting, its justification, and its differences from solipsistic, retributive theories.

## 2.5   THE IRREDUCIBILITY OF ACCOUNTABILITY

I have argued so far that the responses agents warrant in virtue of how they act, what they cause, and who they are, cannot be understood simply in terms of their individual capacities to act and the effects of their acts. Rather, the moral responses agents warrant manifest the complexity and specific character of their moral and social relations to others, as refracted through the perspective of the particular respondent.

One important dimension of accountability might be thought to be nonrelational, however: the scalarity, or degree of accountability that an agent bears for an act. This notion of degree of accountability is often explained in terms of the nonrelational notion of degrees of responsibility. Agents are often said to warrant mitigated responses because they bear only a small degree of responsibility for a harm, or to be largely responsible and hence deserving of especially hard treatment. If I help you with your plan to rob a store by hiding the loot, I am perhaps less responsible for the robbery than you who initiated the plan.[67] Or if my negligent monitoring of the controls of a poorly designed nuclear reactor results in meltdown, I may be said to bear little, but significant, responsibility for a very great harm. Degrees of responsibility play a central role in mitigating liability in tort law, in the guise of principles of contributory negligence, and an overt role in retributivist moral theories, such as Nozick's.[68]

In this section, I want to show that, with limited exceptions, the notion of degree of responsibility must itself be interpreted relationally, that is, as a function of the character of agents' relations with their respondents. In particular, I will argue that the notion of an agent's degree of responsibility, and therefore also accountability, cannot generally be reduced to or explained by facts about that agent alone.

The nonrelational understanding of degrees of responsibility works best in the case of mental capacity, for mental impairment is in many cases scalar.[69] The capacity of rational self-governance, the prerequisite of Quality of Will theories, comes in various levels of functionality and can be interfered with to various degrees. We may think someone is wholly causally responsible for a harm, but only partially accountable for it. Agents' accountability for their conduct may be mitigated when they are under the influence of a drug or a disease. My resentment at a friend's outburst may weaken when I learn that my friend is taking mood-altering medications, because I attribute some share of the responsibility for the outburst to the drugs.[70] Beyond a certain threshold, impaired mental function negates responsibility altogether. As Strawson observed, the objective attitude dominates our relations. (The only genuine significance of the distinction between moderate and extreme psychosis is therapeutic.)

Age is another seemingly nonrelational scalar factor. My reaction to an act of vandalism will depend on whether the culprit is five, twelve, or twenty. As with mental illness, age tends to make more a polar than scalar difference. With few exceptions, children are treated as not responsible and hence not accountable for serious harms, and adults are treated as fully responsible and so accountable. Even in the cases of age and mental illness, however, there are two important ways in which these factors are relationally dependent. First, as I argued while interpreting Strawson in Section 2.3.1, the reason immaturity and illness are significant forms of excuse lies in the nature of the relationship one has with immature or incompetent agents. That is, they are only persuasive forms of excuse because of a background assumption about the nature of the relationship the respondent has with the agent, namely objective rather than participatory. Second, and relatedly, a partial basis for accountability may be established within the context of a particular relationship with a nonresponsible agent. The case is clearest with children, but is presumably true of those who live and work with the mentally ill. Often when parents blame their children, they do so educationally (or "therapeutically"), in order to teach them to become responsible agents. But teaching is not all that parents do, and a teacher's reactions are not all they feel. It is, for example, virtually impossible not to resent the willful brattiness of a three-year old, or not to be charmed by the gift of another Crayola masterpiece.

We should also note the extreme variation among particular respondents in even these cases of limited responsibility. A child, while in the schoolyard, bullies, pushes, and so hurts another child. Imagine now the response of the first child's parents, for whom the child's violent tendencies may mark a worrisome trend and so must be countered sternly. Now compare this response with the corrective but largely superficial response of the supervising teacher, for whom playground fights simply mark a phase of childhood aggression; and with the response of the victim's parents, who do not regard the first child as an autonomous agent at all, but only take that child's act to be symptomatic of the pathologies of public education. None of these responses to the child's act depends upon a deep assessment of the metaphysical or psychological autonomy of children generally, or even of this child in particular. (And consider as well the response of the victim, who is unlikely to take any sort of abstracted view of the tormentor.) It is far better to say these responses mirror the hopes, expectations, and fears that structure the particular relationships among these adults and children.[71]

Distinguishing degrees of causation is another way people sometimes try to reduce the notion of degrees of responsibility. In theory, a probability could be assigned to some causal factors and forms of conduct indicating their likeliness to cause or exacerbate harm when taken in isolation, and from this an assessment of culpability can be derived when the forms of conduct are combined. If the example is a collision between a speeding car and a car making an illegal left turn, some estimate of the dangerousness of each act is presumably derivable, allowing for an apportionment of causal responsibility and perhaps legal damages.[72] But in many cases of joint or multifactor causation, no such estimate will be possible. Consider an airplane crash in which pilots, weather, and machinery combine to produce a disaster. But for the severe weather, the wing flaps wouldn't have bent. But for the wing flaps' bending, the pilot wouldn't have steered the plane manually. But for the pilot's inability to steer with bent wingflaps, the plane wouldn't have crashed. Whether a better pilot, or better weather, or a newer plane might have each made the difference, or whether each factor was necessary, it is sheer bluff to claim that estimates of the independent riskiness of each factor can be assessed and then combined. While differential degrees of responsibility might be assigned for instrumental reasons – little can be done about the weather, liability is lower when pilot error is minimized as a factor – the actual judgment of the accountability of human actors is largely independent.[73]

Once again, it is important to note the positional character of these causal assessments. Compare the response of the surviving pilot, or the pilot's family, with that of the mechanics, or of a potential passenger, or of the airline's financial officer who has been strongly urging cost cutting in all areas. Clearly, all of these differently placed respondents will disagree in the significance they attribute to the various causal candidates. The causal assessment, and so the resulting evaluative response, of any of these parties to the harm will be inflected by the character of their actual or potential relations to the various actors, situations, and interests involved in the tragedy.

I do not mean to suggest that no morally relevant distinctions among causal factors can be drawn, or that all such distinctions reflect overt policy interests, in law or morals. Rather, my point is that the indeterminacy intrinsic to the notion of causal responsibility precludes any reduction of degrees of accountability to causality. Contributory, necessary causes are metaphysically equal and only normatively unequal.[74] When accountability is assigned in degrees ostensibly relative to causal responsibility, independent normative interests are doing the real work. These interests are themselves derived from relationships between agents and respondents, namely relationships of control, reliance, risk, and capacity to compensate.

The attempt to reduce accountability to causality becomes even more puzzling in the case of marginal or unnecessary individual contributors. Consider a pollution case. If all polluters are individual drivers, is each slightly causally responsible for the whole cloud of smog, or wholly responsible only for a tiny burst of emissions? If normative consequences are to follow upon causal analysis, then indeterminacy arises, for what each does both entirely brings about that tiny burst and contributes negligibly to the whole cloud. It could be (and has been) argued that each contribution is necessary to the formation of the particular smog cloud, and hence each driver is fully responsible for the cloud. But such a view individuates smog clouds and other entities implausibly finely.[75] An individual driver must, then, be trivially responsible for the pollution itself, and wholly responsible for a trivial contribution to it. If accountability is measured by causality, then no polluter is nontrivially accountable for what is in fact a very great harm. (I will take up this point at length in Chapter 6.)

A final suggestion for understanding the notion of degrees of responsibility is to interpret this notion in purely moral terms. Responsibility varies with the moral egregiousness of the conduct. If an accident occurs through one party's negligence and another's gross recklessness, the latter might be said to be more responsible because his conduct was more reprehensible. This judgment might rest upon an implicit presumption that recklessness is riskier than negligence, but might also simply express extra condemnatory force at the greater flouting of standards of conduct.[76] My driving the getaway car may be an essential part of our successful bank robbery, but the additional wrongfulness of your instigation of the crime, and willingness to use force, exposes you to greater condemnation in the eyes of others (if not in the eyes of the law). Put another way, the significance attributed to my causal contribution will, as I argued in Section 2.3.2, reflect the position of the respondent assessing that contribution. Given the characterization I have offered of moral standards, as principles structuring interpersonal relationships, it follows that interpreting degrees of responsibility in terms of moral egregiousness is also thoroughly relational. Initiating wrongdoing is only worse than complying with wrongdoing if the first represents a more aggressive affront to the standards governing particular moral relationships than the second. (Whether this is indeed so is my topic in the following chapters.)

## 2.6  ETHICAL FUNCTIONALISM WITHOUT CONSEQUENTIALISM

My conception of accountability is broadly functionalist, in that it explains and justifies practices of accountability in terms of their role in maintaining and fostering certain moral, social, and political relationships, and the interests those relationships protect. The relational and positional nature of accountability manifests this functional justification, insofar as relationality and positionality express the significance different respondents attribute to these interests. My conception might therefore seem to be in keeping with a general category of consequentialist moral theories, insofar as the practices of accountability are justified by the states of affairs they make possible. In this section, however, I want to suggest that it is a mistake to conflate the global instrumental value of practices of accountability with the local warrant individuals have for responding to wrongs and harms. Unlike consequentialist theories, in which all accountability responses maximize, directly or indirectly, aggregate states of well-being, in my theory responses are warranted only by the role they have in sustaining relationships among discrete individuals.

Functionalist theories of accountability have been offered by a broad ideological range of philosophers. Direct and indirect utilitarians such as David Hume, Jeremy Bentham, and J.J.C. Smart have argued that the practices of blame and praise maximize aggregate welfare or some other form of general social well-being.[77] The sociobiologically inclined, notably Allan Gibbard, have argued that blame and praise maximize inclusive fitness by enabling members of social groups to coordinate their behavior.[78] And legal positivists such as H.L.A. Hart and Guido Calabresi endorse instrumentalist theories as justifications for our practices of criminal and civil liability, where these practices maintain social order, lower transaction costs, and maximize liberty, among other institutional goals.[79]

Although my account justifies our practices of accountability in terms of their contribution to well-being, it is not a form of consequentialism. There are several ways my account is nonconsequentialist. First, I make no claims that the practices we have or we should have maximize an aggregate social utility function. While I do not dispute that our practices of accountability have some form of general social utility, I see these practices as justified primarily by their role in sustaining particular relationships that make our lives good. Even if the relation between practices of accountability and general welfare could be well defined, there is no reason to think that it would or should be a relation of optimization. The relation between act and response in my theory is intrinsic, or organic. The relation between them in consequentialist theories is contingent.

Thus, my objection to consequentialist theories is that they fail to attribute the right kind of significance to the relations between agents and harms. Consequentialists claim that the relation between the question of whether an agent's act "objectively" maximized welfare, and the question of what response to that act is warranted, is wholly dependent upon whether the responses will have optimal consequences.[80] As a result, the propriety of blame and guilt are contingent upon extrinsic considerations of aggregate welfare. Because the responses of accountability have no independent conceptual role, consequentialist accounts are fundamentally noncognitivist: There is no independent fact of wrongdoing which it is the point of a response of accountability to get right.

Because of their instrumentalism, consequentialist theories define an enormously flexible scope of accountability. There is no need to track an actual index of harm or responsibility unless tracking it is optimal relative to the goals of the system. In principle, if the environmental demand is right, any individual, no matter how competent, bearing any relation to a harm, no matter how tenuous, is subject to blame. There is, for example, no principled objection to punishing the incompetent or immature or to vicarious punishment, whether administered *pour encourager les autres,* or to augment the stakes for an individual.[81] Even when, as Russell Hardin has argued, the inevitable fact of informational constraints allows theorists to dispose of the most extreme counterexamples, consequentialist theories still fail to make the relations among agents, victims, and onlookers matter at the foundational level.[82]

The second reason my own account is not consequentialist is that whether or not consequentialist theories can provide an objective justification of practices of morality, they cannot explain the significance those practices have from the point of view of the participants. I take it as now widely agreed that a consequentialist interpretation of our moral practices and psychology cannot be fully transparent to the subjects of those practices and psychology: They cannot regard themselves under the description of "agents who maximize aggregate well-being."[83] In Strawson's terms, agents who deliberate in subjectively consequentialist terms must take an objective attitude towards those to whom they respond. The response such agents offer is fundamentally therapeutic, or manipulative.[84] Though some agents, while occupying specific roles, or dealing with nonresponsible others, may have reason to maintain an objective attitude, the objective attitude is neither desirable nor sustainable over the broad range of social interactions. Perhaps some form of objective, two-tiered consequentialism can perform the difficult triple task of maintaining its optimizing credentials, allowing agents to view their relations to others in nonoptimizing terms, and still permitting agents some form of reflective understanding of the consequentialist point of their responses to others.[85] My account, because it is nonaggregative, presents no such problem: Agents understand the point of their practices in terms of the relationships those practices sustain.

## 2.7 NIETZSCHE'S CHALLENGE

Finally, we should consider an alternative functionalist conception of accountability – a conception that might, with equal justice, be labeled counterfunctionalist. This is Friedrich Nietzsche's argument in *The Genealogy of Morals*. Our practices of accountability and the values they serve have a psychological origin not in a conception of rational autonomy or social harmony, but in a peculiarly sly form of imaginary revenge.[86] According to Nietzsche, those who feel weak and vulnerable suffer not so much absolutely but relationally, because they must compare their plight with the proud and the strong. So they devise a form of compensation, a new scheme of values whose effect is to devalue the currency by which the worth of the strong is measured. Their strength and spontaneity become vices of wantonness and cruelty, while the inaction of the vulnerable become virtues of self-restraint and humility. This is the effect of what Nietzsche calls *ressentiment*.[87] The account is clearly functionalist insofar as our moral practices are explained by reference to the interests they serve, and counterfunctionalist insofar as it suggests these practices weaken the strongest even as they protect the weakest.[88]

Nietzsche's critique of the egalitarian and pacific values of morality that I have stressed has been much discussed, and I will not dwell on it. Suffice it to say, the Homeric values he endorses do not wear their justifications on their sleeves either, and it is dubious whether we would (or could) do better with the Homeric scheme than with merely a more light-handed endorsement of our own. What I want to focus on is his suggestion that our practices of accountability manifest the workings of *ressentiment*. On this account, resentment, blame, guilt, and the rest of the responsive and reparative attitudes are not aimed at restoring equilibrium but rather at redescribing the relation between agent and victim from subjection to equality.[89] Nietzsche's target is the way the concept of blame presupposes a metaphysical conception of freedom, a deliberative space in which the agent could have – should have – acknowledged the moral status of the victim:

[N]o wonder if the submerged, darkly glowering emotions of vengefulness and hatred exploit this belief for their own ends and in fact maintain no belief more ardently than the belief that *the strong man is free* to be weak and the bird of prey to be a lamb – for thus they gain the right to make the bird of prey *accountable* for being a bird of prey. . . . The subject (or, to use a more popular expression, the *soul*) has perhaps been believed in hitherto more firmly than anything else on earth because it makes possible to the majority of mortals, the weak and oppressed of every kind, the sublime self-deception that interprets weakness as freedom, and their being thus-and-thus as a *merit*.[90]

Blame is, accordingly, a form of magical thinking in which the normative force of blame – how blame claims the attention of the agent – reconstructs the agent's view of the victim as someone to whom respect is owed. In the idealized account of blame, as we saw with Kant, the victim's blame directs the agent's attention away from the injury itself, towards the moral norms the agent has violated.[91] On the account I have offered as well, blame's function is ultimately productive: It forces confrontation between agent and victim in the form of a demand to restore the proper relations between them. But this normative story, Nietzsche insists, has a psychological base. Blame supplements the victim's weakness, it cloaks him in the power of the "ought" because he lacks the power of the "is." Like all devices of repression, the actual hurt remains to rankle; doubtless Aesop's fox still craves the grapes as well.[92] And when punishment is possible, the story is darker still. Blame allows the agent to "participate[]] in a *right of the masters:* at last he, too, may experience for once the exalted sensation of being allowed to despise and mistreat someone as 'beneath him'. . . . The compensation, then, consists in a warrant for and title to cruelty."[94]

The story of guilt follows suit, for guilt is the internalization of blame by means of punishment. In the idealized story, guilt, like blame, turns the agent's attention to the moral norms he has violated. But, Nietzsche suggests, the institution of guilt is equally fraudulent. The immediate content of guilt is not an awareness of the norms one has violated but rather fear at the anger of the victim.[94] So long as the device of guilt (and the memory of the pain by which it was induced) operates, it preserves the social order. But its very constraining force generates an opposite reaction among the strong: a surge of cruelty and rampage when the strong break free of its claims, thus supplying further though fallacious support for the idea that morality's constraints are required.[95]

Nietzsche's subversive story of blame and guilt is deeply troubling, because it suggests that while blame and guilt may suit and soothe each other like hand and glove, the ensemble is not worth the price. It renders covert conflict which must be overt if it is to be discharged. Note that his is also a relational and positional theory of accountability, but with a crucial difference. According to Nietzsche, the power relations that determine the appropriate responses undermine the ostensible ambitions of those responses. Because blame arises out of weakness, it merely displaces rather than replaces anger; and because guilt arises out of subordination, it displaces rather than replaces fear. By contrast, Nietzsche's counterideal is far more attractive than the strong but ruthless Homeric "blond beast" that he also mentions: It is Mirabeau, "who had no memory for insults and vile actions done him and was unable to forgive simply because he – forgot." This is the mark of those "strong, full natures in whom there is an excess of the power to form, to mold, to recuperate and to forget."[96] Here is the obverse of Spinoza's dictum that "[r]epentance is not a virtue; i.e., it does not arise from reason; he who repents of his action is doubly unhappy or weak."[97] We cripple ourselves, on this account, by demanding acknowledgment of our injuries in the form of guilt. Far better would be to note the wrongs we commit and those committed against us – note them, learn from them, and move on.

The question, then, is whether our practices of accountability can survive Nietzsche's scrutiny of their underlying motives. When the dark satisfactions of blame are exposed, for example, can it be warranted in the strong sense, not just as supported by relevant norms, but as a response whose expression and discharge are part of a model of human relations we can reflectively endorse? I believe the answer is clearly *yes*, but only so long as Nietzsche's suspicions are incorporated into our practices. The institutions of accountability are not the only ones vulnerable to exploitation; so too are the institutions of trust, promise in particular, and cooperation in general. Such institutions work for two reasons: The practices they consist of are not engaged in blindly, and the good they promote – the gains from collective endeavor – is worth the risk of their possible exploitation. We recognize the temptation to make and then renege on a promise, or to free-ride on others' efforts, and so we demand signs and surety of our own and others' good will by cultivating and checking reputations for fidelity.

We also use accountability to make cooperation possible. So what was true of promise and collaboration is true of blame, guilt, and the rest of the panoply: these practices are open to both fruitful and resentful exploitation. We desire the security of body and possession that comes through the moralization of injury, from the demand that we each constrain our wants by reference to shared norms.[98] Likewise we desire the possibilities of intimacy and community that accountability makes possible. So, aware of the workings of *ressentiment*, we can exploit blame and guilt with a clear eye upon vengeful motives. We can, for example, demand of ourselves that attitudes of blame and other demands of accountability come with the possibility of forgiveness, expiation, and forgetting. This demand is at its strongest in the case of demands for punishment, for it is here, as Nietzsche rightly notes, the finer trappings of cruelty most easily take the form of righteousness. Guilt too may be inculcated in the light of the ideal of repair, not submission. To be sure, not all is forgivable and not all relations ought to be restored.[99] Some acts, both grand and domestic, lie so far beyond redemption that forgiveness amounts to a kind of complicity.[100] But if, as I have claimed, the accountability system has a point chiefly in terms of the goods it promotes, then we must act with a reflective conception of those goods, specifically a conception of the relations worth wanting. Perhaps we can display power in forgiveness.

## 2.8  LEGAL ACCOUNTABILITY AND THE LIMITS OF RESPONSE

Accountability, in descriptive terms, reveals how agents understand themselves and their relations to each other. A normative conception of accountability describes the limits to the responses warranted by what agents do, cause, and believe, in virtue of the relationships between agents and their respondents. So far I have not tried to distinguish carefully between how people do respond to others (the response they believe is warranted) and how people ought to respond (what is in fact warranted). One reason I have not done so is that I believe moral standards underdetermine the character of responses agents are warranted in making, whether those standards are the general ones that I suggested serve as default guides of conduct towards strangers, or even the more determinate standards that govern the relations we have with others. Within the limits of warranted response, the intersection and overlap of particular moral and social relationships create complex possibilities of positionally dependent response.

Because states can use violence to coerce and to inflict punishment, the question of the limits of warranted legal response to harms and wrongs is far more important than in the case of moral accountability. And although modern legal systems are also characterized by normative underdeterminacy, the permissible range of response is far more circumscribed.[101] Indeed, unlike the highly positionally dependent responses of social and moral accountability, legal responses to wrongs tend to be univocal or bivocal, consisting in criminal sanctions and/or judgments of civil liability.[102] I will argue in this section that these two striking features of legal accountability, the tightly controlled use of violence and the univocality of its responses, are best understood in terms of the special position of the state with respect to its citizens. I do not intend to elaborate upon the full nature of the state's responsive relations to its citizens; even the very limited topics of criminal complicity and civil associative liability will occupy Chapter 7. Here I merely want to suggest the nature of the position from which the state offers its responses in a range of domains.

Within morality's broad limits, variety reigns. Friends and family members can reproach each other for minor defects of character as social acquaintances cannot. The fury and rage expressed by lovers at betrayal, well warranted though it may be, would be wholly out of place even between friends. Likewise, the poignant guilt properly felt at the betrayal of a friend might well be considered self-lacerating if it were directed at all moral transgressions. Beyond verbal reproach, glowering resentment, and social exile, it becomes difficult to determine the genuine limits of morally permissible response. Agents of contemptible character may be shunned, but may they be publicly ridiculed? May broken promises of gifts be enforced by theft? If a neighbor carelessly runs over my cat, may I deface his car with a spray-painted "Murderer!"? Though the norms governing warranted response have shifted enormously through time and across cultures, and have depended crucially upon the state's eagerness and capacity to keep the civil peace, there have always been limits to appropriate response, even if those responses have greatly transgressed the generally pacific borders of contemporary western elite social morality. I will stipulate here, however, that absent circumstances of self-defense, the limits of moral response are the limits of language and feeling. Physically violent or coercive responses to individuals are only morally permitted to the state.

Why are violent or coercive responses warranted when, and only when, they come from a state authority? Put otherwise, how do citizens internalize the state's claim to its monopoly on force? The answer is found by looking to the nature of interests protected by the different domains of accountability. All forms, I have said, maintain and protect social harmony; but they do this at very different levels of resolution. Social accountability maintains ongoing, concrete, and emotionally invested relationships. Highly charged responses to wrongdoing (or "wrongbeing") not only indicate the seriousness of the relationships in question, but themselves repair and maintain those relationships. By contrast, legal accountability and what I have called background moral accountability do not directly maintain participatory relationships. Both serve, rather, to make inhabitable those social contexts in which concrete participatory relationships (among other pursuits) may have a place. They also provide protection when social relationships turn foul.

Legal systems protect the interests that morality protects, centrally the means and liberties necessary to live well as a rational and reflective, project-centered agent. Unlike the view of morality I sketched earlier, in which moral standards and relationships are seen as having intrinsic and agent-neutral value, this view of legal institutions is almost purely instrumental. Law is good because the interests it protects are valuable; and legal responses are warranted by the importance of those interests. But if liberties and well-being are values within the law, then legal responses that compromise those values are suspect. While the restrictions upon moral wrongdoing and free riding that legal institutions dictate are not objectionable compromises to agents' interests, the use of threats and application of sanctions to guarantee those restrictions do compromise autonomy.[103]

It follows that if coercive measures by the state are warranted at all, they are warranted because no noncoercive measures are adequate to protect social interests once moral and legal forms of accountability have failed. Unlike social and moral responses, whose verbal or emotional nature is only of concern to those for whom the relationships they protect have value, coercive responses are of concern to any self-interested agent. While legal systems may depend primarily, as J.L. Mackie suggests, upon the efficacy of an adverse legal characterization of certain acts, coercive threats play an essentially ancillary role in motivating those unswayed by a desire to maintain morally appropriate relations.[104]

The interests that justify legal responses themselves limit those responses. If, as under liberal regimes, legal systems aim to protect meaningful forms of individual autonomy and social cooperation in general, then individuals' autonomy interests will be of concern as well in the administration of legal sanctions. As Hart (and Scanlon following him) has argued, this concern for autonomy, rather than a concern for rectifying moral wrongs, best explains the general restriction of penal sanctions to cases of voluntary conduct.[105] By making the infliction of those legal sanctions that severely infringe individual autonomy depend primarily upon the choices individuals make, the state has done what it can to ensure the autonomy of each citizen. Due process considerations also serve to protect individual autonomy from undue state interference. The concern for autonomy also explains the criminal law's "act requirement," that only attempts and commissions are punishable, and not inchoate plans.[106] Because who an agent is and what an agent causes are far less sensitive to choice, criminal punishment on these bases is far more restricted.[107]

In other domains of law, the nature of the compromise between the goods protected by law and the interests offended by coercion can vary, because legal sanctions are less invasive of individual autonomy. Noncriminal domains of law – contract, tort, property, environmental, civil rights – concern collective goods of varying levels of importance and therefore justify varying grades of response (and varying forms of excuse). The collective goods of contract law, namely fostering wealth-maximizing exchanges and protecting reasonable reliance between individuals, are significant enough to warrant the enforcement of commercial transactions or their equivalents in monetary damages, but insufficient to warrant compulsory personal service or punitive damages for nonperformance. And because the several goals of tort law – rectifying wrongful losses to individuals, optimizing efficient forced exchanges, minimizing the aggregate cost of accidents, protecting vulnerable consumers – can be met with transfers of wealth rather than direct invasions of individual autonomy, individual choice need not play a dominant role in dictating legal responses.[108]

The point I would like to stress is not just that considerations of choice and autonomy play very different roles in different domains of law. Rather, I want to emphasize that legal responses can only be seen as warranted by a particular set of social and moral relations, and the distorting effect that individual wrongs or harms have on these relations. For example, the need to show an agent's fault as a basis for recovery in tort law had a relatively brief history in Anglo-American law. That fact is explained by the specific historical formation of a conception of the moral and social relations between agents and victims, and the relations of agents and victims with society at large. More importantly, the normative proposition that faulty conduct alone warrants a claim of compensation is made true, if it is true, only by the expectations, patterns of wealth, and standards of conduct that ought to govern relations among citizens. In the absence of a conception of such relations, the idea that an agent deserves to pay compensation is empty. The same point can obviously be made about the other domains of law.

The second point I would like to emphasize is that the appearance of a univocal response delivered by the law is deeply misleading, insofar as it suggests that legal findings of guilt and liability are nonpositional.[109] In the first place, it is primarily the criminal law that appears univocal, delivering a single response of guilty or not guilty. It is not merely a legal conceit that while the prosecutor represents "the people," the court represents impartial justice. For the position of justice taken by the law is very special and circumscribed. Impartiality, in other words, is a specific position. When legal institutions assume the partialist position of the victim and the posture of resentment, the rights and liberties of defendants are severely compromised, a situation of which the sedition trials of the twentieth century are the best exemplars.[110] The warranted response of victims to hostile behavior is resentment; but resentment is wholly inappropriate from the institutions of justice.[111] The position the criminal law represents is not simply an integration over all social and moral positions, and legal responses do not represent whole, overall responses to wrongs. Instead, legal responses are ideally made from a particular position, that of the state, and represent one form of response among many. Regardless of what individuals deserve, the state's responses flow from the relations that tie each individual to one another, agent and victim alike, and are limited by the claims internal to those relationships.

## 2.9 CONCLUSION

Systems of accountability define and structure the moral, social, and political relationships that make our lives good. It is only within the context of relationships between persons that the responses of accountability have meaning and value. Reciprocally, it is only through the responses of accountability that our relationships with others have meaning and value as well. Our practices of accountability may, then, be regarded as a form of interpretation of those relationships. Through reflecting on the terms and character of our relationships with others, we give significance to what we, and they, plan, feel, and do. But accountability does not only give structure and meaning to relationships among individuals. Accountability also structures the character of the individuals within those relationships. Understanding who I am is a matter of understanding what I have done: and "what I have done" is only meaningful in virtue of the responses of accountability.

I have stressed what I call the positional dependence of accountability: the way that individuals' various perspectives on and relations to harms inflect the responses they give and are warranted in giving to those harms. With a relational and positional conception of individual accountability for individual harms now worked out, I can show how the accountability of individuals for structured and unstructured collective harms functions in virtue of their several and varied relations to the harm.

# Chapter 3

# Acting Together

## 3.1 INTRODUCTION

Two partners plan to rob a bank. The first recruits a driver while the second purchases a shotgun from a gun dealer. The driver knows he's taking part in a robbery, although not a bank robbery. The gun dealer should have checked his customer's police record before the sale, but failed to do so. The bank is robbed, a guard is killed, and the robbers escape, only to be caught later. "They committed bank robbery," a prosecutor will say. But does "they" include the gun dealer, whose lax standards made the robbery possible? "They conspired to rob the bank" – but does "they" here include the driver, who didn't know it was a bank they were robbing? "They killed a bank guard" – but does it matter who pulled the trigger?

These difficult questions of accountability raise issues I did not pursue in Chapter 2. There, I argued that individual accountability for individual harms depends upon the relations among agents, respondents, and harms. Warranted responses depend upon the preexisting moral and social relationships among the parties, and vary with the position of the respondent relative to the agent and the harm. But I assumed that agents were individuals acting as individuals. That is, I did not consider the accountability of groups or of individuals intentionally acting as members of groups. In this chapter I will set out and justify an analytical basis for ascribing acts to those individuals, and sets of individuals, who act together. More narrowly, I want to determine what makes true such statements as "They prepared the picnic for tomorrow," "She participated in their robbery by acting as a lookout," and "The City Council decided to fix the east-side potholes first." Later chapters will examine the further question of how ethical and legal accountability track the action ascriptions at issue in this chapter. I will argue that intentional participation in a group's activities is the primary basis for normative evaluation, both when agents contribute to collective harms, and when they fail to contribute to collective goods. Intentional participation establishes a special evaluative position, transforming prior social and ethical relations.

The general intuition I shall be exploring at length is that collective action is the product of individuals who orient themselves around a joint project. The particular form of the analysis I will defend makes use of the notion of an individual *participatory intention,* or an intention to act as part of a group. When suitably combined, individuals acting upon participatory intentions achieve jointly intentional action, and the group of which they are a part can be said to have acted. Section 3.2 is a methodological discussion and argues for an analysis of joint action which is both general enough to cover a wide range of cases, and is formally individualistic. In Section 3.3, I argue that many cases of joint action are best explained by the intentions with which individual agents act. These intentions are what I call *participatory:* Individuals act with the intention of contributing to a collective outcome. Section 3.4 elaborates on the content of these intentions. Next, Section 3.5 challenges the claim, made most prominently by John Searle and Margaret Gilbert, that joint action can only be explained in terms of a special collective *form* of intention. I argue instead that participatory intentions are ordinary individual instrumental intentions whose *content* is irreducibly collective. Section 3.6 urges a *minimalist conception* of joint action, namely a conception that requires agents to have only weak expectations about each other's plans, so long as there is sufficient overlap among their participatory intentions. In Section 3.7 I argue against taking what I call the *executive perspective* of collective actions, which attributes to each member an intention regarding the group's performance as a whole. Often, I suggest, participants intend only their own contributions; they do not conceive the group effort as within the ambit of their control. Finally, Sections 3.8–3.9 explain how joint action permits the ascription of acts and events to collectives, and even to individual members who did not directly produce those acts and events.

## 3.2  METHODOLOGY: GENERALITY, REDUCIBILITY, AND FUNCTIONALISM

In this chapter, I aim to give an account of collective action, collective intention, and individual participation in collective action. Indeed, I will argue that the first two items on the list can be explained by the third. But *collective action* (or *joint action*, as I will often refer to it) is a slippery notion: two drivers jointly navigate a four-way stop without crashing into one another; you and I play a chess match; a baseball team makes a double play in the bottom on the ninth; Exxon posts its third-quarter earnings; a hostile mob storms the Bastille. These joint acts involve very different kinds of groups, whose individual members engage in very different activities, with different degrees of mutual interaction.[1] I want to lay out the methodological structure of my approach to these disparate phenomena: I seek an explanation that generalizes over a broad range of collective acts, explains those acts in terms of individual mental states and, in particular, in terms of individual intentions and beliefs.

### 3.2.1   *For Generality*

Are the myriad forms of collective action in which we continuously engage susceptible to a single analytical account? We can easily identify at least five dimensions of variation in types of joint action, beyond the infinite variations among particular species of joint action. The first is the *number* of agents, ranging from the minimal two, to populations of hundreds of millions, as in general elections. The second dimension is that of *task-intricacy:* Many coordinated activities, such as negotiating a four-way stop sign, involve few choices (I'll go if you wait). Other activities, such as conversing or playing tennis, involve great responsiveness, the evaluation of many options, and sophisticated individual skills. Third, collective activities will vary in *cooperative spirit*. That is, some activities require degrees of goodwill, or willingness to put forth extra effort or incur extra costs for the sake of others (playing a team sport), while other activities can be conducted with little goodwill on the part of others (merging onto a freeway). Fourth, joint actions can involve different levels of *agent autonomy,* or individual (nonresponsive) discretion in how to perform one's task. And fifth, collective activity can be more or less *egalitarian.* Individuals can vary in the influence they actually or properly have over the direction taken by the collective, in choice of ends and means.

I will argue in this chapter that although various elements of organization and interaction are essential to particular types of joint action, most forms of collective action share a common structural feature: individual members of a group intentionally do their parts in promoting a joint outcome, or engaging in a joint activity. Participatory intentions explain both the nature and possibility of joint action, and its distinctive normative contours. I seek a general explanatory framework in order to make sense of the commonalities in our normative responses to individuals who participate in wrongful or harmful collective acts. Although forms of individual participation may vary greatly – from the role of a criminal kingpin to that of an investor in a predatory corporation – intentional participation generally shapes agents' normative relations to the consequences of collective action, as well as their relations to other members of the group. Because of their participation, agents can be accountable for acts and outcomes attributable to the group as a whole, as well as for acts attributable to other participating members.

### 3.2.2  *For Individualism in the Explanation of Collective Action*

Perhaps because as a matter of social fact we often hold individuals accountable for what groups, or other members of groups, do, it is tempting to think collective action is in some sense prior and irreducible to individual action. That is, accountability appears to accrue first to the jointly acting group, and then derivatively to its individual members. This feature of our practices of accountability has suggested to some that individual action is also explained by collective action, so that, for example, my stepping left is explained by our dancing a waltz. On such a *holistic* view, individual action is seen as a product of a collective will (perhaps embodied in individuals), such that the latter explains the former and not vice versa.[2] By contrast, on an *individualistic* view, collective action is explained by individual intentions and actions: our waltzing is explained by my dancing my part and you dancing yours. Individualists typically claim that collective action can always be "reduced" to individual action.

So the focal issue in analyzing collective action appears to concern the possibility of the reduction of claims about groups to claims about individuals.[3] Take the sentence, "Because Exxon posted a third-quarter loss, its share price fell." This sentence predicates an act of a collective entity, Exxon, and attributes an effect to that act. Methodological individualists suggest that such sentences may be replaced in many contexts, perhaps for the sake of social-scientific explanation, by sentences referring only to individuals and individualistic predicates, that is, predicates that do not relate individuals to social institutions.[4] Individualists would claim *Exxon* refers only to a set of individuals (some subset of Exxon employees and shareholders); that the sentence could be replaced by a (very large) set of sentences about those individuals, as well as about individuals trading Exxon stock; and the best explanation for the lower share price can be deduced from sentences about those individuals.[5] Holists, in contrast, might claim Exxon's posting of a loss can only be explained by reference to a collective plan for notifying the public about the company's performance. Though Exxon's act necessarily involves the actions of certain company officials, a holist might say, their actions can only be explained by reference to the collective, insofar as the officials both conceive of themselves as acting as their institutional offices require and because their acts are only regarded as authoritative in virtue of those offices. Holists do not deny that individuals act; they deny that the best explanation of social facts is couched solely in terms of facts about those individuals.

Since explanatory adequacy is always a function of the interests motivating the explanation, the success or utility of explanatory reduction is inherently relative to a particular investigative frame.[6] If, for example, a macroeconomic fact such as the unemployment rate is what is to be explained or predicted, then for many purposes it would be pointless to try to derive an explanation from an account of the behavior of individual managers within individual firms, rather than more straightforwardly from facts about interest rates, the money supply, and so on. On the other hand, for theoretical purposes it may well be worth investigating the interface between macroeconomic phenomena and microeconomic, individual, behavior.

The position I will defend with respect to collective actions is a form of explanatory reduction in the following sense: statements about collective acts may be rephrased always as statements about individual agents, because all collective action is explicable in terms of the intentionality of individuals – their motives, beliefs, and plans. If Exxon posted a third-quarter loss, then this fact may be explained in terms of the acts and intentions of individuals who saw themselves as acting on behalf of Exxon, as well as the expectations and beliefs of other individuals regarding what Exxon is and what acts it is capable of. Furthermore, the corporate policy these individuals saw themselves as promoting can itself be explained as the product of the deliberations and negotiations of and between individuals. Here the adequacy of such a reductive explanation is relative to a particular theoretical purpose, namely understanding the causal history of Exxon's act with the smallest gaps between intermediate explanatory events. Other purposes may be better served either by ignoring individual mediating events or looking to more distant original causes. For example, citing unrest in the Middle East might provide a better explanation of Exxon's posting a loss than would simply resting with unexplained facts about individual pricing and buying behavior. My claim is only that individual intentional action always implicitly mediates the causal explanation of collective acts and events, not that referring to individual acts always provides the most useful explanation.

This very weak form of individualism does not generalize to any strongly individualistic position in the philosophy of the social sciences.[7] Indeed, it is compatible with many moderate forms of holism. In particular, I deny that a full explanation of collective action can be given without reference to collectives or social facts, because reference to irreducibly holistic facts and entities must occur in an account of the mental states of individual agents. For example, if a group overcomes free riderism and collectively provides a public good, the explanation may be that individuals accept fairness norms, modifying their preferences. However, accepting an individualistic explanation of the act does not commit one to the further view that acceptance of these norms is in any strong sense a choice of the individuals. The best explanation of the inculcation and acceptance of fairness norms might be nonindividualistic, for example, it might be a form of group-level evolutionary adaptationism.[8]

In addition, many social groups cannot be reduced to sets of their members, because some groups can persist through changes in their membership (Exxon would be Exxon with a new bookkeeper). That is, certain structured social groups have nonextensional (or nonmereological) identity criteria. In many cases, the identity of a group is grounded in individuals' dispositions to identify themselves (and certain others) as members of that group.[9] In other words, group identity is explained in terms of individual participatory intentions. These dispositions include not just inchoate, romantic feelings of group solidarity, but a willingness to assume obligations taken on by other group members, to speak, decide, and act on others' behalf, and to deliberate about how to act so as to further collective plans and intentions. The identity of Exxon is independent of the extensional composition of its membership, for example, because newly arriving insiders understand themselves to be joining the Exxon organization, and outsiders attribute representative authority to self-proclaimed Exxon members.

### 3.2.3 Intentionalism and Functionalism as Methods in the Theory of Action

My account of intentional actions generally, and individual intentions in particular, is *intentionalist* and *functionalist* in form, and thus in keeping with a large body of philosophy of action. Following Donald Davidson, I will assume intentional action is action (body movements) that is both causally and teleologically explained by an agent's goals, as those goals are embedded in networks of intentions, desires, and instrumental beliefs.[10] Describing an action as intentional is appropriate because of the logical and causal role of the goal in explaining the actions in question.[11] Goals teleologically explain actions so long as there is a possible deliberative route from what an agent wants or intends to what the agent does; the agent need not actually have deliberated. My making a tuna sandwich is causally and teleologically explained by my intention to have lunch, as well as my belief that tuna would make for a good lunch. By contrast, while my making a salmonella-contaminated sandwich is causally explained by the same intention and belief, it is not rationalized, or teleologically explained, by them. As long as what the agent does satisfies a goal nonaccidentally, an intentional action is performed, and the action is intentional under a description appropriately related (or identical) to a statement of the agent's goal.[12]

The possibility of teleological explanation makes an intentional action the type of action it is – that is, it makes appropriate certain intentionalistic descriptions of that action. The goal cited in a teleological explanation may also be thought of as the conditions of satisfaction of the intentional action.[13] Actions (or attempted actions) are characterized and individuated by their motivating intentions, and hence by their goals.[14] A film noir villain's arrested hand motion is a reach for a handkerchief rather than a reach for a revolver just in virtue of the intention with which the agent acted.[15] Intentional actions that are a means to an end may be redescribed in terms of their ends, either as contributions towards that end, or, if closely connected, as realizations of that end. My intentional turning on of a switch to light a room may be redescribed as my intentional lighting of the room. My opening the refrigerator to get the mayonnaise may be redescribed as my preparing to make a sandwich.[16] In the collective context, this aspect of intentional action allows us to re-describe individual contributions in terms of a collective end: The musician, for example, is not just playing the viola, but is performing – along with the others – a certain symphony. The musician's intention to participate in a collective act, playing the symphony, both causes and rationalizes the viola playing, and so licenses our redescription. The possibility of legitimate redescription will be central to my account of individual accountability for collective acts.

My approach to intentions and intentional action is also generally functionalist, in that term's sense as a method in philosophical psychology.[17] Mental states in general, and intentions in particular, are defined by their role in a causal theory that maps agents' psychological inputs (perceptions, intentions, beliefs, and desires) onto their outputs (actions, subsidiary intentions, further beliefs, and desires).[18] Intentions mediate between agents' beliefs and desires (their reasons) and their practical reasoning and action. Functionalists attribute content to individuals' intentions by interpreting their planning and action in terms of reasons that explain and rationalize that deliberative behavior. Although individuals are presumably introspectively aware of the content of their own intentions, we can also attribute intentions on the basis of behavioral observations coupled with a general theory of human rationality.[19] Because functionalists identify the content of intentions according to the best interpretation (or most coherent theory) they can offer of agents' planning, dispositions, and behavior, functionalist analyses deny a strong first-person epistemological privilege. Other interpreters may be in equally good positions to make sense of an individual's behavior. Functionalists may, therefore, ascribe intentions in virtue of unconscious or explicitly disavowed goals and motives if an interpretation making use of those motives is better than the interpretations offered by agents themselves. This point will be important in Chapter 5, when I consider those cases in which individuals claim to be alienated from a collective activity, but in fact contribute to its realization.

## 3.3  COLLECTIVE ACTION AS INTENTIONAL PARTICIPATION

I will defend an account of collective action in which what makes a set of individual acts a case of jointly intentional action is the content of the intentions with which the individuals act. In particular, I will argue that jointly intentional action is primarily a function of the way in which individual agents regard their own actions as contributing to a collective outcome. I call this way of regarding one's own action, acting with a *participatory intention*. In this section, I will show why participatory intentions are ineliminable elements of any account of joint action.

### 3.3.1  *The Necessity of a Collective Conception*

How must individuals act, and be disposed to act, towards one another so that they may be said to act collectively? What conditions on their beliefs and actions must they satisfy? As I suggested before, certain kinds of joint activity – playing chess or tangoing – will require great mutual interdependence and sensitivity: for example,

close monitoring of one another's behavior, as well as highly determinate expectations of each other's plans. Other kinds of group action, such as filing through a narrow door into a theater, or voting
absentee in a general election, require much less of participants,
perhaps only a general sense one is acting concurrently with others,
coupled with adherence to conventions that minimize mutual interference. The great variety of collective actions can be misleading,
since what appears to be a necessary condition for an exemplary type
of collective action, such as the solution of simple coordination problems like entering a theater, will turn out not to be necessary after all
in more attenuated, yet still plausible, collective action examples,
such as a joint scheme in which the individuals deliberately fail to
coordinate. Thus, attempts to generalize an analysis of collective
action from analyses of specific types will often meet with
frustration.

This raises the obvious suspicion that there simply are no universal conditions constitutive of collective action as such, that collective
action types simply hang together in a familial fashion. I will argue in
this section, however, that all forms of collective action share a common element in the form of overlapping, individual participatory
intentions. My strategy is first to try to elicit the individually necessary and jointly sufficient conditions for a case which is under-
detailed enough to generalize plausibly, yet determinate enough to
guide our intuitive assessment of the analysis. Then I will show
whether these conditions remain necessary for other collective action
types.

In this section I focus on one of the simplest forms of collective
action, one-shot coordination or matching. It is obvious that coordination requires that individuals be somehow aware of the attempt by
others to coordinate, and that they make their own choices on the
basis of expectations about the choices to be made by those with
whom they wish to coordinate. I will argue here that these basic
strategic conditions on individuals are not enough; even simple coordination is best explained in terms of individuals acting on participatory intentions. Later, in Section 3.7, I will pare back this analysis
further, and argue that the core, minimalist, notion of collective action
requires only that individuals act on overlapping participatory intentions. We can imagine cases of spontaneous collective action in which

there is neither mutual responsiveness nor mutual awareness beyond what is implicit in the idea of a participatory intention – a conception that one is doing one's part in a collective project.

Consider first some examples that resemble jointly intentional action but are not genuine – examples where it would be false to say some group of agents jointly did G, where G stands for either a joint act or activity (such as playing softball), or for an outcome brought about by several agents (such as the performance of a symphony). You and I may go to Chicago together by happening to go there in the same plane or train, but it would not be true to say that we went to Chicago jointly if our coming on the same flight or train was sheer coincidence.[20] Jointly acting individuals do not merely act in parallel: Each responds to what the others do and plan to do. Thus, our going to Chicago jointly requires that the presence of each of us on the plane or train somehow depends upon the presence of the other. Unless my choice of transportation somehow depends upon your choice (or my expectations regarding your choice), and similarly for you, we will not have coordinated our going to Chicago. Let us call agents' intentions *strategically responsive* if what they intend to do is sensitive to their beliefs or predictions about what others intend to do. Joint action will often – and coordinated action will always – require strategic responsiveness: Individuals acting jointly decide to act, and do act, in light of their beliefs about other potential or actual joint actors.

You and I satisfy another plausible condition on joint action: We share a goal. Let us say two agents share a goal if there is at least one token activity or outcome involving the actions of the other whose performance or realization would satisfy the intentions of each.[21] Both of us share the goal of going to Chicago on the same mode of transportation. Even competitive forms of joint action involve some shared goal. You and I may each be trying to beat the other at chess, and hence no ending of the game will wholly satisfy the goals of each of us. But, at a lower degree of resolution, there are some goals we do share: We each seek an orderly game with the other, played by the rules, and so on. If we did not share these goals, we could not compete with one another, for there would be no background against which to assess the other's performance. Sharing goals, in a sense that I specify further in Section 3.7, is a necessary condition across all forms of joint action.

But even sensitivity to each other's choice coupled with sharing a goal is not enough to make it true that we go to Chicago jointly. Suppose you and I are Spy and Counterspy, each trying to keep tabs on the other's trip while hiding our presence from the other. Our choices are strategically sensitive, obviously. Somewhat less obviously, we may be said to share a goal, for the state of affairs involving our actions in which we both take the train or both take the plane satisfies the intentions of each. Even if we do manage to choose the same mode of transportation, it would be odd to say we have jointly gone to Chicago. This seems odd because each of our choices will have been made with the hope and aim that the other be unaware of that choice. If Counterspy knew of Spy's choice, Spy's secret espionage project would be thwarted, and vice versa.

Conversely, it seems that for our going to Chicago together to be joint, we each must believe it at least possible the other knows of or will try to predict our choice, and be favorably disposed to the other's knowledge or anticipation of that choice at least in the sense that no one would modify his or her plans in virtue of disclosure. As friends rather than spies, each knows or hopes the other got notice of the planned means of transportation, or was otherwise able to predict the other's choice. If, in fact, the messages did get through, or if we are able successfully to anticipate the other's choice, then each will be acting consistently with the other's preferences: our individual aims are furthered rather than frustrated by the other's awareness. So for our trip to be a joint production, each must not only act in light of beliefs about the other's plan, but each must also be favorably disposed towards the other's possible knowledge of this strategic sensitivity. More simply, each must be open to the possibility of joint action. Call this a condition of *mutual openness* concerning our interaction. Mutual openness is a much weaker condition than common knowledge of our situation: it can accommodate those cases of joint action that come off despite inchoate expectations about the other's plans or awareness.[22] Yet it is strong enough to exclude cases of fully adverse strategic interaction, cases like the spy example that are not plausibly regarded as joint.

Strategic responsiveness, shared goals, and mutual openness are necessary for our jointly going to Chicago together. But they are not sufficient. A further intentional commitment of the participants to promoting the group act is required, an intention by each to do his or her part of promoting the group activity or outcome. This further intentional component, by which agents conceive of their actions as standing in a certain instrumental relation to the group act, both satisfies common linguistic intuitions about when we may say that individuals act jointly, and – more importantly – explains how many forms of joint action are possible.

To see that the elements of strategy, shared goals, and mutual openness are insufficient, return to Spy and Counterspy. Suppose now that each of us knows the other is trying to keep tabs; so long as we can satisfy our missions, this mutual awareness does not matter. So each of us has the goal that we go to Chicago together and is disposed to act in response to expectations about the other, while all this is potentially or actually manifest between us. Nonetheless, it seems odd to describe our going to Chicago together as joint, because each of us essentially regards the other as an object of pursuit rather than as a partner in the enterprise. The distinction emerges once we realize each spy's aim is satisfied by the mere presence of the other on the flight. As Michael Bratman points out, if a third party were to kidnap us and put us on the same flight, our shared goal of keeping tabs on each other would be realized even though we did not need to rely upon our strategic dispositions.[23] By contrast, if we are friends trying to go to Chicago together, our goals will not be fully satisfied by a third party's intervention. For we do not (presumably) simply want it to be the case that we arrive in Chicago on the same plane. Rather, we want our traveling together to be the product of the decision of each. That is, we go to Chicago jointly when we go there together, and our going there together is the product of each of us acting with an intention of contributing to our joint project of getting to Chicago together. We act jointly when we act as members of a group who act together.

The crucial role of participatory intentions is also revealed in an important strand in recent philosophical literature about the foundations of game theory. A number of writers have argued convincingly that the purely individualistic components of game theory – namely the strategic dispositions and common knowledge requirements I have outlined – cannot determine optimal individual choices even when it is intuitively obvious what course of action individuals

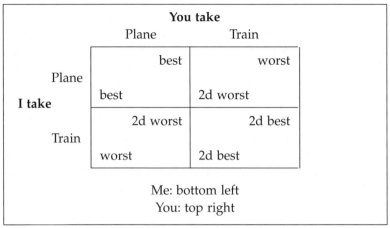

Figure 3.1 Matching Game

ought to pursue.[24] These writers claim cooperative game theory must be supplemented by certain assumptions about what is collectively preferable.

Take the easiest case, coordinating on a single, clearly preferable outcome. Suppose you and I have not been able to coordinate our travel plans for Chicago, but each knows the other is intent on traveling together, and given the satisfaction of that end, prefers planes to trains. The structure of the problem confronting us can be represented graphically (see Figure 3.1). Intuitively, it is obvious each of us should choose to take the plane, since that is both better for each and better for both. The trouble lies in showing why we are justified in relying upon this intuition. For I cannot just assume you will take the plane, since I know you will only take the plane if you think I will also (you prefer our taking the train to your taking the plane alone). Therefore, I should only choose the plane if I think you will choose the plane too. But if your choice depends upon mine, then you are in no better position to make a determinate choice of planes over trains. Each of us most prefers to match the other, and this preference for mutual matching fails to converge on a single choice. The only point of convergence in our expectations is simply a preference for matching the other, and that preference is indeterminate with respect to both the plane and the train, each of which is an equilibrium.[25] Strategic reasoning will get us nowhere.

Of course, actual agents will not be stuck in an infinite regress: Each sees that both prefer planes to trains, and so will choose planes. Moreover, this is clearly the rational course of action. How could it be at odds with game theory? The answer is that this choice is not inconsistent with game theory, but that game theory fails to determine the collectively optimal outcome as *the* rational choice. In order to justify choosing planes, we have to import a crucial further assumption: each of us will, in anticipation of the other, opt for the collectively rational outcome.[26] Unless I see you as wondering what we should do in this context, and assume you see me in the same way, we have no substantive point of convergence in our expectations. But once I conceive of each of us as choosing for us, it is obvious I should choose planes, because it follows from my conception that you will do so as well. This assumption is natural, and consistent with though an addition to, cooperative game theory.[27] The important point is that this additional requirement in the cooperative case distinguishes it from competitive game theory. In competitive contexts, each attempts to achieve the most preferred outcome, based on the most likely choice of the other (or, in the absence of any further information, based on the choice of the other that would make for the worst outcome). Each player is like Spy and Counterspy: the other's choice is simply part of the background against which strategy is formed.[28] In cooperative contexts, by contrast, each must act in accordance with a conception of the other as committed to joint resolution of the problem. In Gerald Postema's expression, each "deliberates from the first-person plural."[29] Each sees the other as an intentional participant in a collective action.

So when we try to coordinate our going to Chicago together, we need further material for our deliberations, external to but consistent with our expectations about each other's preferences, to bring those expectations to converge. A participatory intention can fill this role, providing a sufficient and parsimonious basis for choice. I will do what you would expect me to do, assuming we are mutually searching for an optimal means to our joint goal of going to Chicago together. Deliberating in this way amounts to my doing my part of our going to Chicago together, since I make my choice sensitive to the achievement of our joint goal. Given that we both prefer planes to trains, it is reasonable for me to expect that a choice of plane would follow from joint deliberation over an optimal means. I, therefore, do my part of what would be our solution to the problem and take the plane. If you also deliberate in terms of what we jointly ought to do, then we will have coordinated by means of cooperation: by determining our actions in accordance with a joint goal.

If each of us deliberates in this manner and we do both take the plane together, then it will be true that we went to Chicago jointly. What makes this claim true is how we each conceived of the choice, as one in which each intends to do his part in promoting our group act, not any prior agreement or concert on our part. Call this way of conceiving of action a participatory intention: an intention to do my part of a collective act, where my part is defined as the task I ought to perform if we are to be successful in realizing a shared goal. This conception of oneself as contributing to a collective, as manifested in one's deliberation and action, is what lies at the heart of collective action generally, from simple coordination to complex cooperation. It would be impossible to show that there are no forms of individual interaction in which the agents lack such a conception of themselves as contributors to a collective end. Doubtless there are highly routinized forms of coordination in which agents see their actions as contributing entirely to their own ends; economists' idealized competitive markets may be such creatures, although actual markets reveal cooperation and altruism. But an interpretation of apparently coordinating agents' behavior that attributes to them participatory intentions makes better sense of their deliberations and dispositions than any purely self-regarding attribution of intentional content. I now turn to the task of refining the content of participatory intentions, and then deploying that concept across a range of collective activity.

## 3.4 THE CONTRIBUTORY CONTENT OF PARTICIPATORY INTENTIONS

A participatory intention has two representational components, or sets of conditions of satisfaction: *individual role* and *collective end*. By *individual role* I mean the act an individual performs in order to foster a collective end; and by *collective end* I mean the object of a description that is constituted by or is a causal product of different individuals' acts. This is to say that individual participatory action aims at two goals: accomplishment of a primary individual task that contributes to a secondary collective achievement, be it an activity or an outcome. The collective end might be a state of affairs whose realization depends upon several agents acting together, such as the movement of a heavy object; or an activity, such as dancing a tango; or it might be a social group with characteristic behavior or internal culture, such as a university faculty.[30] Some joint activities can be performed jointly intentionally or unintentionally, such as going to Chicago together. Others can only be performed jointly intentionally if they are performed at all, such as playing chess or dancing the tango.[31]

The defining characteristic of a participatory intention, then, lies in the form of relationship between individual act performed and the group act or outcome that rationalizes the part. Contributory relations might take instrumental form if what the agent does helps cause the collective outcome (my pushing helps to move the car), or if the agent's part is a constitutive element of the group act (stepping this way is part of dancing a tango). The relation might be expressive if by doing one's part, one thereby exemplifies one's membership in a group or participation in an activity, as when by voting I express my membership in a political community. And the relation might be normative if one performs one's part because of norms internal to some group or institution that demand certain behavior (I wear a dark suit as an IBM employee). Of course, a single act may stand in many contributory relations to a group goal or activity. If I am a member of a criminal conspiracy, my refusal to cooperate with the police furthers the success of the conspiratorial objective, adheres to the norms of criminal honor, and expresses my solidarity with my co-conspirators.

What makes my behavior participatory is nothing more (and nothing less) than my conception of what I do as related to the group act, whether that conception is explicit in my deliberations, or functionally implicit in my actual or counterfactual behavior. Merely wearing appropriate clothing is not what constitutes my willing participation in IBM's corporate culture, but rather wearing dark suits with the intention of being a part of that culture. Of course, I need not suit up in the morning thinking, "Better put on this blue suit today if

I'm to show my loyalty to IBM." But it must at least be true that my putting on a dark suit is counterfactually sensitive to my acceptance of the norms that structure life in that organization: if I worked at Apple, I'd wear jeans and a tee shirt instead.[32] Similarly, pushing a car only counts as participating in a group effort given an intention to participate in promoting the group outcome; otherwise, it's isometrics.

Indeed, given an appropriate context, a participatory intention alone can be sufficient to transform individual acts into jointly cooperative activity. Adapting an example of John Searle's, imagine an announcement to factory workers during an economic crisis that they can best help the nation by continuing to work industriously at their posts. Each goes back intending to do his or her part of supporting the nation's economy by doing exactly the same as before.[33] Now, however, all the workers are cooperating in producing what was before merely a peripheral effect of their individual acts. The invisible hand has now been supplemented by individual participatory intentions.[34]

Typically, both individual part and joint act are complete descriptions of acts or states of affairs, as when I intend to push the car as part of our getting it out of the snow bank, or when you intend to promote our picnicking by bringing the sandwiches. But the formal concepts of individual role and joint activity have enough independent content that they can also stand as placeholders within intentions, simply noting the fact that one aims at a coordinated effort. Seeing you standing by your car, I can intend to help you out of your trouble without knowing what the problem is or what role I will play, and you can intend to help our picnic without knowing whether you'll bring drinks or sandwiches. Indeed, one can imagine a Beckett-like scenario in which a group of individuals gather, intending to do their parts in some mysterious venture, waiting to find out what their parts are and what the joint activity is. Given a suitable background story, attributing participatory intentions requires only that individuals regard themselves as acting for the sake of some joint goal; no more content is necessary.

When the individual part is incompletely specified, participatory intentions present agents with problems of practical reasoning, namely what one should do as part of the group act.[35] Jointly acting agents must reason backwards from the nature of the group act to an understanding of what each should do if the group act is to be achieved.[36] If the decomposition of the act is obvious, then no deliberation is needed: I see you trying to push your car out of the snow bank, so I get behind the bumper and push too. But if the goal is complex, or the roles are unobvious, then deliberation may be necessary. Here is how the deliberation might run. If we are to have a picnic, then we need drinks, sandwiches, and a blanket; I ought to bring one of these; I have a nice blanket and the others do not; everyone realizes this; therefore I ought to do my part of bringing a blanket in order to promote our having a picnic.

The part an individual ought to perform will depend not only upon the content of the group act, but upon that individual's incidental attitudes and dispositions. For any group act G, there are cheaper and more expensive, fairer and less fair, surer and riskier means of achieving it. If, for example, I am worried about my bad back, then I may both sincerely intend to do my part of helping to extract your car by pushing, and intend not to try very hard to do so, or intend to give up if the resistance is more than minimal. I intend to participate in our "G-ing," even if what I intend to do in fact makes little difference, or even hinders, G's realization. (Whether I deserve credit or blame for my part in G's realization is an independent question, which I will broach in the Chapter 4.) The bare instrumental structure of participatory intentions cannot supply the needed practical determinacy. Pragmatic, contextual features of both agent and situation must fill in the deliberative lacunae. This is, of course, no different from the ordinary individual case, except perhaps to the extent that collective action increases the possible dimensions of practical indeterminacy. If rational reconstructions of individual, noncollective, action are necessarily holistic, adverting to ever-wider circles of explanatory reasons, then so will be participatory action.

Participatory intentions can thus be seen as merely a species of ordinary, instrumental intentions, differentiated by the group-oriented content of the goal they specify. However, the phenomenology of jointly intentional action accentuates features less commonly found in the purely self-regarding case. First, participatory intentions involve a reflective or deliberative self-awareness of the instrumental relation of one's part to the group act that is its end. In contrast, I do not usually think of myself, when pulling on a door knob, as doing something that will result in a door opening. Rather, I simply open a door. This reflective or deliberative component may just be a function of the complexity of much joint activity, which tends to be interactive and dynamic rather than "pre-programmed" and one-shot. Complex, nonparticipatory action will also occasion instrumental deliberation, while well-rehearsed joint action may require no conscious deliberation or reflection. But the complexity arising from problems of coordination renders collective activity especially salient, making it stand out against a background of unreflective, self-regarding activity.

A second noteworthy feature of participatory action is that the very possibility of free riding on others' efforts often adds a salient normative dimension to agency. Because joint action often occurs in a context of implicit or explicit agreement, others' expectations are raised, generating obligations of trust and reciprocity.[37] If, however, my preferences diverge from a straightforward desire to perform my part, then a motivational gap may open between part and group act: it may become a prudential question whether I ought to perform the part, given my preferences and despite my obligations.[38] In the case of purely self-regarding action, on the other hand, normative questions are usually resolved (if they are raised at all) during prior practical deliberation. Once I have already determined the moral permissibility of the course of action I attempt, there is no conceptual room for asking myself whether I morally ought to go ahead and perform that act, simply because the issue of free riding does not arise.[39] As with complexity, the possibility of free riding, or cheating, contributes to the special salience of our collective activity. Both of these aspects of the phenomenology of collective activity distinguish it from self-regarding activity only in degree, not in kind.

## 3.5 THE REDUCIBILITY OF COLLECTIVE ACTION TO INDIVIDUAL INTENTION

The account of joint action in terms of participatory intentions takes a middle line on the question of the reducibility of collective actions to individual actions. On the one hand, collective activity is an ineliminable part of the content of agents' participatory intentions. Someone playing chess intends to do his or her part of playing a chess match, and thus intends to perform the jointly intentional act of chess playing. On the other hand, participatory intentions are simply a special class of ordinary intentions, differentiated by their group-oriented content. This approach might raise two opposed worries: first, that including the idea of jointly intentional action in the content of individual intentions makes my analysis uninformatively circular; and second, that by insisting on an individualistic form, my analysis fails to take seriously the distinctive nature of cooperative intentions. I will now argue the content of agents' intentions can be irreducibly collective so long as the structure of their intentions is straightforwardly individualistic.

The worry about circularity is more methodological than substantive. As Bratman suggested in an earlier work, if the analysis of intentional collective action merely shows that individuals intend to act collectively, we will be left with the problem of understanding what these individuals intend to do.[40] We ought rather, he suggested, seek an analysis of collective action built out of components that do not themselves presuppose the concept of collective action.

The methodological point is important, but it can be too strictly applied, and Bratman has since relaxed his strictures.[41] The problem is that the intentions to perform many kinds of jointly intentional acts cannot be made sense of except in collective terms: noncooperative chess is not chess but something else – mutual chess solitaire. Likewise, there is no way to characterize the intention of an individual planning to dance the tango except as an intention to engage in jointly intentional tango dancing. What we need, then, is not an analysis that tries to show how each instance of collective action is built out of noncollective materials, but rather a genealogical account that shows generally how the capacity to engage in collective action emerges out of capacities explicable without reference to collective concepts.

Consider first the individual case. There are many purely individual actions that agents intend to engage in intentionally and for which any analysis must presuppose the concept of intentionality. For example, when I intend to play a waltz on the piano, I intend to play it intentionally; that is, I intend to engage in the intentional activity of piano playing. At some level my action must be explained in terms of intentions to move my body, but it would be neither analytically helpful nor accurate to characterize my intention as an intention to move my fingers in ways that will produce the sounds of a waltz. Rather, in learning to play the piano, I come to incorporate the skill of nonintentional piano playing – that is, pure finger-movements – into my skill repertoire, such that once I have the skill the concept can occur ineliminably in attributions of my intentions.[42] Once we have learned to walk, we can learn to run. We need not start with the fundamentals of balance and leg movement but can presuppose those in the next iteration.

We can make use here of a more general distinction, between *executive* and *subsidiary* intentions. An *executive intention* is an intention whose content is an activity or outcome conceived of as a whole, and which plays a characteristic role in generating, commanding, or determining other intentions and mental states in order to achieve that total outcome. A *subsidiary intention* is an intention generated and rationalized by an executive intention, whose content is the achievement of a part of the total outcome or activity. This is a functional distinction, and a relative one: Executive intentions are executive relative to the subsidiary intentions they command, determine, or generate, and vice versa. Subsidiary intentions may therefore be thought of as elements of the plans generated by the goals established by executive intentions; they are causally explained by and make instrumental sense in relation to that goal. For any complex task, we will act on the basis of a broad and hierarchically structured set of executive and subsidiary intentions.[43]

My executive intention to play a waltz commands a range of subsidiary intentions regarding my finger and toe movements, not to mention intentions to sit down at the piano and pull out the Chopin score. So my claim is that the content of executive intentions can be irreducibly intentionalistic, and even jointly intentionalistic, so long as the subsidiary intentions they command have nonintentional objects. Accordingly, when I play chess, my subsidiary intentions can be explicated without relying on the notion of joint intentionality, such as intending to move my queen in response to the threat from your rook. In learning to play chess, I first conceive of the elements of the game in nonjoint terms: the knight moves so and so; it is best to open with pawns; and if you threaten my queen, I should check your king. As I learn to play, these constituent elements of chess come to be represented and internalized as "my playing chess," or, alternatively, "my doing my part of our playing chess together." By such a bootstrapping process, the collective joint activity thus becomes the object of an agent's executive intention, having been built out of noncollective elements. Cooperation does not have to be a basic, unlearned capacity, for it is entirely plausible that children (and certain animals) learn to act jointly in pursuit of a common goal through, for example, initially self-involved play activity. To borrow Schiller's terms, we move from the naïve ability to play to the sentimental capacity to conceive ourselves as participants in joint endeavors.

Even though my account makes room for irreducibly collective content in executive intentions, it is also subject to challenge as overly reductive in its construal of joint action as a species of individual action. John Searle offers such an objection against the reductive account offered by Raimo Tuomela and Kaarlo Miller.[44] Tuomela and Miller explain jointly intentional action in terms of individuals who act with the intention of doing their parts in a collective act, although they add conditions I believe are superfluous.[45] Searle argues that jointly intentional action can only be explained by positing a distinct, "irreducible" form of intending that he calls "we-intending." We-intentions are individual intentions to engage in collective activity, distinct from "I-intentions" to perform one's own acts. The difference is not just the difference in content I have already mentioned – the goal of participating in collective action differs, tautologically, from the goal of engaging in individual action – but also in form.

Searle's argument is important, not because it shows that collective action demands a separate form of intending, but because despite his actual claims, it reveals how collective content is necessary to distinguish cooperation from merely parallel behavior. He proposes the following counterexample: a group of business-school students has been indoctrinated to believe one can best help humanity by pursuing one's selfish interests when others do so also. Furthermore, each student believes that each student believes this to be true and will act upon it. Since "each believes that his selfish efforts will be successful in helping humanity," Searle claims each "intends to do his part" of helping humanity by pursuing selfish interests.[46] He objects that even if the business students knowingly do something that, taken together, helps humanity, they are not acting jointly. Contrast this with the case of business-school students who form a pact to help humanity by individually pursuing their selfish interests.

There surely is an important difference between the two cases. If the first students pursue their selfish interests in the belief that they jointly will help humanity, but without intending to promote that end, then they will not be acting with the intention of jointly benefiting humanity. By contrast, if the second group of students forms a pact to help humanity by acting selfishly, then they are acting with the intention of jointly benefiting humanity. But the difference between the two groups is not one of form. It is instead the familiar difference between intending a certain result and acting with the knowledge the result will obtain. The first group of students believes humanity will be helped because of their (collective) selfish efforts, but they do not intend that end; their actions are not counterfactually sensitive to its achievement. Presumably they would act selfishly even if they came to believe humanity was rendered worse off. Members of the second group, however, act selfishly in order to promote an end that can only be brought about collectively. They would not act selfishly if their selfish acts were likely to be fruitless, since they aim at the end of benefiting humanity and not merely of acting selfishly.[47]

So the difference we need to capture is simply one of intentional content: Jointly acting groups consist of individuals who intend to contribute to a collective end, whether outcome or activity. Groups of individuals, all of whom merely know they happen to be contributing to a collective outcome, cannot be said to act jointly. So long as we see individual actions as aiming at the achievement of a collective end, we can attribute to them participatory intentions, defined in terms of their goals rather than their form. Or, to put the same point another way, we can have irreducible content and reducible form.

## 3.6  COLLECTIVE ACTION: THE MINIMALIST APPROACH

I have claimed jointly intentional action is fundamentally the action of individuals who intend to play a part in producing a group outcome. Other conditions will have to be met as well, depending upon the type of activity in question. Going jointly to Chicago requires a mutual expectation about one another's dispositions and goals, as well as mutual sensitivity to the other's likely means of transportation. Playing chess or dancing the tango together requires not only a willingness to play or dance, but basic knowledge of the constitutive rules of the activity, as well as dispositions to respond to the other's movements as the play or dance progresses. In the analysis of particular group activities, a great many more conditions may be needed in order to support claims that a group engages in an activity jointly intentionally. If we attempt to generalize from these highly interdependent activities, we may arrive at an account of collective action that makes very strong demands upon agents' dispositions and expectations of one another.

I believe, however, that it is a mistake to emphasize the kinds of interdependencies constitutive of particular types of joint action in a general account of the phenomenon. Groups can act jointly although members of the group have only very weak expectations about each other's intentions, do not and are not disposed to respond strategically to one another, and do not intend that the group act be successfully realized. So long as the members of a group overlap in the conception of the collective end to which they intentionally contribute, they act collectively, or jointly intentionally. I call this the *minimalist conception* of joint action. In this section I will defend this conception of joint action against the more demanding accounts of some other philosophers.

The superior descriptive coverage of the minimalist conception is only part of my reason for favoring it. My principal reason is normative. Ethically complex cases of joint action rarely involve perfect common knowledge, wholly shared conceptions of the joint act, or highly responsive strategic interaction. Indeed, the genius of organized criminality lies precisely in obscuring the interrelations of participants by removing the need for frequent interaction. And the enterprises responsible for significant unintended harms are likewise typically distinguished by the dispersion of task responsibility. Conspirators, for example, often compartmentalize knowledge of individual tasks and identities; corporate officers and engineers may understand themselves to pursue very different goals; and executive officials may shield themselves from specific knowledge of the acts

or omissions of subordinates. If joint action is to have special normative significance in such cases, either as a basis for holding individuals accountable for the acts of others, or for aggravating the seriousness of individual offenses, then an account of joint action must not
rely upon high degrees of interaction or mutual knowledge.

The relativity of jointly intentional action to the description of the
joint acts demonstrates the way cooperating agents can have very
different conceptions of what they do, while still acting jointly. Here I
will show cooperating agents can have varying or nonexistent expectations about one another's likely performance of their parts. As
discussed earlier, joint action also often involves strategic responsiveness and mutual favorable awareness, at the stage of both intention formation and execution. Individuals decide to act jointly because of their beliefs about others' similar intentions, and modulate
their pursuit of a joint project in response to the actions of those
others; they further hope their intentions to act jointly are manifest to
the others. Thus, a standard way of preparing to cooperate is to
announce a conditional participatory intention: I'll do my part of
carrying the sofa if you will do yours.[48] My intention actually to
carry the sofa is formed only in response to my beliefs about others'
participation. Indeed, strategic interaction and responsiveness are
essential to many paradigmatically joint activities, such as going for a
walk together. As Margaret Gilbert points out, if we are walking
together, then each of us must be matching our paces to the other,
searching the other for hints that a change in direction would be
welcome, taking turns fighting off the brambles, and so on.[49] Persons
not inclined to so respond are not genuinely going for a walk together, any more than is a crowd moving down a city sidewalk.

Gilbert, Bratman, and Tuomela and Miller therefore suggest that
mutual expectation and responsiveness are essential to jointly intentional action as such. Gilbert argues that a participating member of a
"social group" must first accept that others have committed themselves to the group project.[50] Bratman requires that each agent intend
that the group effort be realized in part because of the intentions of
the other participants, with these intentions commonly known.[51]
And Tuomela and Miller claim that jointly acting agents must believe
a sufficient number of themselves intend to do their parts, and that
this is commonly known.[52]

But it is crucial to recognize that mutual and universal responsiveness are not necessary to joint action as such, at the stage either of intention formation or execution. Two types of ostensibly collective action show that individuals need only have very weak hopes or beliefs about each other's plans. Some collective acts emerge when an entrepreneurial agent begins doing what will be part of a joint effort, but only if others follow suit. A member of the Bastille mob starts throwing rocks at the prison guards; soon others join him, and they collectively storm the prison. While the subsequent participants intended to do their parts of storming the prison in response to the sight of the first, the actions and intentions of the first stone thrower were neither responsive to nor predicated upon definite expectations about the others' conduct. Nonetheless, the leader's intention must be characterized as participatory, for he surely would not have thrown stones if he thought it impossible that others would join in. It is unnecessary to attribute to him the determinate expectation that others actually would join in, fomenting revolution being the risky business it is. Rather than requiring participants to have positive beliefs about the prospect of others joining in (i.e., regarding others' participation as more likely than not), we need only require they not regard the prospect as impossible.

No member of a group need form an intention in the light of expectations about the others. Suppose while we are having a picnic, it begins to rain. I jump up, grab the sandwiches, and head for the car. I intend to do my part of our saving the picnic, hoping you will simultaneously grab the drinks and the blanket.[53] If you do, then it is reasonable to say we will have jointly saved the picnic. We might not have acted jointly, if, say, you had been dozing when the rain hit. But if we do both act with participatory intentions, then we will have jointly intentionally saved the picnic though neither had formed an intention to save the picnic in the light of expectations about the other's intentions.

My claim that nonresponsive or independent action can be jointly intentional does depend upon a disputable thesis: agents need not believe beforehand that they will be likely to succeed in their aims for their actions to count as jointly intentional. For example, two agents might jointly and intentionally dislodge a heavy car without believing they will be successful in their attempt. This general principle seems to me well established for the individual case, as when I try to make a difficult basketball shot, make it, and claim that I hit the basket intentionally.[54] Just as a joint attempt to dislodge a car may be unsuccessful because the car is too heavy, so a joint attempt to save a picnic may be unsuccessful because it is not sufficiently joint.

The putative requirement that agents respond to one another dynamically in execution is equally implausible, for it is clear joint acts can be fully planned beforehand. You and I may agree to do our parts of watering Beth's plant while she is away: you on Mondays and I on Fridays. Once we have planned together, we simply stick to our individual schedules. At the end of the week, it would seem reasonable to say that we cooperated in tending to her plants, and not just that we cooperated in planning, even though we may not have communicated at all during the week.[55]

Note that the picnic and plant-sitting examples do satisfy the condition of mutual openness I suggested earlier. Each of us will regard our individual intentions as furthered, or at least not hindered, by their becoming mutually manifest. But this mutual openness just follows logically from the very concept of participation. For it seems impossible for me to conceive of my act as contributing to a collective end while also intending that my contribution never become known. If I do intend that my contribution to some collective end be secret, for example surreptitiously stuffing a ballot box to help a candidate, then the natural thing to say is not that I am doing my part of our electing the candidate, but rather that I am acting as a rogue, trying to get my candidate elected.[56] By contrast, when I merely cast my ballot, I do conceive of the act as my participation in our common act and so potentially open to public view, whether or not anyone actually knows of my act. (Arguably, it is only this sense of participation that explains the individually irrational behavior of voting in the first place.) So rather than describing mutual openness as a separate necessary condition, it may be more economical to treat it as merely explicating the notion of a participatory intention.

So joint action as such requires neither positive belief about others' intentions nor dispositions of responsiveness, since we can conceive of genuinely joint, if simple, forms of collective action in their absence so long as agents nonetheless act with participatory intentions. Only one further general condition seems to be required as part of the very concept of joint action: a condition of extensional overlap. It must be the same joint enterprise in which agents intentionally participate. Because objects of intention are intensional, however, the question of whether agents' intentions overlap depends upon the way their joint activity is described. Here I discuss some of the complexities attending the notion of overlap.

Agents' participatory intentions to do their parts of a group act overlap if there is common ground in the states of affairs that satisfy the intentions of each. To be precise, agents' intentions overlap – they share goals – when the collective end component of their participatory intentions refers to the same activity or outcome and when there is a nonempty intersection of the sets of states of affairs satisfying those collective ends. So, for example, if you and I each have an intention of playing tennis together, then our intentions overlap: The state of affairs in which we play tennis together satisfies the participatory intentions of each, to do his or her part of our game. Matters are more confusing when the collective end component refers only to an activity or outcome generically, and does not refer to the other participants. If each of us merely has the intention of playing tennis with whomever shows up at the courts, then our intentions are in a state of merely potential overlap: potential because the state of affairs in which I play tennis with Beth while you play with Charlie also satisfies the intentions of each, but our intentions as realized do not actually overlap. When in fact what each of us does satisfies the participatory intentions of the other, because we play with each other, then the potential overlap of our intentions will be actual, and our action is joint. So the condition of overlap is one of actual, and not merely potential, overlap. But the actuality of overlap, like the success of speakers' indirect reference more generally, will rely on a contribution from the world as well, namely whether the other's acts in fact do partly satisfy one's participatory intention.[57]

Clearly, some degree of overlap is necessary in order to characterize an act as jointly intentional. It might even be thought that in paradigm cases of joint action, overlap is perfect: There is only one state of affairs that satisfies each agent's intentions, and it is commonly recognized. But perfect overlap is rarely, if ever, the case. If we intend to go for a walk together, then the state of affairs in which you and I stroll together, responsively and conversationally, satisfies the intentions of each. But I may further intend that as we walk, we talk about my ill health, while you have no set conversational agenda. Thus, while a broad range of states of affairs will satisfy your intention that we stroll together, only a subset of those will satisfy mine.

So overlap is essentially a pragmatic concept and always a matter of degree, given inevitable differences in each agent's expectations and conceptions of the group act. Agents will have more or less determinate conceptions of the group act, they may be more or less willing to compromise after bargaining on the character of that act, and they may have very different ideas about the scope of the group act, its duration and membership. As a result, a group act can be jointly intentional under one description and not jointly intentional under another. You may believe we are going to a friend's house for a quiet dinner, while I believe we are going for a surprise party. While our going to the surprise party is not jointly intentional, our going to the friend's house is.

This point is critical for the legal treatment of group acts, where the grading of penalties depends upon whether acts can be considered matters of common intention. An act, described one way, can fail to be jointly intentional because of insufficient overlap, while it is jointly intentional when described otherwise. Here is a typical example: A shows up at the airstrip intending to help unload a plane; he doesn't know the nature of the cargo, but knows it is illegal. B delivers the contraband to A, knowing it is cocaine destined for the Miami market, intending that it be sold to C. C receives the cocaine from A in unmarked crates and sells it. D launders the proceeds from the sale, not knowing whether it is drug money or untaxed profits from otherwise legitimate business, and deposits the clean money in A's Cayman Islands bank account.[58] Now, there is overlap among the intentions in all five at quite a low degree of specificity. Each intends to do his part of helping distribute and profit illegally, presumably with the awareness that some others were also involved in the operation. Thus, the smuggling of the contraband is jointly intentional. But the crucial question in a conspiracy trial would be whether smuggling cocaine was jointly intentional, given that only three members of the conspiracy knew of the drugs. Relatedly, it might be asked whether A, who intended to participate in smuggling contraband, could be said to be party to a drug smuggling conspiracy, given his ignorance.[59] Many more acts and more individuals can be considered parties to a conspiracy at a low level of specificity than at a higher level. Because the choice of appropriate descriptive level is a normative (or "policy," in lawyers' terms) issue, the question of whether someone is a member of a jointly acting group is always both normative and factual.[60]

## 3.7 PARTICIPATION AND THE PERSPECTIVE OF COMMAND

The central reason that Gilbert, Bratman, Tuomela and Miller claim that participating individuals intend to act in light of their positive expectations about one another's plans is that they explain joint action in terms of individuals' intentions that their group perform an act. I will refer to these intentions as *group-intentions*. Group-intentions are ordinary, instrumental individual intentions whose subject is the individual agent and whose object is a collective act or outcome: I intend that we will dance the tango. Clearly some paradigmatic forms of collective action incorporate our action as the direct aim. I as a participant in a group act do not always contemplate our actions from a perspective suggesting that what we do is up to me. When I do, I occupy an *executive perspective*. But it is a mistake to conceive collective action only from the executive perspective because collective action often incorporates the contributions of participants who have no views, let alone intentions, concerning what the group as a whole should do. And it leads to normative confusion, because the executive perspective implicitly threatens to locate accountability for collective acts only with those who assume that perspective.

Participating individuals necessarily orient their conduct around a collective end, and so participatory intentions must have collective content. But participants need not intend to achieve that collective end. It is sufficient that participants regard themselves as contributing to a collective end. Two arguments support this claim, one based on collective activity in hierarchical contexts, and the second based on making a knowing contribution to a collective end that one disavows.

Bratman and Tuomela and Miller's group-intentions differ in content as well as in syntax from ordinary individual intentions, because individual group-intentions cannot be directly transformed from intentions that P to intentions to P. (My intention that we paint the house is not the same as my intention to paint the house.) As Bratman notes, the notion of group-intentions sacrifices a tight fit between intentions and actions. One might ask whether there really are such nonstandard intentions, or whether they are instead figures of speech, either expressing a hope we will do something, or standing in for an individual intention to promote our doing something.[61] Bratman defends group-intentions by relying upon the "planning" face of intention. Although group-intentions are not directly linked to action in the way that self-regarding intentions are, they may still play identifiable roles in practical reasoning and planning. For example, the content of my intention that we paint the house can be realized functionally, through my dispositions to check on your schedule, to ensure that you have the same color scheme in mind, etc. Group-intentions thus generate directly action-linked self-regarding intentions, such as an intention to call you tonight, to meet you tomorrow, and so on.[62]

The introduction of group-intentions is permissible, and perhaps even required in order to explain the practical reasoning and planning of some members of jointly acting groups. In general, when agents act so as to realize the collective outcome, to the extent of aiding others in their contributions, we should attribute to them the group-intention to achieve that collective end. However, I think that Bratman and Tuomela and Miller have been misled by their reliance on examples of collective action where such planning is universally shared, namely cases of small-scale, highly interdependent, and non-hierarchical cooperation, in which each participant plausibly aims at everyone's achievement of the group goal. Although individuals who intend "that we do G" intend to do their parts of "G-ing," the converse is not true. Individuals may intend to do their parts of our "G-ing," and thus jointly G, without intending that we G. The result is that collective action need involve only individuals acting upon participatory intentions, not upon group-intentions.

Ordinary language provides a clue to the inappropriateness of routinely attributing group-intentions. If you and I paint a house together, it seems reasonable to attribute to each the intention, "that we paint the house together." After all, each has agreed to the time and place for the house painting, we are disposed to agree on a color scheme, and there is even the suggestion that we'll make a pleasant day out of an onerous chore. But there are many contexts in which attributing group-intentions to the participants is out of place. It would ring false to attribute to an individual cellist in an orchestra the intention that "we play the *Eroica*," or to a single running back the intention that "we win the football game." (A cellist or running back who said this might be thought to take too grandiose a view of his or her role.) Rather, it is far more natural to attribute to the cellist an intention to perform his or her part in the symphony, and likewise to the running back. In contrast, we might say of a conductor, orchestra manager, or coach, that each intends that his or her group perform or win, given the ability of each to influence these total outcomes.

Recall the distinction I offered between executive and subsidiary intentions. The distinction between executive and subsidiary intentions also cuts across the interpersonal/intrapersonal distinction. Just as my executive intention to lose ten pounds by winter commands my subsidiary intention to go easy with the mayonnaise on my sandwich, so a conductor's executive intention that the orchestra quicken the tempo commands the cellist's subsidiary intention to play faster. The executive intention, whether intra- or interpersonal, causes and rationalizes the subsidiary intention, of course against a causal backdrop of dispositions to comply with executive intentions. The cellist, if asked why she sped up, can truly say it was because the conductor wanted it so.

In large groups, individuals whose contributions are marginal will typically not have an executive intention with respect to producing the total outcome or activity. Instead they will have a subsidiary, participatory intention, an intention to do their part of achieving the executively determined goal. They may have an intention regarding the whole but they don't need such an intention to identify with and act for the sake of the main goal. Their individual participatory intentions will in turn serve as executive with respect to further intentions and actions. The cellist, for example, has a subsidiary intention to perform the cello part of the *Eroica*, which generates further intentions to play in tune and tempo, and to show up for rehearsal on time. And the cellist's participatory intention may be subsidiary not only to the music director's intention that the orchestra perform the symphony, but to the cellist's own self-regarding intention to make a career out of music, to play as much Beethoven as possible, and so on.

The principal reason for distinguishing between group-intentions and merely participatory intentions is that both kinds of intentions are needed to show how individual cooperation is intentional, even when an individual's efforts are marginal relative to the collective act. Marginal individuals display planning and action directed towards the goal of performing their roles, not towards securing the group outcome, since there is nothing they could do to make a non-marginal difference. The cellist plans to attend rehearsals, practice the cello part, attend the conductor's signals, and so on. But the cellist need not, and likely will not, engage in planning directed at ensuring that others will accomplish their parts, or worry about whether the bassoonists have properly realized the mood of the conductor's interpretation.[63] The cellist's participatory intention is fully explained by citing the conductor's executive intention: But for the conductor's intention, the cellist would not know what to play. So while the cellist's conduct is fully explained by positing an intention to contribute to the orchestra's performance, nothing the cellist has done suggests an intention whose scope includes the entire performance. Thus it would be superfluous to posit an executive group-intention.

By contrast, a conductor's planning and action is aimed at the goal that the symphony together perform the *Eroica*. The conductor is therefore disposed to choose suitable rehearsal times, to ensure that replacement players can be found in case of illness, to study scores and previous performances so this performance can be novel or traditional, and so on. I do not want to suggest that the cellist could not have these dispositions as well, but only that there is no independent justification for positing such an intention. By contrast, it is hard to make sense of the conductor's behavior unless we posit such a group-intention.

Compare the hierarchical case of the orchestra with the egalitarian project of going for a walk together. When I go for a stroll with you, I intend our stroll together as the end of my action, and do not merely play my part in our walking. Although I do play my part, by taking care to heed your direction, following when you decide to lead, and showing up at the appointed time and place, I also am disposed to coordinate with you in the first place, to choose a meeting place and route, leading the way as you become distracted in conversation, ensuring that you have a pleasant time as well. My intention that we walk together explains my doing my part of this project. Indeed, in this context, we need to attribute to me such a group-intention in order to explain my participatory intention. Because there is no obvious leader, each of us must engage in collective-directed planning and behavior. Each solves the associated coordination problems by considering first what we ought to do, then doing one's own part of that solution. Where centralized authority or planning is lacking, individuals must plan and act on the basis of collective intentions. But such collective action is by no means universal. In the orchestral case, as with many other hierarchies, someone is vested with authority in order to resolve coordination problems; subsidiary participants play their parts in the solution. I take this point as important, because I seek an account of collective action that can accommodate both hierarchical and nonhierarchical contexts. Collective action always involves intentional participation; it does not always involve group-intentions.

A second reason to think that jointly intentional action is possible in the absence of group-intentions arises from the general distinction between intentional and intended action. I will now argue that individuals can intentionally contribute to a collective end even though they do not intend the realization of that end. This claim conflicts with what might seem to be an analytic principle of action: who wills the means wills the end. Nonetheless, I will defend the claim that agents who intentionally perform their part of some joint act, but who lack a group-intention of realizing that joint act, nonetheless intentionally perform an act as a means to the joint end.

We can distinguish the notion of performing an act because it is a means to an end, and performing an act in order to realize an end. For me to intentionally perform an act M as a means to end E, the following counterfactual must be true:

(1) If I did not believe M was a way of providing E in such circumstances, I would not do M but would do some other act M'.

For it to be true that I intend to do E by doing M, however, a stronger counterfactual must be true:

(2) If I did not believe M was a way of producing E in such circumstances, *and* I did not believe M actually would produce E, then I would not do M but would instead do M', or call the whole thing off.[64]

I might therefore perform an act that is a means to an end, because it is a means to that end, but would perform it whether or not I believed the end would be produced.

For example, say that I live in a country ruled by a ruthless dictator, and I am a famous neurologist with secret dissident political sympathies. The dictator has just had a stroke. Because of my skills, I am called in by the dictator's aides to administer the appropriate medications. I follow my ethical commitment as a doctor to offer appropriate medical care, all the while hoping that the drug will not, in fact, save him. I do not do M (administer the drug) in order to produce E (save the dictator's life), although I perform M because it is a means to E. Similarly in the joint action case, the following counterfactuals diverge:

(1) If I did not believe P was a way of contributing to G's occurrence in such circumstances, I wouldn't do P but would do P'.
(2) If I did not believe P was a way of contributing to G's occurrence in such circumstances and I did not believe G could be realized in these circumstances, I wouldn't do P (but would do P' or might call the whole thing off).

When I intend to do my part of G, but do not intend that G be realized, the first counterfactual is true and the second is false. I need not intend that the group act be realized in order to do my part intentionally.

It could be objected that my examples do not require a wholesale denial of the principle that who wills the means wills the end, for all of these cases can be redescribed in terms of an end the agent does have, for example, "going through the motions" or "putting on a show" of achieving the unwanted end. But my point is that an agent's acts can be nonaccidentally related as means to end (or part to group act), and the agent can intend that that relation obtain, without intending that the end (or group act) be realized. It may also be true that the agent necessarily intends some other end to be realized, but this does not impugn the validity of the counterfactuals expressing the means-end relationship.

I insist upon this point because many cases of collective action involve contexts where agents are alienated from the end to which they contribute, whether because of coercion, willful ignorance, or moral qualms. A pacifist takes a job at the nuclear weapons plant, because it is the only job available; an accountant processes the astonishingly large receipts of a pizza parlor, not inquiring too carefully into their explanation. These are cases in which the collective activity is jointly intentional and the product of individual intentional participation, for they involve individuals who see themselves as acting in concert, contributing to a collective end though they disavow that end. The collective nature of the activity is sufficiently explained here by the group-oriented content of their participatory intentions. It would be false to these participants' self-understanding, as well as to the most plausible rationalization of their behavior, to view them as intending to realize the collective end rather than merely to contribute intentionally to it.

The minimalist account is weak enough that it can accommodate intentional participation by cognitively vague, alienated, or dyspeptic agents. It can make sense of collective action in our familiar circumstances of routinized cooperation, hierarchical authority, and compartmentalized information. Some might, however, worry that the minimalist account is now too weak, for example because it treats cases like the picnic rescue as genuinely collective, where we have no interaction nor determinate beliefs once the rescue is underway, but only hopes about each other's intentions. One might well think such putative cases of collective action are really simply collections of individual acts, and that more structure and interdependence is required for genuinely collective action.[65] Merely linguistic intuitions are unreliable here, for the claim that "We saved the picnic" is ambiguous between collective and noncollective interpretations of we, as in "We commuters crossed the bridge together at rush hour."

The principal defense of this broad theory of collective action lies in the force of the examples, for it seems natural to regard the picnickers as acting cooperatively in saving the picnic, even though this particular form of cooperation required no interactive structure. Furthermore, it would be consistent with the general contours of my account to rule out some of the borderline cases, assuming a nonarbitrary condition of interaction could be established, a condition that does not rule out cases an even narrower view would want to keep in. But what is decisively in favor of a broad theory is that characterizing the picnickers' rescue as joint simply mirrors the content of their individual intentions, intentions to do their individual parts of together rescuing the picnic. When their actions taken together really do amount to a rescue, the insistence that their rescue was not joint would entail that they would be mistaken in claiming they had achieved their aims of together rescuing the picnic. And so, absent a compelling intuition or argument that points in a narrower direction, it makes great methodological sense to map the category of collective action directly and transparently onto the intentions that produce it. Conversely, there is no evident explanatory advantage in circumscribing the notion of collective action to a domain less ambitious than that of the conceptions of the individuals who endeavor to act together.

## 3.8   ASCRIBING COLLECTIVE ACTIONS

So all collective action, hierarchical and nonhierarchical, preprogrammed and dynamic, planned and spontaneous, admits of a common analysis: A set of individuals jointly G when the members of that set intentionally contribute to G's occurrence by doing their particular parts, and their conceptions of G sufficiently and actually overlap. Put negatively, a set of individuals can jointly intentionally G even though some, and perhaps all, do not intend that G be realized, or do not even intend to contribute to G, but only know their actions are likely to contribute to its occurrence. Depending upon the particular type of act, these requirements on individuals may need to be strengthened, by adding stronger requirements of responsiveness, common knowledge, and executive purview. Individuals' overlapping conceptions of the collective act to which they contribute is the basis of joint action. This common analysis forms the basis for our ascriptions of actions to groups, and to the individuals who compose them.

We also need an account of collective intention. What are the conditions for attributing to groups claims such as "Exxon intended to drive Gulf out of Venezuela," and "The Bastille mob intended to express political claims rather than economic resentments"?[66] In the following section, I argue that intentions may be attributed to groups in virtue of individuals' intentions to participate in forming a collective intention, when their intentions overlap adequately and when their participation is recognized, formally or informally, as legitimately contributing to the collective endeavor.

A group acts because its members act, and so the causal explanation of a group's act consists in the motivating intentions of its members. Furthermore, a group's act is determined by the goals, or conditions of satisfaction, of its members' intentions. It does what they mean it to do when they perform their parts of a collective act. If I make sandwiches for our picnic, and you buy the drinks, then we have prepared for a picnic. Our collective act is causally explained by our intentions, and is describable as preparation for a picnic because that was the overlapping joint goal we individually promoted. So the following general principle for attributing collective acts seems to be true: A group intentionally acts (performs G intentionally) when its members do their parts of intentionally promoting G and overlap in their conceptions of G.

This principle, however, is both too narrow and too broad. It is too narrow because it assumes that only acts performed by all a group's members may be redescribed collectively as the group's acts. But some collective actions may be just the actions of a single member: when Exxon announces its plans for oil exploration, only the spokesperson for Exxon has acted. And we made sandwiches for the picnic, although I, in fact, was the only one to make them. The principle is also too broad, because it fails to exclude acts done by agents with participatory intentions that do not, nonetheless, count as the group's actions. If someone posing as Exxon's spokesperson announces the exploration plan, Exxon has not acted, only this poser has. So there must be more constraints on the attribution of collective actions to groups than simply the presence of overlapping participatory intentions.

It will be helpful to distinguish between two sorts of jointly acting groups: *ephemeral groups*, and *institutional groups*. Ephemeral groups are groups whose identity as a group consists just in the fact that a set of persons is acting jointly with overlapping participatory intentions. When we push a car out of a snow bank, we are an ephemeral group, whose identity is given by our mutual goal of pushing the car. Our overlapping participatory intentions distinguish each of us as insiders of that group, while excluding from membership those watching from the sidewalk.[67] But there is no further criterion of membership. Institutional groups, by contrast, have identity criteria that do not wholly consist in the presence of overlapping participatory intentions. I cannot make myself a member of the Giants by running out onto the field and catching a line drive, or of the U.S. Senate by intentionally participating in its deliberations. In the case of some institutional groups, recognition of one's membership by other members may be sufficient. Other groups, like the U.S. Senate, have additional necessary membership conditions: Even if other members regard me as a Senator, if I did not win a majority of the vote, I am not a member of that group.[68]

In the case of ephemeral groups, the acts of each and the acts of all are the acts of the group, in the sense that they can be ascribed to each and all of us, considered as members of the group. For they are, after all, nothing but the actions of each of us, and not the actions of some supra-individual entity.[69] Within the modality of collective action, the acts of the group can be ascribed to each. We can expand the domain of ascribable actions by using either the *we* pronoun, or adding a *qua group member* modifier. Take the following example: "Russell and Whitehead wrote the *Principia*." The sentence is puzzling because while ordinarily each conjunct of a true conjunction is also true, Russell did not write the *Principia* alone; and it would be false for him to say "I wrote it." But Russell did write the *Principia* as a member of the Russell-Whitehead team; and he could truly say "we wrote it." You and I can each say "we bought wine and cheese, and so prepared for our picnic," though neither of us did all of these things. Statements about joint action are made true by agents' overlapping participatory intentions and their consequent individual actions.

Let me now introduce a terminological distinction to mark the modality of collective action. I am the *exclusive author* of the actions I perform myself, as well as of the events caused by those actions. My authorship is exclusive because I and only I can say of an action or event, "I did it,", or "I caused it to be done." By contrast, I am an *inclusive author* of the actions of the group in which I participate, inclusive because I am one among those who can say "We did it." I can say, "We bought Chianti rather than Chardonnay," though I played no part in selecting those wines, so long as I am a member of the group with the shared project of selecting wines. You, in contrast, can say both that you picked out Chianti, and that we did. This is the semantics of collective action.

Now, I noted earlier an important complication to this picture: the description-relativity of action ascriptions. By description-relativity, I refer to the principle that actions may be intentional as described one way, and unintentional under another description.[70] I intentionally let out the cat, but a wasp flies in. My letting out the cat was the same action as my letting in the wasp, but only letting out the cat was intentional. This feature of action-ascription is especially marked in the context of collective, or joint action, ascriptions, since actions are only ascribable to a group when they reflect overlapping participatory intentions. Our joint picnicking may also be, in your view, a chance to discuss our work. But if I do not share this view, then we do not jointly prepare an occasion for discussing our work – only you do that.

Furthermore, our shared intention may be indeterminate in some respects. As the shared intention becomes less determinate, it becomes more difficult to say whether a particular action can be ascribed to the collective. The limits on ascription are largely implicit, a function of shared tacit preferences and constraints. We may not have discussed which wine you would buy; but whether you pick Chianti or Chardonnay, this act can plausibly be ascribed to us as a group. However, if you pick out Night Train instead, that might be considered your aberrant action rather than ours, because it falls outside the scope of any plausible refinement of a goal we share. These complications will be especially relevant in the context of the legal discussion of conspiracy, in Chapter 7.

In the case of ephemeral collective action, where no party commands another but all cooperate, the participatory intentions of each allow the mutual attribution of actions, but only inclusively. Because

I did not command others' acts, I cannot claim exclusive authorship of them, only inclusive authorship.[71] Though I did not do either what you did or what we did, I am part of the group that did those things. My claim of inclusive authorship is licensed indirectly by my membership in the group, and directly by the fact that I pursue the same goal that explains your, and our, actions. The presence of the shared goal, and its derivative intentions, therefore is the basis for collective attributions. This case should be distinguished from merely vicarious or expressive claims of authorship, as when I say "we won the Superbowl!" This claim states no fact about my role in producing (or intending to produce) the outcome, but only expresses my imaginative solidarity with the hometown team.[72]

The case of institutional groups is similar, though more complex. Here, too, the action of each and the actions of all are the actions of the collective. Exxon pays a bill when its treasurer writes a check, and prospects for oil when its geologists survey and its engineers drill. However, because group members are not identified solely by their participatory membership, but by additional membership criteria, only the actions of bona fide members of the group can be attributed to the group. (The group's actions do not include those of posers, even posers who act for the sake of the group.) Furthermore, the actions performed by bona fide group members must be consistent with the particular powers and limitations on the member's role. When IBM's executive negotiates a sale of its microcomputer division, IBM sells its division. But if an IBM computer salesperson negotiates a sale of the division, IBM does no such thing; the salesperson merely tries to sell the division.[73] Any member of the institutional group can claim inclusive authorship of acts done by other members, so long as those actions were done for the sake of the institution's goals, in conformity with restrictions on those members' participatory powers. As in the ephemeral case, claims of inclusive authorship are licensed by the fact that each member's acts are explained by the overlapping goal of realizing the group's plans.

## 3.9  ATTRIBUTING COLLECTIVE INTENTIONS

My account of collective action may seem to present a problem for attributing collective intentions. For if collective action is nothing but appropriately motivated individual action, then collective intention is nothing but individual intention. And I have just argued that sets of individual actions may be conjoined under a collective description, and ascribed inclusively to a group, as when we prepare a picnic. But sets of individuals intentions would not seem to be combinable in the same way, as one collective intention, except as a purely functional characterization of interagent plans. What, then, is the intentional equivalent of a collective act, that is an intention that can be attributed inclusively to a collective as a whole?

I want to restrict discussion of genuine intentions to individual mental states, rather than absorbing functionally characterizable individual and interpersonal planning and action under the same term. By *collective intention* I mean essentially a figure of speech, referring not to a supra-individual mental or functional state, but to the region of overlap among individual participatory intentions.[74]

A collective intention is attributable to a group when the following three conditions are met:

(1) Members of the group are intentionally members of that group. That is, they are disposed to participate as members of the group in deciding upon a shared plan and then in acting in conformity with that plan.
(2) There is an explicit or implicit collective-decision rule by which a collective intention may be assigned to the group in virtue of individuals' intentions to participate in forming and abiding by that collective intention.
(3) The participatory intentions of the individuals overlap sufficiently to meet the constraints of the collective-decision rule.

Condition 1 excludes groups of individuals who are not disposed to act as members of groups, either because they do not think of themselves as taking part in making a collective decision, or are not willing to conform to a collective decision. Condition 2 presupposes a method or rule for assigning a collective intention. Among formal bodies, the rule may be an explicit voting rule or a rule that vests decisive authority in some subgroup; among informal bodies, the rule is likely to be an implicit principle of consensus. Condition 3 acknowledges that even when individuals are disposed to act in conformity with a collective decision, there may be so little overlap among individual intentions that no collective intention will be well-defined.

I will explore this characterization of collective decision and intention through two examples, one of executive, future-directed intentions, and one of participatory, present-directed intentions. First, the City Council votes, 20–12 to repave downtown streets. Ten of the winning council members intend to garner the support of downtown businesses by ordering the streets paved, and ten intend to throw construction business to struggling local contractors. Furthermore, ten intend that the city pave with concrete, and ten with asphalt. The losers intend to back the city decision, at least to the extent of noninterference. It is surely appropriate to attribute to the City Council an intention to pave the downtown streets, even amid such disagreement and dissent. Why?

The first reason, given by Condition 1, is to note that the individual members understand themselves to be contributing to a collective decision. Each member, voting pro or con, intends to do his or her part of enacting a city street policy.[75] Furthermore, presumably individual members have the ancillary intention to conform with the collective decision, whether their own preferences win or lose. Such a disposition (related to cooperativeness) may not be necessary to collective decision making, for some members may intend to conform on the condition that their own preferences dominate. However, a disposition to compromise or conform is surely a necessary attribute of enduring formal bodies whose decisions occur amid disagreement.[76]

The second basis for attributing a collective intention is the existence of a collective-decision (CD) rule, that is a method for combining individual intentions into a single plan of action. The CD rule is like an interpretive principle: a schema for organizing an array of intentional behavior into a thematic whole. The City Council has a majority CD rule: If more than half a quorum approves a plan of action, then that plan becomes the collective intention. Clearly, the collective intention can only be as well defined as the plan of action upon which individuals converge. If the plan is left partially open (say, the medium for the resurfacing), then the collective intention is undetermined with respect to that element. In the absence of a formal rule or group policy, the character of an implicit CD rule depends upon the context of attribution and the structure of the group. A rule of near consensus among members seems to serve as a default CD rule for informal groups. If most members of a group conceive of themselves as acting in order to promote the same end, then that end is the collective intention.[77]

This brings us to the third basis for ascribing a collective intention: there must be sufficient overlap among individual intentions. In Section 3.6, I explained that agents' intentions overlap if the collective end component of their participatory intentions refers to the same activity or outcome and when there is a nonempty intersection of the sets of states of affairs satisfying those collective ends. As I suggested there, whether intentions overlap depends upon those pragmatic features that govern the level of specificity with which intentional objects are described. Suppose that Andy intends that, by voting for repaving, he can help the Council curry downtown support; he also intends that the city use asphalt, because it is cheaper. Berenice intends that, by voting for repaving, she will help the city throw business to desperate contractors; she intends that the city will use concrete, because it is more expensive. Although Andy's and Berenice's intentions differ with respect to several ends, they overlap with respect to the city's repaving downtown. Together with eighteen others, a voting majority on the Council overlaps with respect to this goal, and so the bare goal of repaving the downtown is attributable to the majority.

My second example is of a present-directed joint intention in an ephemeral group. Return to the Bastille, where a crowd of some 800 hungry and angry petitioners has assembled.[78] The initial plan of self-appointed leaders of the gathering crowd was to demand the release of 250 barrels of gunpowder stockpiled within. Presumably, however, many of the crowd members had arrived instead with intentions of freeing the (nonexistent) multitudes of state prisoners, with more inchoate demands for lower bread prices, or simply with a taste for spectacle. After failed negotiations with the commandant, a member of the uneasy crowd begins to saw through the drawbridge chains so as to gain access to the inner courtyard. Soon others join in, the drawbridge falls, and the mob rushes within. Fighting between the mob and the guards ensues, and leaders of the crowd organize separate parties to demand surrender from the captain of the guards, to gather weapons from local gunshops, and to set fire to carts of dung and straw so as to mask the attackers with smoke. At the close of the day, the crowd has variously disarmed, arrested, and executed the guards and their commandant. They have, thus, jointly and intentionally taken the Bastille.

At the beginning of the siege, no joint intention can be attributed to the crowd, given the swirl of beliefs and grievances among them – at most, perhaps, a collective mood of anger and resentment. While some hoped to storm and destroy the prison, others simply wanted its powder store. Members of the crowd did not thus initially conceive of themselves as participating in a collective act. But as newcomers observed the initial assailants, as they began to identify themselves with a goal that could only be achieved by collective means, they began to do their parts of storming the Bastille. They understood themselves to be acting as a part of a group in order to achieve an end they believed was widely shared. Thus, Condition 1 was fulfilled: agents acted as participants, and were disposed to modify their actions to the achievement of the collective end.

It seems clear the mob can be attributed the collective intention to storm the Bastille, so long as most of its members thought of themselves as acting for the sake of that end. Although there is no CD rule for the ascription of an intention to a mob, there would appear to be general consensus among the mob members. Note that there must have been insufficient overlap among intentions, in which case there might have been joint action of some kind but no collective intention. For example, many of the members of the crowd might have been royalist *agents provocateurs,* who did not intend to storm the Bastille, but only to entrap the more subversive members of the mob. Even where a formal CD rule exists, the ends of participants may diverge so much that any unity of purpose is purely illusory.

As with the attribution of jointly intentional acts, the attribution of collective intentions is always in part a function of the level of descriptive specificity. For purposes of history, weak overlap may be sufficient; for criminal prosecution, a narrower standard should obtain. The important point is to acknowledge that joint intentions are largely interpretive artifacts, shorthand ways of relating individual agents' participatory intentions and behavior to one another. Attributions of collective intention may play a pragmatic role in narrative description, a functional role in cooperation with outsiders, even perhaps a psychological role in instilling feelings of communal solidarity and identification. But a nonreductive realism about collective intentions is always misplaced. We always do better to keep in mind that collective action and intention is nothing but the action and intention of participating individuals.

### 3.10  CONCLUSION

I have argued for a conception of collective action that is both individualistic with respect to agency and irreducibly holistic with respect to the content of agents' intentions. Groups are nothing more or less than agents who intend to participate in collective action. I have also argued for a minimalist conception of the conditions of collective action. Although particular types of joint activities may require high degrees of responsiveness and robust mutual expectation, joint action as such merely requires there be sufficient overlap among the objects of agents' participatory intentions. From these few elements, we can do much: We can explain what we do together.

In the following chapters, I will draw out the normative consequences of this minimalist and individualistic conception of collective activity. Because all collective action is reducible to individual action, accountability for collective harms can be nothing more than the accountability of individuals who participate in collective acts. Because participating individuals orient themselves in acting with respect to collective outcomes, they may be warrantably accountable for acts done by other group members in pursuit of the collective object. Among structured groups, therefore, accountability can be simultaneously collective and individual.

# Chapter 4

# Moral Accountability and Collective Action

## 4.1  INTRODUCTION

We turn now to the central issue: individual moral accountability in the context of collective action. The most important and far-reaching harms and wrongs of contemporary life are the products of collective actions, mediated by social and institutional structures. These harms and wrongs are essentially collective products, and individual agents rarely make a difference to their occurrence. So long as individuals are only responsible for the effects they produce, then the result of this disparity between collective harm and individual effect is the disappearance of individual accountability. If no individual makes a difference, then no individual is accountable for these collective harms. And since institutions and social groups consist ultimately in nothing but individual agents, no one is accountable for what we do together.

The disappearance of individual accountability is both a description of our current state and a predicament whose practical and theoretical dimensions I have already indicated in Chapter 1. The following three chapters treat this problem. The present chapter and Chapter 5 discuss the moral accountability of individuals for harms that are the result of jointly intentional action, or what I will call *structured collective action*. Chapter 6 then extends the discussion to collective harms that are not the product of jointly intentional action: cases of facilitation, when one individual aids others in their wrong without intentionally promoting that wrong; and cases of environmental harms, which are the products of the unconcerted actions of many individuals.

Section 4.2 introduces the problem of overdetermined, collective wrongdoing, in the context of certain commonsense principles of individual moral accountability. The central example I treat is taken from history, not literature: the incendiary bomb raids of cities in World War II, particularly of Dresden at the end of the European war. The firestorm was a result of the actions of thousands of combat flyers, and many more thousands of planners and support crew; no individual below command levels made a difference. (Because the example is real and the issues it raises still raw, I develop it in considerably more detail than is customary in analytical ethics.) In sections 4.3–4.5, I discuss the difficulties of individually oriented consequentialists and Kantians in explaining accountability for marginal or peripheral participation in collective wrongdoing. I then examine revisions of consequentialism, suggested by Derek Parfit and Frank Jackson, that take collectives as subjects of moral evaluation. I argue that these collectivist approaches fail to provide a satisfying model of accountability, through which individuals can understand the normative significance of their collective acts affecting others. This is a theory in which individual agents remain the subjects of accountability, but the objects of their accountability can include collective harms.

Section 4.6 then presents a theory that explains how individuals can be morally accountable for the acts of others. This is a theory of *moral complicity*, or individual accountability for harms brought about in part by others. My theory of complicity will draw upon the last chapter's analysis of collective action. I argue that this analysis of collective action provides a basis for moral accountability, whereby participants may be deemed morally accountable for the actions of others. For those who like slogans: "No participation without implication." But slogans do not capture the difficulties of making ethical judgments. And so Chapter 5 completes the analysis of moral accountability by applying the slogan in the contexts that obtain in modern ethical life, as we muddle through, alienated, uninformed, "just doing our jobs."

## 4.2 COMMON SENSE AND THE DISAPPEARANCE OF MORAL ACCOUNTABILITY: DRESDEN

In my discussion of accountability thus far, I have spoken primarily of the accountability of individuals. I have presumed that what individual subjects are held accountable for, or what I have termed the object of accountability, is also individualistic: a form of conduct, consequences of that conduct, or an aspect of character. Many of our practices and responses of accountability treat aspects of what individuals alone do, and who they are. However, if we restrict our discussion of accountability to just these individualistic objects, we lose sight of an important category of harms and wrongs. We ignore those harms and wrongs that result essentially from collective action, and that could not be the product of any one individual.

I suggested in Chapter 1 that philosophical discussion of collective accountability has confused two importantly distinct claims. The first is the thesis that the basis of a judgment of accountability must be individualistic. By the basis of accountability, I mean the facts about agents that warrant holding them accountable for a harm or wrong. Judgments of accountability have an individualistic basis when they are warranted primarily by facts about individual subjects, who they are, or what they have done. It is rightly thought unfair to hold an agent morally accountable on the basis of what another agent or agents have done. Holding agents morally accountable on the basis of what others have done fails to respond to those agents as distinct persons, with their own characteristics, decisions, and commitments. Just systems of moral accountability serve the purpose of relating agents harmoniously to one another, and protecting the interests that make their lives good. Ignoring individual differences among agents undermines these purposes, for the resulting responses of accountability do not attach to agents in such a way that they can be integrated into an understanding of their position with respect to their victims or bystanders. The relationships that systems of accountability are supposed to foster (and, in part, constitute) instead are sapped by undiscriminating reproach.

115

This thesis about the need to restrict judgments to individualistic bases is often confused with a more disputable claim. The disputable claim is that the object of accountability must also be individualistic, and in particular that what agents are accountable for must be an act, consequence, or characteristic of the subject of the judgment of accountability. The object of accountability is analytically distinct from the basis of accountability. If I willfully hit you, then I am accountable for that blow and its consequences. I am also accountable for the attitude of hostility I manifest by that action: you will rightfully take my attitude into account in your future dealings with me. My decision to strike you, assuming my capacity to govern myself according to moral norms, warrants you in holding me accountable. By contrast, if I tell my little brother to hit you, then the object of my accountability will be his blow and the harm it does, while the basis of my accountability will still be a fact about me, namely my telling him to hit you. Responses of accountability are always functions of the basis and the object of accountability – as well as of the position of the respondent.

### 4.2.1 Commonsense Principles and the Object of Individual Accountability

Confusion between the object and basis of accountability is responsible for the difficulties common sense and moral theory alike have in dealing with collective harms in particular, and complicitous accountability in general. In Chapter 1, I noted two principles that are deeply rooted in commonsense moral thinking, and that restrict the object of accountability to individual harms. I separate these principles here into the basis they specify of accountability, and the object of that accountability:

**Individual Difference Principle:** (Basis) I am accountable for a harm only if what I have done made a difference to that harm's occurrence. (Object) I am accountable only for the difference my action alone makes to the resulting state of affairs.

**Control Principle:** (Basis) I am accountable for a harm's occurrence only if I could control its occurrence, by producing or preventing it. (Object) I am accountable only for those harms over whose occurrence I had control.

Let us consider how these principles tend to rule out any substantial notion of complicitous accountability. In an attempt to give my discussion ethical and psychological texture, I will discuss a real example: the Allied strategic bombing of Dresden on February 13–15, 1945.[1] The attack on Dresden involved a series of mainly incendiary bombing raids that combined with meteorological conditions to produce a firestorm that devoured the city's residential sectors. The bombing – indeed, much of the Allied strategic bombing campaign – was seen by many at the time as falling well outside the pale of legitimate warfare. A figure of 35,000 civilians killed is now generally accepted, although some estimates have run higher. More significant than the number of deaths was their manner. The firestorm killed through a combination of intense heat and asphyxiation, the latter attacking those who had taken refuge in shelters, when the oxygen was sucked out by the fires. In the words of a German witness to the 1943 Hamburg firestorm, "The calamity is as much perceived in the process of destruction as in the accomplished fact."[2] Indeed, the ghastly destruction the survivors witnessed constitutes a second great violence.

The Dresden firestorm was seen by planners as a welcome, if fortuitous, occurrence – Bomber Command had been trying to repeat its success in the 1943 Hamburg firestorm raid.[3] However, the decision to bomb the city with incendiaries was not a singular product of pure malice, but was instead the culmination of the technique of "Area Bombing," itself a product of more and less respectable purposes.[4] First was the general aim of quickly winning a justified, defensive war against Nazism, a war that many regarded as a defense of civilization against total barbarity. This was a motive shared across the Bomber service, from ground crew to high command. Second, and also widely prevalent across all groups, was a fair measure of retaliatory anger at Germany's own indiscriminate – if far less lethal – bombing of Coventry and London. The remainder were motives more particular to the planners and leadership: using bombing to avoid the trench warfare of the First World War; bureaucratic imperatives within Bomber Command to mitigate the failures of its attempts at precision bombing raids through area bombing; and demonstrating Allied power to the Soviets, who were finding far quicker success in their land campaign.

The Dresden firebombing is a difficult example, in part because of its contemporary status as a *cause célèbre* among Neo-Nazis (although also among pacifists, German and non-German), and more generally because it was carried out in a war against a state whose acts dwarfed Dresden in horror, major segments of whose populace condoned those acts. But two features make the Dresden bombing peculiarly appropriate for a discussion of complicity in collective harm. The first is the counterpart to the fraught place the raids occupy in postwar thought, namely their very ethical complexity. I do not want to take up systematically the question of whether, in the anguished circumstances of the war, British and U.S. authorities should have ordered the targeting of civilian populations. I accept the general consensus, among both historians and philosophers, that the Dresden raids in particular, which came after an Allied victory was already assured, were both strategically valueless and inhumane.[5] I also believe that, despite the difficulties of thinking clearly in times of war, the wrongfulness of the raids should have been and almost certainly was apparent to the wartime military and political leadership.[6]

The second apt feature of the Dresden raids is the massive extent of individual participation in a force of destruction as overdetermined as can be imagined. The city was bombed in three raids, and at least 1,000 planes and 8,000 crewmen were directly involved in the raids, in various roles as pilots, navigators, bombers, and gunners. The firestorm was already raging before many crews dropped their bombs.[7] Each crewman's causal contribution to the conflagration, indeed each plane's, was marginal to the point of insignificance. Many thousands further were involved in planning and support at Bomber Command – what Freeman Dyson, the physicist and peace activist, would later call "a huge organization dedicated to the purpose of burning cities and killing people, and doing the job badly."[8] (A consequence of this mass participation is the wealth of personal accounts about Dresden as well as Hamburg and Tokyo, in which participants reflect on the nature of their responsibility for the events, materials I draw upon.) It is of course only too easy to find examples of fully deliberate mass participation in collective evil, from the increasingly well-documented extent of the complicity of "ordinary" Europeans in Nazi crimes to the massacres in Rwanda in 1994 and in Srbenica in 1995.[9] But the very purity and enormity of the evil involved in those cases obscures underlying moral structures. The wrongfulness of work as a field executioner, concentration camp guard, or a radio announcer urging bloodbath resonates throughout action, intention, and character. Despite the occasional difficulties of tracing causal connections between individuals and atrocity, the moral calculus of accountability nonetheless is overdetermined.[10] By contrast, the Dresden bombing constitutes an evil that was more inhabited than made, where individuals discovered themselves on the verge or in the course of participation in a great wrong through the flow of obedience and circumstance.[11] I concentrate here on inhabited evil, because the philosophical and psychological questions that arise are both less tractable and more pressing. If individuals are accountable in such circumstances, it will have to be by way of a more subtle argument than one that directly links homicidal intent to massive wrong, an argument that attends to the competing pulls of cooperative action and causal insignificance.

The philosophical question is what follows ethically from individuals' participation in a wrongful collective act, an act whose underlying harm is overdetermined with respect to individual contributions. The question is manifestly practical as well as theoretical, for reflective agents might come to understand that they have obligations of disobedience, repair, or prevention; victims must decide whether they can legitimately press their claims; and bystanders must decide whether and on what terms to return the perpetrators to the fold. In the specific case of Dresden, the question is whether and why the individual flyers and planners acted wrongly in participating in the raids; and how they must account for their roles to their victims, to themselves, and to the broader world that looks upon them in question and judgment. The number of individuals involved in the Dresden bombing and the nature of the destruction license a stipulation close to, if not coincident with, the historical facts. No one rank-

and-file individual made a difference to the evil that occurred, and no one could control the devastation that resulted. I will therefore focus on two aspects of the example: the imperceptible marginal difference made by each individual contribution, and the cooperative structure of the bombers' interaction.[12]

Now, as a matter of historical fact, many of the individuals involved were indifferent to the moral issues surrounding area bombing.[13] But among those whose ethical sensibilities had not been deadened by terror, boredom, and wartime's general inuring to cruelty, reactions were more complicated. Some simply regarded themselves "a force of retribution," and were frankly glad of the destruction they caused a hated enemy.[14] Many others, though, expressed a sense they had brushed and so been marked by real evil.[15] Witness the claim of an RAF navigator who participated in the Hamburg firebombing: "I expect no mercy in the life to come. The teacher told us clearly. We disobeyed." And a gunner who flew in the Dresden raid recounted, "The whole city was just one raging inferno. Years later, I thought about the people. . . . This was the only raid that really mattered to me. It preyed on my mind afterwards."[16] Freeman Dyson helped plan the raids, along with countless others at Bomber Command. He grieved over his participation:

I felt sickened by what I knew. Many times I decided I had a moral obligation to run out into the streets and tell the British people what stupidities were being done in their name. But I never had the courage to do it. I sat in my office until the end, carefully calculating how to murder most economically another hundred thousand people.[17]

Another planner offered a more complex reaction, after seeing the devastated cities:

I began to think, "Oh my God, what have I done in taking part in all this?" I remember being appalled at what I saw, feeling that I ought to have a sense of shame and being surprised that I didn't. But I don't think I would be honest if I said that I regretted it now. I still think that what we did was a major factor in bringing about the eventual defeat of Germany.[18]

All of these men believed themselves retrospectively accountable for their roles in a great harm. Some concluded they had done wrong, period. The last could accept his responsibility as part of a nasty but necessary job. Their sense of accountability was grounded not in an assessment of the differences they had made as individuals, but in an act they had performed together. Their thinking thus manifests the complexity of actual ethical life. The task now is to see whether moral theory is adequate to that complexity.

Imagine a young flyer, a pilot, who must decide whether he can participate in the night's raid. He has just been informed that the aiming point in tonight's raid is the residential district of Dresden, and that there are no industrial targets in the area. He realizes the civilian population is his target, and he is perhaps troubled by this, for he is aware of the terror felt by the people of Coventry and London at the sound of German bombs. He knows, or at least suspects, that wars are not won on the bodies of the very young and very old, the only ones likely to be remaining in the city. But Nazi Germany is a threat to what he holds good, and he hates it for the violence it has brought to him. Moreover, flying is what he joined the R.A.F. to do, and the price of dropping out of the mission is high: he'd be labelled "LMF," for "Lacking Moral Fibre," and drummed out or sent to desk duty.[19] Finally, his is only one of a thousand planes. If he does not go, another will fly in his place, and even if he does go, his plane's load of bombs will make no difference to the success of the raid. It does not matter to my argument where and when his reflection takes place. Perhaps it is during the raid – if he has qualms about participating, he may consider dropping his bombs over the countryside, as at least one plane did.[20] Or he may fly eagerly, roused by Churchill's words to make "the German people taste and gulp each month a sharper dose of the miseries they have showered upon mankind."[21] But later, seeing pictures of the devastated city, he wonders whether he did wrong, and what he must do to atone.[22]

His commonsense reflection will likely be indeterminate, for intuitions conflict. On the one hand, if the Dresden bombing is a great wrong, then each person who participated voluntarily will be complicit in that evil. Each person is accountable in some way for the collective wrong. This is the view of Dyson and some of the others I quoted above; it is surely also the view of many of the firestorm's survivors. They are pulled by what I will call:

**The Complicity Principle:** (Basis) I am accountable for what others do when I intentionally participate in the wrong they do or harm they cause. (Object) I am accountable for the harm or wrong we do together, independently of the actual difference I make.

No participation without implication. Where the individualistic principles exculpate, the principle of complicity implicates. It specifies an individualistic basis (participation) that grounds, rather than precludes, accountability for collective harms.

The Complicity Principle is well-grounded in our intuitions, ethical practices, and psychologies. But it is clearly inconsistent with the commonsense Individual Difference and Control principles I mentioned earlier. By hypothesis, no bomber makes an individual difference and no bomber has control over the total outcome. Even if one (and probably many) of the flyers or planners failed to participate, the firestorm would still have been raised and the massive casualties would still have happened. Therefore, there is no basis for holding an individual bomber accountable, nor any morally significant object of accountability. We might have contempt for a bomber who reveled in the destruction and killing, but there is nothing he has done for which response is warranted. Each bomber can truly reply to the victims or their survivors, "Why blame me? I have not caused your suffering, nor made you worse off." Since all of the bombers are symmetrically placed, none is accountable for the wrong. Individual accountability has fled the scene of collectively induced suffering.

Note that common intuitions are highly positionally dependent. The Difference and Control principles seem most natural, and are most compelling, from a third-person point of view, a perspective that emphasizes the objective causal relations that underlie the principles. The principles may also seem convincing to the individual agents themselves, at least to the extent that they also view their actions in terms of their causal properties.[23] By contrast, the Complicity Principle is best supported from the second-person perspective of the person who is harmed. The victim's experience is dominated by the fact of suffering, a fact saliently linked to what the Allied bombing forces together do, not to what the individual pilots do.

How do we reconcile these apparently inconsistent moral principles and responsive perspectives? Commonsense morality fractures along their lines. But we must reconcile them unless we are willing to accept the disappearance of individual accountability. That is the task I set for this chapter. I seek a theory of individual accountability that will help to foster and constitute the moral, psychological, and social relations among agents that make their lives good. Such a theory must meet several criteria. First, a theory of individual accountability must provide individual agents with reasons to avoid and reasons to respond to even marginal participation in harmful acts. In the absence of such a theory, there is little social hope of controlling the essentially collective harms that threaten individual interests. This is in part a normative goal, but it is one that is sensitive to the actual psychology and ethical life of moral agents. This implies two further conditions. A theory of individual complicit accountability must be psychologically feasible: it must be generally capable of motivating (or restraining) action, and it must be able to survive individual moral reflection. As I will discuss later, this condition rules out purely institutional approaches to the problem, for such approaches fail to accommodate themselves adequately to individuals' own conceptions of themselves and others as moral agents. And finally, at least for serious harms, a normative theory of complicitous accountability must have a political component: Such a theory must justify the coercive application of penal and compensatory institutions.[24] In this and the next two chapters I will try to satisfy the first two of these demands. In Chapter 7, I will discuss the political morality of complicity, that is, its role in a system of legal liability.

This challenge is best met first by considering the ways the two dominant contemporary moral theories, consequentialism and Kantianism, fail to justify complicitous accountability. The failure of these theories will be instructive for the later construction of an approach to individual accountability for collective harms.

## 4.3 THE INADEQUACY OF MORAL THEORY TO COLLECTIVE WRONGDOING: INDIVIDUAL CONSEQUENTIALISM

I begin with direct or "act" consequentialism. On most forms of direct consequentialism, agents act wrongly when they fail to perform the action, among those physically possible, that would result in the best consequences, "best" having been determined by a prior ranking principle.[25] Consequentialist theories present two initial complications to discussing their conception of accountability, both stemming from the purely instrumental role played by responses of accountability. I have defined *accountability* as the responses warranted by an agent's relation to a harm. According to commonsense thinking, a necessary and sufficient condition of warranting a response of (critical) accountability is that an agent has acted wrongly.[26] But consequentialism challenges this supposition at a fundamental level. First, since the responses of accountability are themselves acts, they can be assessed by the consequentialist calculus. Whether an actual response of accountability is warranted depends entirely upon the instrumental value of the response. Second, many consequentialists make a distinction between "objective" and "subjective" forms of the theory. Objective consequentialism assesses agents' actions solely in terms of their actual consequences. Subjective consequentialism assesses actions relative to what agents actually or reasonably ought to have believed the consequences would be.[27] Agents can therefore be said to have acted objectively wrongly though subjectively rightly, if they mistakenly but reasonably believed the act they chose would have the best consequences. Though consequentialist theories care ultimately only about the instrumental value of expressions of accountability, as behavior-modification devices, I treat them as though they also cared about the noninstrumental warrant they provide for those expressions. That is, I will discuss the theoretical question of whether consequentialist approaches provide adequate grounds for a judgment of accountability. We will therefore say that agents are potentially accountable if their action contributes to a less good state of affairs than other actions reasonably available to them.[28]

Our pilot presents an obvious problem for direct consequentialist theories, which are by definition unequipped to explain the relevance of marginally insubstantial participation. Since the victims' suffering is as severe whether or not his plane drops its bombs, the direct consequences of his participation (towards them) are the same as the consequences of refusal. Let me rule out two considerations that might lead consequentialists to answer differently. First, if the choices of individual agents depended strategically upon the choices of others, or if individuals were uncertain about the participation of others, then there is a consequentialist basis for accountability. For example, some with qualms might be monitoring each other's willingness to fly, so that many will refuse to go if a few break ranks at first. This could be the case, but is not necessarily. I will assume each acts independently, on the supposition that a significant number of others will participate, whatever he does. Second, consequentialists frequently point to the significance of considerations such as the habituating and corrupting effects of single choices upon the agent's (or others') character. The history of warfare is testament to how acts of violence, individual and collective, spawn further atrocities, both in aggressors and in their victims.[29] But while these factors can make a significant difference in actual cases, they fundamentally miss the central theoretical question: whether an agent acts wrongly by virtue of marginal participation. The answer is that direct consequentialism is indifferent to marginal participation.[30] For we have now excluded all of the considerations that do make a difference.

Such puzzles about collective harms are sometimes thought to stem from general metaphysical problems about causal overdetermination, namely how to account for potential causal contributions that in fact make no difference. But the problem of marginal contribution is not primarily a problem of causal overdetermination, for we can stipulate solutions to the relevant metaphysical causal riddles without illuminating the ethical questions at all. For example, if we are willing to discriminate very finely among different blast- or flame-paths, then we may say the actions of each bomber were necessary to that particular pattern of destruction, even though indefinitely many other patterns would have resulted in the same number of dead.[31] So long as we allow token events to be differentiated purely by their causal antecedents, we may say that each bomber's act was a necessary condition of the set of elements sufficient to produce that very token.[32] So each bomber did in fact make a causal difference to the raising of the particular set of fires and explosions. Each was a metaphysically necessary condition of the firestorm that actually occurred.[33]

But metaphysical differences are not (always) moral differences. An event can be normatively overdetermined though not causally overdetermined, insofar as a given individual's action may make no difference to the normative properties of a given event.[34] Among the relevant normative properties of the Dresden firestorm are tens of thousands of deaths and much additional suffering. Even if a given bomber had failed to drop his incendiary bombs, and so a fractionally different pattern of fires and explosions had occurred, the firestorm would still have had these normative properties – indeed, the number of deaths might even have been greater. The purely metaphysical difference between event-tokens is not susceptible to consequentialist evaluation.[35] Nor can consequentialists avoid this conclusion by simply identifying normative with metaphysical differences. As David Lewis and Kenneth Kress have noted, this strategy threatens to make too much out of a difference between token events, for then not only is each actual contributor fully causally and morally responsible for that token event of destruction, but so is each potential bomber who instead refrained.[36] Each agent's refusal to participate was an equally necessary condition of its being that token event. But this surely spreads negative responsibility too far even for a consequentialist theory. In circumstances of conflagration, a few bombs more or less are just bits of kindling at the periphery of a raging bonfire. They don't make the moral difference consequentialism requires.

I will not belabor direct consequentialism's difficulties with the bombers. It is, however, worth considering indirect consequentialist strategies for dealing with multiagent problems, such as Rule Utilitarianism (RU) and Donald Regan's Cooperative Utilitarianism (CU).[37] According to RU, an agent ought to act in accordance with a rule such that general acceptance of the rule would have the best overall consequences. According to CU, an agent first ought to ascertain other potential cooperative utilitarians, and then join in the best collective pattern of behavior with those cooperators, taking into account the likely behavior of noncooperative utilitarian agents.[38] These indirect theories work well prospectively, especially among a community of utilitarian agents. In these contexts, individual agents will be directed to refrain from participation, since general nonparticipation would have the best consequences.

But the problem is not whether some scheme of rules can lead uncertain agents to act optimifically. Clearly, some scheme could. The problem is whether a consequentialist agent has any ethical reason to refrain from participating in a collective act of firebombing that will inevitably take place. And here the indirect theories must either agree with direct consequentialism, or lapse into instrumental irrationality. RU would still prescribe nonparticipation, but it is then vulnerable to the familiar objection of "rule-worship."[39] Since nothing is gained from actual nonparticipation in no-difference circumstances, there is no rational basis for the application of the rule prohibiting participation. And if the behavior of other agents is already fixed by hypothesis – in other words, they are engaging in strategic bombing – then a cooperative utilitarian will have no one with whom to cooperate in not participating. So again, there is no reason not to participate. Consequentialism, both direct and indirect, is committed to the Individual Difference Principle and thus to the denial of the Complicity Principle.

Is this conclusion necessarily troubling to consequentialists? They might well respond that if participation really does not make matters worse, then the objection to participation must rest on nonmoral grounds, or at least on grounds that do not involve the assessment of actions. This, in effect, is Jonathan Glover's position.[40] While Glover is at pains to argue that the side effects of individual actions will often add up to a moral difference, he concedes that an agent has no intrinsic moral reason not to contribute to overdetermined harms. Those who nonetheless believe it wrong to participate are, Glover says, attached to the nonconsequentialist "Solzhenitsyn principle," according to which one must not allow wrong to be done through one's own agency.[41] Glover acknowledges that attachment to this principle is often admirable, though it can in its more self-reflexive forms lead to "a possessive attitude to one's own virtue," that is, a reluctance to act in ways that are beneficial in the aggregate, although they involve moral costs.[42] But Glover is careful to insist that our admiration for a purely principled objection to participation is not part of strict consequentialism. Our admiration reflects an aesthetic or morality of character rather than of actions.

At a purely descriptive level, consequentialism's indifference to complicity is deeply at odds with the intuition that participation in wrong is itself wrong, and in a direction that does consequentialism no credit. More deeply, a moral theory that countenances overdetermined wrongdoing fails to acknowledge the interpersonal nature of morality. The responses of accountability are fundamentally the responses of individuals to one another. These responses are essential constituents of the relationships through which individuals flourish, and by which they retain the values that help give their lives purpose. Participation in wrong invites response, from both agent and victim, in virtue of what the act means about their relations to one another. As long as consequentialism is unable to ground criticism of complicity, it cannot provide a basis for sustaining and repairing the relations among agents that make their lives good. Finally, complicity poses purely operational problems for consequentialists. In conditions of uncertainty, how should agents evaluate the decision to participate against alternatives? If a utilitarian penal system is in place, how severe should the sanctions be to deter marginal wrongdoing?

A consequentialist would answer these criticisms in purely instrumental terms, by saying agents might be encouraged to think of themselves as doing wrong in cases of marginal participation, both in order to prevent collective wrongdoing, and in order to maintain appropriate relationships between victims and bombers. But this response raises two further problems. In the first place, it exposes a consequentialist theory to the familiar objection of the unfairness of holding faultless agents accountable on extrinsic grounds. The problem of fairness is, of course, particularly acute for penal institutions, but it is of concern even with respect to the milder sanctions of social morality. And in the second place, it is unlikely that any purely instrumental form of accountability is psychologically feasible. The reason for this is that the basis for a purely instrumental response must be opaque to the subject of that response. Since the judgment of accountability here would be divorced from the judgment of wrongness, complicitous agents must not reflect on the justification of the responses to which they are subjected. Ideally, responses of accountability ground and motivate claims of repair. But as the logical gap increases between the responses of accountability and judgments of wrongfulness, the motivational force of those responses is undermined.[43] This internally inconsistent pattern of reaction is unlikely to spur individuals to make amends for the past or to alter their conduct in the future. And the divergence will generally sap the ability of a system of moral accountability to perform its elementary function of social control. Even if consequentialists wanted to accommodate the problem of marginal wrongdoing, their theory does not provide the resources required to do so.

## 4.4 THE INCOMPATIBILITY OF COLLECTIVE CONSEQUENTIALISM AND INDIVIDUAL ACCOUNTABILITY

Consequentialist theories that take individual acts as their objects cannot adequately treat complicity because they cannot account for the moral significance of contributing marginally to a collective wrong. What about consequentialist theories that instead evaluate sets of individual acts? Derek Parfit's solution to the problem of overdetermination involves such a procedure. Considering the claim made by a "harmless torturer," one of many simultaneously acting torturers who each applies to the same individual an individually unnoticeable but aggregatively awful electric shock, Parfit recognizes that traditional consequentialism entails that no individual acts wrongly, because no harmful consequences can be traced to any given torturer's act. So, in order to ground the plausible claim that the "harmless torturers" do wrong, he offers the principle that an act may be wrong even if it harms no one, "because it is one of a *set* of acts that *together* harm other people."[44] Rather than assessing individuals' actions in terms of the differences their actions alone make, we assess individuals' actions in terms of the pattern of actions of which they are a part. According to Parfit's principle, a harmless torturer acts wrongly because the torturers collectively act wrongly; and they collectively act wrongly because their actions together cause harm. The object of accountability becomes the set of all torturers' acts, while the basis of accountability remains the individual act. The principle is still consequentialist, for the wrongness of the act is derived from its effects. But those effects are now assessed as an interpersonal aggregate.

Parfit argues for this principle by examining the case where his harmless torturers collectively torture 1,000 victims, each contributing imperceptibly to the suffering of each victim. He compares this situation with one in which each torturer causes a single victim to suffer, and wonders why the fact of dispersion should make a significant moral difference, since the aggregate level of suffering is identical. Parfit presumes, therefore, that it is as wrong to engage in collective torture as to engage in individual torture, if the aggregate suffering is the same. But since no collectivized torturer makes an individual difference, the wrongfulness of participating in collective torture must flow from the consequences of the collective act. Therefore, each harmless torturer acts wrongly, because each torturer's act is among a set of acts that together are wrongful.[45]

Parfit's principle seems on firmest ground in cases of suffering dispersed over many victims. One thousand aerial bombers collectively firebombing a city and causing 35,000 casualties seems practically equivalent to 1,000 individual saboteurs, each dynamiting a building with 35 inhabitants. All that differs is the technology.[46] But his collective consequentialist principle is neutral with respect to both the dispersion of harm and the number of victims: It simply tells us to aggregate consequences and determine whether that aggregate is bad. Consider the case of 1,000 bombers killing just one victim. Here no reallocation in which each bomber is imaginatively assigned his own complete killing is possible. So, when we look at the case of a single victim, we see that Parfit's principle succeeds only by fiat. It leaves unanswered the fundamental question of why a nonconsequential relation between one act and a set of acts should be morally significant within a consequentialist theory. If a torturer's act genuinely makes no difference, then there is no consequentialist basis for judging that act wrongful, though it may well be part of a set of acts that together make a difference. Furthermore, as a number of critics have noted, Parfit's principle leads to inconsistent or incoherent conclusions in comparative contexts.[47] How, for example, is an individual to decide between contributing marginally to a great harm or individually bringing about a lesser harm? A consequentialist ought to endorse such an individual's decision to participate marginally in a great harm when that choice will provide a significant but small benefit, since no one is made significantly worse off and someone is made better off. But Parfit's principle makes no room for this reasoning.

Frank Jackson has attempted to repair Parfit's treatment of collective harms.[48] Jackson agrees that an individual torturer acts permissibly if the individual's contribution is insignificant. But he points out that a consequentialist logic can be applied directly to sets of actions and actors as well as to individuals. That is, consequentialists may ask whether a set of persons jointly produced the best state of affairs, distinguishing this question from the question of whether individual members of the set acted well. In many cases, a group may have acted wrongly, in the sense that a different set of actions would have had better consequences, even though no individual member of the group has acted wrongly, because any individual change might have made the situation worse yet. Jackson gives the example of a highway filled with speeders. Collectively, they ought to drive slower, though any individual law abider would merely endanger others further. Each driver therefore acts rightly, given the behavior of the others, while all collectively act wrongly.[49] In the case of the Dresden bombers, Jackson would hold the line at the level of the collective: We act wrongly by firebombing the city, but no individual acts wrongly.

Jackson's position has considerable theoretical integrity, but it comes at a high price: He concedes the disappearance of individual accountability. No individual bomber has moral reason to act differently if others will cause harm anyway, although the bomber will act as part of a group that does wrong.[50] It may be true the group

131

ought to have acted otherwise, in the sense that its members ought to have coordinated on a plan of nonparticipation. But no individual acts wrongly once the opportunity for coordination is past. So Jackson leaves us with two options with respect to the question of individual accountability.[51] We may criticize the character of marginal contributors, or we may fault them for having entered the group in the first place. The latter may be an especially appropriate option in cases of concerted, overdetermined wrongdoing, when the acts of preparation are themselves culpable. But Jackson is clear that the act of participation in an overdetermined harm is not itself wrong. An individual deciding whether or not to participate in a harm that will occur anyway has no moral reason not to participate, nor have others any reason to fault this participation. So Jackson's group consequentialism is silent with respect to individual moral deliberation and response. Since Jackson's goal is precisely to distinguish between individual and collective evaluations, this is not necessarily a criticism of his own project. But if we are looking for a framework within which individuals can deliberate about and assess their relations to collective harms, Jackson's is a nonstarter. We still have no way to cross the bridge from collective to individual accountability.[52]

## 4.5 KANTIAN UNIVERSALIZATION AND MARGINAL CONTRIBUTIONS

Surprisingly, Kantians have as much trouble with complicitous wrongdoing as do consequentialists. This is surprising because Kantians' focus on agents' intentions, as opposed to the consequences of their intentions, would seem to give them an important advantage. Kantians evaluate actions by testing the maxims, or intentions underlying those actions, for permissibility. Permissible maxims are universalizable. That is, agents can conceive of and will their maxims "without contradiction" in a world in which everyone acts upon a similar maxim.[53] The general point of the universalization test is to constrain agents to act intentionally in ways consistent with regarding others as moral equals. Nonuniversalizable actions are actions that distinguish invidiously among moral agents, typically treating the agent's own ends as more important than those of others.

It is a disputed question among Kant scholars what "conceiving" or "willing without contradiction" means; but for present purposes an inclusive view of possible interpretations will do.[54] Let us say an agent cannot conceive of a maxim without contradiction if in the universalized world, the agent could not possibly act successfully upon the maxim.[55] Kant refers to this as a "contradiction in conception" (CC) test. The CC test generates what Kant calls "perfect" or strict duties: Agents can never permissibly will maxims that fail this test. Taking Kant's familiar example, an agent could not successfully act upon a maxim of welshing on promises when convenient, because in a world in which everyone kept their promises only at their convenience, no one would rely upon a promisor's words in the first place. Thus, since there is no universalized world in which agents act upon a maxim of keeping only convenient promises, no agent may permissibly act upon such a maxim.[56]

Some maxims, however, can be conceivably universalized without being willable as universal laws. Therefore, maxims must also be subjected to the "contradiction in will" test (CW), according to which a maxim cannot be willed if the world of its universalization does not make possible the basic exercise of rational agency by all subjects. According to Kant, agents have an "imperfect" duty, or a general but occasionally defeasible obligation, not to act on such maxims. Taking another Kantian example, we can imagine a world in which all agents act upon a maxim of never giving aid to others, nor seeking it when themselves in need. This is, however, a world in which life is nasty, brutish, and short for almost all. It is not a world in which agents may be reasonably confident of being able to fulfill the ends which they, as rational creatures, necessarily seek for themselves. That is, acting successfully upon this maxim would undermine the conditions which make possible rational agency as such. Agents' wills would be "in contradiction" because they would simultaneously be willing a particular project in a world in which they might not be able to pursue effectively any projects whatsoever. It is, therefore, a world that can be conceived but not willed. Accordingly, agents must not have a strict, general policy of never seeking aid (nor giving it, giving being a precondition of seeking), although they need not respond to every request for aid whatever its effects upon their own projects.

The Kantian tests are not to be understood as a kind of trap laid for the immoral but rational agent, who finds his or her vicious plans thwarted by the contradictions the tests reveal. They are, rather, rigorous but helpful aids to moral deliberation, addressed to agents who are basically morally inclined but perhaps puzzled by what the world demands of them. So imagine again our flyer, who is trying to decide whether he can fly the mission. First he formulates what his intention would be were he to accept the mission. This statement of his "maxim," in Kantian terms, must be an honest characterization of his plans and motive, not tailored to the test. Here is one candidate: "I will drop my incendiary bombs on the city, in order to avoid the criticisms of my commander and fellow crew, but only because I know these few bombs won't make a difference to whether a firestorm arises." To apply the CC test, he now asks whether he can conceive of a world in which everyone acts on that maxim – in which all participate in a possible atrocity of war, in order to preserve reputation and promote the cause of victory, but only when each one's contribution is negligible. A Kantian would have to say that he can, for the envisioned world involves no logical incoherence or practical impossibility. Unlike the paradigm Kantian cases of impermissibility, such as making a lying promise, the possibility of making only a marginal contribution is enhanced rather than undermined by universal practice. The more who join in a cooperative scheme, the more negligible the contribution of each. Although this would be, on intuitive grounds, a morally deplorable world – alas, it is our own world – Kantians cannot resort to these intuitions. Rather, it is the task of the universalization test to vindicate moral intuitions on non-moral grounds.[57] Note that the test would give the same result whether the flyer's attitude towards the mission was reluctant or eager, perhaps out of a desire for revenge. Since we can imagine a world of universal, marginal participation in firebombing cities, it is not necessarily impermissible to engage in complicitous acts of terror.

Already it is clear that Kantian ethics has a problem, since if firebombing cities is impermissible, it is presumably strictly impermissible – that is, it ought to fail the CC test. It might be thought that the problem with the CC test is the problem the test generally has in dealing with actions that do not exploit others' adherence to a convention, the way lying promises do. Acts of violence escape the CC net because the harm they inflict is independent of the behavior of other agents. In contrast, lying promises do harm only when other agents generally keep their promises. What the CC test serves to bring out is the absence of social transparency, that is, occasions when individuals elicit cooperation from others through misplaced trust rather than reasonable agreement. (The undermining of others' reason is for Kant the gravest insult). But cases of massive complicity involve no duplicities or opacities. Each member of the bomber fleet not only lays open his intent, but indeed relies on the mutual awareness of this intent. For only if each flyer is assured that others will bomb will it be reasonable for that flyer to participate. Thus a world of universal participation in firebombing is fully conceivable. The problem such harms pose for the Kantian stems from the marginal character of the agent's contribution, not the nature of the harm to which the agent contributes.

The CW test can do a little better. The CW test asks whether a world in which some harm is universalized is incompatible with the universal exercise of rational agency. In the firebombing case, if the universalized maxim entails the claim that all participating agents would also be subjects (or potential subjects) of civilian massacres, then this is clearly not a world in which rational agency can be exercised.[58] So if agents have an imperfect duty not to participate in acts that have the effect of interfering substantially with the agency of others, then they must have an imperfect duty not to participate in firebombing. Complicitous agents are morally criticizable insofar as they will a world in which agents cannot pursue their ends.

The problem with applying the CW test is not just that agents should presumably have strict rather than imperfect duties not to participate in firebombing, although that is a problem. The main problem is that the contradiction revealed by the CW test fails to illuminate what is wrong with widespread participation in collective harm. This test misses the point in contexts of marginal participation. For the problem posed by collective action is that it introduces a gap between act and harm. In the standard case, where individual agency is sufficient to produce the harm, universalizing the act universalizes the harm. In the case of marginal participation, universalizing the act is no longer the same as universalizing the harm, in light of the fact that the act requires universal (or at least very widespread) participation for there to be any harm. Since universalization is already built into the collective act, a universalized harm does not simply follow logically from universalizing the individual act. Ruling out participation by reference to the horrors of a world of global firebombing invites the objection that the world of global firebombing has simply been stipulated, rather than following naturally from the CI test procedure, as in the paradigm cases.

What we need is to link the individual act of participation to the prospect of universal harm in a way that escapes the charge of stipulation. What we need, in other words, is a modified form of the CW test that justifies universalizing the effects of what we do together while retaining the connections between what each does and what we together do. The CW test does still get something important right. It supplies a moral link between individual agents and states of affairs that is independent of the causal links between the two. Unlike forms of collective consequentialism, the CW test provides a framework for justifying that moral link: An agent who wills even a remote connection to a nonuniversalizable harm wills a world incompatible with relations of cooperation and reciprocity. The test, therefore, fixes appropriately on the marginal participant's identification with the collective act, even if its apparatus of universalization fails to explain the significance of that connection. I now want to pursue the insight that marginal participation is wrong primarily by virtue of the will of the participating agent, rather than the effects of that will. In order to explain the special moral relation of complicity, Kant's procedure must incorporate the logic of collective action. Only thus can the test reveal how individual participation in collective harm transmits accountability for that harm.

I have said that contemporary moral theories share a common problem. They proceed from the premise that the basis of ethical evaluation must be individualistic, an agent's intentions or actions, to the conclusion the object of assessment, the consequences of an action or its underlying intention, must also be individualistic. The strict consequentialist reasons from the fact that agents control only their own actions to the conclusion that the effects of those actions are the only appropriate object of evaluation. The Kantian certainly recognizes the special interest we take in how individuals see themselves as members of a community of equals, as manifested in their intentions and actions. Strangely however, Kantians, in their strictest CC test, then assess the meaning of individuals' actions for the community in terms of their individual effects when hypothetically universalized, rather than in terms of their actual collective effects. But an individual marginal effect universalized remains both individual and marginal.

Parfit's Collective Consequentialist principle, and Jackson's Group Consequentialism, solve the problem of complicity by allowing for collective objects of assessment. However, they thereby forfeit an intelligible and internalizable link between individual agents and the object of moral assessment. A theory of accountability must take as its basis individuals' actions and intentions if it is to serve as a source of reasons for action and deliberation. Simply asserting an ethical link between individual acts and collective harms, as Parfit does, or severing it altogether, as Jackson does, undermines the capacity of an accountability system to regulate reflective behavior. The Kantian CW test likewise forges largely by stipulation its link between individual agents and the harms in which they participate. Without an adequate way of conceiving the relation between individual and collective act, the CW test likewise loses its grip on the individualistic basis of accountability, which resides in the agent's will. All these approaches obscure or ignore the relation between individuals and collective harms.

## 4.6 UNDERSTANDING COLLECTIVE ACTION AND INDIVIDUAL ACCOUNTABILITY

In order to vindicate the complicity principle, we need a form of ethical assessment that takes collective harms as objects of accountability, while retaining a solid basis in features of an individual – intentions, actions, and characteristics. The problem with Kantianism and consequentialism is that they do not provide the link between the collective harm and the individualistic basis. And this problem, in turn, is due to their failure to understand the nature of collective action. Both theories see collective action as essentially *parallel* rather than *cooperative* behavior: each agent is envisioned as pursuing a private end. On this picture, collective acts are mysterious emergent effects. The end result of the victims' suffering, in the Dresden example, seems to be a remarkable coincidence, a result unexplainable in terms of the bombers' intentions, for no one intends to do harm. This picture fails to reflect the way in which jointly acting individuals see themselves as promoting a common end.

The Complicity Principle assumes a different view of collective action. Intuitively, marginally effective participants in a collective harm are accountable for the victims' suffering, not because of the individual differences they make, but because their intentional participation in a collective endeavor directly links them to the consequences of that endeavor. The notion of participation rather than causation is at the heart of both complicity and collective action. Chapter 3 presented a theory of collective action based upon the notion of individual participation. Because Chapter 3 was concerned largely with the analysis of collective action rather than with its normative implications, I did not pursue the relation between intentional participation and complicity. Now it is time to probe that link. I will argue here that the normative relations among participating agents, and between them and their victims, are given by the analytical structure I have already developed. Intentional participation provides a special basis for ascribing individual members' actions to the group as a whole, and to the group members individually. When we act together, we are each accountable for what all do, because we are each authors of our collective acts.

In Chapter 3, I argued that individuals act collectively when they intentionally do their parts of what they conceive as a collective project, and when their conceptions of that group project overlap sufficiently. When these minimal conditions obtain, we can ascribe actions both to a group and to the members of that group. Collectively acting agents render themselves the authors of their groups' actions. Take the earlier example: We prepare for a picnic, with me buying cheese while you buy wine. Our individual actions are each explained by our respective participatory intentions of promoting our joint picnic. Note that my conception of the picnic as *our* – that is, in part *your* – project plays an essential role in rationalizing, or explaining teleologically, my particular action. If I did not believe you would also do your part towards our picnic, I would not buy cheese – cheese having little point without wine.

So our sharing a goal, in the sense of having overlapping participatory intentions, teleologically explains our actions, taken both individually and collectively. While the causal explanation of our actions is intrapersonal, stemming from the beliefs and intentions of each, the teleological explanation is interpersonal. This teleological explanatory link provides the basis for collective action ascription. My buying cheese and your picking out wine can be ascribed to us as a group, in virtue of the explanatory role played by our shared goal. They are our actions, because they are explained by our shared intention, which is causally efficacious through our individual participatory intentions.

In the terminology introduced in Chapter 3, I am the exclusive author of the actions I perform myself, as well as of the events caused by those actions. By contrast, I am an inclusive author of the actions of the group in which I participate – inclusive because I am one among those who can truly say *we* did it. As I will now explain, the semantic, or modal, difference between inclusive and exclusive ascription also marks an important normative difference. Though I am accountable in some form for the actions and events inclusively ascribable to me, inclusive authorship constitutes a fundamentally different responsive position from exclusive authorship.

The ascription of actions (and their consequences) to us, as individuals or as members of groups, provides a basis for accountability. Chapter 2 detailed the ways in which ascription grounds accountability in the individual case. Responses are warranted to what we do and who we are, not because of some deep metaphysics of causal responsibility, but because of what our actions and gestures of repair indicate about the view we take of our relations with others. I emphasized in Chapter 2 that these responses are not generated from abstract moral principles. Like the norms they protect, the responses of accountability exist and make sense within particular concrete social relationships.

Our intentional activity manifests our attitudes towards others because of the teleological relation between our aims and our actions. Responses to conduct are not so much responses to actions as to the intentions and attitudes underlying those actions. This is why a central feature of ethical life is our practice of demanding reasons from those whose acts infringe upon our interests. The salient connection between agent, act, and victim is essentially one of meaning rather than causality.[59] I do not mean to suggest that causal connections are entirely irrelevant to either ascription or accountability. Causal relations are presupposed in the paradigm case of individual, exclusive ascription. If I push a button in order to signal an elevator, and an elevator comes, its coming can only be ascribed to me if my button push in fact caused the elevator to arrive.[60] Strong causal connections are also presupposed when we ascribe one agent's acts exclusively to another agent, as in actions brought about through duress or deceit. If I send my unwitting accountant false receipts that he then submits to the government, I may be said to have caused the deception. Because my actions merely played upon his settled expectations and habits, and involved no autonomous exercise in judgment, it is I who have defrauded the government, not my accountant.[61]

So causal connections are presupposed by exclusive ascriptions, and exclusive ascriptions are presupposed by inclusive ascriptions. If I may claim inclusive authorship of your actions or their consequences, this is only because what you did is causally explained by your intentions and beliefs. But within the modality of collective action, teleological relations play the primary role in relating actors to events. There need be no question, for example, that I caused you to buy wine for our picnic. It may be either likely that you would have done so anyway, or unlikely that my suggestion to do so would have moved you on its own. But your buying wine is something I can say we have done just because the goal I share with you explains your action. Inclusive ascription is fundamentally teleological rather than causal.

Inclusive accountability follows suit. It too is based in the teleological rather than causal relations between group members' intentions and the collective act. We are properly held accountable for the actions of groups (and of individual group members) in which we participate, because these actions represent our own conception of our agency and our projects. This conception, embedded in our participatory action, is thoroughly normative: it expresses what we desire, what we will tolerate, and what we believe.[62] If a set of agents' participatory intentions overlap, then the will of each is represented in what each other does qua group member, as well as what they do together. The logical overlap permits us to say they manifest their attitudes through one another's actions. I help to persuade you to fool your boss into allowing you to go to our picnic. Though you alone actually enact the deception, I am also accountable for it, for your deception manifests my will as well. The coincidence of our intentions grounds my accountability for your actions. Note that because the accountability link is teleological rather than causal, there is no room to apply the Individual Difference and Control Principles. Whether or not you would have played hooky anyway, my will is manifested as a matter of logic in your actions. My inclusive accountability for those actions is therefore independent of the difference I make or the control I have.

Let us return to the case of area bombing, imagining now that the flyers are united, all eager for their mission, hot with thoughts of revenge and righteous anger – a description that fairly fits the United States' Tokyo bombing raids. Each intends, wholeheartedly, to do his part of together laying waste to the city. In this guise, the area bombing provides the most perspicuous example of complicitous accountability, for each agent intentionally does his or her part of realizing a collective goal, raising the firestorm. Each flyer is wholeheartedly committed to the shared goal, understands that goal in detail, and endorses the role each other participant will play. Since all want the end of raising the firestorm achieved, and this end depends upon most successfully doing their parts, each flyer at least hopes others will do their proper parts. What the bombers do together is the object of the will of any given bomber, and so what the bombers do together is a potential object of inclusive individual accountability. The Individual Difference and Control Principles are inapplicable, since the basis of accountability is the content of an individual's will and not the particular causal contribution. Although, in fact, no individual bomber made a difference to the death and suffering that all produced, nor could any control the outcome, the will of each was manifested in the acts of all. And so a victim may rightly focus on the effects of the joint act while blaming an individual.

We now have the proper materials for conducting the Kantian tests of impermissibility. Rather than simply universalizing an individual intention to contribute marginally to a bombing raid, we should universalize an intention to do one's part, albeit marginal, in a collective act of bombing. In the former case, only individual marginal participation is universalized. In the latter case, both individual participation and the collective act must be universalized: our bombing by way (in part) of my participation. Only this question accurately reflects the structure of the moral agent's intentions. As I noted earlier, even vengeful individual firebombing may escape the CC net, because it does not exploit a convention for its success. But at least with the CW test, we now have an intelligible way of linking the agent's will to the unwillable world. An agent who wills participation wills the collective act as well.[63] Since we know a world in which firebombing occurs is a world in which agency cannot be universally exercised, we now can see how each bomber's will contradicts itself. The bomber wills a world in which rational agency is condemned to be ineffectual. The world of universalized firebombing is now treated as the object of the individual agent's will.

Accountability for unintended consequences can also be made sense of in terms of participatory intentions. In the individual case, consequences are ascribed to me when they are causal products of my intentional actions, like the wasp that entered when I let out the cat. Now, I argued in Chapter 2 that, because the universe of consequences flowing from our actions is potentially infinite, our accountability for subsequent events is normatively delimited. Considerations rooted in the primitive phenomenology of action, as well as various moral and social conventions, determine the boundaries of consequential accountability – of what are considered, in lawyers' jargon, the "proximate consequences" of our actions. Though the field of response-worthy events varies with the particular ethical culture, in every culture some unintended consequences warrant some response. By taking responsibility for the consequences of our acts, we demonstrate to others a concern for their projects and interests, and thereby work to ensure their respect for our own. Within this delimited set of consequences, normative questions of individual response arise: whether to apologize, compensate, or repair. The wasp I let in stings you badly, and so I have a special obligation to give you comfort, as well as reason to express my sadness at your pain. Fault is not essential to the response. There may be no reason for you to feel resentment or for me to feel guilt. My response is rooted in the more primitive basis of causality, in the simple fact that my agency has led to your suffering. My response to your suffering, or the claims upon me to respond, is an indication of the importance I attach or ought to attach to your interests within our community.

So accountability for unintended consequences manifests an acknowledgment of the fact that one's projects have interfered with another's interests. This relation is present at the collective level as well. The collective actions that may be ascribed to us as a group, and inclusively to us as members, have unintended consequences. These consequences too can be ascribed to us as a group, or as individuals qua group members. Suppose while picnicking we inadvertently set our blanket down on a flower bed. Though we did not share the goal of ruining the flower bed, ruining it is a direct consequence of what we did intentionally, namely choosing a nice spot for a picnic. We are, therefore, accountable for the damage to the gardener, at least in the form of apology, and perhaps compensation or help in its restoration. This is a duty owed not just by us as a group, but by us as individuals. Ruining the bed was a consequence of the project each of us engaged in, and so acknowledgment of the costs of that project flows directly to each. Each of us is complicit in the ruined bed just because of our intentional mutual engagement. That is enough to render us authors of and accountable for the consequences of what we do together.

Consequential complicity, as we can call it, forms a central part of our ethical experience. Whether or not we act on the moral reasons that obtain in virtue of our participation, and however others respond to our complicity, the (by us) unforeseen and unfortunate actions of our groups give us pause. Alexander McKee was a young Canadian infantryman in World War II, with no direct part in the Dresden bombings. He went to war in a just cause, joining his will with others. At war's end, having learned about the firebombing, he wrote:

[T]here was no sense of exultation or victory (except perhaps among those who had been far from the fighting). Confronted by the reality one felt soiled by the evil which had been done; distinctions between opposing forms of atrocity seemed meaningless, when in effect one had been an unwilling part of it. That is what I felt, anyway.[64]

And so he wrote a book about the bombing, collecting the accounts of others. We can surely disagree with his assessment of the comparative evils involved – as he might do today – while recognizing the importance of participation.

## 4.7 CONCLUSION

I have attempted in this chapter to vindicate the Complicity Principle, grounding it in an interpretation of individuals' actual ethical experience and in the more abstract claims of action theory. Both the individualistic strand of commonsense morality and standard moral theories obscure the deep role played in ethical life by the principle that collective responsibility entails individual accountability.[65] I have also, therefore, attempted to show how consequentialist and Kantian theories can reconcile themselves to this central ethical datum, by expanding the scope of possible objects of accountability to include what we together do while maintaining the individualistic basis of evaluation.

In defending my claim that participation entails implication, I have relied upon the broad but thin analysis of collective action that I provided in Chapter 3, according to which collective actors are merely agents with overlapping participatory intentions. Bombers, planners, infantrymen, harmless torturers, picnickers: Each engages in collective action because each intends to his or her part in together destroying cities, winning wars, inflicting suffering, passing the afternoon. Each is an inclusive author of the group's deeds. The theory of accountability I have so far offered is correspondingly broad and thin, assigning to each inclusive author an unmeasured basis of accountability. I have shown, I believe, why it is true that we are accountable individually for what we do together. But I have not yet shown how it is true: how norms of response distribute accountability among different participants and respondents, reflecting the variety of circumstances and perspectives on which claims of repair and reproach are grounded. That is the task for the next chapter.

# Chapter 5

# Complicitous Accountability

## 5.1 INTRODUCTION

In the last chapter, I described all of the participants in the Dresden bombing as implicated in the firestorm's rage. Because the collective act of firebombing is ascribable to each individual bomber, the collective act is an object of individual accountability. A participatory intention thus satisfies what we might call the "threshold condition" of accountability: an agent who participates intentionally in a wrong is accountable in some form for that wrong. Moral philosophers have often been content to rest at this threshold condition. But the chief argument of Chapter 2 was that it is a mistake to ignore the particularities of the responses of accountability, their dependence upon the specific relations and positions of agents, victims, and onlookers. How, for example, do we assess the accountability of agents who participate in wrongs, but who do not know which others are also participating? I now want to amplify my claim that individual participation in collective action means individual responsibility for collective harm. I want to show how it can be squared with the variety of circumstances in which we find ourselves as participants in the collective structures of everyday life. In particular, I will explore the positionality of accountability in collective wrongdoing by probing the moral difference between direct action and complicit participation, that is between exclusive and inclusive accountability. I also take up the problem of complicitous accountability in cases of ignorant or psychologically compartmentalized participation, when agents fail or refuse to see the systemic contribution of their actions to collective harms.

## 5.2 WHETHER COMPLICIT ACTORS ARE LESS CULPABLE THAN DIRECT ACTORS

The first question to be considered is whether and how participatory, inclusive accountability differs from direct, exclusive accountability. Inclusive accountability is predicated primarily upon a teleological relation between the subject's will and the harm or wrong, exclusive accountability upon a teleological and a causal relation. Does the existence of a direct causal linkage have ethical significance? To simplify matters, compare the accountability of a group of eager Dresden bombers, who collectively and wholeheartedly inflict suffering upon the residents of the city, with the accountability of a single pilot with a nuclear bomb, whose act brings about the same number of deaths. Does the inclusive authorship of the incendiary bombers warrant a mitigated response?

Many would answer yes, regarding mere participants as less culpable than solo practitioners, and implicitly judging it permissible to participate in a wrongful act even when they would not perform the same act alone. It is, however, surprisingly difficult to justify these claims. Both the incendiary bombers and the nuclear bomber have the same ultimate goal, namely the victims' deaths. Since the victims are dead in both cases, the difference cannot lie in some quality intrinsic to the wrong done them. The world that both incendiary and nuclear bombers intentionally promote is in this sense morally identical. One might even argue that the incendiary bombers contribute to a morally worse situation, since it contains more perpetrators of harm.

The most obvious ground for distinguishing between participatory and direct accountability lies in the Individual Difference Principle. I have said the Individual Difference Principle plays an important role in commonsense moral thought. It is a source of the intuition that participatory wrongdoing is, while not faultless, still better than direct wrongdoing. But if we attempt to make room for the principle, we will quickly fall into contradiction, since the basis for complicitous accountability is inconsistent with the Individual Difference principle. If accountability is relative to causal contribution, then the Dresden bombers ought not be accountable at all. Once the Complicity Principle has been invoked to satisfy the threshold condition of accountability, it cannot simply be disregarded in judgments of the form or degree of accountability. If the Individual Difference principle is to do any work here, it must first be shown to be consistent with the Complicity Principle.

A second strategy for illuminating the moral difference between inclusive and exclusive accountability is also ultimately unhelpful. We could resort to the distinction between judgments of character and judgments of actions. While the acts of incendiary bombers may be no better than those of individual bombers, their characters may be morally better, perhaps because they are less vicious or more squeamish.[1] Because their characters are better, they may warrant less severe condemnation for what they do. But it is not obvious our responses would change even if we held questions of character constant – if, for example, each Dresden bomber would be equally willing to drop the nuclear bomb. Participation still seems less culpable than direct commission, in virtue of the relation between agent and event and regardless of the agent's character.

We will never find a single argument for distinguishing between participatory and direct wrongdoing, for the simple reason that there is no single framework for assessing accountability. And so a more supple argumentative tack is called for. My argument now proceeds interpretively, by eliciting intuitions and judgments that I take to reflect what variously positioned respondents really would think in specific situations. As I noted in Chapter 1, this approach may seem to confuse the normative with the descriptive. But we do have means for evaluating particular responses. I suggested in Chapter 2 that the general test for the warrant of a particular response is whether the respondent would endorse that response under full ethical reflection – that is, reflecting on the intelligibility of the response given the relationship-fostering goals of the accountability system. In cases of collective action, we can try to engage each responsive position to see whether it would hold up under ethical reflection. The test has two questions. First is the question of whether the response accurately captures the ostensibly complicitous agent's role in the collective act, for example, whether the agent must be seen as having intended to participate in something that did harm. Second is the question of whether the response coheres with other responsive

positions. If I am disposed to care whether my response is warranted, then I must care that other interested parties can see its
ground and its point, whether or not they fully endorse it. Otherwise,
it becomes hard for even me to see it as appropriate. In other words,
the warrant of a given response to complicity depends both on its
grounding in the logic of inclusive attribution, and in its coherence
with the responses of other interested parties.

Begin with the point of view of the victim: The content of the
bombers' intentions, to promote my death, stands out as the object of
my response. The causal distinctions highlighted by the Individual
Difference Principle are irrelevant, because my interests and person-
hood are under attack, equally and by all participants, and whether
they act individually or in concert. For incendiary and nuclear
bombers alike, their intentional promotion of my suffering defines
our relationship; it manifests the hostile or contemptuous view they
take of me and my interests. My response to any given agent reflects
this general hostility, amplified by the degree of my suffering. If my
response is one of resentment, or of a demand for respect, then
differences in the particular causal relationship between me and any
given bomber are insignificant, compared with the salience of the
attitude manifested towards myself by all participants. Or, like an
actual survivor of the Hamburg firestorm, I may look to the firestorm
as retribution for the sins of my nation, feeling a kind of "wild joy" at
the raids.[2] This view treats the attackers as a unified force, not
distinguishing among them.

Contrast this with the view naturally taken by the agents themselves. Now one's conception of the link to the victim takes on a
different character. The deeply personal nature of the relationship
emphasized by the victim is shifted, and instead the actual causal
pathways between our actions and the victim's suffering become
salient. The Individual Difference Principle has greatest force within
this perspective, emphasizing the difference between causal and logical links to the harm.[3] As a nuclear bomber (or a commander ordering the bombing), I know I alone will cause this suffering. This
knowledge may be either a hurdle to overcome, or an enticement. In
either case, my causal power is a central element of my conception of
my action. As an incendiary bomber, I can reflect that my actions do

not in fact add appreciably to my victims' suffering, and so whatever significance my participation has for me, it is not an expression of my power over the victims. My feelings of accountability are not wholly undercut, since I am still intentionally invested in the consequences of bombing. But I can honestly regard the world as unmarked by my participation, and so can see my wrongful act as metaphysically shallow, demanding no great efforts at repair.

There is another powerful reason why, from the perspective of the agent, the distinction between direct and participatory wrongdoing seems to have great normative force. When we act together, it becomes easy to inhabit an essentially *bureaucratic* frame of mind, in which ultimate ends are less salient than the instrumental procedures used to effect those ends. In my construction of the example, the incendiary bombers are as set upon their objective as the lone nuclear bomber. But if we enter again into the perspective of the marginal, incendiary bombers, the fact of cooperation, of mediation by the agency of others, tends to displace the victim from the center of attention. The instrumental action of dropping my bombs simply as part of our collective raid looms instead as the proper object of moral evaluation – and this act is causally innocuous. Consider now the perspective of the nuclear bomber. It is now far harder to distinguish between my actions and their consequences. I cannot retreat from the immediacy of what I do, and so my response to my wrongdoing is invested with greater focus and significance. Of course, other forms of mediation between agent and effect can also play this psychological role, making it far easier for individuals knowingly to cause harm and do wrong. (Bombers undoubtedly would find it harder to kill in the same numbers were they asked to do so with small arms.) And collective actors can focus single mindedly upon the object of their collective effort, regardless of their particular roles. My point is not that this psychological distancing is peculiar to or inevitably accompanies collective activity, but only that collective activity often provides a framework hospitable to it.

Finally, as onlookers to the transaction between victims and bombers, we find material for our responses by trying to project ourselves into both perspectives, to identify the harm from the victim's point of view, and to discern the motives of the agents. Because of the disparities between the perspectives, any projective identification will be inherently unstable. It is generally easier to imagine oneself a part of a fleet of bombers, without a strong causal connection to a great harm, than to think of oneself as singlemindedly and individually destroying a city.[4] We project ourselves more easily into the perspective of a participant, for whom the fact of others' participation is a considerable inducement. As onlookers, our responses are, therefore, likely to be more lenient towards participants than towards direct actors, because we are inclined to be most lenient to ourselves, or the selves we can most imagine being.

On the other hand, we can imagine circumstances in which the indirect actors would seem to warrant more bitter responses than the direct agent. Consider Othello's murder of Desdemona. The scheming Iago has manipulated circumstance and passion in order to build up a volcanic jealousy in Othello and has guided him in every detail. "Do it not with poison; strangle her in her bed, even the bed she hath contaminated."[5] Othello's dual role as agent and instrument complicates our assessment of him, and of Iago. For Othello is clearly wronged, although he in turn wrongs Desdemona. Indeed he is wronged in part by having been led to wrong Desdemona. Iago brings about the killings by manipulating Othello; but it would be dramatically and linguistically too simple to say he causes Othello to kill Desdemona.[6] If Othello had been nothing but a dupe, or had killed in a mistaken impression of self-defense, we might simply say Iago has killed Desdemona.[7] To be sure, Iago plays Othello like a harp, but it is a harp already tautly in tune, a product of Othello's arrogance and sexual insecurity, character flaws for which Othello is partially accountable.[8] By the standards of both Shakespeare's imagined Venice and modernity, Othello's act was an excessively passionate response to adultery even if the accusations had been true.[9] And so Othello was doubly wrong, for believing too quickly in the ambiguous proofs he was offered, and in killing on their basis. We, along with Emilia, Iago's wife and Desdemona's servant, hold Othello guilty of the murder.

But our anger at Othello is mixed with sorrow and regret. He is Iago's victim as well as Desdemona's killer. Although Othello is exclusively accountable for the murder, Iago is the "hellish villain" of the tragedy. Iago conceives the killings purely out of resentment. For these reasons, the contempt (and eventual punishment) heaped justly upon Iago would be unjustly applied to Othello. Iago's is genuinely a case of inclusive accountability, since Iago's relation to Desdemona's death is not purely causal. Desdemona's death was something he promoted, indeed engineered, but it did not occur by his hand or by someone who could be reckoned fully his instrument. Our onlookers' sense of Iago's culpability reflects our awareness of the structure of the situation, as well as of his motives, but it is not reducible to any one of the elements of causality, character, and intention, nor is it a simple additive sum. Only by first noting the participatory nature of the killing, and then examining these further considerations, can we reflect adequately upon the particular response warranted by Iago's misconduct.

We are accustomed to assigning strong inclusive responsibility to those who make others instruments of their wills, as Iago made Othello. Indeed, Kant's only discussion of inclusive accountability centers upon the instrumental treatment of another. It culminates in the apparently outlandish claim that you may not lie to the murderer who comes to the door to demand the whereabouts of your friend. Kant, as I mentioned in Chapter 1, says that:

After you have honestly answered the murderer's question as to whether this intended victim is at home, it may be that he has slipped out so that he does not come in the way of the murderer, and thus that the murder may not be committed. But if you had lied and said he was not at home when he had really gone out without your knowing it, and if the murderer had then met him as he went away and murdered him, you might be justly accused as the cause of his death. For if you had told the truth as far as you knew it, perhaps the murderer might have been apprehended by the neighbors while he searched the house and thus the deed might have been prevented. Therefore, whoever tells a lie, however well intentioned he might be, must answer for the consequences, however unforeseeable they were, and pay the penalty for them even in a civil tribunal. This is because truthfulness is a duty which must be regarded as the ground of all duties based on contract, and the laws of these duties would be rendered uncertain and useless if even the least exception to them were admitted. To be truthful (honest) in all declarations, therefore, is a sacred and absolutely commanding decree of reason, limited by no expediency.[10]

Most readers today find his claim puzzling. Surely you would be complicit in the murderer's crime only if you told the murderer where your friend had gone. The mere contingency of the murderer encountering your friend in the street (or being apprehended by your neighbors) ought not – least of all on Kant's anticonsequentialist views – make a difference to your culpability.

As Christine Korsgaard persuasively argues, Kant is not, in fact, insisting upon an outrageously consequentialist allocation of accountability.[11] Rather, his claim is grounded in the fundamental duty to treat others, friends and murderers alike, with respect to their capacity for reason, which means telling the truth, so they may autonomously decide whether to act so as to promote your own projects. By lying to the murderer, you incorporate him into your project, rendering him a mere tool. Like Iago, you are accountable for what your instrument does, in the mode of accountability for consequences.

Nonetheless, Kant's view is puzzling. Most of us intuitively believe that your telling the murderer the truth would implicate you. By deliberately aiding the murderer in his quest you become not merely his tool but his collaborator: You are an intentional participant in his act. (This is surely the view your friend, his victim, would take.) Moreover, joining the murderer's project means violating the tacit terms of the projects you share with your friend, of specially promoting each other's ends, and in particular of keeping your friend hidden. Kant ignores these considerations because he does not take cooperation into account. He sees only two possible states of affairs: the good one, in which he imagines that all agents act autonomously, and the bad one, in which certain agents make others instruments of their own wills. But cooperation complicates the story both in cases when we treat others as rational agents and in cases when we treat them instrumentally. We are the instruments of one another's wills whenever we act cooperatively, in the sense that each of use pursues the goals of another. (This is what it is to share a goal.) This does not exonerate us of culpability for our own actions anymore than Othello can be exonerated of murdering Desdemona. Accountability is not an all-or-nothing matter, resting entirely with the misguided murderer or entirely with the manipulating liar, wholly on the shoulders of each incendiary bomber or wholly reserved to Bomber Command. Instead it is distributed in both degree and kind and, like any element of the real world, looks different from every angle.

## 5.2.1   Accountability for Unintended Consequences Converges for Direct and Indirect Agents

The difference between inclusive and exclusive authorship seems to matter less in the case of unintended consequences, which do not further the group project and so seem especially distant from the participating intentions of group members. Return to the picnic upon the ruined flower bed, and let us suppose it was you alone who set down the blanket, failing adequately to check on its placement. Depending on the care you ought to have taken, I may have a gripe against you, for implicating me in damage I would have avoided. Your feelings towards the gardener are likely to be framed by your consciousness of your fault; you might even make a gesture at exonerating me. The response I owe the gardener is more complicated. Assuming it was reasonable for me to trust your discretion, I am not at fault with regard to the gardener, but it seems I do nonetheless owe some form of response. I could not simply assume the stance of a disapproving outsider, standing with the gardener and chiding you for your carelessness. To take up a purely external stance would be to conceal the relation between my own will and this regrettable event. The relation is oblique, to be sure, but still carries normative weight. Because I have made our picnic mine by my intentional involvement, I have also made its consequences mine. My accountability is therefore intermediate, between what one owes for faultless harms (for I was not at fault), and what one owes for faulty harms (for you, and hence we, were). Your fault sticks to me though not with its full force.

How does this fact affect our relations with the angry gardener? Should he be discriminating in allocating responsibility, or can he hold us both to account for the damage? It may be inappropriate for him to fail to acknowledge the difference in our fault, but that does not seem to oblige him to exclude me entirely from either his anger or his demands of repair. His warrant for his claims upon me is the same as my own: I am a participant in the picnic. It is both a reasonable and a necessary expectation upon agents inhabiting a crowded social landscape that they be prepared to deal with the costs imposed upon others by their freely chosen projects. My relation to the gardener in this respect is identical to yours. It would be inappropriate for the gardener to single me out for blame, for I have not failed to treat him or his projects with due concern. But we clearly have done so, through your sloppy agency, and so some resentment towards us, and hence me, is warranted.

Now I have begged an important question here, which is when and why a collectively unintended act of one group member should be ascribed to the group and its other members. I said previously that actions falling outside the scope of any plausible refinement of our shared goal cannot be ascribed to the group. The same principle holds of unintended consequences: if they flow from behavior beyond the pale of any reasonable collective expectation, then the Complicity Principle does not apply. At the limits of unforeseeability, I genuinely do stand as an outsider to your acts and their consequences, whether or not intended, for they bear no intelligible relation to my will. My response would be that of a shocked onlooker. But ruined flowers are a foreseeable part of a project of picnicking, as a product of any group member's actions. Neither of us needed to expect that we would ruin flowers, but each ought *ex post* to acknowledge that that was a possible consequence of what we did together. And so it is reasonable to ascribe the mess to us, and to me inclusively.

### 5.2.2 *Psychological Compartmentalization and Inclusive Accountability*

Wholehearted and mutually aware cooperation, such as with the firebombers, makes for an easy defense of the Complicity Principle. Agents' participatory intentions transmit accountability from all to each. Even so, we had reason to recognize the positional differences in accountability warranted by direct versus inclusive authorship. These differences are magnified the further we move out from the paradigm of wholehearted participation. Frequently, our knowledge of what others do when we act together is hazy or distorted. Often we do not know the specific character of what we intentionally promote together, but only recognize it under a vague description. Vagueness about the collective end sustains a compartmentalized attitude towards one's own participation; agents regard only the immediate tasks before them. This compartmentalization generates the "just doing my job" explanations of one's role in a nasty business.

At the limit, we are faced with agents who know their actions contribute to harm, but who can truly say they do not intend that harm. Does the Complicity Principle hold in these murky domains?

Chapter 3 argued that collective action can be jointly intentional under some description though the cooperating agents have little awareness of the specific nature of the action, or the identities of their counterparts. Return to *Othello* and now consider the position of Emilia, who has acceded to Iago's request that she procure Desdemona's handkerchief – this will be the "ocular proof" of Desdemona's adultery. Emilia knows Iago's business is mischievous, though she does not plumb its depths: "My wayward husband hath a hundred times wooed me to steal it. . . .What he will do with it, Heaven knows, not I. I nothing, but to please his fantasy."[12] The handkerchief, and hence Emilia, is the instrument of the ensuing tragedy, clinching Othello's suspicion that he has been cuckolded.

Emilia recognizes her own culpability, and attempts what repair she can before dying of grief. She reveals Desdemona's innocence to Othello: "Let heaven, and men, and devils, let 'em all, all, all cry shame against me, yet I'll speak."[13] The theft, Emilia's exclusive act, made her an inclusive author of Iago's treachery. Emilia's response to Iago is complicated. Though she bears responsibility for what she has done as part of the scheme, she is also warranted in her anger at Iago. Hers is not the pure resentment of a victim, nor the dispassionate contempt of an outsider. It has, rather, a self-reflexive component: She holds Iago accountable for making her accountable for a harm. Emilia's complicity is itself an object of accountability, a basis of resentment, repair, and even revenge.

When we act together, we must expect that the group act may have aspects we do not know about but with which we will have to reckon. These are the moral "agency costs," in economists' jargon, of collective action: The possibility of expanding our powers (or rewards) through cooperation entails the risk that the resulting act will not align with our moral interests. We might compare Emilia's situation with that of a mid-level engineer for a large manufacturer, who has reason to believe but does not know that the control modules he is helping to design, which are used by the company in manufacturing consumer products, are also used in manufacturing land mines to be sold in the Third World.[14] The relation between the engineer and the harm is indirect, for he does not promote the mine sales intentionally if he does not know about them. However, there is still a significant basis for his accountability for the mine sales, grounded in his intentional participation in a collective project. Like Emilia, the engineer intentionally performs acts as a means to a collective end, and he intends that collective end under some descriptions, though not under others. Described as "doing his part of producing control modules," or even "doing his part of producing whatever the company sells," he both works toward and identifies with the collective end; described as "doing his part of selling land mines for Third World conflicts," he does not. The engineer need not know of or intend this sale, much less the inevitably resulting civilian casualties. But since he may be regarded as a collective actor just so long as he conceives his actions as a means, he is inclusively accountable for the consequences of the collective act to which he in fact contributes. Indeed, so long as the decision to work with the company is voluntary, and information about the company's activities is available, every employee bears an accountable relation to the victims of the land mines.[15]

Of course, to say that the engineer is accountable, in virtue of his intentional participation in the company's activities, does not specify how he is accountable. His complicity along the dimension of consequences will vary functionally, according to the scope of his contribution. The stronger the links between him and the collective act, the less it matters that he remained ignorant of its nature. At the limit, the ignorance of executive figures in a collective enterprise is often treated as irrelevant in both ethics and law. This is not only to eliminate a possible loophole of accountability, but also because the executives' participation in any collective act runs so deep that they are ineluctably accountable for it independently of their specific knowledge. Knowledge can implicate a participant, but ignorance can never fully exculpate.

The engineer's functional role is significant, not just in the thin, metaphysical sense of providing a necessary contribution to the collective end, but as involving considerable thought, reflection, and adjustment in its execution. The engineer's will pervades the collective act, for in order to explain the (collective) development and production of the mines, we must cite at many points his exercise of skill and judgment. Contrast the engineer with a shipping clerk, indiscriminately sending out blenders to Singapore and landmines to Cambodia; he may also play a necessary role in the collective act. The shipping clerk's participatory role indeed will ground some form of consequential accountability, but it would be mindless to treat him in the same way as someone whose contributions inhabit the collective act more deeply.

The general positionality of response manifests itself in functional assessments of his role, for the engineer may well think his role far grander than does any one else, not just because he knows best the sweat poured into his designs. This is not to assume that his subjective assessment of his role tracks its actual functional significance. He could be alienated from his work, in which case he may see his role as simply that of a cog, while his employers may accurately assess his contributions as far larger. But these two components, functional significance and perceived salience of contribution, combine to ground his own and others' actual ethical responses to his complicity, as well as supporting norms governing those responses. He may say to himself or others, "Look, I'm only making tiny improvements in little black boxes." He is then vulnerable to the response by someone else who cares – a partner, a victim, a campaigner against land mines – that 50 hours of his week are invested in making these tiny improvements, and in fact the black boxes he improves end up in the killing fields. Alternatively, once ethical reflection is sparked within him, his accountability may resonate in his own mind far more strongly than in the minds of others, who see him as merely a part of an ethically irresponsible system of international arms sales. The respondents' particular depth of focus, personal or political, will make different responses apt.

Either way, the engineer is not accountable in the same manner as, say, the vice president in charge of arms sales. The vice president's intention is straightforwardly to promote the sale of the mines. Though both the engineer and the vice president participate and so are complicit in the same act, their complicity is based in very different participatory intentions. The vice president has sought the sale, fully aware of what she has done. Our response to the vice president, therefore, reflects both the fact of her contribution to the harm, and the fact that she knowingly promoted it. The vice president's will is presumably fully engaged with the project of making and selling mines, while the engineer's bears only a contingent connection based in his participation in the company's projects, whatever those turn out to be.

We can characterize the difference between the vice president and the engineer using a spatial metaphor, treating agents who intend the collective end as at the core of the activity, and agents whose roles are merely participatory as at the periphery. Relative distance from core to periphery might then be measured through functional assessments, so the shipping clerk would be said to be more peripheral than the engineer. This spatial metaphor maps the relative difference in our responses to conduct and character. For in the typical case, what distinguishes the engineer from the vice president also distinguishes them both from the shipping clerk, namely the attitudes they take towards the success of the activity. As victims and outsiders we concentrate our responses upon those who seek out the harm, rather than upon those for whom the harm's creation is merely incidental to their focal activity. It is, of course, possible the vice president's intentions relate only obliquely to the project of selling mines. Perhaps she, like the engineer, simply sees herself as in sales, whether the product be land mines or lawn sprinklers.[16] But in carrying out her duty, she must focus on the project of encouraging consumption of the mines, perhaps by stressing their destructiveness or their reliability. As a consequence of her participatory intention, she must identify with their sale and use, and so must associate herself directly with their morally relevant characteristics in the course of doing her job. The engineer, meanwhile, does not care whether the mines are left unsold, but he does care whether the modules he designs perform their functions. This is a precondition of his engaging in the activity at all, unless he is a deliberate saboteur. And finally, the shipping clerk need not care whether the objects he sends work at all; none of their moral characteristics impinge upon his tasks.

The difference in response to core and peripheral agents is often explained in terms of the familiar deontological distinction between the permissibility of intending to produce harm, and foreseeably producing harm as a consequence of one's intended pursuits: the vice president intends the harm, while the shipping clerk foresees the harm as a consequence of his doing his part of the collective act. In Thomas Nagel's terms, we have strict agent-relative reasons not to do harm, while we have only weaker agent-neutral reasons to prevent harm from being brought about by others.[17] By willfully promoting arms sales, the vice president has directly affronted the values that generate the agent-relative reasons that apply to her action; the shipping clerk has only affronted the agent-neutral reasons that support minimizing harm. But I think the difference in response to them is better explained through the distinction between an executive intention, which the vice president has with respect to the company's sale of the mines, and a subsidiary intention, which the engineer and shipping clerk have, to do their respective jobs.

There is a basis for regarding the engineer as accountable, and to a far lesser degree also the shipping clerk. If making land mines is an act within the possible scope of the company's general activities, then they might well be thought guilty of a moral indifference with respect to the mines, and a lack of interest in the consequences of their work. What grounds this judgment is not an estimate of the relative value they place on human suffering, for they may well have all the right nominal sentiments and commitments. Their problem is that they have failed to integrate their values into their everyday lives. The judgment about their character and conduct is grounded in a critical conception of the attitude they ought to take towards their work and life, one which accomplishes the integration of their values with their actions. Our assessment of the functional significance of their participation underwrites criteria of subjective assessment. Given what they do, they ought to think more deeply about the uses of their labor, and are criticizable when they do not. Since the degree of their functional contribution varies, so too does the stringency of this assessment. The engineer is vulnerable in a way the shipping clerk is not. But while it might be unreasonable to expect the shipping clerk to quit his job, he would still rightly be thought callous if the thought of shipping out land mines gave him no pause or regret.

This conclusion of broad complicity in a large enterprise's activities may seem too quick. It is one thing to hold individual members of a tightly knit cooperative group accountable for what the group does, for the actions of each represent the shared will of all. But many employees take jobs with little choice, and exercise little autonomy within their roles. Arguably, it is not so much their wills as the force of their circumstances that is expressed. We may discount the normative significance of choices made amid few material opportunities.

There is also another subtle way in which many employees' wills might not be thought reflected in the collective activities of their employers. Employee roles are usually well defined, and there is little encouragement for lower-level employees to take a broad view of the company's activities. I have described the shipping clerk as intentionally promoting the company's activities, even though he has no concern for the use to which those services will be put. But he might well reply, "I am just doing my job. I do not intend to promote anything but my paycheck." The case of small shareholders is similar. A shareholder might plausibly claim no interest in whether the company makes land mines or baby food, but only in the dividend on the stock or the likelihood of a rise in its price. Collective action requires shared goals, and it is only within the scope of the shared goal that accountability for the actions of others makes sense. Very peripheral employees and small shareholders seem to share no goals.

This objection has two aspects, each of which might defeat the attribution of the collective act to the individual. The first aspect concerns whether the employee or shareholder intentionally participates in anything at all – that is, whether the agent conceives of his or her action as part of a collective action of any sort. The second aspect concerns the scope of the collective end embedded in the agent's participatory intention, assuming we can attribute to the agent a participatory intention. Employees might decide they are not taking part in the activities of the whole enterprise; they view themselves as merely participating in the activities of their own scrupulously moral subdivision. In either case, the agent does not act upon a participatory intention whose scope includes the wrongful acts, either as intended objects or unintended consequences. If so, there might seem to be no basis for accountability for these wrongful acts.

This objection from total compartmentalization has initial plausibility. It is certainly true that one may promote a collective act without participating in it. One may provide aid to another or others unintentionally, or one may knowingly aid others while maintaining absolute disinterest in the success of their venture. A gas pump operator who knowingly fills up the tank of a getaway car may well hope for the capture of the thieves. Though the operator has aided the thieves intentionally, there is little reason to consider the operator as one of them without more information about the operator's intentions.[18] Such agents are not participants, because they do not provide such aid as part of any collective effort, although in fact their aid does further the effort.

It is doubtful, however, that this description really does suit any employees, frequent suppliers of goods, or long-term shareholders. For a continuous and dynamic relation with the group tends to bring with it a conception of oneself as a participant in some form. I am not suggesting that regular association will necessarily bring such agents into sympathy with a collective's acts and goals. Indeed, constant association may make the collective's acts seem more reprehensible, and so lead one to deny all the more strenuously any accountable relation to them. But these familiar psychological facts do not defeat the attribution of a participatory intention. Indeed, they sustain the attribution, for they are motivated by agents' conceptions of themselves as participants.

I suggest that those who contribute to collective acts on an ongoing basis will fall into the category of intentional participants so long as they see themselves as part of a collective act, and whether or not they favor the collective goal. If so, they are subject to the inclusive ascription of collective acts. Employees who say, "I'm just doing my job," are still acting on the basis of a participatory conception of their agency. To do one's job is to be responsive to norms and directives internal to an organization; it is to accept the relevance of collective, institutional norms to one's actions. The shipping clerk may well be indifferent to the success of the company's arms business, may even hope for a disastrous loss. But the shipping clerk intentionally plays his proper role in the company, adhering to procedures and meeting internal schedules. Any employee may disavow responsibility for the company's actions. But such disavowals are betrayed by the employee's own, functionally characterizable, conception of his or her agency. More generally, individual claims of detachment must always be weighed against the patterns of action in which those individuals engage. Insofar as the employees' actions are modulated to the demands of a collective end, he or she is an intentional participant in that end, accountable for it.

A more realistic psychology of participation can also provide an answer to the second aspect of the objection, that agents can restrict their view of those with whom they see themselves acting. Consider an academic research scientist with pacifist inclinations, call her Miriam, who accepts work in a Defense-funded university lab on an electronic communications project, technology not intrinsically destructive but which is likely to find a home in weapons systems. Miriam might be tempted to regard her own lab's work as benign, and distinguish sharply between the lab's work and the broader aims of the military. From Miriam's point of view, although her lab is funded by the Defense Department, she collaborates only with the other researchers in her lab. She regards only their work as what "we have done." She might thus try to disclaim accountability for the ultimate purposes to which her work will be put: "That is what they will make of our work, and I wish they wouldn't."

Given the close relation between participation and agents' conceptions of their activities, Miriam's disclaimer has prima facie plausibility, if she genuinely does think of herself as participating only in the lab's work. But others are less likely to be convinced by its force – notably, the funding officials within the Defense Department, who regard her as working on an essentially military project, and critics of the academic-military alliance, who also note the role Miriam's work plays within national defense policy. These superior officers and critics alike might take Miriam's disclaimer to be a form of bad faith, a failure to recognize the actual subsumption of her work within the larger policy network. For Miriam's disclaimer is vulnerable on three separate grounds, each giving reason to regard her as a participant in the collective defense project. First, and most importantly, the fact that, in functional terms, Miriam's actions are intentional contributions to defense policy dominates any objective assessment of her accountability. Second, her compartmentalized view of her role is not plausibly sustainable psychologically, given what in fact she does – that is, its functional characterization. And third, the best psychological explanation of her disclaimer arises from her prior acceptance of her implication.

The functionalist point is obvious: Whatever Miriam's preferred view of her role, her work is oriented around the ends of the defense establishment. If we ask why she performs the work she does, we must advert to the problems she has been posed, and these are military problems, even if they at the same time have theoretical or civilian counterparts. Her motives for working in the lab may not be those of her underwriters, but the ends she directly pursues and the norms that constrain her pursuit – secrecy, for example – are only intelligible in terms of her funders' interests. Her work is counterfactually sensitive to the promotion of their goals and the observance of their constraints. So the intention we must attribute to her, in order to render her activities functionally intelligible, takes as its object the defense goals of her funders.

This characterization of Miriam's intention, as a contribution to defense activities, must dominate not only the assessments of third-party observers, but also Miriam's own first-personal assessment. This is the reason we regard her disavowal as bad faith. For it simply follows from Miriam's knowledge of the overlap between her own conception of her role and that of her underwriters, that Miriam must see herself as intentionally contributing to their ends. Even if she regards herself as an opportunist merely exploiting the largesse of the defense establishment, she cannot but see the connections between her own work and its eventual military uses.[19] Her preferred narrow conception of her role is therefore constantly undermined by her awareness of the broader role she plays. And given her knowledge of the overlap between these narrow and broad conceptions of her role, the only plausible psychological explanation of her preference for the narrow conception is her sense that she is a participant in the defense work. This is not, of course, to say that any attempted exculpation is itself inculpating. In this context, however, given that Miriam is intentionally responsive to the defense goals, her segregated view of her role has to be seen as a form of recognition of her implication in the collective project she disavows.

## 5.3 CONCLUSION

I have attempted in this and the previous chapter to offer a philosophical vindication of the Complicity Principle, the claim that intentional participation in a collective venture is a basis for accountability for the harms and wrongs that result from this venture. The Complicity Principle conflicts with well-rooted convictions about the necessity of a link between individual accountability and individual causal contribution. Its ground, however, lies not in a consequentialist conception of accountability, but in a conception that relates agents to wrongs and harms in virtue of the content of their wills. Given a proper analytical understanding of collective intentional action and of the nature of intentional participation in a shared project, the Complicity Principle stands secure. When we act together, we are each accountable for what all do.

I have stressed, however, that while the Complicity Principle answers the threshold question of individual moral accountability in a broad array of shared activities, it must be supplemented by a positional theory of complicitous accountability. Therefore, I have also attempted to provide the grounds for the distinctions we make between exclusive and inclusive accountability. These distinctions are especially important when some participants are unaware of the specific nature of the wrong or harm, or when some would prefer that aspects of the shared project go unrealized. I have argued that agents are accountable even in these circumstances, but that the responses due them must reflect the nature of their conceptions of their role and identity within the shared project.

My discussion has been both descriptive and normative: descriptive insofar as it tries to map the obscure territory of our actual responses to complicity, and normative insofar as it suggests considerations that reasonably apply to these problems. In the end, this is the most that philosophical discussion about ethics can do – to suggest further and more fruitful ways to reflect upon the difficult questions that present themselves to everyday life. The next chapter will continue this project by investigating the question of accountability for the acts and consequences of others in the absence of intentional participation.

# Chapter 6

# Problematic Accountability: Facilitation, Unstructured Collective Harm, and Organizational Dysfunction

## 6.1 INTRODUCTION

The last two chapters examined the moral accountability of individuals for the actions and consequences of the collective acts in which they participate. Because participatory accountability is based primarily on individual intentions rather than causal contributions, the individuals I considered, such as the Dresden bombers, were accountable even when their actions made no difference to the resulting harm. Interpreting complicity in terms of participation makes sense of a great variety of contexts, whenever individuals are linked together in a common pursuit, from conspiracy to contract to employment. This understanding of complicity makes considerable headway on the practical problem I posed in Chapter 1: the problem of how to provide individuals with reasons to avoid and repair the collective harms that mar our social landscape. Many of these harms arise from the concerted acts of governments, companies, and cartels. Individual participants in these organizations are accountable for the collective harms that arise, and so have individual moral reason to atone for the past and try better for the future.

At the same time, many of the most serious collective harms are not obviously the products of concerted action. They are, rather, the results of a confluence of individual behavior. Environmental damages that result from an aggregate of marginal individual contributions are the chief example of this genre, which I will call *unstructured collective harms*. As with the Dresden bombers, no individual polluter's contribution makes a significant causal difference. However, unlike the Dresden bombers, individual polluters are not intentional participants in a collective act of pollution. So the usual basis for applying the Complicity Principle does not obtain.

The indifferent provision of aid to wrongdoers presents similar problems for vindicating the Complicity Principle. Intuitively, a merchant who knowingly provides tools for a criminal act, despite a lack of interest in the success of the venture, would seem to be morally complicit in some way for the resulting crime. Yet often the tools are widely available elsewhere, and so the merchant's sale makes no significant difference to the commission of a crime. Here the over-determination of the harm is a product of alternative rather than marginal individual contributors; in both cases, however, there is no significant individual difference. To be sure, the merchant intentionally participates in the transfer of the tools, but not in the criminal use to which they are put, and so there is no apparent participatory basis for regarding the merchant as inclusively accountable.

Can individuals warrantably regard themselves (and be regarded) as accountable for these collective harms, despite the absence of participatory intentions and causal differences? The theoretical challenge is to provide a rational justification for feelings of reproach and responsibility. The practical challenge is to ensure that the theoretical solution is psychologically realizable. Section 6.2 attempts to meet these challenges in cases of both marginal contributions to unstructured harms and facilitation of harmful enterprises. I argue that two distinct bases of individual accountability exist. The first basis is an expanded notion of individual participation, to include participation in a culture or way of life. I suggest that unstructured harms typically arise in contexts in which deeper, systemic, forms of collective action lie. Responses of accountability can be grounded in these systemic forms of collective action. The second basis of individual accountability relies upon the discussion in Chapter 2 of accountability for character. Symbolic considerations of character can support the claim that one ought to refrain from participating in even overdetermined wrongs, and can offer individuals reason to do their part in cooperative solutions to these wrongs. When coupled, these two bases of individual accountability avoid the problems inherent in purely instrumental conceptions of accountability.

Section 6.3 addresses a closely related topic: the intelligibility of

167

purely collective, or holistic, accountability. The problems of accountability posed by unstructured harms are often usefully viewed through a collective, rather than individual lens. When intentional and causal relations between individuals and the collective harm are attenuated, can victims and onlookers warrantably reproach and demand response from the harming group itself, as distinct from its constituent members? I argue that holistic responses of accountability are intelligible, given a theory of collective action and an instrumental conception of accountability. However, holistic responses are only effective when they mesh logically and psychologically with responses to and from the individual constituent members. The group itself may be the primary, but not the ultimate, object of response. The section concludes by examining the relations between individual, inclusive accountability and holistic, exclusive accountability. I defend the filtering of reparative duties to individuals.

## 6.2 COMPLICITY WITHOUT PARTICIPATION

### 6.2.1 *Facilitation and the Marketplace*

In the last chapter, I mentioned the case of agents who knowingly aid collective enterprises but who do not seem to meet the minimal criteria of intentional participation. Such cases are both ethically and legally important and complex. A central feature of modernity is the amoral cash nexus provided by the marketplace: individuals buy, sell, and trade, all seeking to promote their own ends, mostly unconcerned about the ends of their trading partners. This system makes possible and stabilizes the pursuit of individual conceptions of the good despite widespread moral disagreement.[1]

So it is desirable that agents who offer goods and services on the marketplace not police each other's motives too scrupulously. Nonetheless, moral questions necessarily intrude when it becomes clear that the goods or services one provides will be used in an uncontroversially wrongful pursuit. Imagine a gun seller who sells a shotgun to someone who has indicated he will use it in a robbery. The seller has no interest in the success of the robbery; indeed, he may well hope the robber is caught. The shotgun is then used in a robbery, and a guard is killed as a result. Is there a sense in which the seller is morally complicit in the event, inclusively accountable for the crime and the death?

There is reason to think he is not complicit, at least not on grounds of inclusive authorship. Unlike employees whose actions are dynamically related to the goals of the enterprise, or long-term shareholders whose retention of an ownership stake links them to their corporations, the gun seller's participation consists only in the single transaction. The seller is an intentional participant in the purchase/sale of the shotgun, for that act does involve his doing his part of the collective act of commerce. But, by hypothesis, there is no plausible description of his attitude towards the crime that would include it as a goal shared between him and the purchaser. Though he aids the robbery, it is not an act of his, considering him as a member of the group. By contrast, a friend of the robber who went to purchase the shotgun for the robbery would intentionally participate in the crime, and so would be accountable for it. In the absence of a participatory intention, there is no basis for consequential or conduct-based accountability. There is no outcome that can be identified with the agent's will.

Yet there seems to be something to the idea that the gun seller is morally complicit in the crime – indeed, intuitions are strong when injuries or death result. In some cases, there is a causal, Individual Difference basis of accountability for the crime, when the seller's act made a difference to the commission of the crime. Let us assume the sale of the gun was counterfactually necessary to the crime: If the sale hadn't occurred, no crime would have taken place. The sale of the gun was, then, a causal factor in the crime, one that might be used in an explanation of how the event came about. If the crime was a foreseen consequence of the seller's act, then it might make sense to treat it as an unwanted but intentionally promoted event.

In applying a consequential basis of accountability, we must note a serious difficulty in drawing a causal connection between the seller and the crime, since any causal relation is mediated by the criminal's autonomous act. We might be inclined to say that the seller's act was a causal factor in the robbery (and death). But does it make sense to say that the merchant caused the criminal's act? Noninterpersonal causal chains typically allow for a kind of reverse transitivity: if person A causes event C by way of event B, then A causes B. For example, if I cause my wife to wake up by switching on the radio, then I also cause the radio to go on. But in the interpersonal context if I cause tenants to be unjustly evicted by asking my lawyer to evict them, I do not cause the lawyer to act.[2] In general, an agent A is only said to cause a second agent B's act when B's act is nonautonomous because of what A has done. When B acts voluntarily, uncoercedly, and with reasonably complete information, we are very reluctant to say that A has caused B's act. This breakdown of transitivity undermines the use of causal notions for ascribing accountability in interpersonal contexts.[3]

Philosophers have adopted various maneuvers for getting around the problems of describing interpersonal causal chains, but none is really satisfactory. H.L.A. Hart and Tony Honoré, for example, distinguish a special interpersonal sense of causality, used for cases where one person provides the occasion for another's act (e.g., by leaving a car running and unlocked, so that someone else can easily hop in), and for when someone provides reasons to another for acting (e.g., telling someone that he has just been betrayed and ought to vindicate his honor).[4] Hart and Honoré's special kind of causality may be tenable as an account of the incoherent "ordinary" language and practice of the courtroom, which tries to shoehorn relations of accountability into a causal slipper. But it provides little help for an attempt to make sense of interpersonal accountability in causal terms. J.L. Mackie, in contrast, says that any relations between events meeting the logical condition of counterfactual necessity thereby instantiate a single type of causal relation, but he says we often should not say that the relations are "causal" in interpersonal cases, lest doing so give rise to the mistaken implication of nonautonomous action.[5] David Lewis, like Mackie, says any relations meeting the counterfactual condition are causal, but suggests that causative verbs, such as "kill" or "hurt," may have further normative criteria of application.[6] So, for example, only those who cause death by means of a "stable and durable structure" can be said to kill; intervening, autonomous agents are rarely thought of in such mechanistic terms.[7] Lewis seems right that ethically loaded causatives have additional criteria of application, and so may not apply even if bare metaphysical causality would.[8] But even if we forgo causative terms in these contexts, we still have not determined the ethical significance of the relation that does exist.[9] For we do still want to say that knowing facilitation of another's autonomous act warrants some response, if not the response due on standard causal or intentional grounds.

These problems of interpersonal causation are compounded in the most common contexts in which the good or service is easily available elsewhere. A merchant declines the sale; the customer just goes on to the next shop. Even when there is a law (generally obeyed) that restricts sales knowingly facilitating criminal acts, not all merchants will or ought to have the requisite culpable knowledge.[10] We are back to the overdetermined universe of the Dresden bombers. And the lesson of the bombers was that overdetermination defeats consequential accountability, which is tightly wedded to the Individual Difference Principle.[11]

### 6.2.2   Environmental Harms and Coordination Problems

Before attempting to solve the case of the indifferent merchant, I want to shift attention to a related set of cases: environmental harms. Environmental damage is typically the result of the knowing but uncoordinated activity of disparate individuals, each of whose actions contributes only imperceptibly to the resulting harm. To take a typical example, it is now well accepted that chlorofluorocarbon (CFC)-based coolants, of which freon is the most common, contribute to the destruction of the ozone layer, and in particular to the widening of "holes," or thin patches, of the ozone layer. There also appears to be a significant link between skin cancer rates and residence under one of these ozone holes. Automobile air conditioners are a significant factor in the release of CFCs, and so are a prime contributor to the widening of the ozone holes. Fortunately, CFC-free coolants are available, but at a much higher cost and with substantially less cooling power.

Let us say, for the purposes of the example, that American drivers of CFC-cooled cars contribute 25% of the CFCs released into the atmosphere, and that the increased CFC emissions globally have been linked to 4,000 additional skin cancer cases in Northern Australia because of a hole in the ozone layer. And so, let us say 1,000 skin cancers can be causally attributed to American drivers. American drivers as a group make a difference for the worse, and could do better if more expensive, non-CFC-based refrigerants were widely used. At the same time, it is clear no individual driver makes a difference, for one car's contribution of freon is negligible. Furthermore, any individual switching unilaterally to CFC-free coolant would simply be wasting money. Only if most American drivers shifted to the more expensive coolant would there be a reduction of skin cancer rates. Applying the Difference and Control Principles, we find no individual accountability. No one makes a difference, nor could any one (nondictatorial) individual affect the outcome. We are all accountable for the 1,000 skin cancers, but none of us is individually. I am assuming in this example that American drivers do not intend to promote the widening of the ozone hole or the resulting skin cancers. Nor do they see themselves as engaged in any other well-defined joint project with other CFC-using drivers, of which the ozone damage is an unintended consequence. Unlike in the cases of the Dresden bombers and corporate employees of the last chapters, here the Complicity Principle also does not apply.

Not everyone accepts the essentially collective nature of the problem. Derek Parfit, for example, has claimed there are often individualistic grounds of consequential accountability even when the harm is dispersed over many victims.[12] Parfit argues that although an individual agent does not perceptibly harm any victim, the sum of imperceptible harms to all victims is morally significant. Were the effects of the agent's actions concentrated upon a single victim, that victim would suffer greatly. Thus, on Parfit's model of aggregated harm, an agent acting alone acts as badly as an agent acting with others.[13] But there are several problems with this model. First, in cases like the CFC example, it makes no sense to segregate, even conceptually, the harm done by a single agent from that done by the collective. Each individual contribution of CFC refrigerants only has causal and ethical significance given the contributions of many others.[14] Second, Parfit uses a highly controversial notion of aggregation. The unobjectionable sense of aggregation, at least in the context of consequentialism, involves the summing of significant harmful events suffered by many agents: It is worse for more rather than fewer agents to suffer harms of the same type, and worse if the harm each suffers is severe rather than mild.[15] Parfit, however, invokes a more contentious notion of aggregation, whereby imperceptible contributions to many individuals' suffering combine into a significant contribution of harm. So, if agent A creates an imperceptible harm to each of victims $V_1$–$V_n$, A is said to act very wrongly towards $V_1$–$V_n$ as a whole, even though A's action made no difference to any individual $V_i$.[16] But, in the absence of a superagent who can experience this aggregation of imperceptible harms, it is unclear why we should regard A's act as harmful.[17] Even if single agents could (counterfactually) make a difference by focusing their actions upon single victims, there is no reason why this should make a difference to ethical assessment of the actual case. In the absence of any victim to whom an individual driver's act makes an actual difference, there is simply no purchase for the Individual Difference Principle. And in the absence of any structure of participation, there is no purchase for the Complicity Principle either.

Therefore I will assume no individual action makes an ethically significant difference. The vocabulary of decision and game theory provides us with a useful way of considering the problem, as well as an explanation of why the world is rife with collective harms. Both the gun merchants and the CFC-users examples have the structure of what are called "Collective Action problems" (CA problems).[18] Let us say that individuals comply when they do their part of a cooperative solution to the problem, and that they defect when they do not cooperate.[19] Individuals face a CA problem when they most prefer not to comply when enough others comply, but prefer general compliance to general non-compliance. Note that this is not an especially self-interested attribution of preferences. We can imagine drivers who would strongly prefer for there to be no massive freon discharge or its incident harms. But so long as these drivers realize that their own use or nonuse of CFCs makes no difference, and that nonuse involves a cost, they will naturally most prefer both global compliance and their own defection. Figure 6.1 sets out the choice faced by each individual with these preferences.

I will use the CFC example. The algebraic expressions and numbers in the boxes represent the cardinal preferences of any individual choosing whether to continue using CFC-based coolants. The benefit (b) is a moral benefit, that there be no collective harm, to which I am assuming any individual assigns significant weight. I have arbitrarily assigned it a value of 3. The only other value here is the cost of moving to CFC-free technology, here –1. This cost is significant but

**If I believe others will**

|  | | comply | defect |
|---|---|---|---|
| **and I** | comply | $b - c_1$ <br> 2 | $-c_1$ <br> $-1$ |
| | defect | $b$ <br> 3 | 0 |

(My payoffs in box.)

**Variables and assumptions:**

Comply: use new CFC-free coolant
Defect: use old CFC coolant

VC: Expected value of compliance
VD: Expected value of defection
NV: Net expected value of compliance = VC − VD

p: my subjective probability of others' general compliance

b: my benefit from general compliance = 3

$c_1$: my compliance costs = 1

**Calculation of payoffs:**

$VC = p(b - c_1) + (1 - p)(-c_1)$
   $= pb - c_1$
$VC = pb + (1 - p) \cdot 0 = pb$
$NV = pb - c_1 - pb = -c_1$

$NV > 0$ when $c_1 < 0$

**Here, I never comply.**

Figure 6.1 Collective Action Problem

much less than the benefit of no ozone destruction. Thus, this chart represents the values of a morally interested individual, with a respectable amount of self-regarding concern. The equations below the box model the deliberations any individual with these preferences would make, assuming the individual chooses consistently with these preferences.[20] Rational individuals will choose as if they were maximizing the expected value of their choices. That is, they will choose the state of affairs that will produce the most good, discounted by the likelihood they attribute to that state of affairs. Here individuals would assign a probability (p) to the likelihood of global compliance. So, an individual choosing whether to comply will decide whether complying has greater expected value than defecting, given the likelihood of general compliance (or defection). If the net difference (NV) between these expected values (VC–VD) is positive, individuals will choose to comply; otherwise to defect.

Trouble arises because individuals with this preference schedule have reason to defect from any proposed cooperative scheme, since their own defection will leave them better off regardless of what others do.[21] Indeed, they need not assign probabilities to global compliance at all, since whatever others generally do, it will always pay not to comply, insofar as individuals will save the cost of the forgone compliance device. Assuming most individuals in the population have such a preference schedule, most will have reason not to use the more expensive CFC-free technology. The result is that there will never be global compliance, as long as individuals are at all sensitive to the cost of compliance. In game theory jargon, defection strongly dominates compliance in CA problems: individuals in CA problems always have reason not to comply (or to feign compliance), whatever others do. Otherwise put, universal defection is the unique equilibrium in this game, for no one facing the prospect of universal defection has reason to act otherwise. Given this preference schedule, not only will there be a collective harm, there will be no collective solution. Everyone will continue to use the cheaper technology.

### 6.2.3  *Facilitation and Marginal Harm: The Systemic View*

It may seem an odd juxtaposition to discuss the indifferent gun merchants with the CFC-using drivers. But the structure of overdetermination, coupled with the absence of participatory intentions, makes joint treatment appropriate. Both gun merchants, facing violence-prone customers, and drivers, facing the high cost of cleaner technology, realize alike that however they choose, and however they deplore the consequences of their collective pattern of behavior, their individual actions make no difference. The irony of the situation is that even the most ethically inclined of merchants and drivers can find little basis in ethical thought for not simply following the path of least resistance. I have just explored the difficulties consequentialists have in this domain, and, as in Chapter 3, Kantians fare little better. Let an individual's maxim be: I will sell guns or discharge freon for economic gain, but only as long as my individual action makes no difference. The universalized world is the world we live in now. And sadly, this world is fully conceivable. As with the Dresden bombers, universalization enhances rather than undermines the efficacy of the individual maxim. Nor does invoking claims of interpersonal fairness suffice for the moral argument.[22] In the first place, in the absence of a functioning cooperative scheme to control the harm, no individual defection is unfair to any other agent. Second, it is difficult to build content into the relevant notion of fairness. For if no one suffers additionally by an individual's defection, and no one would otherwise gain, how does the defector act unfairly?[23] Explaining fairness in terms of an *ex ante* reasonable agreement begs the question, because it must first be shown why it is reasonable to object in the circumstances to an individual's noncompliance.[24]

The difficulty in determining precisely what makes individual contributions of Uzis and freon morally problematic has led Joel Feinberg to the conclusion there is nothing wrong with overdetermined contributions – at least, in the absence of a legal scheme for resolving the collective problem.[25] But this answer is intuitively unsatisfying. We are – at least in our more reflective moments – often troubled by our participation in collective harms, in spite of our superfluous roles in producing them. This inchoate sense of unease can, I think, be seen as having two components: a sense that we, as individuals, do wrong in perpetuating the harm, and a sense of accountability towards those who suffer from it. It should not be surprising that we have difficulty articulating this unease, for the difficulty arises from the basic structure of the situation. Although there is pressure to regard ourselves as part of the collective that does harm, the ethical links between us as individuals and us as members of the collective dissolve under reflection. The result is what I called in Chapter 1 an "I-We" problem. There is no intelligible normative link between the accountability of any "I" and the causal responsibility of "we."

I have so far posed the problem in theoretical and individualistic terms. What is the ethical significance of the fact that an individual's act lies in the causal path of a harm, even though the act is neither necessary nor sufficient for the harm or wrong? An answer to this question ideally will provide agents with reasons to make repair to the victims of the collective harm, and to avoid such actions in the future. The theoretical question is closely linked to a practical question with a systemic rather than individualistic cast: How can we avoid these collective harms? What motivations will lead individuals generally to shun contributing to such collective harms?

Now, it is of course possible to answer the practical, systemic question in purely instrumental terms: Individuals should have whatever motivations are sufficient to avoid the collective harm. But answering the practical question purely instrumentally fails to respect the constraints we noted in the last chapter. Any such motivations must be psychologically feasible, which is to say they must be internalizable and stable under ethical reflection. For this reason, simple indoctrination in the personal benefits of CFC-free coolants will not work; agents' unsupported motivations will be quickly undermined by the realization that their actions make no significant difference. In other words, the theoretical, individualistic challenge places constraints upon practical, systemic solutions. Feasible motivations must be grounded in structures of moral reasoning, namely conceptions of wrongdoing and accountability.

Here enters a complication specific to CFC-like cases of marginal contribution. Not only must we provide individuals with reason to shun contributions to the harm, but we must provide them with reason to cooperate with a collective solution. Because defection strongly dominates compliance for individuals with CA preferences, there is no hope for a sustainable cooperative solution to the problem. Since no individual discharge of freon makes a difference either way, individuals would seem to have no more reason to comply with a cooperative scheme for reducing the harm than reason to shun contributions to the harm in the first place. By contrast, if gun merchants were generally to avoid sales to the disturbed, any individual defector would make a significant difference, by providing a gun to someone who would otherwise not have one. Assuming gun merchants would prefer not to have blood on their consciences, we can attribute to them a preference for universal compliance (i.e., including themselves) over general compliance and their own defection. Gun merchants are still, however, assumed to prefer universal defection over their own individual compliance and general defection, since compliance amid defection carries a cost and no corresponding benefit.

Figure 6.2 is the structure of the gun merchants' collective action problem. The new addition is represented by $c_3$, which I have called a "defection cost." It represents the unease felt by a gun seller who breaks rank to sell. Even though the seller still has the benefit of generally safer streets – a benefit secured by others' compliance – this benefit is sharply eroded by the moral pangs that follow a sale that does make a difference. Of course, this quantification of moral costs and benefits and its link to economic costs is utilitarian fantasy. But if it can be useful as a depiction of how rational and moral individuals assign different weights to different considerations, then the fantasy shouldn't make a difference.

The important point to note about the structure of the gun merchants' choices is that how they choose depends crucially upon both how likely they believe general compliance to be, and how they weight the costs of their defection. Unlike the collective action problem earlier, gun merchants who believe others will comply, or who assign very great disvalue to breaking ranks, do have reason to comply. As I have represented it, they will choose to comply in proportion to the probability they assign to others' compliance, and in inverse proportion to the degree to which they regret defection. Let us assume significant but not immoderate regrets about defection, here represented by 2; that is, more than they regret a missed sale and less than they value safer streets. Given these values, gun merchants will refuse to sell when they think it more likely than not that others will also comply. Conversely, gun merchants will sell whenever they

**If I believe others will**

|  | comply | defect |
|---|---|---|
| **and I** comply | $b - c_1$  2 | $-c_1$  $-1$ |
| defect | $b - c_2$  1 | 0 |

(My payoffs in box.)

**Variables and assumptions:**

Comply: refuse sale
Defect:  sell gun

VC:  Expected value of compliance
VD:  Expected value of defection
NV:  Net expected value of compliance = VC − VD

p:  my subjective probability of others' general compliance

b:  my benefit from general compliance = 3
$c_1$:  my compliance costs = 1
$c_2$:  my defection costs = 2

**Calculation of payoffs:**

$VC = pb - c_1$
$VD = p(b - c_2) + 1 - p) \cdot 0$
$\quad = pb - pc_2$
$NV = pc_2 - c_1$

$NV > 0$ when $p < \dfrac{c_1}{c_2}$

**Here, I comply when $p < \frac{1}{2}$.**

Figure 6.2 Assurance

expect general defection, for there is no point to forgoing a sale if general mayhem will result anyway. This interaction among gun sellers thus has two stable equilibria, universal compliance and universal defection. No individual can unilaterally improve his or her position by choosing differently amid general compliance or defection.

Although this structure tells us much about how individuals with these preferences will conditionally behave, it is not clear how they actually will choose, because there are two stable equilibria. If we assume that all individuals have and act upon these preferences, and that this is common knowledge among them, then we cannot assign a priori probabilities to general compliance. Rather, in deciding, each person must ask how the others will choose in this circumstance. But since each person's choice depends upon anticipating the acts of others, this chain of reasoning gives out in regress. In order to give individuals a basis for their choice, assurance about others' compliance must be imported from further assumptions. If assurance is provided – in other words, if individuals have reason to think others will generally comply (or defect) – then they will have reason themselves to comply (or defect). Amartya Sen calls such interactions "Assurance games."[26] In Assurance games, it can be difficult to initiate a general pattern of compliance, but once achieved, universal compliance will be stable (it is an equilibrium), since no one has an incentive to depart from compliance. If gun merchants can come to have reason to believe others will comply, then they will forgo arms sales to madmen. Even the CFC-polluting drivers might achieve compliance within such a structure, if individuals assign disvalue to free riding on others' compliance. As I argued earlier, the notion of fairness in overdetermination contexts is not well-enough defined to motivate individual compliance on its own, as a matter of ethical argument. But reputational concerns about being viewed as a free rider, or the undeniable instinct to join in collective behavior, may supply some basis for cooperation. The more likely they believe others will comply, the more likely they are to comply individually. And, conversely, the more likely they foresee general defection, the more likely they too will defect.

The Assurance game is important, because many actual social problems involve a significant number of individuals who prefer universal compliance, often out of a sense of fairness. (I will discuss possible theoretical bases for this preference in the following text.) Second, it can be shown that even when all individuals have CA preferences, the prospect that they will be in similar straits of harm-production indefinitely can make it rational for them to choose as if they had Assurance preferences in the one-shot situation.[27] The critical task is providing the desired assurance. A distribution of preferences not to defect amid general compliance makes possible universal compliance, but it is insufficient to guarantee that general compliance will result.

One traditional means of supplying the requisite assurance is political: a coordinating authority can be established in order to channel agents into collectively rational patterns of action.[28] In pure Assurance games, the authority need only signal the desired form of coordination and show evidence that others will be willing to comply; agents are then independently motivated to conform their behavior to that standard. More realistically, the state can simply change the payoffs individuals face, by attaching a significant penalty to individual defection, or subsidizing individual compliance. If the penalties (or subsidies) are substantial enough, individuals will choose without regard to their predictions of others' behavior, and so universal compliance can be expected. Individuals who had CA preferences may come to have Assurance preferences, and knowledge of the sanctions will move them to select the desired equilibrium.

Many collective action problems call for political solutions.[29] But in most cases, political solutions are necessarily supplementary. They cannot do all the motivational work themselves.[30] If the solution is punishing defection, enforcement costs would explode whenever many people are involved.[31] And subsidies are not only expensive on their own, but also raise the prospect of fraud, adding monitoring and enforcement costs. Furthermore, in many cases adverting to a political solution simply defers the problem, for we must then explain why individuals had reason to create and fund the political authority in the first place, given that it could only be realized under general compliance.[32] More generally, stable political solutions to collective action problems are successful when and only when they operate in conjunction with preferences. Individuals must be assumed to be disposed to act upon their directives, to have reason to comply. Political assurance and sanction are both effective at the margins; we seek here a motivational solution at the core of the problem.

One possibility is to seek to extend the Complicity Principle to cases of unstructured collective wrongdoing. If agents are individually morally accountable for the harms that result when no one cooperates, then each has reason to ensure that harms are mitigated or prevented. Figure 6.3 shows the structure of interactions among agents who take seriously their involvement in collective harms. This chart represents agents with CA preferences, but with the addition that they attach disvalue to having contributed to a collective harm. They do not, on the other hand, attach disvalue to free riding on others' general compliance, since there is in those cases no harm with which they would be associated. The result is what is sometimes called a "Chicken" interaction, named after the dangerous road-race game. Each individual would like the advantage of noncompliance, but each finds universal noncompliance worse than his or her own individual compliance amid general defection. Each would, in other words, prefer to bear a consequentially pointless cost in order to keep clean hands.

As with Assurance, the Complicity interaction has two equilibria, representing the two modes of nonconformity. Individuals will act on the basis of their expectations of others. If they expect general compliance, they will choose to defect, and will choose to comply if others defect. With the payoffs I have selected, each agent has reason to comply when they think it more likely than not that others will defect. More generally, the incentive to comply varies inversely with the likelihood of general compliance, and directly with the disvalue attached to complicity. (I will discuss possible reasons for attaching disvalue to complicity later). Again, as with Assurance, it is very hard to predict the outcome of a Chicken or Complicity interaction. Assuming all agents have this preference schedule, and this is common knowledge, the Complicity pattern makes the timing and monitoring of choices crucial. Since everyone prefers general compliance to general defection, everyone has reason to force the others into compliance by defecting preemptively. The result is either general noncompliance, if too many act preemptively, or a waiting game to

**If I believe others will**

| | comply | defect |
|---|---|---|
| **and I** comply | $b - c_1$ <br> 2 | $-c_1$ <br> $-1$ |
| defect | $b$ <br> 3 | $-c_3$ <br> $-2$ |

(My payoffs in box.)

**Variables and assumptions:**

Comply: use new CFC-free coolant
Defect: use old CFC coolant

VC: Expected value of compliance
VD: Expected value of defection
NV: Net expected value of compliance = VC − VD

$p$: my subjective probability of others' general compliance

$b$: my benefit from general compliance = 3
$c_1$: my compliance costs = 1
$c_3$: my complicity costs = 2

**Calculation of payoffs:**

$VC = pb - c_1$
$VD = pb + (1 - p) \cdot (-c_3)$
$\quad\; = pb + pc_3 - c_3$
$NV = c_1 - c_3 - pc_3$

$NV > 0$ when $p < \dfrac{c_1 - c_3}{c_2}$

**Here, I comply when $p < \frac{1}{2}$.**

Figure 6.3 Complicity

see who is willing first to incur the compliance costs. However, if preemptive defection is not possible and agents attach substantial disvalue to complicity, then general compliance is more likely. And if the choice to comply is irrevocable (you wouldn't switch back to the cheaper technology), then general compliance will be as stable as that provided by Assurance.[33] But as long as uncertainty prevails or agents attach only moderate significance to complicitous involvement, the risk of general defection is very high.

So both Assurance and Complicity preference schedules provide hope for avoiding collective harms, but neither is adequate on its own. We have much better results when we combine both types of preferences – or, better, both sorts of moral scruples (see Figure 6.4).

This interaction is the reverse of CA. Given these payoffs, compliance strongly dominates defection, since defection entails either substantial complicity or free-riding costs. It is, I believe, a realistic assumption that individuals will weigh the moral costs of complicity and free riding approximately equally, so the choice between the two is just a matter of compliance costs. When these costs are equal, individuals will always have reason to comply, however they assess the likelihood of others' compliance. A population of such individuals will be a population of universal compliance. And even a substantial core of such agents can provide the requisite assurance to those who shun free riding.

### 6.2.4 Symbolic Utility and Quasi-Participation as Grounds For Accountability

So we now have an idea of how to solve the practical problem. If we inculcate both Complicity and Assurance preferences, then gun merchants will have no incentive to sell Uzis to madmen, and drivers will be willing to pay more for CFC-free coolants. The challenge is to provide internalizable, reflectively stable grounds for these motivations. And so we return to the theoretical considerations of the earlier chapters, to see what can warrant responses of accountability in the absence of causation and simple intention. Recall that we seek accountability in both its negative and positive senses. Individuals must reproach themselves for contributing to collective harms, and must identify affirmatively with efforts at their prevention and

**If I believe others will**

|  | comply | defect |
|---|---|---|
| **comply** | $b - c_1$ <br> 2 | $-c_1$ <br> -1 |
| **and I defect** | $b - c_2$ <br> 1 | $-c_3$ <br> -2 |

(My payoffs in box.)

**Variables and assumptions:**

Comply: use new CFC-free coolant
Defect: use old CFC coolant

VC: Expected value of compliance
VD: Expected value of defection
NV: Net expected value of compliance = VC − VD

p: my subjective probability of others' general compliance

b: my benefit from general compliance = 3

$c_1$: my compliance costs = 1
$c_2$: my defection costs = 2
$c_3$: my complicity costs = 2

**Calculation of payoffs:**

$VC = pb - c_1$
$VD = p(b - c_2) + (1 - p) \cdot (-c_3)$
$\quad = pb + pc_3 - pc_2 - c_3$
$NV = pc_2 - pc_3 + c_3 - c_1$

In general, if $c_1$ is greater than $c_2$ or $c_3$, NV < 0 for all p. But as $c_2$ increases relative to $c_1$, NV > 0 for smaller p; and as $c_3$ increases relative to $c_1$, NV > 0 for larger p.

**For these $c_1$, $c_2$, $c_3$, NV > 0 for all p.**

Figure 6.4 Assurance and Complicity

repair. More generally, individuals must come to think of themselves as inclusively accountable for what they do together, to see themselves as participants in a group.

The grounds I will offer are two-fold, neither element alone sufficient to ground individual accountability. Taken together, however, they can account for the warrant individuals have in holding themselves and others accountable for facilitation and unstructured harms.[34] I consider the problem in two parts, first from the point of view of the victims, and next from that of the agents.

Note first that from the victims' perspective, the source of the harm is clearly identifiable: a people engaging in a concrete way of life that generates these harms. To a member of the environmentally affected population, or to a member of a community ravaged by violence, a systemic view quickly becomes salient, and collective agency is attributed to the group causing the harm. In the CFC case, the agent of the harm is the set of drivers of luxury cars, or perhaps more generally the inhabitants of Western nations.[35] These drivers and inhabitants depend upon one another for the maintenance of the infrastructure that allows their way of life. More generally, they abide by and reinforce in one another a sense of accountability that treats collective and distant harms as off the moral map, so to speak. In the gun-seller case, the culpable "agent" is not the individual merchant, but the set of gun sellers who are routinely indifferent to the violence that flows from their trade.[36] These merchants are unified in part by shared trade networks, lobbying efforts, and manufacturing standards. And they are united by a shared universe of values, here regarding the permissibility of selling such deadly instruments. Thus, to the victims, a community of accountability is identifiable: a set of individuals who jointly cause harm, against a background of interdependent activity and shared values. Furthermore, from the victims' abstracted, systemic point of view, claims against individual agents make sense. Individual agents are, broadly speaking, participants in a shared venture that does harm, and so are inclusively accountable for the unintended consequences of what they do together.[37] Call this a *quasi-participatory* basis of accountability, "quasi" because there is no specific project to which individuals contribute.

The trouble with extending this argument to the position of the agents is that the systemic, collective view it depends upon only rarely coincides with agents' own first-personal perspective. It is therefore unclear whether these conclusions from the victims' position can be motivating for agents. Individuals can and do think of themselves as members of vast social and political networks, and they can prepare themselves to act upon that conception, particularly in times of crisis such as war. In these cases, a deeply sedimented conception of an integrated "way of life" can give individuals a sense of unity and purpose. But it is difficult to awaken that consciousness for altruistic ends when no crisis looms. In these contexts, the purely individualistic point of view tends to dominate, because the threatening activities are generated by self-interested motives.[38] Individual merchants, when they sell, do not think of themselves as in alliance with other merchants. They simply make their sales and feed their families. Similarly for drivers. Indeed, if moral criticism does generate feelings of participatory solidarity, they are likely to be unhelpfully defensive: "We'd better band together to defeat this threat to our way of life."

It is not necessarily futile to hope that a systemic, collective perspective can come to have moral saliency for agents. Samuel Scheffler has argued that the universalistic perspective of consequentialism is too far removed from the phenomenology of individual agency that gives the traditional conception its psychological bite.[39] The consequentialist position, that one is as responsible for what one fails to prevent as for what one does, misses the special significance of individual causation. So it is true that the homogeneous landscape of sentient agents invoked by consequentialism gives little purchase to psychologically realistic conceptions of accountability. Still, there are other alternatives besides a purely individualistic perspective on moral agency. The disappearance of individual accountability is not simply a product of a confrontation between the traditional individualistic conception of accountability and a world of large-scale effects. Rather, it is also a product of a kind of ethical *anomie*, of a tendency to regard one's moral relations to the world as essentially isolable. If we can look to and cultivate the groupings in which agents actually do find themselves to be participants, then perhaps there is material for generating a sense of accountability.[40]

One plausible route to eliciting this sense of accountability and collective identity lies in returning to the victims' observation that the agents of their suffering share an objectively determinate and highly interdependent way of life. For the socioeconomic structures noted by the victims are neither self-originating nor self-sustaining. They emerge, rather, from unreflective confluences of habit and sentiment, tacit agreements upon, for example, the value of private transportation. These manifest themselves in myriad public policy choices and private behaviors. Indeed, to the extent that the offending socioeconomic structures are social, they must arise from the motivations of individual agents, for all social activity is individual activity. This is what Bernard Williams calls the minimal truth of methodological individualism.[41] I claim that if collective harms can be ascribed to social and economic structures, then those harms can also be traced to individual motivations. And it is to these individual motivations that we can appeal in constructing a motivating sense of accountability.

By noting the individualistic source of social structures, I do not mean either that these motivations rise easily to the level of consciousness, or that they may be invoked as foundational causal explanations of the social structure. Pierre Bourdieu, the sociologist and philosopher, has provided the most searching investigation of the reciprocal relationship between individual motivation and social structure. He uses the term *habitus* to refer to the durable complexes of dispositions of thinking, acting, and feeling that unify and individuate members of social groups.[42] The crucial point for Bourdieu is that these *habitus* are not self-defining, but rather emerge out of individual experience with the objective circumstances of social life, in much the way that the inarticulable skills of baseball emerge out of individual experience with gravity and momentum. More to the point, the individual *habitus* of a given social group – for example, drivers of luxury cars – are both shaped by and shape their social and natural environment, just as (it is often said) the Aristotelian personal virtues were shaped by a slave economy and a patriarchal politics, and contributed to the maintenance of that social order. In the example at hand, the values drivers put upon personal comfort and privacy are only realizable given cheap fuel and disguised public subsidies of automobile travel. Reciprocally, those social conditions themselves reflect valuations by driver-citizens.

So one part of the task of dealing with collective harms is emphasizing the moral significance of preexisting networks of collaboration. This invocation of community may seem utopian in the fragmented condition of postmodernity. But it is less utopian than the form of moral reflection proposed by consequentialists, and it is susceptible to social reinforcement. In general individuals do not and need not conceive of themselves as either isolated units or as members of humanity writ large. Rather, they inhabit middle-sized, overlapping fields of shared meanings and political identifications. These shared bases of identification can in turn provide the requisite basis of individual accountability. Drivers can come to be aware of the damage done by a way of life that ignores atmospheric effects. Gun sellers can realize that their trade, taken as a whole, occasions a climate of violence. More generally, the regional and institutional arrangements and roles that orient agents in social space can be used as foundations upon which to build structures of accountability.

So even in the absence of a discrete identifiable collective act whose unwanted consequence is the harm in question, agents can think of themselves as participants in a collective venture. As moral critics of our own and others' actions, we can draw upon preexisting contexts of social interaction in order to create a sense of shared venture. We do not need to adopt a radically different conception of each one's agency, but rather to extend the determinate and meaningful views we already share. The basis of accountability is still individualistic, and indeed is reinforced by individual moral reflection, because we are asked to reflect on the interactions that already, concretely, structure our lives. Thinking of the damage that I and my fellow American drivers do confirms me in a regional identity I already hold. Against this background, we can each foster a sense of accountability for what we do together.

Granted, agents' identification with the harms they produce will be weaker than the identification grounded in the specific shared intentions I have been discussing. But even a weak sense of participation may move individuals to act from Complicity and Assurance preferences, rather than CA preferences. While it remains true that what an individual does makes no consequential difference, this thought is not immediately relevant to consideration of what we ought to do together to resolve the problem.[43] Individuals who think of themselves as working towards a shared goal of reducing harm will reject individual noncompliance as a dominant strategy, because noncompliance is incompatible with seeing oneself as a member of the relevant community. Drivers can come to accept CFC reduction essentially as a shared enterprise. Gun sellers can accept closer scrutiny of their customers as the cost of jointly protecting a culture from violence.[44]

The nascent sense of common venture I am invoking can be linked to a second basis of accountability for unstructured collective harms: *symbolic,* or character-based accountability. In Chapter 2 I discussed accountability for wrongs done by others, from which one has benefited. I said that agents can feel and are held accountable for the wrong "subjunctively." By their acceptance of the benefit, they can be thought to indicate their tolerance for the conduct that produced it. Agents are accountable not only by virtue of what they have done or caused, but for what they might have done or caused. They are accountable in virtue of who they are.

The cases of facilitation and environmental damage invite a similar form of subjunctive accountability. In overdetermined contexts, agents can have reason to refrain from participating in a harm, not because of the relation between this choice and an actual outcome, but because of what the choice symbolizes in their characters and commitments. Agents who show no concern for their participation in collective harms in overdetermined contexts make themselves vulnerable to the suspicion they will be indifferent even when they could make a difference. By contrast, agents who distinguish themselves from other participants demonstrate a commitment to the value of the lives of those they harm.[45] A driver can demonstrate concern for ozone levels, and awareness of the harm we do together, by preemptively moving to the non-CFC coolant. A gun seller's refusal to associate himself with even inevitable crime identifies him with the interests of those who will be harmed. The motive in these cases is not, or is not necessarily, causal. That is, agents need not believe that unilateral nonparticipation will lead others to follow.[46] Rather, they choose to act as a way of expressing meaning.[47]

Such concern for the symbolic character of one's act, independent of its effects, may bespeak an annoying priggishness or high-mindedness. I do not endorse martyrdom, or the absolutism of the Solzhenitsyn principle by which one's hands must remain clean at all costs. But acts do have a powerful symbolic dimension of choice, and agents who are attracted by the principles or values at stake may come to prefer individual compliance for symbolic reasons. Acting from principle, in defiance of circumstances, attracts most criticism in its "Let justice be done, even if the world should perish" form. It is also criticizable when motivated by an overly self-reflexive concern with one's own integrity. Neither criticism applies here. So long as agents' reluctance to participate is focused on the harm, and not on the purity of their consciences, acting from principle should not attract criticism.[48] Furthermore, although symbolic motives may have the character of absolute demands, I do not try to represent them as demands of morality as such. It is doubtful whether any plausible construction of morality could require outcome-independent self-sacrifice. But it is plausible that some agents may require this of themselves, especially when the individual costs are not great in comparison with the harm that is done. Like other supererogatory actions, symbolic actions fit awkwardly with a pure ethics of obligation. Nonetheless they have a firm place within a broader ethics of value.[49]

A piecemeal solution may seem unsatisfying. But solving any real social problem requires a mixture of political and ethical motivations and institutions. We are not without ethical resources for confronting these problems. Taken together, a sense of individual quasi-participatory accountability and of symbolic accountability can make the difference between insoluble collective action problems and stable Assurance game motives. A further important point about these motives is that they appear to be immune to Scheffler's worry about adapting an individualistic conception of responsibility to collective harms. For both of these motives rest soundly on individualistic bases: our participation in the social structures and our expression of the shared values that give our lives meaning. Reflection on who we are can thus supply accountability for what we together do.

## 6.3 COLLECTIVE ACCOUNTABILITY AND HOLISTIC RESPONSES

The very difficulty of linking individuals directly to unstructured collective harms invites an alternative response: ignore the relations between individual agents and victims, and focus instead upon the unmediated accountability of the collective. If, for example, we are unwilling to think of individual American drivers as accountable for ozone depletion, or of individual gun dealers as worthy of reproach for the mayhem on the streets, instead we might focus our resentments and demand repair from supra-individual, collective entities: the American people as a whole, or the trade association of gun sellers. In this section I explore the intelligibility of responses of accountability directed at collectives as collectives, rather than at individuals as members of collectives.

This exploration of collective accountability is not only of theoretical interest.[50] For commonsense language and thought already makes a home for holistic (or collective) forms of accountability. For example, Exxon is accused of destroying the Prince William Sound, and compensation is demanded; criminal charges are brought against Operation Rescue for its interference with abortion clinics; and the Republican Party is accused by the President of heightening racial divisiveness in America and its leadership is called to respond. Individuals are implicated in all of these events, but the accusations and demands are not made of individuals in particular. Such accusations are directed primarily at the organization, in light of the goals it pursues and the consequences of those goals. Political and legal life would be unintelligible and unrecognizable without such holistic talk of groups, and without holistic systems of accountability.

I turn only now to address these issues of collective accountability because the strongest pressure for collective accountability arises when, as with facilitation and unstructured harm, it is difficult to connect individual agency with the collective harm. Only the collective is left to be blamed. Furthermore, with the analytical apparatus developed in the previous chapters, we are now in a position to see how collective action is necessarily mediated by individual practical deliberation and action. It follows that any theory of collective accountability must be intimately related to a theory of individual accountability, since any theory of accountability has ultimately to operate through the motivations and normative commitments of individual actors. As I stressed in Chapter 3, this form of individualism is not reductive in any substantive explanatory or ontological sense. The best theories of organizational behavior may make use of irreducible, structural (or "emergent") properties of the organization in question; the best explanations of individual behavior may be couched in social terms. Indeed, a major lesson of the organizational theory of the last 50 years is that many structured collectives can only be treated adequately from an essentially holistic, or structural, point of view.[51] I do not claim, therefore, that a theory of collective accountability must be reducible to a theory of individual accountability. I claim only that a theory of collective accountability must tie into a theory of individual accountability if the judgments of collective accountability are to have any role within a social system of ethical deliberation and action.

Now that we have in hand a theory of individual moral accountability, we can pursue questions of collective accountability. In particular, I want to examine two questions: first, whether organizations are appropriate subjects of accountability; and second, if so, whether the accountability of organizations differs from the accountability of their members. There are two reasons for this inquiry. The first concerns the ethical justification of applying holistic legal sanctions to groups. Although I regard the question of the application of legal sanctions to collectives as largely pragmatic, there are issues of justice related to the effects of collective sanctions upon the disparate individual members of these collectives. The second reason is the hope that distinguishing a level of collective accountability may help us to gain further ground upon the problem discussed in the last section, that of individual accountability for unstructured collective harms. If a relevant collective can be identified as the appropriate accountable subject, then it may be possible to justify a set of indirect reparative duties binding upon the individual members of the collective.

### 6.3.1  *Collectives as Subjects of Accountability*

Much of the philosophical literature on collective and corporate accountability treats the question of whether social groups can be liable to moral blame as an essentially metaphysical question: Are social groups moral persons?[52] While this question has some independent conceptual interest, its application to the problem of accountability raises problems that do not need to be solved. I have urged an essentially instrumental view of accountability. Our practices and responses of accountability perform the task of sustaining and repairing certain interpersonal relationships.[53]

The question of whether structured collectives are possible holistic subjects of accountability is, on my view, the question of whether there is a point to treating them as such. This question still has a conceptual component, since the coherent application of judgments of accountability depends upon the defensibility of relating structured collectives to possible harms and wrongs. In particular, if structured collectives are possible subjects of accountability, then two things must be true. First, it must be possible to ascribe intentions and actions to the group as a whole. And second, the collectives must be in principle responsive to expressions of accountability. Unless the first is true, there is no basis for accountability. Unless the second is true, there is no point to our responses. Granted, it can make sense in particular cases to express blame or resentment of even an incorrigible wrongdoer, because of the symbolic resonance of these responses in our own lives. However, the rationale of our practices of accountability quickly evaporates when they become entirely expressive.

I have already explained in Chapter 3 how intentions, actions, and events can be ascribed holistically to groups.[54] Indeed, the ascription of actions and events to groups is logically prior to their inclusive ascription to other members. Collective intentions are interpretive constructions of the shared goal that explains individual agents' actions. Future-oriented collective intentions can be ascribed to groups when their members are disposed to allow a shared goal to govern their future deliberation and action. When these conditions are met, then actions, intentions, and events can be ascribed to groups as a whole. Thus, if the members of a robbery gang severally stand guard, break in, cause a guard's death, and fence their loot, each with the intent of promoting the joint robbery, then these acts can be ascribed to the gang as a whole. Their collective intention of robbery is manifest in the actions of each, for it explains those actions. And they could be said to collectively intend the robbery beforehand, insofar as the individual members were disposed to promote it. The "intentionality" of the group is wholly derivative, a function of the intentionality of its members. To put the point in Daniel Dennett's terms, we observers can usefully take an "intentional stance" in interpreting the behavior of a firm in terms of holistic decision and intentional action.[55] The legitimacy of taking such an interpretive stance is grounded in the actual intentionality of the individual members of the organization. So there is nothing fallacious about the use of intentional language to describe holistic behavior, as long as we keep in mind the derivative nature of our judgments.[56]

The second condition on holistic accountability is that there be a point to the practice of holding collectives accountable. In pragmatic terms, the main point of holistic responses is to change a collective's behavior for the better. But this is only a general condition. There will usually be expressive value in criticizing the wrongful behavior of a collective. There might even be instrumental value in delivering a holistic reproach or punishment even if that particular collective's behavior is unlikely to improve. (For instance if the punishment has the effect, intended or not, of destroying the collective.) A stern response towards one collective might send a message to others, or it might signal to that collective's actual or potential members that they should locate their loyalties elsewhere. In the standard case, however, the holistic reproach will be met with a holistic response. For example, the E.E.O.C. announces its suspicion that Texaco has racist employment practices, and Texaco institutes an internal review and adopts new policies.

Institutional collectives take many forms, of course, and there is little consensus within organizational theory literature on even the proper typology, much less on the best theories for explaining the behavior of various forms of organization.[57] I do not want to evaluate the success of various organizational theories, which is basically an empirical task, albeit essential for designing an effective system of external sanctions. Even without carrying out this project, we can still safely assert that there is no principled reason that a regime of sanctions cannot be designed to achieve some of the goals of a system of accountability. Economic or regulatory measures are probably the most effective in modifying organizational behavior, but even individual expressions of moral condemnation can form a basis of response. A climate of public opinion that regards strip mining as unacceptable will not have the same effects on a mining firm that a strict regulatory regime would. But individuals within the firm can still be influenced by moral argument, and can bring these influences to bear within the organizational structure as they deliberate about what the firm ought to do.[58]

The derivative intentionality of structured collectives makes possible a broad panoply of moral response as well as economic and legal sanction. One might judge Union Carbide, say, to be careless with respect to the risks it imposed upon overseas populations. This judgment might be expressed in moral indignation or even rage. (It certainly would be by a Bhopal survivor.) The holistic judgment would be warranted by the presence or absence of company policies regarding health and safety. Warranted anger over these policies does not depend upon discovering which individuals in the company are responsible for their implementation. It is sufficient that someone was or could have been. A longtime assembly line worker, downsized out of General Motors, could well feel resentful, and think the company has betrayed him. Again, this response could be warranted in terms of company policies and the expectations those policies have raised. I will return to the issue of attributions of systemic fault in the following text. For now, the point is that victims' responses to the collective agents of their suffering can mimic their responses to individual agents. As long as intentional actions are ascribable to a collective, all forms of responses to those actions can be warranted.

There is an important difference between expressing recrimination at an organization and expressing it at an individual. Individuals who are the subjects of response respond affectively, ideally (from the perspective of the victims) with shame and guilt, perhaps with resentment. But a collective cannot respond affectively to these expressions, only its constituent members can. The lack of an affective counterresponse is troubling, because the efficacy of responses of accountability partially depends upon affect.[59] The responses of shame, guilt, and regret help to register the significance of the harm. When responses focus primarily upon the collective rather than upon individual agents, some degree of misfire is inevitable. The sting of collective blame will often be felt least where it is needed most, in the head office. To the extent that blame focuses upon an organization as a whole and its substandard procedures, individuals within the organization have little motivation to do better. Practices of accountability bear fruit only when some individuals within a group seize the initiative and pursue both more specific sites of accountability and modes of rectification. For instance, the Bhopal disaster seems to have been the product of lax supervisory and maintenance standards at the plant, undertrained employees, understaffing as a result of low profits, the absence of effective regulatory authority within the relevant Indian ministries, and inadequate oversight by U.S. headquarters.[60] The duty of compensating victims can perhaps only be borne by the company as a whole.[61] But in order to prevent such accidents in the future, very specific individuals and office holders must be held and hold themselves accountable as well. Blame focused upon the company as a whole is overly diffused with respect to its proper targets, the individuals whose conduct really did fall below acceptable standards.

Economic and legal sanctions face a different version of the same problem. The responsiveness of an organization to fines and regulations depends upon the inclination of the firm to maximize profits and to comply with a regulatory authority. These inclinations do not need to bear any strong relation to the emotions of accountability, and so are not undermined by the absence of a holistic level of affect. Nonetheless, firm-oriented sanctions can be difficult to structure efficiently, given the proven ability of managers and high-level bureaucrats to deflect their costs onto more vulnerable subordinates or unorganized shareholders.[62] When the burden of punitive damages and fines is not borne by outside insurers, their brunt is taken primarily by stockholders and eliminable employees.[63] I do not want to take up here the complex subject of the design of legal sanctions that optimally reduce collective wrongdoing.[64] I want only to note that the principles of design are by no means straightforward. Aside from the palpable unfairness that can result to individuals whose culpability is slight – a problem I discuss subsequently – poorly targeted fines can be tremendously counterproductive, encouraging the inefficient diffusion of task responsibility or the compartmentalization of knowledge.

### 6.3.2  Holistic Accountability and Individual Accountability

In the absence of a coherent basis of individual moral accountability, recriminations directed at collectives can be ineffectual or unfair or both. Holistic responses of accountability must therefore engage with individual responses – they must provide individuals with reasons. But there are two ways of construing this demand that holistic responses tie into individual responses. The strong interpretation is eliminative of holistic accountability. Once individuals are properly subjected to a response and have offered the response due, no response is owed by or to the group as a whole. On this view, accountability is functionally "translatable" into individualistic responses. A weaker view holds that whenever an organization is accountable, then some response is owed by and to the members of that organization. This weaker view seems more plausible, even in cases of uniform levels of culpability among the organization's members. Say a golf club has a practice of excluding racial minorities, and this practice is supported and enforced by each member. Here it seems each member can be faulted for being a racist, and each shares in a duty to make amends to the subjects of discrimination and to the community at large. But we might also think a collective response from the organization is due: a public apology, creation of programs friendly to minorities, and so on. This is not simply because the organization is logically different from the sum of its members. The need for a two-tiered response arises from the nature of the organization as a shared project, and the racial exclusion as a product of that project. The logic of collective action suggests that the response be in part a shared project as well.

Already I have discussed a clear case of a distinction between individual and collective accountability, that of Emilia and Iago. The fraud on Othello is ascribable to the group, since both intentionally participated in the theft of the handkerchief, and so there is a basis for holding the couple accountable as a couple – faulting their partnership in the fraud. But we also saw that Emilia's accountability differs radically from Iago's. While – within a poetic scheme of justice – Othello might be warranted in trying to kill Iago, a "volunteered" death from grief is just relief and expiation for Emilia. It follows that any poetic collective sanction upon the couple would either fall too easily upon the one or too heavily upon the other.

The culpability of an organization may also be greater than the culpability of its members. This is typically the case when the harm is a consequence of a complex of omissions, no one of which was sufficient for the harm. To return to Bhopal, the released gases would not have had nearly the tragic consequences if any of the following had been true:

(1) The refrigeration unit for the methyl isocyanate (MIC) had been functioning according to the manual;
(2) the emissions scrubber at the plant had been repaired sooner;
(3) a properly trained employee had not washed out a connecting pipe with water;
(4) the tanks containing the MIC had been built of the appropriate nonreactive steel alloy;
(5) the Bhopal authorities had enforced the rules restricting habitation close to the plant;
(6) the plant had been staffed with its precutback complement of twelve rather than six;
(7) reliable instrumentation had been in place; or
(8) local health officials had been informed that simply placing a wet cloth over a victim's face greatly reduces the lung damage.

A number of people at all levels of the organization acted badly before, during, and after the gas leak, and it is only because many of them did so independently that the tragedy arose.

I have argued in Chapter 5 for the claim that in cases of foreseeable industrial accidents, all participants in the venture – here, Indian and U.S. shareholders, employees, the engineers who designed the plant – are accountable for the tragedy, because it is a consequence of their shared endeavor. Each bears a special responsive relation to the harm and its victims – perhaps a sense of regret, shame at their company's carelessness, and a special duty to contribute to the aid of those who have suffered.[65] To say all are accountable is not, however, to say all are to blame. Most of these individuals have in no way failed to act responsibly. The accountability of the blameworthy is more complicated. Each is at fault with respect to the tragedy, but the tragedy only ensued because of different pieces of bad luck, most of it consisting in the negligence of other agents. Although each negligent employee is accountable on the basis of what all did together, and although each is specially accountable because of his or her own lapse, no one individual is exclusively accountable for the tragedy.

Nothing that anyone did warrants full recrimination for the 2,000 deaths.[66] The responses of agents, victims, and bystanders alike must be tempered by an awareness of the systemic nature of the failure. Indeed, the responses of the nonnegligent members acknowledges this fact. They feel accountable precisely because of their company's negligence.

It is clear that if we confine ourselves to the arena of individual accountability, we have a problem. For it still seems that only one subject is rightly accountable for the full extent of the tragedy, namely the company as a whole, or – better yet – the industrial-governmental complex that operated the plant. Given the systemic nature of the failure, it seems appropriate to say the complex as a whole was at fault in the sense that it should have instituted better procedures and better safety equipment. The judgment of systemic fault does entail a claim about individuals, namely that some individuals should have made sure the plant's procedures were up to snuff. But this claim about individuals cannot be further localized – the culpable "individuals" are simply placeholders for whoever would have, counterfactually, operated the plant safely. No one within the organization had the duty of monitoring safety precautions, but someone ought to have done so. The inadequacy of the system as a whole is an emergent property, one explicable only in terms of the structure of the organization in relation to its environment.

Because the wrong that lay behind the gas leak is emergent at the group level, it makes sense that the duty of compensation should emerge at the group level too. The company's wrongful discharge caused the harm, and so the company owes compensation to its victims. This may seem to lead to a difficulty. The members do not uniformly owe compensation, yet the burden of any compensation the company makes will be borne by them. Any duty of compensation of the company becomes, in effect, a further duty of the individual members. But now we seem to have multiplied reparative duties, from a collective duty to numerous individual duties. Is this either incoherent or double counting?

Not necessarily. It is true that nonfaulty members of the organization have no exclusive, compensatory duties. This is a consequence of their individual, noncomplicit accountability: They have neither acted badly, nor caused harm. But they owe an inclusive duty as group members. They should share in the collective task of compensating their victims. Their obligations after the accident mirror the nature of their participation beforehand, as members of a venture that was foreseeably capable of doing great harm. Their inclusive duties as company members entails a derivative obligation to help make good their company's debts to its victims.

Given that all members individually owe an inclusive duty of compensation, insofar as the organization as a whole has a duty to compensate, how ought the burden of this duty be allocated among them? Answering this question would seem to require a hybrid theory of distributive and corrective justice, one adequate both to the task of compensating victims and to the fair distribution of burdens among differentially placed participants. In the next chapter, I will discuss this issue in more detail, with respect to the actual regime of corporate tort liability. Here I want to raise the general ethical question of whether there is any particular distributive pattern that victims can claim as a right, or that the injurers owe as a duty. For it might be thought that the victims' interests stop at compensation – that the distribution of its burden is wholly an internal matter of fairness within the organization.[67]

The answer, I believe, is that the claim of victims to compensation has lexical priority over the claims of organizational members to fairness. In cases of grossly disparate fault among insiders, it might be fairest for the most faulty to contribute most towards compensation, with some faultless members owing nothing. But if compensation can only be achieved by having all contribute some, then the claim of the victims upon the collective as a whole requires this pattern of distribution. On the other hand, there is no necessary affront to the victims if some members contribute nothing so long as these members were in the potential pool of contributors. The Complicity Principle requires that participation in a common endeavor generates claims of accountability for all members. It does not follow that the claims be uniform, or that all be nonempty with respect to any given form of response.[68] Relative ability to pay, voluntariness of the association with the organization, fault, role-bound duties, and causal contribution can play a role in determining an inclusive compensatory scheme, if they are part of a distributively fair allocation of burdens. The important point is that the grounds of complicitous accountability are logically prior to these considerations, and are not reducible to them.

We can now return to our discussion of individual accountability for unstructured collective harms. I said that a systemic view of the source of the harm is especially salient from the point of view of victims, and that reflection on this view could be a partial source of motivation for agents. A different way to put the point is to say that victims can claim a holistic response from the people whose way of life harms them.[69] The responsibility of meeting the burden of this claim then falls upon the members of these societies. As a CFC car driver, I have no direct or exclusive duty to mend my ways, for my ways do not make a difference to anyone. We CFC drivers, however, together have a duty to mend our ways, for we do harm. Our collective accountability admits of only one response, namely our individually coordinated effort at CFC reduction. And so I have an inclusive duty to comply with the coordination scheme, in virtue of my membership in this group.

If the notion of an emergent, holistic obligation is troubling, for metaphysical or other reasons, then there is an alternative conception of such obligations that may be more palatable. From the perspective of the agent, one may see holistic obligations as inputs to practical and ethical reasoning. They pose deliberative problems for participants, forcing them to think through the significance of their relationship to the collective structure, and to act on the basis of that understanding. Each participant individually, and all participants together, must deliberate about what they owe in virtue of what they have done. From the point of view of victims, the obligations are the source of claims against individuals, but claims whose basis likewise reflects the structure of participation. Responses of accountability, are owed ultimately by and to individuals, but the content of those claims is irreducibly collective. Complicity is a property of agents, linking them to one another and to their victims.

## 6.4 CONCLUSION

The discussion of this chapter has ranged over several individual relations to harm: facilitation of another's autonomous act, making a negligible marginal contribution to a public bad; and being a fault-less member of an organization systemically at fault in causing harm. What links these various individual relations together is their setting in a concrete social context of interdependence, institutional coopera-tion, and shared norms. Agents, victims, and onlookers who look to the social or institutional background of cooperation can find grounds for inclusive, individual accountability. Attention to the symbolic resonance of one's choice whether or not to participate in a pattern of wrong can further strengthen an individual's sense of accountability. So, individually accountable for what they jointly do, agents can work together to repair the past and improve the future.

There is, however, a residual worry about the approach I have sketched here. Namely, it would be an intolerable world if we were to take too great an interest in policing the activities of those with whom we deal or live. There is, after all, some moral truth to the hoary legal principle of *novus actus interveniens,* that relations of ac-countability are severed by the independent acts of others. At a certain point, except under the most demanding consequentialist ethic, it must be appropriate to say, "Enough. The acts of others are theirs to account for and theirs alone."

The principle that others' autonomous actions delimit individual accountability marks out a desirable range of moral freedom for individuals, one necessary in an environment of rational and irre-solvable dispute about the boundaries of the good and the right. While we ought to be reluctant to lend our efforts and our products to the wrongful designs of others, we must take care not to impose overly controversial conceptions of wrongfulness on others. I do not mean simply that a liberal political regime may not criminalize doing or facilitating morally controversial acts.[70] Rather, my point applies to moral agents directly. A proper concern for the actions in which one plays a role must be tempered by a respect for the decisions made by others about their own courses of action. It is not easy to accommodate the conflicting goal of a free and pluralistic social space to that of a community of moral involvement and mutual concern. I only have tried to indicate the grounds upon which such concern might be justified.

# Chapter 7

# Complicity, Conspiracy, and Shareholder Liability

## 7.1 INTRODUCTION

Participation means implication. It is the basis of individual accountability for what others do. But participatory accountability is inclusive, attaching to individuals as members of groups, and so differs from exclusive attributions of accountability. In Chapter 5 I showed how the moral responses to participatory wrongdoing by victims, onlookers, and participants properly reflect the difference between inclusive and exclusive accountability. However, because the diffuse domain of moral accountability finds its substance in the prior and particular web of moral and social relationships, few generalizations about moral accountability are both true and informative.

As H.L.A. Hart and Lon Fuller have argued, the domain of legal accountability is necessarily more determinate, especially in liberal regimes.[1] Committed to fostering the autonomy of its citizens, a liberal state must narrowly tailor its punitive and reparative responses. Unless citizens can reasonably predict and control the imposition of legal sanctions, they cannot lead good and meaningful lives within the law's constraints. So, in order to lend determinacy to my discussion of participatory accountability, I turn now to the domain of law. I will focus on criminal liability for complicity and conspiracy, and on shareholders' civil liability for the torts of the companies in which they invest. These are all examples of the law's treatment of indirect liability. I will argue that the law's treatment of participatory accountability is dogged by the same problem as individualistic consequentialism and Kantianism. The law too fails to understand the nature of the normative and logical relations between groups and their members. We need instead a system of criminal and civil liability attentive to the distinction between inclusive and exclusive accountability, a system that can distinguish between "we did it" and "I did it."

My aim in this chapter is not to provide a comprehensive doctrinal analysis of the criminal and civil law of associative accountability. Apart from being dull, such a project would threaten to obscure the main point I want to make: the theory of participatory complicity, grounded in the notion of participatory intentions, enables a critique as well as an understanding of central features of our legal practices, as these relate individuals to collectives. Accordingly, Section 7.2 opens with a methodological argument for distinguishing clearly between a normative theory of legal accountability and a theory of moral accountability. Theories of legal accountability must be sensitive to epistemic constraints as moral theories need not. My focus in this chapter is primarily upon criminal rather than civil liability, and in Section 7.3 I try to lay out in a philosophically perspicuous way the structure of criminal complicity and conspiracy doctrine, as well as its presuppositions. Next, in Section 7.4, I briefly assess the problems in attempting to justify accomplice liability on the basis of analogies drawn from the civil law of agency and offer instead a theory of accomplice liability grounded in participatory intentions. While my theory captures the heart of actual doctrine, it is explicitly revisionary in an important way. We must resurrect the fundamental distinction between principals and accomplices, a distinction that will usually entail lesser punishment for accomplices.

I turn finally, with a frankly polemical intent, to a central example of the civil liability of individuals for collective acts: the limitation of personal liability of corporate shareholders. In Section 7.5 I argue that our general practices and norms of moral and legal accountability lie at odds with our treatment of corporate shareholders. Instead I argue that we have ethical reason to treat shareholders as liable for their company's deficiencies in meeting its reparative duties to accident victims. (I leave open the question of whether countervailing economic or procedural reasons override the ethical argument.)

## 7.2 EPISTEMIC CONSTRAINTS UPON LEGAL ACCOUNTABILITY

We have discussed moral accountability so far, and presumed a knowledge of individuals' motives and goals. But legal authority is exercised in doubt. Motives are inferred from scatterings of evidence and causal explanations are shaped by the interests of the contesting parties. Unfortunately, just resolution of cases requires good information and good information is frequently too expensive or difficult to obtain. Criminal law presents the most serious epistemic problems, given its focus upon individual intentions. No individual accused of a crime can be expected, practically or normatively, to divulge a culpable state of mind. The legal distinction between premeditated and spontaneous homicide, for example, can be the difference between execution and incarceration. Premeditated homicide can be proven by evidence of advance planning. However, courts have held that killing can count as premeditated in the absence of planning, so long as the accused has the opportunity to reflect on the decision to kill.[2] Since most killers will not admit to premeditation, and since there is rarely a surviving witness to the crime, the judge or jury's decision is often only a construct teetering upon a scaffolding of circumstantial evidence and psychological inference.[3]

Despite pervasive doubt and uncertainty, decisions must be made and distinctions drawn. It is no wonder evidentiary matters play a central role in the criminal process. Some of the restrictions upon the evidence that can be procured by the state and brought to bear in the courtroom, such as the requirement of a duly authorized warrant for a comprehensive search, stem from a generalized concern about the limits of police intrusion. But other restrictions reflect fundamentally epistemic concerns, such as the exclusion of evidence of a defendant's prior criminal history, or of hearsay reports of the defendant's statements. Although prior criminal history is clearly relevant to the proof of the crime in question, such evidence is rightly excluded in many cases on the grounds that its effect upon juries is more prejudicial than probative.[4] Without these protective evidentiary rules, a system of criminal (and civil) law could not possibly be applied in justice.

Contrast the circumstances of criminal justice with those of moral theory. Although moral philosophers since Kant have warned of the inscrutability of individual intention in the first as well as third-personal cases, most moral theories ignore the epistemic problems, including Kant's own.[5] Deontologists such as Thomas Nagel and Barbara Herman still focus on agents' underlying intentions and self-conceptions. Utilitarians such as Richard Brandt and John Harsanyi resort to the idealized fiction of fully informed, "ethical" preferences in order to justify their criterion of right action.[6] Whether agents have acted wrongly and are accountable for so acting thus depends upon deep facts about their deliberative and motivational capacities, fine-grained attributions of intentional content, unequivocal motivation, and empirically adequate predictions of future consequences. With these idealizations, it is no wonder theorists tend to rest their arguments upon extreme moral types – Hitler, murder, and desert island promises. Outside the comfort of extremes, it is unlikely the idealized criteria of moral judgment can be realized. I do not mean to suggest that outlandish cases can play no role in testing moral principles, but only that the successful ones apply unclearly, if at all, to the messy domain of actual moral practice.[7] Some idealization is unavoidable. My own discussion of the morality of collective action has been guilty of idealization, in its reliance upon attributions of participatory intentions, and the simplified schematics of the Dresden bombers.

I must also acknowledge that moral theorists' judgments about accountability mirror our ordinary interpersonal reactions. In general, the moral judgments we make and the responses we offer may be out of line with the evidence necessary to support them. We routinely blame and condemn on the basis of a small portion of the available spectrum of evidence. Our estimates of each other's intentions are as much interpretive constructs as are the theorists'; and we rarely take the time to weigh all possible exculpatory factors. The jerk who cuts me off on the highway may in fact be distracted by great personal loss. But this possibility is unlikely to stop me from thinking him a jerk. My carelessness at a neighbor's party may manifest a deep, simmering resentment rather than clumsiness. But I am unlikely to dwell on this possibility either – I simply make my apologies and put the matter out of mind. Moral theory and practice can live by idealized epistemic standards because the stakes in the moral game are low in any particular case. The relationships protected by social morality can usually be repaired through apology and understanding. I may unfairly resent your failure to arrive at our meeting, not realizing you had a sick child to take care of. When you have a chance to explain, or when I otherwise discover the reason for your absence, all is again put right between us.[8]

By contrast, the belated acquittal of someone unjustly convicted cannot put things right, for nothing can repair the violence done to one's sense of autonomy and worth by unjust punishment. To be imprisoned, publicly despised, and stripped of elementary civil rights is to lose one's political, social, and moral identity. It is to become an object of the state's power, rather than a subject who authorizes the state's exercise of that power.[9] Freedom and perhaps compensation may be valid claims stemming from an unjust process or sentence, but they are not a means of repair. Given the moral and human costs of wrongful conviction, it surely follows that a necessary condition of a just penal institution is that it make very few mistakes. Whatever the moral propriety of, say, a rule against premeditated killing, the enforcement of this rule can only be justified so long as it rarely results in false positives: only those who actually do premeditate a killing should actually be subjected to the sanction that backs it. Legal judgments have little point unless actually applied and enforced; they are nearly worthless merely as indicators of moral norms. But in order to be justifiable applications of state force, legal judgments must be well rooted in both fact and political morality.

Therefore, the task of justifying a penal institution (or of justifying particular concepts within the institution) makes epistemic principles as fundamental as normative principles. The question of whether a given legal rule or concept is normatively defensible is always in part a question of whether it can be fairly operationalized. It is a mistake to treat the principles and rules of criminal liability simply as the instantiation of abstract justice. The legal theorists and moral philosophers who distinguish sharply between normative and evidentiary issues run the risk of ignoring the social space, with its costs and limitations, in which legal rules are necessarily embedded.[10] The problem is that an awareness of the law's epistemic constraints can quickly become a license for cynicism about alibi and excuse. To the extent exculpatory considerations are narrowed because of difficulties of proof, the scope of legal intrusion broadens. Attention to epistemic constraints must ensure the just application of the laws rather than extend their unjust dominion. The approach I will offer in the following sections therefore mixes normative and epistemic considerations, in order to produce a framework of complicit accountability maximally sensitive to the actual application of justice.

## 7.3 CRIMINAL COMPLICITY DOCTRINE AND THE SCOPE OF LIABILITY

In Anglo-American criminal law, complicity is not an object of accountability – that is, unlike conspiracy, complicity is not a distinct, substantive crime in its own right. It is instead a basis of liability, rendering one person liable for the acts of another. Generally speaking, an individual is complicit in another's crime if the first intentionally encourages or aids the second in the commission of that crime. Once a complicitous basis of liability is established, criminal law does not further distinguish between direct actors and accomplices: both are treated as perpetrators of the crime and punished accordingly.[11] Because liability as an accomplice is based in another agent's commission of a crime, complicity is often called a form of "derivative" liability.[12]

In U.S. federal law, international war-crimes law, and in many states, this principle of complicitous accountability is extended to all of the participants in a conspiracy.[13] Conspiracy, unlike complicity, is a separate, substantive crime: It is the crime of agreeing to participate in committing a crime. But conspiracy is also often treated as a basis for complicitous liability, on the grounds that any coconspirator is intentionally aiding or encouraging the crime he or she has agreed to commit. A conspirator – anyone who agrees to the commission of a crime or set of crimes – is liable for all reasonably foreseeable criminal acts and omissions of others in furtherance of the jointly undertaken criminal activity.[14] It is not necessary to show that conspirators in any way aided the commission of the crime, but only that they agreed to its commission, or to the commission of another crime giving rise to it. This stringent principle of coconspirator liability is generally known as the *Pinkerton* rule; it was first explicitly stated in a Supreme Court opinion upholding the conviction of one Daniel Pinkerton for six moonshining-related tax crimes, all of which had been committed by Daniel's brother Walter while Daniel was in prison.[15] In a notorious California case, also from the 1940s, *Anderson v. Superior Court,* the Court of Appeal permitted the prosecution of a woman named Alta Anderson for twenty-six counts of performing illegal abortions, both for cases in which she directly procured patients for the doctor and for cases procured by another woman, personally unknown to Anderson.[16]

The undifferentiated liability of direct and indirect actors under complicity doctrine, and the wholesale liability of conspirators, will be the subject of Section 7.4. Before offering a criticism of the doctrine, however, I want first to elaborate the conceptual content of complicitous liability in law. As we will see, the framework of participatory intentions provides a helpful way of making sense of the doctrinal requirements of complicity.

### 7.3.1 The Doctrine of Complicity

Liability for most crimes is based upon a combination of *subjective* and *objective* criteria. The terms *subjective* and *objective* are a matter of much confusion in criminal law, as they are used both to distinguish between individualized and normalized standards, and between mentalistic and behavioral or causal criteria. In the first sense, subjective criteria predicate liability upon the actual capacities and beliefs of the agent, while objective criteria predicate liability upon the capacities and beliefs that could reasonably be expected of a generally competent rational agent.[17] Departing somewhat from standard legal usage, I will use the terms *individualized* and *normalized* for this sense of subjective and objective criteria. The second sense of subjective and objective criteria refers, respectively, to the mental (called the *mens rea*) element of a crime, and to the result or conduct element (called the *actus reus*). I will continue to refer to the *mens rea* element as the subjective aspect of the crime, and the *actus reus* as the objective aspect, for these usages are closer to their philosophical counterparts.[18]

Standardly, criminal liability requires that a single agent perform the specified acts or cause the specified harms, with and because of a specified mental state or states.[19] First degree murder, for example, requires the subjective element of a premeditated intention to kill, as well, of course, as the objective result that the agent has caused another's death in acting upon that intention. Similarly, larceny requires not only the objective taking of another's property, but a subjective intent to deprive the other permanently of that property.

The standard model of criminal liability breaks down in the case of accessorial, or complicitous, liability. In the standard model, the criminal actor, his or her mental states, and the acts and consequences of those states form a sort of self-contained liability "package."[20] Within the institutional relations defined by the criminal law, criminal liability thus approximates the solipsistic retributive model of accountability I discussed in Chapter 2. But complicitous liability requires that we look to the liability of other agents, for by definition someone can only be complicit in the criminal act of another. For this reason, complicitous liability is inherently relative to the liability of another.[21] Call the accomplice "S," for secondary actor; and the principal actor "P." S is complicitously liable for P's act if and only if P's acts, mental states, and their consequences prima facie satisfy the requirements of some crime and S has intentionally acted (or failed to act in violation of a legal duty) in such a way as to encourage or promote P's performing that very crime. There is no liability for S without at least prima facie liability for P.[22]

The general statement that criminal complicity consists in the intentional promotion of another's criminal act leaves obscure the specific contours of the concept of complicity. Before we can assess the institution of complicitous liability in philosophical terms, we need to know more about its doctrinal boundaries. There are two central questions, relating respectively to the subjective and objective components of complicity doctrine. First, what intentional overlap must there be between S's and P's plans for the crime? Second, what causal or counterfactual relation does the law require between S's and P's actions?

### 7.3.2    *The Subjective Component of Complicity Doctrine*

The subjective aspect of complicity consists in the requirement that S intend to aid or encourage another in committing a criminal act, with the mental state required for that criminal act.[23] Judge Learned Hand gave the classic formulation of this subjective requirement. Considering a claim of complicity against a defendant who sold large amounts of sugar to someone who was obviously running an illegal still, Hand wrote that a genuine accomplice "must in some sense promote their [the principle actors'] venture himself, make it his own, have a stake in its outcome."[24] Note that Hand's "stake in the outcome" condition does not require that S stand to gain or lose by P's crime according to an objective metric. Rather, Hand's "stake" just means S has taken P's criminal end as S's own by volitionally investing (or identifying) himself or herself in that act. S succeeds when P commits the criminal act just because S's own end will have been satisfied. To take a standard example, S hoists P through a window so P can steal something. S satisfies the subjective condition for complicity in P's theft simply by having the intention of promoting P's act of permanently depriving the victim of property.

A complication in stating the subjective condition comes from the requirement that S satisfy the mental requirements for P's criminal act. So, in the example I just offered, liability for theft requires that one take property one believes belongs to another, with the aim of permanently depriving that person of the property. If S had mistakenly believed P to be retrieving P's own property, or thought they were merely borrowing the item, then S could not be liable as an accomplice to the theft – whatever P's own beliefs or aims.[25] Overlap between S's and P's intentions is necessary in order to protect S from liability for crimes S never contemplated. So, for example, courts have held there is no liability when P so departs from the criminal conduct contemplated by S as to commit a different crime, such as when P, in the course of subduing a watchman as part of a plan with S to rob a business, also stops to rob the watchman. Although S was complicitously liable for P's robbery of the business (and for the assault upon the watchman), he was not liable for the robbery of the watchman, since S had no intention that the watchman be robbed as well as subdued.[26]

We can recharacterize this subjective requirement in terms of the theoretical apparatus developed in Chapter 3. Let P perform some act C that can be described so as to satisfy the law's requirements of a crime of that type. For S to be complicitously liable for C, S must have the participatory intention of promoting P's performing C; that is, S must see C as something S seeks to realize. Second, S and P must overlap with respect to their intentions – in S's case, a participatory intention, and in P's case, simply the intention to perform C. (This is to say that P need not have the participatory intention of performing C, since P may be unaware of S's intentional assistance.) C, in these cases, will not be a jointly intentional act, though both S and P will be liable for it. Third, S must satisfy the volitional and cognitive requirements of the criminal act of which P's performance of C is an instance. Here is an illustration: S wants V dead and knows of P's proclivities towards violence. So, as a fistfight between V and P rages, S hands P a knife with which P stabs and so kills V. S is liable for P's killing V because (1) P's killing of V is the crime of murder, the intentional, inexcusable, and unjustified causing of another's death; (2) S and P both had the intentional object of V's death (or, better, of P causing V's death); and (3), though S did not cause V's death, S intended that V die, and knew that V's death was a likely result of P's stabbing.[27]

This account of the subjective condition for complicity is still not quite adequate, in two important respects. First, courts have occasionally relaxed the requirement that S satisfy the mental requirements for C when S merely knowingly facilitates P's performing C, for instance by supplying materials. In these cases, S need not intend that P successfully perform C, but only be aware that P does intend to perform a criminal act, and be aware that S's own actions will facilitate C. (In my own terms, this is a case of S intentionally participating in C, without intending to promote C.) Theoretically, S could be indifferent to P's success, and stand only to profit from providing the materials. One famous case is *Regina v. Bainbridge*, in which defendant Bainbridge stood accused of purchasing a cutting torch for P who then used it for breaking and entering. Bainbridge was held complicitously liable for the breaking and entering once it was determined he knew of the other's plan in its essentials – in other words, with respect to the type of crime contemplated by P. No

evidence was offered as to whether Bainbridge intended the breaking and entering, rather than merely intentionally facilitating it.[28] A
slightly easier example is *Direct Sales Co. v. United States*, a case
involving a mail-order drug company that made large sales of mor-
phine to a physician over an extended period, who was in fact resell-
ing the drug illegally. The Court held that not only must the company
have known it was facilitating the illegal sales, but that the "pro-
longed cooperation" between company and physician was sufficient
to find it a conspiratorial partner in the business.[29] In effect, the
Court reasoned that the large volume of business brought in by the
errant doctor supported the inference that the company had an interest in the success of the crime – that it sought the success of the
doctor's enterprise.

A more equivocal example of supplying materials is *People v. Lauria*, a California case involving the owner of a telephone answering
service obviously and widely used by prostitutes. Here the court
found Lauria not to be a conspiratorial partner in the acts of prostitution he had knowingly facilitated. The court phrased its holding in
terms of the illegitimacy of an inference to the intent of the accomplice. But in fact the court made clear that the real basis of the decision was the misdemeanor nature of the crime of prostitution. Knowing facilitation of a felony, the court made clear, could be sufficient to
convict.[30] A minority of jurisdictions have accepted *Lauria*'s pragmatic invitation to evaluate complicity on the basis of the seriousness of
the crime rather than intention: Rarely does causally significant but
merely knowing aid to even a serious crime suffice for accomplice
liability.[31] There is a troubling asymmetry between the accomplice
and the principal: P must satisfy both act and mental requirements of
the crime, while S can be equally culpable having satisfied only the
mental requirements. Any move, as in *Lauria*, to allow knowing aid
as a basis for conviction as an accomplice would further exacerbate the asymmetry between the positions of S and P. For in almost
any felony case that does find mere complicitous knowledge sufficient, S will not satisfy the mental state requirements of the crime,
since almost all felonies require more than mere knowledge on the
part of P.

The second caveat to this account of the subjective condition
stems from the rule that S may be liable for P's criminal acts when

those acts are a "reasonably foreseeable" consequence of a criminal act of P's that S does intend to promote.[32] For example, two robbers plan to use stealth rather than force in robbing a warehouse. But if one robber ends up assaulting a guard in the course of the robbery, both are liable for the assault, since it was a foreseeable development of the jointly planned robbery.[33] The rule of foreseeable consequence liability amounts to a major extension of the traditional rule of felony-murder/misdemeanor-manslaughter liability, according to which any party to a felony (or misdemeanor) becomes liable for murder (or manslaughter) for any death that occurs as a consequence of the intended crime; a night watchman's accidental death while chasing two robbers could suffice for their liability for murder. But with accomplice liability the foreseeable-consequence rule is found outside of murder contexts, as in the assault example. When accomplice liability is predicated on foreseeable consequences, the normal subjective conditions are not met in two respects. First, S is typically at most reckless, and usually negligent, with respect to P's crime, rather than having intended or intentionally facilitated that crime. Second, S manifestly fails to satisfy the mental state requirements of the crime, since S usually does not know of its commission in advance.[34] As I will argue shortly, foreseeable-consequence liability is very hard to justify.

### 7.3.3   Objective Doctrinal Requirements

If anything, the objective aspect of complicity – the causal or counterfactual relations between S's and P's actions and the resulting harm – is even more ill defined than the subjective aspect in the cases and statutes. Direct liability requires a causal relation between a defendant's actions and the legally proscribed events. An attempt to kill does not suffice for liability for murder, even with the victim's subsequent death, unless the attempt is directly causally linked to that death.[35] It might thus be thought that the law would extend this general causal requirement, expressed in counterfactuals, to the domain of complicity. And indeed, the paradigmatic examples of solicitations, promises of assistance, orders, and strategic discussions would probably satisfy a counterfactual requirement: But for the solicitation or order, say, the hitman would not have made the hit.

Provision of substantial material or technical assistance – weapons, money, building plans, getaway cars – also would satisfy a counterfactual requirement.[36] Without the getaway car, the robbery would not have taken place.

The problem is that courts have traditionally allowed contributions to suffice for complicitous liability in the absence of any plausible counterfactual link between S's contribution and P's act. In the leading case, *State ex rel. Tally,* the defendant Tally tried to aid a murder plot by instructing a telegraph operator not to deliver a warning message to the intended victim. Tally's efforts were independent of, and unknown to, the actual murderers, the Skelton brothers. Though Tally's aid could not, therefore, have encouraged the Skeltons, and did not, in fact, give them any significant advantage, the court ruled that Tally had rendered himself an accomplice to the murder: "The assistance given . . . need not contribute to the criminal result in the sense that but for it the result would not have ensued. . . . It is quite enough if the aid merely rendered it easier for the principal actor to accomplish the end intended by him and the abettor, though in all human probability the end would have been attained without it."[37]

Even more extreme is the English case of *Wilcox v. Jeffery.*[38] In 1949, Coleman Hawkins, the great jazz saxophonist, visited England on a visa that did not allow him to perform publicly, paid or unpaid. Hawkins attended a jazz show as a member of the audience, during which he was spotlit as a distinguished visitor, and then went on stage and performed. One of the paying members of the audience was Herbert Wilcox, editor of *Jazz Illustrated,* who had been covering Hawkins's visit and later wrote up his performance in the journal. Wilcox was punished with a fine and charges of £46 for his complicity in the illegal performance. Wilcox was one of many presumably enthusiastic members of the audience who might have hoped but did not most likely know that Hawkins would perform despite the ban. There is no evidence that Hawkins performed only because of Wilcox's or any other individual's presence, though doubtless if no one had bought tickets, he would not have performed. There is thus no plausible causal or counterfactual relation between Wilcox's act (or any other audience member's) and Hawkins's performance. Nonetheless, the court claimed that Wilcox's paying presence constituted "encouragement" and so a sufficient basis for complicitous liability, despite the absence of any causal link.[39]

The upshot of these cases is that causal responsibility is not necessary to complicitous criminal liability. True, in many cases it is possible to find a causal condition in the manner we saw in earlier chapters, namely by describing the token criminal act in finer detail. For example, if someone else had driven the car, the robbery would have taken place slightly later (or a slightly different robbery would have taken place). But, as we saw earlier, then we must ask why a causal relation to a token act suffices for criminal liability when a normatively similar act would have been committed anyway. And the task of providing justification for an affirmative answer to this question is far more difficult when punishment is at stake. Furthermore, actual doctrine goes beyond even this weak causal condition, as in *Wilcox:* on the basis of the evidentiary record, we have no reason to think Hawkins played in any way that was sensitive to Wilcox's presence or intention to provide coverage.[40] In cases like *Wilcox* that are not susceptible to causal analysis, courts have instead looked to such liability bases as approval or authorization, bases that are standardly invoked for civil liability.[41] On Glanville Williams's interpretation, the principal requirement of doctrine is subjective – S's participatory intention – and the objective requirement is only that S act in some way upon this intention. There need be no further objective link to P's criminal act.

Sanford Kadish has suggested that while complicity doctrine cannot be reconciled with a causal or counterfactual condition, it can be reconciled with a weaker objective condition. Relying primarily on the *Tally* case, Kadish claims an implicit condition for S's liability is that it must have been possible for S's act or encouragement to have made a difference, even if in fact it did not.[42] By this Kadish means that "without the influence or aid, it is *possible* that the principal would not have acted as he did."[43] This condition is easy to meet when S's liability is predicated on manifest encouragement or attempts to aid, since these bases could have made a significant difference to P's decision to act, even when they in fact did not.

The trouble is that a condition of physical possibility may rule out cases that courts typically include within the net of complicity. Perhaps S's attempt to aid could not, by contingency, be effective. But it is easy to think of examples where courts would find liability anyway. Say guard S believes he has successfully deactivated a plant's security system with the intention of aiding P's theft. In fact, S physically could not have deactivated the system alone, but P is anyway able to defeat it. I believe courts could still find S liable for P's act, on the basis of his acting decisively with the intention of promoting it.[44] It is also difficult to say whether the condition would rule out superfluous attempts at encouragement, as when P's mind is resolutely made up. Could S's encouragement have made a difference to P's act? Perhaps if P's resolution were wavering; but it is not, by hypothesis. Still, liability for S seems clearly justified.

We might modify Kadish's condition and require instead that S act or be prepared to act in a way intended to promote P's performing C, with S's act of a type that would ordinarily make P's successful performance of C more likely, or make it more likely that P would attempt C, even if S's act or preparation to act would not do so in the particular circumstances. More particularly, in cases of S's providing encouragement, S must intentionally and successfully communicate to P the proposition that P ought to perform an act that is of the same criminal type as C, whether or not S's communication makes a difference to P's decision.[45] And, in cases of assistance, S's aid, or readiness to render aid, must be reasonably calculated to promote P's successful performance of C.

Let me now schematize the results of this survey of doctrine:

S can be criminally liable for the commission of some other person P's act if:

(1) P performs a criminal act of type C, meeting its act and mental state requirements; and
(2) (a) S has the participatory intention of promoting P's performance of an act of type C, with respect to which S also satisfies the mental state requirements; or
　　 (b) S has the participatory intention of promoting P's performance of some other act C', such that C is the reasonably foreseeable consequence of C', and S satisfies the mental state requirements with respect to C'; and
(3) S acts or is prepared to act on this participatory intention; and

(4) The aid or encouragement that S intends to render is of a type that would typically enhance the likelihood of P's committing C successfully.

As I mentioned previously, conspiracy law under the federal *Pinkerton* rule further attenuates the connection between S and P. S is liable for any crime committed by any coconspirator that is in furtherance of the conspiracy and is a reasonably foreseeable consequence of the conspiratorial objective.[46] There is no objective requirement that S's membership in the conspiracy either encouraged or provided assistance to the coconspirator, nor must S have intended to promote P's act. Membership in the conspiracy does proxy service for both objective and subjective complicity requirements. Typically, S can only be found to be a party to a conspiratorial agreement on the basis of some act or expression, but these need not be communicated to coconspirator P.[47] This doctrine is strongly criticized by the Model Penal Code and many commentators, and rejected by many state jurisdictions as well as by England, but it is securely lodged in federal criminal jurisprudence, as well as in international war crimes law.[48]

So, schematically, when the basis of S's liability is membership in a conspiracy, then S is also complicitously liable for coconspirator P's act of C if:

(1) P performs a criminal act of type C, meeting its act and mental state requirements; and
(2) P has a participatory intention of promoting some group act $G_1$, meeting the mental state requirements for $G_1$; and
(3) P's act C is a component of $G_1$, or is a reasonably foreseeable consequence of $G_1$, and is committed in furtherance of $G_1$; and
(4) S has a participatory intention of promoting some criminal group act $G_2$ and meets the mental state requirements for $G_2$; and
(5) S has in some way manifested the participatory intention by word or act; and
(6) There is sufficient overlap in the sets of states of affairs that satisfy $G_1$ and $G_2$, such that S and P may be deemed to each promote the same joint act G.[49]

## 7.4 JUSTIFYING COMPLICITOUS ACCOUNTABILITY

The problem of justifying complicitous liability is exacerbated with conspiracy when, under the *Pinkerton* rule, a conspiracy charge is taken as a basis for accomplice liability. This may explain why, while the justification of complicitous liability is simply assumed for aiders and encouragers, only conspiracy jurisprudence attempts to offer an explicit justification of liability. I want to take up the justifications offered by courts and commentators and show where they fail. I will suggest that the justification offered in Chapter 4 of ethical complicity can go some distance towards justifying complicitous liability, though nothing like the liability currently authorized by doctrine. I will also argue that the current regime of treating primary and secondary parties identically, as well as all members of a conspiracy, essentially ignores the relation of individual participation to the group project. Doctrine has tended to "naturalize" the conspiratorial or complicitous group, treating it as the primary wrongdoer and then simply deriving individual liabilities from collective liability. This misconception of the relation of individual parties to the joint act has been the source of the incoherence in attempts to justify accomplice liability.

### 7.4.1 Failed Justifications: Causation and Consent

Since standard criminal liability is often linked to causal responsibility, it is unsurprising that the first efforts of justification attempted to assimilate complicity to the causal-responsibility paradigm.[50] In what follows, I offer my own justification of accomplice liability, grounded in participatory intentions. But first I will examine briefly the efforts that have been made, and offer a diagnosis of their common error. One of the most prominent early accounts is by Francis Sayre in 1930, who claimed that even accomplice liability based on mere knowledge plus acquiescence was straightforwardly causal.[51] Oddly he offered in support of this claim the case of *Moreland v. State*,[52] in which the defendant Moreland was riding in a car being driven by his chauffeur too fast and on the wrong side of the road. The car crashed, killing someone; the chauffeur fled, and Moreland was convicted of manslaughter. Though Sayre notes that there was no evidence that Moreland had "authorized, commanded, or incited the chauffeur to drive at an illegal speed or on the wrong side of the road," he approvingly reports that the decision was based "not upon *respondeat superior*" – a noncausal basis of vicarious liability in civil law – "but upon actual causation."[53] The conclusion is a nonsequitur. Though Moreland may have caused his chauffeur to drive, there is no evidence of a causal or counterfactual relation between his passive presence and the respect in which the chauffeur's conduct was criminally culpable. Only if we take Moreland's omission to intervene – assuming he had been sober enough to do so – as a proximate cause of the accident, can a causal analysis go through, in which event the case would not generalize.

Similarly, *Pinkerton* liability for coconspirators is sometimes justified on the causal grounds that merely joining a conspiracy strengthens the resolve of other conspirators and makes successful execution more likely.[54] Given the attenuated relationships typical of criminal conspiracies, it is very hard to take this claim seriously. In the *Anderson* case, for example, there was no evidence that Anderson's procurement of abortion patients bore any causal relationship to the doctor's performance of abortions on patients procured by other conspirators.[55] If anything, any one agent's participation in a conspiracy would seem to decrease the probability of success as much as to increase it, since each new member increases the exposure of the group to law enforcement. Then there is the further, and much more general, problem that accomplice liability is found even when the actor's contribution is marginal, as in *Wilcox*, or unnecessary, as in *Tally*.

Indeed, Kadish has argued forcefully that the very point of complicity law is to ground liability when causation cannot. Kadish's diagnosis of the problem points out the peculiar approach of the criminal law to issues of causation. He claims that criminal law reflects a deep-rooted jurisprudential and philosophical distinction between the world of events, to which causal analysis applies, and the world of agents, each of whom is a (potential) uncaused causer, an original source of events through whom chains of causation cannot be traced.[56] Nothing some S does, Kadish says, can be the cause of an

221

autonomous act of P, because no antecedent condition is ever necessary to P's autonomous choice – it is always possible that P would
have chosen differently.

Kadish is relying upon a metaphysically controversial conception
of agent autonomy. He claims that agent autonomy, a precondition of
criminal liability, entails the modal claim that the agent could have
acted other than as he or she did. Kadish does not endorse this
libertarian conception but rather gleans it from doctrine. But we
should pause to wonder whether it is necessary to read this conception into criminal law. The criteria for autonomy usually stressed in
the criminal law are psychological rather than metaphysical: Autonomous agents are well-informed as to the physical and moral/legal
properties of their actions, are relatively conscious rather than som-
nambulistic, are not drugged or drunk, are generally capable of reasonable reflection, deliberate choice, and derivative action, and are
not subject to such coercive pressure as constitutes duress. Certainly
this conception of psychological autonomy is compatible with causal
necessity, whether or not it is also compatible with a metaphysically
ambitious conception of moral desert.[57]

By contrast, with overdetermination – so often present in complicity cases – there really is no resort to causation analysis. Instead
we need a basis for criminal liability independent of causal responsibility. Courts and commentators who recognize the inadequacy of
causation often turn to the civil law of agency. In agency law, the
consent or authorization of one party to act or deal through another
(the agent) justifies liability for the acts of the other. Justice Douglas
invoked this basis in *Pinkerton:* "So long as the partnership in crime
continues, the partners act for each other in carrying it forward."[58] In
civil law, partners in business are individually personally liable for
the full amount of the torts and contracts resulting from other partners' actions, so that plaintiffs can sue any or all.[59] This is known as
joint and several liability: The act of one is regarded as the act of all
and the act of each.[60] This civil liability rule is in turn usually justified
on three grounds. First, the rule ensures the recovery of outsiders
who deal with or are hurt by members of the partnership; second,
since partners stand to benefit together, they should in fairness bear
risks together as well; and third, partners are usually in a better
position than any outsiders to monitor each other's behavior, and so

are effective pressure points at which the law can seek to minimize aggregate costs.[61] Finally, in choosing to go into business, partners can be said to have consented to be bound by the consequences of each other's actions.

Joint and several liability works reasonably justly in the agency context, despite the possibility that a wealthy (or easily suable) defendant who personally did nothing to incur the particular liability will nonetheless become wholly responsible for his more elusive partner's acts.[62] This potential unfairness is set off by the value of ensuring the recovery by the even more blameless plaintiffs – more blameless because they are not members of the group that collectively incurred the tort or made the contract. The tort or contract loss must lie with someone, after all. But we are talking about the distribution of criminal punishment, not tort or contract liability, and that need not fall on anyone.[63] Justice Rutledge, dissenting in *Pinkerton,* complained that conspiratorial liability violated the principle that criminal liability, unlike civil liability, must be "personal" – that is, solely a consequence of one's own active wrongdoing.[64] Although Rutledge limited his disagreement to conspiracy, it extends equally to accomplice liability. For there too, we find liability though the agent has done nothing that is otherwise criminal. The agent may, for example, only have provided a legal weapon to another, who then uses it in a killing. The accomplice to murder, however, is liable not for providing assistance to the killer, but for the killing itself – a violation of the "personal" requirement invoked by Rutledge.

It should be unsurprising that justifications for distributing civil liability do not work nearly so well for criminal liability. For example, "shared-benefit – shared-risk," a principle whose ground is a principle of distributive justice, would seem to apply only when the benefits are legitimate, and when those benefits are to be distributed equally. A gang of muggers fans out across a city, each performing one mugging with the same weapons and causing the same amount of physical harm. It ought not matter in allocating punishment among them how they planned to divide up the loot, whether equally or as a percentage of individual take. Rather, what matters is just what each intended and did, as individuals and participants. Furthermore, the suggestion that all conspirators are partners to one another implies an egalitarian structure that is probably as out of place in a large conspiracy as in any large legitimate enterprise. The fact that each stood to benefit from the scheme in some way will ground some form of associative liability, but it does not determine a principle of equal punishment. While it may be fair to hold criminal ringleaders fully liable for the acts of subordinates, there is little equitable basis for holding the subordinates fully liable for the acts of their superiors, and less yet for holding them liable for the acts of coconspirators of equal rank, over whom they exercise no control and from whom they may extract no benefit.

The third basis of agency liability is its effect in stabilizing expectations about agency arrangements. As a species of a more generally instrumental attitude towards allocating liability, this basis carries some weight in the criminal context. Although the state has no interest in enhancing the efficiency of criminal joint ventures, joint and several criminal liability does have a desirable incentive effect. For if each conspirator is liable for the most serious acts of any other, those with potentially minor roles and smaller payoffs have less incentive to join groups and greater incentive to defect and cooperate with the prosecution. However, this observation shows only that the accomplice liability rule serves a desirable social function, not that it is fair or reasonable to serve this function at the cost of punishing accomplices.

The final agency ground, that partners have consented to joint liability, does the most to justify liability in the criminal context, although it too does not go far enough. Kadish has suggested that consent is, in fact, the main justification for accomplice liability in the absence of causal responsibility: "The intention to further the acts of another, which creates liability under the criminal law, may be understood as equivalent to manifesting consent to liability under the civil law."[65] The initial trouble with this justification is that it is unclear even in the civil context what normative role consent plays. As a purely logical point, and as many commentators have pointed out, there is no direct inference from the claim that agents have consented to engage in activities they know bear certain risks, to the conclusion they have thereby consented to those risks.

What follows from the fact that agents have made an informed and free choice to incur risks is, at most, that there is no unfairness in their suffering the realization of those risks. But not always. I may have chosen to get money at night from an ATM fully cognizant of the attendant risks, but I surely have not consented to be mugged, nor is my being mugged fair.[66] To show that the harm is not unfairly borne, we must explore the nature of the risks and the opportunity set presented to the choosers. When it is not unfair, we may wish to call this conclusion *hypothetical consent*. In the commercial context, the circumstances for legitimating imposition of liability, and so for inferring hypothetical consent, generally obtain straightforwardly. Business partners have genuinely consented to engage in commerce jointly, against a background framework of liability rules relating to third parties. Though partners do not affirmatively choose those liability rules, their deliberate choice to do business jointly, as well as their ability to divide liability among themselves by contract or to shift their liability through insurance, can make it acceptable to hold them liable. But these legitimating circumstances will not always be in place. One can easily imagine circumstances in which asymmetries in bargaining power vitiate the fairness of a joint and several liability rule, or even of an allocation of liability explicitly agreed to by the partners themselves. (A gang initiate may agree to tag along on a criminal venture out of fear of reprisal, but surely he should not be punished as severely as the gang leader.) Without examining this background, consent – hypothetical or actual – has little independent normative force. In Judith Thomson's phrase, consent is epiphenomenal from a moral point of view – only the underlying facts make a difference.[67]

In the standard criminal case, only hypothetical not actual consent is at issue, and the factors that would ground an inference of consent would also directly legitimate punishment. Consent legitimates punishment when there is a legal code justifiable to the defendant, a sufficient background level of moral and social education, and alternative opportunities for satisfaction of material needs. If the criminal has voluntarily engaged in conduct that he had reason to believe violates a legal standard, and it is not unreasonable to expect his compliance with that standard, then some kind of punishment is fair. (But only some kind: a barbaric punishment would remain unjustifiable even if the criminal had explicitly consented to it.)[68] We need not invoke the notion of consent to reach this conclusion. Moreover, there are no grounds for inference that the criminal has consented to any particular punishment, for there is no objective presumption that he knows the penalty schedule for his crime, but only that he is generally subject to liability – a conclusion we can reach independently. More to the point, while business partners do literally agree with one another to share liability, conspiratorial "agreements" are usually juridical constructs, inferred from a coincidence of interests and actions among the putative conspirators.[69] Meanwhile, accomplice liability predicated upon assistance or encouragement need involve no agreement at all. All these forms of criminal liability involve is an individual defendant's intentional participation in a joint act.

So consent, like causation, is manifestly too thin a reed to hang complicitous accountability upon. There is usually no factual basis for its inference, and little or no legitimating force to its presence. My claim is not that we cannot justify conspiracy or accomplice liability. Rather, in order to justify punishment for joint criminal activity, we need a theory of liability that draws only upon the soundest available materials, relative to the courtroom's epistemic straitjacket. These materials are the objective acts performed by the defendants and the intentions that best explain those acts. The burden of this book has been to show how these materials can suffice for moral accountability. When we can best make sense of someone's individual actions by relating those actions to a collective project – that is, when we ought to attribute to him or her a participatory intention – then we have a basis for individual moral accountability for collective acts. In such a case, a person can be personally morally accountable to victims and bystanders for what others do, in the absence of causation and consent. The warrant for moral accountability is strongest in the circumstances characteristic of complicity and conspiracy, when one person intentionally promotes the wrongdoing of another (or others). If the Dresden bombers are individually morally accountable for their victims' deaths although none made a difference, then Tally can be morally accountable for a murder to whose commission he does not, in fact, make a difference.

But this point about moral accountability applies only indirectly within the criminal law. First, any adequate theory of complicity must justify liability for purely regulatory offenses, such as Wilcox's supposed encouragement of Hawkins's illegal concert.[70] Here, liability to the penal fine cannot plausibly be justified in terms of moral culpability for an independent harm – the wrong just is the legal violation.[71] Second, it was a major theme of my discussion in the earlier chapters that moral accountability is positional – the responses warranted by direct and indirect wrongdoing differ significantly. In this sense moral accountability is "personal" – individualistic in basis. We need to be able to justify not only punishment in principle, but also a specific level of liability. For even if some form of criminal complicitous liability is justified, it does not follow that accomplices should be punished as perpetrators, or that conspirators should be treated alike. The content of individual participatory intentions must be considered, so that accountability varies among the participants. And, third, even if moral accountability is a necessary condition for severe criminal punishment, it is obviously not a sufficient condition. I am, for example, morally expected to repair or apologize for unintended property damage that arises through ordinary negligence, and I will likely be found liable for damages in a civil court. But no one would say the state ought generally to punish me for negligent but unintended harms.

### 7.4.2   Accomplice Liability and Liberal Theory

In order to justify the imposition of any form of complicitous liability, even if not of current doctrine, we need to show how such liability is consistent with the more general goals and constraints of the criminal law in a liberal regime, among which may well be deterring (and punishing) moral wrongdoing. Rather than look to causation, consent, or moral accountability, we should start fresh, by considering the purposes of punishment.

As I argued in Chapter 2, the central function of law in a liberal regime is the protection and promotion of the interests that make its citizens' lives good. More specifically, a central goal of the criminal law is the promotion of agents' autonomy, and their protection against wrongful intrusions by both the state and other agents. The infliction of punishment is not conceived as a good within this system, but as an evil that is nonetheless preferable to more managerial or totalitarian alternatives.[72] By stressing the importance that a liberal legal regime ascribes to the autonomy of its subjects, Hart and

T.M. Scanlon have provided a good explanation of the reason we generally restrict criminal liability to intentional wrongdoing.[73] This restriction maximizes agents' control over whether or not they are punished, and so maximizes their autonomy.[74] If punishment were not triggered by the affirmative and cognizant choice of individuals, individuals would find it difficult to shape their lives around the law's constraints. Choice thus serves, in Scanlon's terms, as a kind of protection against the unexpected incursions of the state into individual autonomy.[75] In positive terms, intention functions as a justification of criminal liability only in the context of an institution generally devoted to enhancing and protecting the interests of self-governing, deliberative agents. Agent choice, manifested in intentional criminal acts, legitimates punishment because it reflects an awareness and acceptance of the risks that attend a given course of action. So long as the choice is meaningful, insofar as it is based upon a foundation of factual and ethical knowledge and defined against a reasonably accessible set of noncriminal alternatives, it is fair to impose punishment based upon that choice.

Note that this justification of punishment depends upon there being a close relation between the content of agents' choices and the wrongs for which they are punished: Their choices have to explain the commission of the crime. When agents directly cause harm by their intentional action, the relationship between choice and wrong is as tight as possible. They have chosen to commit a wrong, and brought about that wrong's occurrence. Complicity, or intentional participation, frequently lacks that causal connection. The question is whether the teleological connection that remains is sufficient to justify punishment. I argued in Chapter 3 that the teleological connection between joint act and individual participatory attention can warrant the ascription of collective acts to even marginal participants. When a given act or event is the product of jointly intentional action, in the sense that it lies at the intersection of the states of affairs sought by two or more agents, then it can be ascribed to each agent inclusively, as something they together have done. In a paradigm example of conspiracy or complicity, when two or more agents agree with one another to perform some well-defined criminal act with each other's aid and encouragement, these conditions are fully satisfied. A getaway driver who waits in the car outside the bank is as much the inclusive author of the heist as the gunman who enters the bank.

When these conditions of inclusive authorship are satisfied, we can justify criminal liability of each inclusive author for the jointly criminal act. The twin goals of a liberal theory of punishment, protecting the community against dangerously disposed members and ensuring that individual members have maximal control over their susceptibility to legal sanctions, are both served. The relation between individual intention and criminal act is close enough that each agent fairly can be said to have chosen to risk the law's penalties that attend the particular criminal act. Though a given individual accomplice may not have made a difference to the resulting harm, the harm squarely reflects the accomplice's will, and so is an index of the danger that individual poses to the community.

### 7.4.3   *Accomplice Liability and the Positionality of Perpetrators*

Inclusive authorship does justify some form of complicitous liability for aiders, encouragers, and some conspirators. This does not mean we must punish accomplices to criminal acts when their actions do not independently meet the criteria of criminality. The necessity of accomplice liability is a pragmatic question whose answer is ultimately empirical: Would punishing only exclusive criminal actors adequately protect the relevant interests?[76] But it is not unfair to punish accomplices, given a tight logical nexus between their intentional acts of aid or encouragement and the principal's criminal act. However, inclusive authorship justifies nothing like current complicity doctrine. First, it provides no reason in support of the criminal law's refusal to distinguish the culpability of principals and secondary parties. Second, if liability is justified only when there is a tight connection between S's participatory intention and P's act, then the foreseeable consequence rule of liability is likely to violate that requirement. And, third, the uniform sentences passed on coconspirators wholly fail to take into account the specific content of individuals' participatory intentions. I take up each of these points in turn.

First, in my discussion of moral complicitous accountability, I suggested several reasons for thinking mere participation warranted a less severe response than direct wrongdoing. Generally speaking, a mere participant may be less committed to bringing about the wrong than the direct actor is, for it is often true that agents will participate in wrongs they would not bring about themselves. When present, such squeamishness or ambivalence about the wrongful act modify the assessment we make of the participant's character, forcing us to see moral complexity in place of undiluted evil. From the victim's point of view in particular, the encounter with the participant, as compared to the direct actor, is less personal. One's response is more to the moral qualities of the act ("I have been wronged by this person") than to the direct malevolence displayed. Of course, as I noted earlier, the malevolence may be wholly on the side of the participant, who has ordered or solicited an indifferent direct actor into committing the wrong. But otherwise, more focussed and severe responses, from bystanders and victims alike, are warranted towards the direct actor.

Under my instrumentalist interpretation, it is not the job of the criminal law to make fine assessments of character, and the rage and resentment appropriate to a victim are out of place in a juridical context.[77] Rather, the job of the criminal law is to protect important individual and social interests through the channeled and justified allocation of violence. But a variation on the above moral considerations does have application in the criminal context. For malevolence and commitment to wrongful action are indicia of a threat to those social interests, and where they differ between direct and indirect actors, so too should the law's penalties.[78] When there is no reason to think the actions of a primary actor would have been performed by an accomplice, the law should mitigate the accomplice's liability. And, in the absence of a basis for thinking otherwise, such as that displayed by instigators, complicitous defendants are entitled to the evidentiary presumption that they intend to assist another's act, and nothing more.

Here is an example drawn from a recent English case, *Regina v. Hyde*. Three individuals, Hyde, Sussex, and Collins, were charged with murder: After drinking too much at a pub, they attacked another customer, Gallagher, beating him badly. Collins acted particularly viciously, by giving the prostrate victim a running "place kick" in the skull with a steel-toed boot. The victim died two months later, never having regained consciousness.[79] Let us assume Hyde and

Sussex only intended to injure Gallagher, while Collins became so excited during the assault that he formed the intention to kill him, and moreover, that Hyde and Sussex knew beforehand of Collins' excessively violent tendencies. In that case, it would be true of Hyde (and of Sussex) that he intended to and intentionally did participate in a serious assault, and he knew it was possible Collins would kill. Because Hyde would not have seen his own actions as a means to the end of Collins' killing, he cannot be said to have intentionally participated in the killing. Though Hyde has done something worse than simply joining in an assault – he has joined in an assault that could foreseeably issue in death – he has not done what Collins did, namely intentionally killed. And indeed, there is no reason to think Hyde would have killed on his own, but only that he was willing to participate in a process that results in death.

Despite the discrepancy between Hyde's (S's) and Collins's (P's) intentions, the court decided that Hyde's realization that Collins might kill in the course of a different criminal act, coupled with Hyde's willingness to participate with Collins, amounted to "a sufficient mental element" for Hyde's liability for the killing.[80] That is, Hyde's realization that Collins might kill not only renders him accountable for the ensuing death, but renders him accountable in exactly the same way as Collins. This seems to me to confuse precisely the issues it is the task of criminal law to distinguish. For if Hyde did not, in fact, intend to kill Gallagher, then it is wrong to treat him as though he has chosen to risk the penalties attendant upon a killing. It is fair to treat him as having chosen to participate in an act that might result in a killing, and so to treat him as inclusively accountable for the ensuing death. But simply equating Hyde's culpability with that of Collins is mistaken on both normative and conceptual grounds. The act he has chosen to participate in differs too greatly from the act for which he is punished.

Though current Anglo-American law makes no explicit room for the concept I am suggesting it needs – purely inclusive accountability – we can accommodate the normative and conceptual concerns to some degree through existing categories. For example, the crime of manslaughter requires conduct that, under circumstances known to the defendant, involves a high risk of death or serious bodily injury to another, and that the defendant consciously courts this risk through his or her own conduct.[81] Hyde's participation in the assault genuinely does satisfy this definition, and we need only rely on the notion of inclusive authorship in order to bypass the issue of causal responsibility. By treating Hyde as a reckless killer rather than as a murderer, we properly calibrate the punishment to the deliberate choice made by Hyde, and recognize the noncausal basis of responsibility that intentional participation creates. Looking to the specific content of Hyde's participatory intention, in other words, provides both a justification of his liability for a death that he did not personally cause, and a basis for distinguishing between the culpability of Hyde, and that of Collins.

Compare *Hyde* with Iago.[82] Having manipulated circumstance and played upon Othello's volatile temper and sexual vulnerability, Iago seems to be both morally worse and socially more dangerous than Othello. Where Iago reveals a general ruthlessness in the advancement of his own interests, Othello's crime displays a particularity that makes him an unlikely repeat offender – that is, even if he had not killed himself, he would have been unlikely to kill again. Criminal law, tracking both commonsense morality and future risk, distinguishes between the cold-blooded, instrumental killer and the passionate, expressive killer, grading the former worse even when both have premeditated their crimes.[83] So, although both are murderers and both warrant serious penal response, Iago's culpability in literature, morals, and law is far greater than Othello's.[84]

Kadish explains this intuitive conclusion on grounds of causation. Though it cannot be said that Iago caused Othello to act, since Othello acted on the basis of a deliberate and autonomous decision to kill,[85] Iago's actions are a counterfactual condition of Desdemona's death. This analysis gets something important right: We regard Iago, more than Othello, as the author of the deed. The trouble with this analysis, however, is that it fails to distinguish the culpability of Othello, who also caused Desdemona's death. We need to know why the counterfactual relation between Iago's deceit and the death is so salient that we hang liability for murder upon it. In one sense, the answer to this problem is obvious. Iago, not Othello, sets the whole tragic machinery in motion; in the law's terms, he instigates the killing. But I think examining the intentions of each explains better yet why we think Iago warrants more severe treatment.

Iago represents himself to be promoting Othello's killing of Desdemona, and so to be holding a participatory intention whose content involves their joint killing of her. The success of his attempt to convince Othello to kill Desdemona depends upon Othello accepting this representation. Othello trusts Iago's words not only because they confirm his fears, but also because Iago presents himself as a confederate, aiming to help Othello reclaim his cuckolded honor. But, of course, this representation is false. Iago's intention that Othello take him to be a sympathetic confederate is purely instrumental, a device for misleading the Moor. Unlike an intention to communicate actual good faith and trust, Iago's intention is not transparent. It is not founded on an underlying attitude of communicative openness and veracity. It is an intention to manipulate and deceive.[86] Iago, in other words, doesn't conceive the killing as a joint act, but rather as something Iago brings about via Othello. Our intuitive responses capture the nature of Iago's manipulative intention.

In general, then, instigators warrant greater punishment than accomplices because their intentions in acting with others are not so much participatory as individualistic. To the extent they actually make a difference to what the directly acting party does, instigators are accountable on the ordinary, fully individualistic, grounds of causality and intentionality. Kadish is right that causality rather than complicity explains the liability of instigators. But causality must be combined with intention to distinguish instigators from accomplices. A rational law of complicity would recognize this fact, by mitigating the accountability of accomplices and aggravating that of instigators.[87]

The *Hyde* case also reveals the problem of varying individual contents of participatory intentions with respect to the foreseeable consequence rule. Consider another aspect of Hyde's liability. There is at most evidence that Hyde should have known of Collins' potential to kill intentionally. Even if we conclude on the basis of this evidence, as the jury seems to have, that Hyde did in fact consciously court the risk of Collins killing Gallagher, this would only constitute recklessness on Hyde's part. We may, on this basis, want to hold

Hyde accountable for Gallagher's death, but it would seem that the only bases for doing so are (a) his participation in the joint project of beating Gallagher, whose actual outcome was unintended by him and (b) his recklessness in engaging in a joint project that could issue in death. It would seem, then, that Hyde could only be liable for either intentional involvement in an act causing an unintended death, or reckless involvement in a killing. On either theory, Hyde should not be charged with murder, which requires an intention to kill and not mere recklessness.

This point holds even if we grant, as J.C. Smith urges, that we should punish an intention to participate in an act that might result in murder more severely than an intention to participate in an act that might result in death.[88] It hardly follows from this point that recklessness with respect to murder is tantamount to murder. Unless killing Gallagher was part of Hyde's participatory intention, overlapping with the intention of Collins who actually did the killing, Gallagher's death is not ascribable to Collins as an intended outcome. As long as the law recognizes a distinction between intentional and reckless homicide, it is simply inconsistent to hold Hyde liable for murder. Participatory intentions can furnish a basis for the liability of accomplices for even unintended outcomes. But the liability that follows must reflect the unintended nature of those outcomes. The gap in these cases between agent choice and actual outcome is too great to warrant the severe punishment predicated upon intentional wrongdoing. In Scanlon's terms, the foreseeable-consequence rule means that accomplices will not have gotten the protection from the state they deserve.

The foreseeable-consequence rule is justified more by epistemic concerns than by concerns of justice. Criminal defendants are unlikely to acknowledge their awareness of each other's plans, especially if such an acknowledgement will substantially increase their liability. The foreseeable-consequence liability rule amounts, in practice, to a presumption that defendants intend (at least conditionally) what their confederates intend. This presumption is frequently well supported in fact although difficult to prove. It is, for example, reasonable to suppose that one who engages in a robbery with another known to be armed has manifested a willingness to engage in armed robbery. Similarly, in the individual case, the old rule that defendants were presumed in law to intend the natural and probable consequences of their acts prevented defendants from defeating prosecution by claiming they only intended some incidental or antecedent aspect of the culpable harm – for example, someone who shot another in the head intended only to penetrate the flesh, and not actually to kill.

But the rule of natural and probable consequences in the individual case is in retreat, in both England[89] and America,[90] largely on the procedural ground that it violates the requirement that the state affirmatively prove every element of its charge beyond a reasonable doubt. The foreseeable-consequence rule in complicity prosecutions ought to disappear as well. For while it may be reasonable to suppose that accomplices intend the likely actions of their confederates, or at least those acts in furtherance of the joint goal, it is also reasonable to doubt whether they intend those acts, particularly if they have shown no independent propensity toward them. So, in the armed robbery example, S's willingness to participate in a robbery with a P whom S knows to be armed should implicate S as an accomplice to P's armed robbery, even if S does not intend that weapons should be used. But S should not be treated as an armed robber himself. Liability for armed robbery is only justified when S can be shown to have placed himself in that zone of risk from the law's penalties. The foreseeable-consequence rule ignores this fundamental principle of penal legitimacy.

There remains one problem with a rule categorically mitigating accomplice liability. Frequently, in murder cases, no witnesses survive the crime, and so, if the murder was the product of a criminal group, there is no way to establish with sufficient certainty who actually performed the killing.[91] If the law did not treat principals and accomplices alike, there would be no one to charge with murder. But the problem is probably not insurmountable. So long as the penalties for complicity in murder are more severe than, say, those for mere armed robbery or assault, and penalties for participating in two or more killings are more severe than those for killing one, then this perverse incentive will be adequately compensated for under the general liability scheme.

### 7.4.4 *Diagnosing the Conceptual Failure of Accomplice Doctrine*

It may now seem that the injustice of actual complicity doctrine is obvious, for it ignores liability requirements internal to the criminal law. More damningly, complicity doctrine fails to consider the accountability of individuals as individuals, and so violates a fundamental liberal condition of the legitimate exercise of state power. So what is the source of the criminal law's confusion? The answer is found, surprisingly enough, in a conceptual or ontological mistake, rather than in evidentiary worries or normative concerns. The law of complicity and conspiracy in effect applies an organicist conception of collective action, treating the jointly acting group as conceptually prior to its individual members. This is, in effect, to naturalize the group itself, treating it as the culpable party, and then simply to impute the accountability of the group to each the group's members.

This reifies the joint intention that underlies all concerted action, treating it as a thing in itself rather than an overlap among individual participatory intentions. Once a mental state can be attributed to a group, so too can an action, and then the criteria of criminal responsibility are satisfied. A robbery in which one member kills is an assault that kills; the group committing the assault is therefore accountable for the killing. And since that group consists in nothing more than the individual members, the punishments devolve upon them. Each of these steps is potentially legitimate – as long as the crucial difference between inclusive and exclusive accountability is kept in mind. But by treating the group as an exclusive author in an ethical sense, and then simply translating that conclusion into liabilities for the individual members, the law ignores the modal distinction that justifies the apparatus of inclusive ascription.

### 7.5 AGAINST THE LIMITED CIVIL LIABILITY OF SHAREHOLDERS

Recall that a standard justification for complicity and conspiracy doctrine comes from an analogy to the civil liability of commercial partners. I now turn to commercial law, in order to examine the domain of reparative tort duties of shareholders under civil law. In particular, I will test the justification for the modern rule that shareholders are not personally liable for the torts and contracts of their companies. Aside from the sheer practical importance of the rules governing corporate and shareholder liability, probing those rules provides an informative contrast to our consideration of criminal liability. For, ironically, while commercial law principles serve to implicate individuals in the conspiracy context, individuals tend to be insulated from liability in the corporate context. I suggest that these opposite patterns of liability have a common source. The law takes the primary wrongdoer to be the collective and then decides how to deal with the individuals associated with that collective – either leniently or harshly – rather than treating them individually.

My claim is polemical as well as descriptive. The disparity between the law's treatment of accomplices and shareholders, and the incoherence of the underlying theories of liability, shift the burden of argument to those who defend limited shareholder liability. Given a general ethical framework of inclusive and exclusive accountability, it makes no sense to except shareholders from the reparative duties of corrective justice. There are certainly substantial practical reasons for favoring the limited liability rule, and those reasons may well be decisive. At the least, however, I hope to provoke a debate about whether those practical benefits are indeed worth their moral cost.

### 7.5.1 *The Background of Corporate Liability Rules*

The privately owned business corporation is a relatively recent arrival to the social and economic landscape, as are the great legal benefits attached to doing business in the corporate form. Corporations are unitary legal entities, created under the aegis of the state, with "personalities," or bundles of legal rights, powers, and obligations, distinct from those held by their constituent members. Until the early nineteenth century, little business in England or America was conducted in the corporate form, largely as a result of the great suspicion with which (nonpublic) corporations were treated by the state. The state-granted special charters empowering corporations imposed strict constraints on their powers and strict accountability for their officers and shareholders. By the late nineteenth century, however, and for an interlocking set of reasons, including the easing of state requirements on incorporation and the development of liquid capital markets, the corporate form became by far the dominant form of business organization.[92] At the same time, German "realist" theories of corporate personality began to take root in American soil and it became conceptually possible to treat the corporate enterprise as an entity distinct from any class of its owners or agents. These factors combined with a view, itself indisputably correct, that corporations are the main engines of national economic growth, at least within a competitive market. The corporate form is far more effective than, say, partnership, for pooling very large amounts of capital from many nonwealthy contributors – capital that can then be invested in expensive production facilities, research, and integrated distribution systems, all of which in turn can further reduce production and transaction costs.[93]

Because corporations are distinct legal entities, they can be the subject of lawsuits in contract and tort by third parties injured by the corporation's conduct. The liability of the corporation to these third-party creditors is often referred to as "enterprise liability"; that is, the enterprise, rather than its owners, the stockholders, is liable to satisfy these claims. Enterprise liability is in principle compatible with liability of the constituent members – plaintiffs might be able to choose among these parties, for example – but in virtually all western economies the principle of enterprise liability has as its concomitant a rule limiting shareholders' personal liability.[94] Individual shareholders are liable for claims against their companies only up to the value of their shares, which are their claim on the corporation's net worth. If a company's debts exceed its assets, the company must go bankrupt, and the shares become worthless.[95] But the deficiency in meeting its creditors' claims will not then be made up out of shareholders' personal assets. Their personal assets are wholly insulated from claims against the corporation, at least beyond the nominal value of their stock. Liability is limited whether the shareholders are many widely scattered individual investors, a small group of individual owners, or other corporations or holding companies. By contrast, as I mentioned in discussing conspiracy liability, members of a business partnership have to make up any deficiency out of their personal assets, each owner being individually liable for the full amount of any other partner's obligations to tort or contract creditors.[96]

The limited liability rule is an even more recent arrival to the economic scene, postdating significantly the triumph of the corporate form. The general justification for the rule is that small investors would not risk placing their money in a company over whose conduct they have little or no control if they faced the prospect of potentially unlimited personal liability. This claim is belied somewhat by the actual history of the rule, for, as Phillip Blumberg has argued, shareholder personal immunity did not arrive in England until a century after the Industrial Revolution, in America generally until the mid-eighteenth century, and in California until 1931. In all of these regions shareholders could be liable for several times the value of their ownership stake; and yet, all of these regions displayed tremendous economic growth and capital formation.[97] But it is certainly true that it would be more difficult for risky firms to attract capital with unlimited shareholder liability: Stocks for risky enterprises would be likely to sell at a lower price or to have to offer higher dividend rates.

As long as a company has assets or insurance sufficient to cover the potential claims against it, limited liability isn't a significant issue, especially not in the contractual context. Most companies in a position to hurt someone seriously also have significant assets that can be sold to meet their liabilities. And third-party contract creditors (e.g., bondholders or suppliers) are generally in a position to take account of the risks of corporate bankruptcy, whether by demanding security or higher prices for the transaction, or by declining it altogether. But there are contexts in which limited shareholder liability presents serious threats to individual and social welfare. First is when a company's product, like asbestos insulation or an IUD, turns out to have unforeseen, very serious and widely spread consequences. At the time of manufacture, it would have been unreasonable for the company to purchase insurance coverage in the amount it would actually need. Indeed, had the company anticipated the harms, it would not have sold the product. As a result, tort victims of the company will recover only a scant portion of their claims in bankruptcy.

The second problematic context stems from the structure of incentives to which the limited liability rule gives rise. In particular, the rule creates a perverse incentive to conduct risky activities through undercapitalized and underinsured corporations. This incentive is powerfully at work in the oil transport, tobacco, and hazardous waste industries and also in the taxi industry. It is, for example, a common practice for individually owned taxi fleets to be divided into many small incorporated units, each with assets of only a few cabs and minimal liability insurance.[98] Owners of these corporations, whether individuals or other corporations, are not exposed to the risks of the enterprise, and so have no incentive to purchase sufficient insurance. The result is that the risks are shifted onto potential tort victims – or, alternatively, that the actual costs of the industry are subsidized by accident victims. Tort victims of such undercapitalized companies can sometimes try to go after shareholders' personal assets by "piercing the corporate veil," in the law's colorful phrase. But unless the incorporators have not played by the basic incorporation and accounting rules, or otherwise used the corporate form to commit deliberate fraud, veil piercers are almost always rebuffed.[99] In fact, *Walkovszky* v. *Carlton*, the actual case behind the taxi example, is frequently cited in support of the claim that it is permissible to incorporate a business "for the very purpose of enabling its proprietors to escape personal liability."[100]

### 7.5.2 Is Limited Liability Morally Justified?

The limited liability rule flouts a number of commonsense principles of moral accountability: "Who stands to gain must stand to lose"; and, more simply, "Clean up your messes."[101] Corporate torts are consequences, accidental or intended, of profit-seeking enterprises. Ordinarily one might well think that the chief beneficiaries of those enterprises – a group identical with their owners – would have to bear the burden of those consequences, as opposed to their being borne by their unlucky victims. Limited liability also flouts the default presumption of tort law of concerted action that I mentioned in my discussion of conspiracy law: "All those who, in pursuance of a common plan or design to commit a tortious act, actively take part in it, or further it by cooperation or request, or who lend aid or encouragement to the wrongdoer, or ratify and adopt the wrongdoer's acts done for their benefit, are equally liable."[102]

The question I wish to pose is simple: is the limited liability rule legitimate? When a corporation cannot cover the warranted claims by its tort victims, ought those victims have a claim for repair against the corporation's shareholders? The relevant alternative to a limited liability rule need not be the joint and several rule that applies in contexts of smaller numbers, but rather an intermediate rule, such as a principle of personal shareholder liability apportioned to the degree of equity. I shall refer to this alternative rule as a pro rata liability rule. So, my question is, does justice demand pro rata liability?

There is a basic and clear general economic argument against limited liability, at least for corporate torts.[103] The rule clearly promotes the pursuit of risky activities at socially irrational levels, since those deciding whether to engage in the activities need pay only a fraction of the expected costs. The result is that profit-maximizing activity in these domains will take place even though the real aggregate (and marginal) social costs exceed the firms' aggregate (and marginal) benefits. A shift to unlimited liability would force owners to include (or "internalize") the potential costs of their firms' accidents, at least up to the point of personal bankruptcy, and so in the *ex ante* perspective would create pressure on firm managers to reduce these risks to the extent possible – so long, that is, as they wish to attract capital to their firms. True, differences in the structure of ownership between closely held and publicly traded corporations will affect the efficiency of this reallocation of risk. But there is at least good economic reason to think that a move towards internalizing accident costs through increased shareholder liability would be socially desirable.

On the other side of the ledger, forcing firms to internalize risks they had previously passed off to potential tort victims would drive up the cost of raising capital, since potential investors would demand higher returns to compensate for their increased risk.[104] And it is, of course, possible that increasing the cost of raising capital would have consequences that outweighed the benefits of risk internalization. (Employment might decrease, for instance, or there might be an undersupply of goods necessarily produced in risky ways.) Not only might such costs tip a distributively neutral assessment of the social value of the limited liability rule, but they might have decisive weight under a distributively sensitive calculation of its value, since they might well be borne by the least well-off in the community.[105] And finally, there's ample room for a wash in costs and benefits whenever the sets of potential tort victims and shareholders substantially overlap. This is especially true today, when pension funds representing large numbers of workers own a substantial portion of the nation's equity.[106]

I cannot assess the economic arguments for and against limited liability, but only mean to point out that the economic logic of the rule is not self-evident. Instead, I want to ask whether so limiting liability is consistent with the general normative principles of justice and fairness structuring tort law. Of course, if the normative structure of tort law is simply identified with an economically optimal set of rules, then the answer to this normative question will depend entirely upon the status of the economic analysis I have gestured towards.[107] But if the normative structure of tort law can be interpreted in terms of a broader view of corrective justice or personal accountability, as Jules Coleman and others have argued, then there is room for an independent philosophical examination of the rule.[108]

According to a corrective justice view, the function of tort law is to compensate accident victims for unexcused incursions into their legitimate interests by imposing reparative duties upon those agents warrantably accountable for those harms. The warrant for imposing these reparative duties derives from an underlying theory of moral accountability. This underlying moral theory may be modified at the level of application by epistemic limitations, and by the desire to satisfy extrinsic economic goals. Nonetheless, it supplies the normative foundation for any application of liability.[109] Corrective justice serves two ethical goals: compensating victims and holding injuring agents accountable. It is a matter of philosophical controversy precisely what relations among agents, victims, and harms give rise to such reparative duties. According to the orthodox view, injurers owe compensation just when the harm is a reasonably direct causal consequence of conduct that fails to meet a normalized standard of care with respect to its potential risks, except for whatever portion of accident costs may be reasonably attributed to causally relevant substandard conduct of the victims. In short, faulty injurers owe compensation to faultless victims. In some other specific domains of accident law – notably, products liability – a reasonably direct causal relation between the injurer's activity and the harm is sufficient to ground a reparative duty.[110]

All of these normative proposals have their work cut out for them, particularly in explicating and defending the relevant notions of fault and causality as necessary or sufficient conditions of imposing liability. I have hinted at the attendant difficulties in the discussion of accountability for individual harms in Chapter 2; and suggested, in Chapters 2 and 4, that despite such difficulties there is no principled reason why a just system of tort law cannot make use of a normatively constrained notion of causation as a warrant for imposing reparative duties. A comprehensive theory of corrective justice is beyond the scope of this discussion. Such a theory would need to take a position on the right way to relate the elements of conduct and consequence across a broad array of cases, for instance by way of a negligence or strict liability rule. Also, such a theory would need to solve many additional problems concerning, for example, how intentional notions like knowledge and care can be attributed to collective entities for purposes of establishing liability. Fortunately, we need not defend a particular conception of corrective justice in order to evaluate the limited liability rule, for we can assume that whatever the best account of corrective justice turns out to be, the injuring company has a reparative duty towards its accident victims, a duty grounded in causation and conduct.

To put the issue in context, let us adapt an illustration from the well-known case of the Johns-Manville Corporation, which produced asbestos insulation for many decades.[111] Long-term work with asbestos causes asbestosis, as well as mesothelioma and lung cancer, all fatal diseases that often do not appear until twenty years after exposure. (For convenience, I will just refer to asbestosis.) Johns-Manville apparently suspected as early as 1933 that work with asbestos caused asbestosis (obviously not so named at the time), and had considerably more evidence by the early 1940s. Nonetheless, it both concealed evidence of asbestos's dangers and continued to have its workers install asbestos without protection. The result, when the diseases began to appear – primarily in shipyard workers – was a large number of lawsuits and a staggering potential tort liability for compensatory damages alone, not to mention punitive damages. In

1982 Johns-Manville filed for bankruptcy, claiming that it anticipated 50,000 liability claims and damages exceeding $4.5 billion, versus a declared worth of $1.2 billion. By 1996, holders of valid tort claims against the company could expect to be paid only about ten cents on the dollar for their claims. These claimants are workers and their families suffering from fatal diseases and their financial consequences, diseases that are a direct consequence of their work for Johns-Manville. I propose that a rule providing that the Johns-Manville shareholders would be accountable to the asbestosis victims for the residue of their justified claims, on a pro rata basis, is demanded by corrective justice.

The Johns-Manville case raises enormously difficult questions of proof, procedure, compensation, financial planning, and the legitimate ends of bankruptcy law. I want to put aside those questions. I will instead make the following assumptions, whose purpose is to create the practical space for, but not determine the justice of, a pro rata rule. First, there are very many holders of valid asbestosis tort claims against Johns-Manville – valid in not just the nominal sense that a court has granted them, but in the sense that their claims generate reparative duties under the best theory of corrective justice. Second, there is no reorganization of the corporation or its assets that will suffice to pay these claims in full. The claimants will be left with a substantial deficit. Third, we will ignore the claims of all other contract and tort claimants upon the company's assets. Fourth, aside from a few controlling shareholders, all of Johns-Manville's stock is held mostly by small shareholders, each with fractional percentage of equity, who actively trade the stock in the secondary market. Fifth, these shareholders could collectively meet the tort claims against Johns-Manville through a pro rata assessment, either from personal assets or from previously purchased portfolio insurance. These costs would on average be burdensome but not ruinous. (If pro rata liability were adopted, portfolio insurance might even be legally required for all investors.) Sixth, information is affordably accessible concerning the identities of all shareholders and the amounts of their holdings at all possibly relevant times – for example, at the filing of each asbestosis claim – and it is procedurally feasible to impose a pro rata assessment. Seventh, potential investors would have prior notice of the risk of a pro rata assessment. Limited liability would not be abrogated retroactively. And eighth, the reorganizational goals of bankruptcy law can be achieved independently of the mode of settling the tort claims, for instance by permitting the bankruptcy to go forward once the shareholders have been assessed their contribution.

The suffering and death of the asbestos workers is unfortunate, and could have been avoided. It is doubly unfortunate they cannot receive the full value of their just tort claims from the corporation. But it does not, of course, follow from their misfortune that they have a special claim upon Johns-Manville shareholders for compensation.[112] These shareholders did nothing to injure the workers, and their causal contribution to the workers' suffering was hardly greater than that of you or me, or anyone else with no special connection to the company. Personal shareholder liability would seem to violate the Individual Control and Difference Principles. The Johns-Manville shareholders, I stipulated, are just anonymous investors with no power to control corporate policy or to ensure that business is conducted carefully.[113] Indeed, the divorce of control and ownership is, like limited liability, a defining feature of the publicly held corporate form.[114] Similarly, any small investor in a large company makes a marginally negligible contribution to the company's capitalization, and hence to underwriting the company's activities. Since no individual investor's action made or could have made a difference to the harms and wrongs done by Johns-Manville, personal liability for those harms might seem unjustified. A rule imposing liability would simply shift the costs of accidents from blameless victims to blameless shareholders.

This argument invokes the Control and Difference Principles as they apply to individual objects of accountability: harms that can be seen to flow directly from the actions of the accountable subject. As I have argued already, however, the Control and Difference Principles only strictly limit accountability in contexts of direct, exclusive accountability. They do not apply in the context of individual inclusive accountability. If we wish to know whether an individual is exclusively accountable for a given harm, then we will need to satisfy the object version of these principles. But if our question is more general, whether a given individual can warrantably be held accountable, inclusively or exclusively, for a given harm, then only the individualistic basis version of the Complicity Principle is relevant. Did the individual have control over the character of his or her relationship to the other agents to whom the harm is causally ascribable?

In the criminal law context, the basis version of the Control Principle was satisfied when individuals had well-informed participatory intentions to contribute to criminal acts. In the mass tort context, an individual's voluntary decision to participate in an intrinsically risk-bearing collective venture should also satisfy the control condition, even if the effects of that participation are indiscernible in the collective's acts. Investors who purchase shares in corporations, or who authorize others to purchase shares on their behalf, as through a mutual fund, do have control over their exposure to the risk that the enterprise's activities will go awry. Their intentional participation in the collective endeavor does not make them blameworthy – they have done nothing wrong by purchasing stock, nor have they failed in any way in their duties as shareholders (whatever those might be). But it does render them accountable in the domain of repair for the company's accidents, when the company cannot meet its warranted claims. There need be no injustice if the victims can receive their compensation elsewhere, either from the company's coffers or through social insurance.[115] We may even assume, following the argument in Chapter 6 that the victims' claims ought first be met by corporate assets. But when those assets are inadequate, there is also no injustice in requiring shareholders to meet the victims' claims, on a basis sensitive to the degree of their inclusive responsibility. There are difficult and important questions about which shareholders are accountable: who held shares at the time of the injury (difficult to know in disease cases like Johns-Manville), when was the first claim filed, and when were the corporate assets exhausted? There are practical reasons for and against each of these proposals.[116] I will simply assume that a reasonably practical and fair rule can be found. Whatever the rule, the conclusion follows that (some of) the Johns-Manville shareholders must pay.

The chief difficulty in this argument is one we encountered in Chapter 4: Many investors do not regard themselves as participants in any collective venture.[117] Rather, they may think of themselves as gamblers simply "playing the market," attempting to maximize the return on their investments. For these investors, a stake in a given company means no more than an entry in their portfolio. The company has no identity for them beyond its cipher in the stock listings. If such investors do not regard themselves as participants in their companies, then there seems to be no reason for holding them accountable on the basis of their participatory intentions.

The claim of the compartmentalizing investor thus raises issues similar to those of the compartmentalizing participants we examined in Chapter 5, notably Miriam, the nominally pacifist academic scientist with a Defense Department-funded research grant. Miriam did not regard herself as participating in the Defense Department's broader project of developing weapons systems, but only as performing her own research work in collaboration with her lab. She certainly did not share the Defense Department's ends. Nonetheless, I argued that she should be considered an intentional participant in the Defense Department's activities, and so accountable for those activities – including, most saliently, the activities in which the particular technologies she developed play a part. I based this conclusion on three main grounds. First, the functional characterization of her activity, which is counterfactually sensitive to the collective pursuit of Defense ends, renders her objectively an intentional participant in those ends; second, her subjective, compartmentalized view was not plausibly sustainable under her own reflection upon the objective conception of her activities; and third, in light of her awareness of the source of her funding, her compartmentalized view was best explained as a response to an underlying guilty sense of participation. Even if her subjective attitude were not vulnerable to disintegration, the objective conception of her activity grounds the demands for response made by victims or onlookers of Defense activities. What she in fact does, as a contributor to Defense research, dominates the responsive perspective.

The situation of investors is like Miriam's in some respects, and unlike it in others. Like Miriam, they have voluntarily provided assets to a collective enterprise. Indeed, their decision to invest only has a point given the collective aspects of the act. In the first place, investment is typically only rational when investors expect many others to invest, so that share prices rise. Second, and more importantly, rational investment presumes those in the company will do something productive with the capital investors provide – something better than what they could do with it on their own. This point is most obviously true in the case of long-term investors, who take profits in the form of dividends over many years of association with the corporation, but it holds true in the limiting case of any investor, even those who buy only to sell immediately thereafter.[118] For under orthodox economic theory, the price of a stock reflects the discounted cash value of the company's profit stream, and so anyone who purchases a share aims to capture directly or indirectly some portion of the collective's productive activity. So all investors are intentionally engaging in an activity whose point is essentially collective. Even if they do not take account of that fact consciously, their actions counterfactually reflect it. If their acts didn't contribute to the collective use of their funds in productive but potentially risky activities, they wouldn't invest.

Second, and also as with Miriam, for investors a fully compartmentalized attitude towards stock ownership is neither sustainable nor credible. It is hard to imagine a Johns-Manville shareholder who regarded the suffering of asbestosis victims entirely dispassionately, from the perspective of a complete outsider (likewise for Union Carbide investors in regards to the Bhopal disaster). These investors might not feel guilty (nor do I suggest they should); they might think the workers assumed the risks of their jobs. But they would undoubtedly regard themselves as occupying a special responsive position, not that of a mere onlooker, but as someone with "a stake in the venture." Similarly, in the 1980s debates over South African divestment, investors argued over whether promoting South African businesses helped or hurt the apartheid system. But few treated the fact they were invested in South Africa as morally irrelevant. There is a further point worth noting about the objection from shareholder compartmentalization. To the extent that psychological detachment is a product of the limited liability rule, which condones (if not encourages) such investor attitudes, it cannot be cited in defense of the rule. For it is obviously possible that a rule of personal liability would encourage the opposite attitude, one of moral connection to the targets of one's investment activity. So on both functional and psychological grounds, investors can legitimately be regarded as intentional participants in a tortious activity, and so accountable in corrective justice for its costs.

That said, the investors are unlike Miriam in that their form of participation does not expose them to the breadth of moral accountability her employment does. Employment is a pervasive relationship to a collective endeavor, both functionally and psychologically, as stockholding is not. Though Miriam lacks malice, her conduct is reproachable by those to whose welfare she is indifferent. Although she intends no harm, she is subject to legitimate claims of repair by those injured by the consequences of the collective ends in which she participates. Although she is undoubtedly a peaceful person, her pacifist commitments are open to doubt in light of what she does. Similar claims might be made of investors who target tobacco stocks because of their profit potential, or those who preach environmentalism but pay no attention to the toxic waste in their portfolio. But for the investors who really do not know the nature of their company's activities, or whose ownership is mediated by pension funds, trusts, or mutual funds, accountability in the personal dimensions of conduct and character is unwarranted. Nonetheless, they are expected to bear the costs of their company's activities.

Call these costs the "moral agency costs" of participation, on analogy to the costs borne by anyone who designates an agent to further his or her will, even when the agent's acts deviate from it. What we are distributing is reparative accountability, not blame or punishment, and its costs are legitimately borne by the personally blameless. Since blame or personal reproach are not at issue, there is no great unfairness in allocating these moral agency costs to investors. They may be regarded by all involved, shareholders and victims alike, simply as the downside of the investment gamble and not as a personal tarnish. Investors who wish to minimize these risks, or diffuse their impact, could avail themselves of the standard means of insurance or diversification. Better yet, they can put pressure on their companies to insure adequately or conduct their businesses more carefully, through investment intermediaries and paid monitors. There are already many groups of "ethical investors" to provide advice on the moral quality of investments, and "socially responsible" investment funds to filter investment choices. At the least, investors might begin to pay more attention to the public reports of their potential investments, refraining from investing in companies engaged in overly risky or socially undesirable activities.[119] Here the moral and economic arguments coincide.

On my account, the chief virtues of a pro rata rule are the just satisfaction of victims and, concomitantly, the reorientation of shareholders towards the full consequences of their activities. But these virtues are not shared by a rule passing on punitive damages. Punitive damages are granted in cases of intentional harms or harms arising from grossly negligent conduct. (e.g., Johns-Manville was liable for punitive damages on the grounds of its willful withholding of information.)[120] In theory, punitive damages are justified as necessary for adequate deterrence when ordinary damages will not suffice, because of uncertain enforcement.[121] They also serve to stigmatize the injurer for a gross breach of standards of conduct. In practice, jury calculations of the sum necessary to send a message are, to put it mildly, erratic. Because their expressive function is directed at wrongdoers, and because their costs are based on a moral assessment of those wrongdoers, there would be considerable injustice in imposing them personally upon shareholders.[122] Punitive damages are primarily a response to the exclusive and culpable actor, be it the company as a whole or specific participants within the enterprise. The deterrent effect is aimed chiefly at corporate managers, and whatever marginal increase in deterrence would result from implicating shareholder assets, that increase is likely offset by unfairness. Furthermore, except in rare cases where a company's gross misconduct is reasonably identifiable by shareholders, it is likely any stigmatizing effect would overreach also. This situation is precisely analogous to that of accomplice liability for the unintended but foreseeable acts of another. As with criminal accomplice liability, tort liability is only justified to the extent it is consistent with the underlying structure of intentional participation.[123]

There is one final worry about a pro rata rule I should address briefly. I have singled out shareholders as intentional participants in the corporation's activities, and on that basis they are indeed inclusively accountable for their company's accidents. But others are also intentional participants – for instance, corporate bondholders or other lenders, and outside but dedicated suppliers of goods and services. This raises the question of the comparative fairness of holding only shareholders liable. It might be thought, for example, that the status of shareholders as owners of the corporation is sufficient to differentiate them from bondholders or suppliers. Ownership is, after all, a concept with significant moral force in the context of corrective justice. But while ownership status is meaningful when shareholders are considered collectively, it is largely empty as applied to a small, individual shareholder. Secured creditors such as bondholders have more of a claim on corporate assets. So perhaps in justice these others ought also to be personally liable when victims' claims exceed corporate assets; or, if no meaningful line can be drawn, liability should end where it does now, with the corporate coffers.

There are two points to make in response.[124] First, the distinctive form of participation by shareholders, as compared to that of bondholders or suppliers, makes a moral difference. Bondholders can expect to gain from their association only the matured value of their bonds. Suppliers can expect to gain only the profit from whatever transactions they have with the company. But shareholders' association is, in a sense, open-endedly optimistic: Their financial stake directly tracks the success of the corporation as a whole. Because their "stake in the venture," to return to Hand's phrase, is identified with the profit-maximizing goal of the corporation as whole, it makes sense to treat them as specially positioned to respond to the corporation's misadventures.[125] And second, even if the potential range of accountable parties is somewhat greater, there is no great unfairness in drawing the line at stock ownership. Just as there would be no injustice if victims' claims could be wholly paid out of corporate resources, so that the assets of potentially accountable shareholders need not be tapped, there is no injustice in not calling to account other intentional participants. I already have said that the expressively thin species of consequential accountability that attaches when conduct is not in question may be regarded functionally and ethically as a simple cost of ownership. Potential investors facing the risk of personal liability will accordingly bid down the costs of shares; and, in a comparative sense, participants such as bondholders not exposed to personal liability will have paid for the benefit of their decreased risk. The result is no distributive unfairness between shareholders and other participants, and the emergence of fairness between shareholders and victims.

### 7.5.3   *Mistaken Realism and Shareholder Liability*

In general, then, a moral conception of tort law that imposes reparative duties upon shareholders beyond the value of their shares has powerful moral standing. Personal shareholder liability indeed seems to be demanded by the structure of participation between shareholders and their corporate agents. Given the criminal law's severe treatment of complicitous participation, what accounts for the leniency demonstrated towards shareholders?

One plausible, albeit philosophically uninteresting, answer to this question is historical. The limited liability rule marks a political victory by the groups whom it benefited.[126] And there is the policy justification I adverted to earlier, that the rule makes it easier to attract investment capital for socially desirably but risky enterprises, especially in the absence of accessible insurance. But I think a major reason for the law's continued toleration of the rule stems from a conceptual error in the law much like the target of my criticism of undifferentiated accomplice liability. Rather than conceiving of corporations as essentially cooperative structures, corporate law takes the separate entity theory as a serious metaphysical proposition, thus reifying the corporation. Although most modern corporate law theorists would claim that the days of high Germanic realism about corporate entities are long gone, I believe there is no other way to explain the near absolutism of the distinction drawn by the law between the corporation's assets and liabilities and those of its shareholders. The reluctance of courts to "pierce the veil" even in cases of obvious inequities to third parties can only be justified on the assumption that the corporation and its members are wholly independent of one another, metaphysically and ethically.

But that conception of shareholder independence cannot be justified on conceptual grounds, as I have shown. Once we realize corporations are constituted, in part, by their shareholders, who are each participating in the common corporate venture, it becomes impossible to distinguish thoroughly between corporate agency and the agency of its members. The corporation is essentially a cooperative structure of contractual relationships among individuals, each agreeing to participate by lending financial or human capital to a common endeavor. The corporation and its goals exist only in virtue of this participatory structure. Restricting liability to corporate assets only makes sense on the assumption that there is some thing, the corporation, and no one else, that takes risks in order to pursue gain. While such a holistic conception of the corporation can make sense in a theory of organizational behavior, and a corporation can be the legitimate subject of accountability, this holistic conception cannot exclude the accountability of the corporation's constituent members. For the corporation is the product of its shareholders. It is *they*, not a separate entity, who risk their money in order to pursue gain. For consequential accountability, there is no principled distinction between corporate assets and the private assets of shareholders.

## 7.6 CONCLUSION

Unlike conspiracy law, which makes the error of identifying the group with each member, corporate law distinguishes the group from each member. But the basic conceptual error is the same in both cases. The law fails to understand the normative and analytical significance of the relations between individuals and the groups in which they participate. In both cases, there is justification for some form of liability for collective harms, so long as that liability is sensitive to individual differences in the scale and scope of participation. I do not mean to suggest that criminal and tort law should simply track underlying considerations of moral accountability. The special responsive position of the state, its epistemic limitations, and the nature of the interests it protects must all radically inform the nature of the responses it offers. In criminal law this can be accomplished by modulating punishment to the specific understandings of criminal accomplices and conspirators. In corporate law, by apportioning tort liability to ownership stake. Taken together, these rules can do justice toward us when we act together, both in sanction and repair.

## Chapter 8

# Conclusion: Accountability and the Possibility of Community

We are by nature social animals, and in the intricacy of our communal life we often do each other harm and wrong. These are the circumstances of morality and justice. Fortunately, our power to hurt one another, whether out of malice or indifference, is but the unhappy side of our other great power – to make a community. Aristotle offers the appropriate metaphor: The hermit may be compared to an isolated game piece, stripped of meaning and function when taken out of its relation to the other elements of the game.[1] A person is given meaning and purpose by the responses of others. It is through praise and blame, reward and punishment, resentment and forgiveness, that we define and thicken the bonds that make us a community.

I hope my attention to matters of harm and repair has not overshadowed my essential purpose in scrutinizing these matters, which was to understand the values that sustain a community. We hold ourselves and each other accountable not because reproach is righteous and shame a virtue, but because in responding to one another we foster the relationships that make our lives good. Much philosophical writing about moral responsibility takes a juridical perspective, from which the disinterested writer metes out the appropriate deserts to the offending agent. This tendency is unfortunate, not just because it often transmutes gestures of repair into punishment, but because it wholly fails to capture the way in which actual agents and respondents are mutually engaged in moral, social, and legal relationships. Out of context, a reproach can be nothing more than an enumeration of an agent's demerits. In its relational context, a reproach can be an expression of the respondent's dignity, a characterization of the duties owed by the agent, and even a preservation of love.

Accordingly, I have emphasized throughout this discussion what I called the relationality and positionality of accountability. Responses to harm are always warranted in part by the preexisting relations among the individuals, and vary with the perspective of the respondent. I have used descriptive moral psychology, and cribbed from literary examples and memoirs, to make a normative point. As we think about the meaning of the harm we have done, and of the response it calls for, we must try to capture the perspectives taken of that harm by its sufferers and witnesses alike. The project of Chapter 2 was to articulate these different perspectives, and to show how they inflect the resulting judgments of individual accountability.

To say we are by nature social animals is simply to say we are disposed to live and act together, in collective projects. As I conceive them, our moral, social, and legal institutions of accountability are themselves collective projects, joint attempts to stabilize and foster our several communities of concern and interest. But, of course, accountability also attaches to individual involvement in other collective projects; and it was a principal task of this book to examine our ethical regard for individual participation in collective acts. This required first an understanding of the analytical basis of individual interaction and cooperation. I grounded my account of collective action on the notion of a participatory intention. Chapter 3 defined collective acts as the acts of sets of individuals who intentionally participate in a joint action, provided they share a common conception of that action. Because I aimed to account for a great variety of collective acts, from dancing a tango to fomenting a revolution to heisting a bank, I defended what I called a minimalist conception of collective action. Joint action as such requires only agents who act on overlapping participatory intentions. The intrinsic complexity of many kinds of collective acts will, of course, require far more coordination, but those are act-specific requirements, and inessential to the concept at the root of cooperation. While collective acts are just the acts of intentional participants, intentional participation is just the action of individuals who understand themselves to be promoting a collective act. The circularity of these concepts is inevitable but tolerable, I argued, if we adopt a developmental rather than reductive approach to understanding the psychological capacity to act together.

Having established the key notion of individual participation, I went on to examine its ethical implications. Both traditional consequentialist and deontological moral theories focus on harms resulting solely from individual acts. This focus, I suggest in Chapter 4, has made their application to collective harms problematic. In particular, it is hard to reconcile the intuitive, commonsensical force of what I call the Complicity Principle – the claim that individuals are accountable for collective acts in which they participate – with the individualistic perspective of traditional moral theories. The dependence of consequentialist theories upon causal links renders them inapplicable to morally puzzling contexts in which individual acts genuinely make no difference. Individuals, in these cases, have no direct, intrinsic moral reason to refrain from participating in collective wrongs. They have at most only indirect, purely instrumental, considerations in favor of refraining. Such indirect reasons, I argued, would not be motivationally effective, for they could always be undermined by the consequentialist thought that one's participation makes no difference. Equally, the Kantian tests of universalizability failed to bar complicitous participation, because the possibility of merely marginal contribution is enhanced rather than undermined by universalization. Since neither Kantian nor consequentialist theories could supply an explanation of the wrongfulness of complicity, neither could provide an adequate basis for individual accountability for collective harms.

Because traditional theories could not make sense of the moral significance of complicity, I turned back to basics – more particularly, to the analytical understanding of collective action achieved in Chapter 3. By making individuals' participatory intentions the key to evaluating their accountability, we can link individuals to collective harms independently of their causal contributions, while retaining ethically significant distinctions among individuals. The links between agents' wills and what they do are as much teleological as causal, and it is the teleological connection that principally grounds ethical evaluation. Just as my actions reflect my will, our actions can reflect my will to the extent I intentionally participate in them. In the terms I introduced in Chapter 3, the products of our collective acts are inclusively ascribable to me as their partial author. An ethical evaluation of me must reflect the collective acts I seek to promote. Only then will it fully encompass my attitudes to others and the way in which I see myself as a member of collective endeavors.

Ethical evaluations based upon individual intentions rather than causal contributions might seem in danger of failing to take seriously morally significant differences among individuals. All members of a collective may will the same end, while each makes very different contributions to its realization, because of differences in power, knowledge, or causality. These factors greatly affect our evaluations and responses in purely individual contexts. It would be odd if they played no role in the collective context. So in Chapter 5 I drew upon the positional and relational nature of individual accountability to show the similarly positional and relational nature of complicitous accountability. Responses to individual participants depend upon the nature of their cooperation in a collective wrong. While guilt and resentment may only be appropriate in cases of direct wrongdoing, peripheral agents bear various normatively freighted relations and reparative duties to the victims of harms in which they participate.

Chapter 6 brought the discussion from cases of clear, individual moral accountability to the more attenuated relations of what I called political accountability, in which collective harms arise from the independent acts of many marginal participants. I made two interlocking arguments. Very large-scale collective harms can only plausibly be brought under control if individuals have internalized collective-oriented motivations of complicity and solidarity and if these motivations can be grounded in the forms of accountability I explored earlier in this book. In particular, we can extend the notion of participatory accountability to encompass participation in the shared norms and practices that define a way of life for a given society or group. One can find expressive significance in cooperating to right collective wrongs, even when one's own actions make no significant causal difference. Taken together, the symbolic and participatory sources of moral reasons can maintain stable patterns of nonexploitation and mutually assured cooperation.

I also examined the other face of political accountability in Chapter 6: holistic accountability, or the accountability of collectives for collective harms. I argued for a limited sense in which holistic, nonindividual accountability is appropriate, such as in cases of systemic failure. In such cases, a collective is the only exclusive author of a given harm. But even such collective accountability must be accompanied by inclusive individual accountability, and ultimately, the responses of collective accountability must map onto responses to and by individuals. Accountability functions through the acts and attitudes of individuals, so even a conception of collective accountability must rely upon an underlying theory of complicity.

Finally, I turned in Chapter 7 to some exemplary legal contexts in which questions of complicitous accountability arise. I first made use of the analytical framework of participatory intentions to explicate murky complicity and conspiracy doctrine in the criminal law. Then I examined the discrepancy between the criminal law of complicity, which presumes the equal culpability of all participants, and the civil law of shareholder liability, which presumes no liability for capital participants. I argued that broad complicitous accountability can be justified, even within the constraints of a liberal theory of criminal punishment, but only so long as we pay attention to the specific participatory understandings and intentions of accomplices and conspirators. That is, the predominant rule of equal culpability must be rejected in favor of a more individually discriminating standard. In the context of corporate mass torts, I argued that we must rethink the limitation on shareholder liability, for it is morally indefensible and probably economically unwise. Shareholders are intentional participants in the activities of their corporations. There is no moral reason to refrain from imposing reparative duties upon them for their companies' torts.

As I remarked at the beginning of this book, the consolidation of social and economic life threatens the possibility of individual accountability. I believe the loss of a negative sense of individual accountability for harms also carries with it a loss of the positive individual sense of self. With respect to the collective harms that threaten our global age, all individual actions are essentially insignificant. These harms pose the great challenge to maintain a sense of the agency of individuals in a consolidated world. It may seem odd to turn for help to the counterideal of complicity. Surely, such edifying concepts as universal solidarity or cosmopolitan justice are more alluring. Reflection on complicity teaches us what it means to act together, when acting together goes badly. But the collective project of living ethically may find as great support in what it deplores as in what it prizes. The hidden promise of complicity is the conception of community upon which it draws: a world where individuals shape their lives with others, in love mixed with resentment, and in cooperation mixed with discord. Such a world is no utopia, which suggests that it can be made real.

# Notes

## CHAPTER 1: INTRODUCTION

1  Aristotle (1984), I.5, 1096a3; III.1, 1110a5–8.
2  Aristotle's treatment of this example is confusing, for his claim that some crimes demanded under duress are so awful that they must be resisted whatever the consequences appears to be inconsistent with his psychological argument that agency simply vanishes against certain threats. Rather, he seems to offer a report on what the community will say about some acts, independent of the consequences of any theory about the limits of the voluntary. For an alternative discussion, see Broadie (1991), 142–45.
3  Kant (1949 [1797]).
4  Ibid., 348.
5  See Korsgaard (1996a), for a persuasive argument that Kant misapplies the Formulas of Universal Law and Humanity to this case, and, more fundamentally, fails to distinguish between the implications of his theory for an ideal world of general compliance, and for the nonideal world that contains murderers at the door.
6  Levi (1988).
7  Aristotle (1941a), 1096a3 (Ross translation).
8  Or to the realization of a risk of harm. I take the term *Difference Principle* from Jackson (1987), 94. Gerald Postema identifies the "act-appraisal thesis," the claim that an act's appraisal depends solely on the causal consequences attributable to it individually. Postema (1995), 49–50. Postema himself rejects this thesis.
9  Douglas Husak offers a version of the Control Principle for the criminal law in Husak (1987), 98.
10  See, for example, Hart and Honoré (1985), 73.
11  Here is the quotation in full:

There is a time in every man's education when he arrives at the conviction that envy is ignorance; that imitation is suicide; that he must take himself for better, for worse, as his portion; that though the wide universe is full of good, no kernel of nourishing corn can come to him but through his toil bestowed on that plot of ground which is given to him to till.

Emerson (1983), 259. For a thorough archeology of the origins of modern individualism, see C. Taylor (1989).

12 A corollary to the Autonomy Principle, common in many conceptions of professional ethics, is something we could call the Agency Principle, according to which one does not do wrong oneself if one does wrong in the service of another. Think of politicians, lawyers, and the problem of "dirty hands."

13 By this term, I mean to suggest the doctrine in philosophical psychology of "methodological solipsism," according to which the intentional content of an agent's mental states must be consistent with the possibility of metaphysical solipsism, which is to say, independent of facts external to the agent.

14 Joel Feinberg explores the metaphor of a metaphysical "account" of responsibility, on which one's demerits are recorded by ascriptions of blame. Feinberg (1970d), 124–25. The metaphor is useful in revealing the impersonality of this conception of accountability: the "charge" of blame retains constant value for all would-be punishers.

15 Defenders of the individualistic conception often beat a retreat to ideal or intended causal relations, when reflection upon the vagaries of actual causal sequences introduces too great a role for luck. See the discussion of "moral luck" by Thomas Nagel, in Nagel (1979); see also the discussion in Feinberg (1970a) of the significance of luck in attributions of responsibility.

16 The causal solipsism of the individualistic conception supports – in at least a purely psychological sense – several other commonsense, accountability-limiting principles:

*Proximity Principle:* I am more accountable for harms to (or failures to help) persons socially, physically, or temporally close to me than for harms to more distant others.

*Positive Acts Principle:* I am more accountable for what I do than what I prevent.

*Direct Causation Principle:* Accountability for harms diminishes with intervening events (especially when events consist in voluntary acts).

*Dispersion Principle:* accountability diminishes if aggregate harms are spread over persons or times. (This is not the claim that harms are lessened through spreading, e.g. through diminishing marginal utility effects.)

*Parallel Acts Principle:* Accountability diminishes if other agents act similarly.

I do not mean to suggest that these principles are uniformly defensible in normative terms, even within the individualistic paradigm.

17 See Scheffler (1995). This observation perhaps forms a virtuous circle with Strawson's semi-Kantian suggestion that we construct our concept of generic causation partly out of the phenomenology of agency, in Strawson (1985), 122–25. The circle could be virtuous if, in the protean agency of our infancy, we come to learn that we can mark our environments, and this discovery leads to a more determinate sense of self and its limits as we practice shaping our world.

18 The obvious failure of metonymic responsibility in organizations is nicely evident in a recent *New Yorker* cartoon. A business executive speaking to an employee seated before him says, "Harper, we'd like you to become the company fall guy. The position comes with a generous severance package." Mankoff, *The New Yorker,* Oct. 5th, 1998, 44.

19 While the CI test can obviously bar free riding on a collectively provided good, it cannot deal well with intentional participation in an activity producing a collective harm, whether the harm be intended or not.

20 This is not to say the dominant neo-classical economic view, that only individual material incentives adequately motivate productive activity, has attained the status of natural law. Firms, families, and other collectives still play significant roles in global and local economies, and their coherence must be somehow explained. For a sensitive discussion of how individual and collective incentives, material and otherwise, might plausibly be combined to motivate collective production, see Riskin (1973).

21 Scheffler (1995), 234.

22 Postema (1995), 35. This article sketches a view with which my own account has deep affinities.

23 Ibid., 64.

24 Williams (1993), 13.

25 See, for example, Dworkin (1986) (although Dworkin rejects interpretivism as a guide to ethics in "What Justice Isn't," in Dworkin (1985b); Walzer (1993); and Jules Coleman's account of tort law in Coleman (1992)). I am indebted in this discussion to Sreenivasan (1998). For discussion of Aristotle's interpretivism, see Broadie (1991), 17–24.

26 H.L.A. Hart's discussion of "the minimal content of Natural Law" is essentially an interpretive rather than a priori argument that leads to plausible universal conclusions. Hart (1997), ch. 6.

## CHAPTER 2: THE DEEP STRUCTURE OF INDIVIDUAL ACCOUNTABILITY

1 There is also the normative but nonblaming sense of causal responsibility. A is causally responsible for B if it is an especially significant element of the set of necessary elements sufficient for B's occurrence. This sense of responsibility will be discussed in Section 2.5.

2 Nozick (1974), 60–63. Although Nozick's retributivist theory occurs in a

work of political philosophy, and hence might be thought to describe conditions for institutional punishment, it is clear he gives it wide moral standing. See also Nozick (1981), 366–93. Among contemporary legal writers, Michael S. Moore has been the most forceful in developing and defending a retributivist account. See for example Moore (1994).

3 Although any intentional act may be described in indefinitely many ways, retributivists privilege one description or set of descriptions to serve as the basis for normative evaluation. This problem of descriptive relativity is common to all nonobjective consequentialist theories. I will take up the problem in more detail in later chapters.

4 They would also owe the same response of praise to a good deed. I will not, however, generally discuss praise and gratitude.

5 It may be some of those standards overlap with moral standards, for instance, some forms of politeness, and some moral standards, cover all social transactions. I only mean to suggest that the basis of response in these cases is not, intuitively, moral, but depends upon other normative standards of conduct.

6 Sidgwick (1981 [1874]), 280–81. See also Joel Feinberg's discussion of Sidgwick's point, in Feinberg (1970b), 68. I do not mean to deny that a primary function of criminal sanctions is nonexpressive deterrence.

7 See Sher, (1987), ch. 5; Morris (1976).

8 Hart (1968a), 234. To put the point boringly, while the notion of desert may contribute to the threshold question of whether some punishment is justified, and may even contribute a further formal constraint of proportionality, the notion lacks the substantive content necessary to determine the appropriate response.

9 Hegel's attempt to rescue retribution from this problem by distinguishing between the "internal" and "external" aspects of the crime, such that the punitive injury to the criminal is equivalent to the injury of the victim, simply makes the notion of balance or equality vacuous. Hegel (1952 [1821]), § 101.

10 Amartya Sen, for example, allows for "evaluator-relativity" in assessing outcomes without making the truth of those evaluations relative to the beliefs of particular evaluators. Sen (1988), 219–21. I do not want to endorse evaluator-relativity in his sense, but only respondent-relativity. That is, there may be no perspective from which an act judged wrong could be judged right, but there may be many different warranted responses to that wrongful act.

11 These possibilities roughly reflect evolutionary psychological, Kantian, and Humean approaches to the problem of normativity. For a lucid survey of such approaches, as well as an argument for the Kantian approach, see Korsgaard (1996e).

12 Otherwise put, the moral and social strands of our relationships, in the sense of the norms governing our intercourse, are so tangled as to be inseparable.

13 My discussion of Strawson is greatly indebted to Bennett (1980), Scanlon (1988), and Wallace (1996).
14 Strawson (1982), 62.
15 Ibid., 66.
16 And Strawson rightly says that our attitudes to children are a complex blend of the two. Ibid., 75.
17 Ibid., 71.
18 Ibid.
19 Ibid., 72.
20 David Hume makes such a claim in his *An Enquiry Concerning the Principles of Morals,* though he grounds the disposition in a notion of self-interest generously expanded by our capacities of sympathetic identification. Hume (1983 [1777]), sec. 5, pt. I. Here Strawson may be thinking of Hume.
21 There is also a strategic, self-interested explanation of this tendency. If one agent acts immorally towards another, the expectations of all agents of morally proper conduct are affected. When moral standards can no longer be expected to restrain behavior, individual incentives to comply drop precipitously, and a war of all against all soon results. Thus, I am directly harmed by another's immoral conduct, because it lowers my expectations of being treated morally by any other agent. But I do not find this explanation sufficient to explain the phenomenology of indignation.
22 Jay Wallace also develops a cognitivist theory although his subtle account of the interdependence of affect and cognition in judgments of responsibility makes him hard to pigeonhole. See Wallace (1996). His book is deeply illuminating in its treatment of responsibility as continuous with, though not exhausted by, a natural, psychological account of our practices of accountability.
23 I mean to leave open what "suitably disposed" means. For Kant, moral agents are disposed to act only on the basis of "objective" reasons, that is, reasons that could serve as grounds for deliberate action by any rational agent. Kant (1964 [1785]), ch. 3. According to Scanlon, suitably motivated agents are disposed to respond to demands to offer justificatory reasons for their actions, and so agents act wrongly when they act in a way that other suitably motivated agents, also seeking common principles for regulating conduct, could reasonably reject. Scanlon (1982), 110, 116–19.
24 I do not, for example, want to argue for, or deny, any particular thesis of the form that concern for strangers' welfare should take, whether it be rescue oriented or welfarist egalitarian.
25 Scabs also threaten workers' concrete interests as general infidelity does not. However, the added element of insinuation seems to make scabs more resented than other threats to those concrete interests, such as overseas competition. I am grateful to Peter Levine for pressing this point.

26 Another way to put the point is to say, in Thomas Nagel's terms, that I regard these background moral standards as having agent-neutral value, that is, as making claims upon any rational agent. Nagel (1988), 152–53. This is not to distinguish the standards of abstract morality from those constitutive of more determinate relationships. It is because I value my friendships that I condemn strangers upon learning they have betrayed their friends.

27 Although the considerations characteristic of these accounts are agent-relative, evaluations of what agents do in light of those considerations are agent-neutral, in the sense they can be affirmed by any rational agent. If I have an agent-relative reason not to kill even though my killing would reduce total deaths, then so long as the agent-relative reason can be defended at all, it can shield me from the charge by anyone, even the victims' survivors, that I have acted wrongly. Compare the discussion in Sen (1988), 207, where he suggests that agent-relative reasons also entail evaluative relativity.

28 Unless a God (or his temporal representatives), who can forgive transgressions against others, enters the picture.

29 Wiggins (1991); and Winch (1965).

30 In the next section I will consider the ethical demands made in light of pure causality. Here I want just to focus on the intentional.

31 Melville (1969 [1924]), 478.

32 Ibid.

33 Ibid., 486.

34 It is a rule form of utilitarianism at issue. Melville earlier has shown his contempt for the general utilitarian principle that the worth of actions is to be measured solely by reference to their probable effects in his mention of Lord Nelson's heroic appearance on the bridge at Trafalgar, an appearance contrary to the cautious rules of the "Benthamites of war." Incautious it may have been, but, as Melville remarks, "the *might-have-been* is but boggy ground to build upon." Ibid., 442.

35 See G. Taylor (1985); and Williams (1993), 219–23.

36 Kant (1964 [1785]), 401 n.**. I have translated *Achtung* as *respect* rather than *reverence*. See Williams' comment that this moralistic form of guilt loses one of the chief advantages guilt has over shame, namely its tendency to draw attention to the victim. Williams (1993), 222.

37 I leave aside the category of victimless guilt, as when I feel guilty at going to the movies rather than working. I also leave aside pure status-shame, such as the shame at being ungainly. Both of these are understood under the more moralized model, where the fault lies in failing to meet the criteria of certain standards whose authority is, perhaps ambivalently, granted.

38 Special relationships, such as those between friends or family members, create special obligations of trust and support. It may be useful to characterize these agent-relative obligations as moral so long as their claims are

universalizable over other agents bearing similar relations to others. Special relationships may, of course, also give rise to nonmoral, nonuniversalizable obligations. See the discussion in Scheffler (1997).

39 This is particularly true if the debt of guilt only can be repaired (or repaid) through punishment. It is not only unwarranted punishment that creates resentment.

40 See Nietzsche (1967 [1887]). Responses to a victim that flow from a sense of *noblesse obligee* are importantly unlike guilt, for the debt is not owed to the victim, but to those who maintain the standards of aristocratic behavior.

41 See Williams' discussion of the Oedipus example, in Williams (1993), 56–60

42 Williams (1981a).

43 As Williams notes, one of the roles played by other moral agents may be to insist upon the rightness of conduct in order to erase the significance of an agent's connection to the harm. Ibid., 28.

44 G. Taylor (1985), 91. It is unclear whether Williams so distinguishes agent-regret from guilt. Williams (1991a) does not discuss guilt; and, elsewhere in Williams (1993) he argues that the archaic Greek response to wrongdoing lay somewhere between shame and guilt.

45 Of course, the driver also now stands in a special normative relation to my friend, owing her at least the courtesy of informing the cat's owner that the cat is dead.

46 This is not to say I would be morally wrong not to feel at all guilty, whatever that could mean. And of course, self-laceration is out of place. But, as Williams has made clear, it is both healthy and desirable that I do have such feelings when they are warranted. Williams (1981a).

47 Hart and Honoré (1985), lxxx. See also Honoré's discussion of "outcome-responsibility" and its relationship to identity in Honoré (1995a), 81–83.

48 This is consistent with a certain understanding of Donald Davidson's claim that "We never do more than move our bodies; the rest is up to nature." Davidson (1982b), 59. The "accordion effect" that licenses further ascriptions of events to my agency relies on causal relations external to me, but the particular relations singled out are, as Davidson would acknowledge, deeply dependent upon our normative concerns. See also Feinberg (1970d).

49 In which there is no more thorough account than that of Hart and Honoré. See also Mackie (1974); Feinberg (1984), ch. 3; D. Lewis (1986). See also my discussion of related causal issues in Chapter 2, Section 2.5 and Chapter 4, Section 4.2 of this book.

50 D. Lewis (1986).

51 That I will see it this way says much about my view of what constitutes appropriate relations among competitors.

52 Williams makes a similar point, in Williams (1981a), 28–29. I do not mean to claim that agents usually will feel this way, except in the most tragic of

circumstances. Few would be aggrieved by the implementation of a general, no-fault insurance pool for auto accidents, as is the case in New Zealand. Cf. Coleman (1992), 401–04, Waldron (1995).

53 This charge of circularity is the standard criticism of tort lawyers' use of the notion of "proximate cause." To say of a party's conduct that it was the proximate cause of the harm is virtually to foreclose the question of liability. Much of *Causation in the Law* can be seen as an attempt to give independent content to the notion of proximate cause. By contrast, Jules Coleman and Arthur Ripstein argue that for purposes of liability the notion of causation must be largely replaced by a conception of the duties of care individuals owe one another. See Coleman and Ripstein (1995). Although I agree with Coleman and Ripstein about the ineluctably normative nature of causal attributions in these contexts, the concept of causation still seems to me to have useful independent force.

54 I mean to suggest that even within a moral theory, such as Scanlon's contractualism, the force of claims of compensation depends upon the justice of other social institutions. In the absence of just economic and social institutions, some compensatory claims will have normative force they would lack under ideal systems.

55 The great English tort case of *Holmes v. Mather*, [1875] 10 Ex. 21, contains the first prominent claim that negligent or willful misconduct is a necessary element in a legal claim for compensation. Horwitz (1977), 85–99, argues that the move to negligence in American law expressed a deliberate social policy of subsidizing emerging industries. He notes also, however, that jurists focused on fault as a useful tool for determining liability in cases of joint collision, of which there were suddenly many. It should be remarked that strict, or no-fault tort liability has in modern tort law expanded far beyond its Victorian borders of keeping cattle, blasting, boiling, and keeping noxious substances, to cover most product liability cases.

Compare Holmes (1963 [1881]), 76–78, for the ahistorical claim that misconduct as a matter of morals and public policy is the appropriate standard for compensation.

56 How victims understand their social relationships also affects whom they identify as the cause of their harm. Whether Guatemalan peasants see United Fruit or their plantation supervisors as the cause of their misery depends upon the scope of their conception of economic relations, as well as their ambitions to become overseers.

57 See, for example, H.D. Lewis (1991). Cf. Adams (1985), which defends accountability for involuntary feelings, such as racist attitudes, and enduring traits of character.

58 This is not an especially communitarian point: Nothing follows about the extent or limits of my obligations.

59 Though it is certainly likely that the mechanics of shame and counterfactual guilt support the urge to repair. What I have called the "German

view" nonetheless makes sense. I may feel a special responsibility to make up for the wrongdoing of a family member without feeling guilty or ashamed by the wrongdoing. Karl Jaspers refers to this sense of accountability as "metaphysical responsibility," in Jaspers (1947).

60 See Tim O'Brien's novel about a witness to the My Lai massacre, haunted by the memory of what his fellow soldiers did, *In the Lake of the Woods* (1994); all of Gunther Grass' fiction, but especially *The Tin Drum* (1990), is an attempt in part to come to terms with the significance of his own participation in the Hitler Youth. While Grass can, of course, be considered a wrongdoer for that membership alone, it is the symbolic relation between the relatively innocuous youth movement and its adult counterpart that delivers the real guilt.

61 G. Taylor (1985), 92; and Feinberg (1970c), 231. Feinberg, however, means that guilt understood as wrongdoing (rather than psychological response) is not vicarious. This is tautological.

62 K. Anthony Appiah is skeptical of the notion of taint, regarding it as essentially atavistic. Appiah (1987), 222.

63 There is a related, prospective, integrity-based phenomenon: not wanting to be associated with an organization or practice one regards as corrupt. But this desire, whether aesthetic or ethical, to separate oneself from what one deplores, is not necessarily a form of accountability. One might not feel accountable for the wrongdoing, or in relation to it, but merely appalled at one's association with it. See my discussion of accountability for unstructured harms in Chapter 6. See Williams (1973), 97–118; and Appiah (1987). See also Glover (1975); and Williams' response, Williams (1981b).

64 C. Taylor (1982).

65 It is also central to the reconstructive historical tale Nietzsche tells about the moralization of the political community in Nietzsche (1967 [1887]), Bk. II. I echo his language here advisedly. See Section 2.10 for further discussion of Nietzsche's challenge to a complacent picture of accountability.

66 Austen (1996 [1816]), 324–25.

67 Although modern Anglo-American criminal law treats all accomplices as coperpetrators, whether they intervene before or during the crime.

68 Nozick (1981).

69 This seems to be Nozick's main use of the "r" factor: He classifies psychotics as having r=o. Nozick (1974), 63.

70 Of course, if the inebriation is self-induced, accountability will not be mitigated although responsibility will be.

71 Again, it is doubtless possible to make a similar point in terms of responses to the severely mentally ill.

72 Hart and Honoré (1985), 233. See, for example, *Spier v. Barker* 35 N.Y.2d 444, 323 N.E.2d 164 (1974) (holding that injured driver's failure to use a seatbelt mitigates the liability of the other negligent driver in the collision).

73 This weakness in the notion of degrees of causal responsibility is acknowledged even by Hart and Honoré, who struggle valiantly to defend the claim that legal notions of causation are more world guided than policy guided. Hart and Honoré (1985), 232–34.

74 Mackie (1974), 128–29.

75 See D. Lewis (1986).

76 Nozick (1981) reinterprets "r" in terms of the "degree of flouting of values," 388.

77 See Hume (1978 [1739–40]), bk 3, pt. III, sec. 1; and Smart (1973).

78 See Gibbard (1990). It must be noted the idea that adaptive pressures are at all relevant to the very recent and quite varied natural histories of these practices is immediately suspect. There are, however, forms of selection which are nongenetic – for example, tradition based. It might be that groups who can maintain coherence through shared norms of cooperation and reproach do better in the race for territorial domination and expansion. For a thorough discussion, see Sober and Wilson (1998). It's unclear, in any event, what normative force these accounts are supposed to have.

79 See the essays collected in Hart (1968); and see Calabresi (1970); and Calabresi and Melamed (1972).

80 Smart (1973).

81 Indeed, the historical efficacy of such principles as the township's liability for murder in medieval England may well have redeemed its social cost, in the absence of policing institutions.

82 Hardin (1988).

83 Even most consequentialists acknowledge this point. See, for example, Railton (1988). Derek Parfit writes of agents "adjusting their sympathies" in line with consequentialist reasoning, but I take it this is not intended as a fully realistic proposal. See Parfit (1984), ch. 3.

84 See Bennett (1980); Morris (1976).

85 Railton (1988) makes an effort to pull off this triple play. But his theory is dogged by the notorious instability of two-tier theories. The theory must endorse, objectively as well as subjectively, nonoptimal responses and dispositions.

86 Foucault (1979) further develops Nietzsche's argument in a historical vein. Foucault's argument, roughly put, is that the disappearance of torture from the penal scene, in favor of such Enlightened responses as incarceration, merely translates rather than transforms the way in which the state seeks to impose order upon the populace. The underlying violence of torture practices is still present. But Foucault does not claim a psychological foundation in *ressentiment* for disciplinary practices.

87 For further discussion, see Bittner (1994).

88 For that matter, Nietzsche's "history" of the slave revolt in morality is little more far-fetched than the adaptationist theodicies favored by evolutionary psychologists.

89 I owe this point to Williams (1995a).

90 Nietzsche (1967 [1887]), Bk. I, ¶ 13, p. 45.

91 Recall that for Kant, an offense against a particular agent is really an offense against humanity in that agent, because the essence of wrongdoing is a violation of the demands of universality, demands originating in our common rational nature. Kant (1964 [1785]), Bk. III.

92 *Cf.* Bittner (1994).

93 Nietzsche (1967 [1887]), Bk II, ¶ 5, p. 65.

94 I have already noted earlier, in Section 2.6, some of the dysfunctions of guilt.

95 Ibid., Bk. I, ¶ 11, p. 40. (The weak are constrained anyway by their very weakness, which moral restraints merely veil.)

96 Ibid., Bk. I, ¶ 10, p. 39. (I have reversed the order of the clauses in the quotation.)

97 Spinoza (1982). For an illuminating discussion, see Bittner (1992).

98 Perhaps Nietzsche was not wholly ironic when he wrote: "With the aid of such images and procedures [of torture] one finally remembers five or six 'I will not's,' in regard to which one had given one's *promise* so as to participate in the advantages of society – and it was indeed with the aid of this kind of memory that one at last came to reason." Nietzsche (1967 [1887]). Bk. II, ¶ 3, p. 62.

99 For a discussion of the relations among forgiveness, mercy, and an underlying conception of moral value, see Murphy and Hampton (1988).

100 For a literary exploration of the dangerous and complicitous urge to forgive when lovers have done great evil, see Bernhard Schlink's novel, *The Reader* (1999). See also Murphy, "Forgiveness and Resentment," in Murphy and Hampton (1988).

101 In Kutz (1994) I argue that normative indeterminacy (or, better, underdeterminacy) is a valuable feature of legal systems, allowing for greater exposure to and reflection upon the evaluative decisions members of a political community must confront.

102 An important exception to this rule is civil rights law, such as school desegregation and voting rights. Legal responses in this domain are characterized by what Owen Fiss has called the "structural injunction," a complexly "polycentric" and systematic attempt to restructure basic social institutions. See Fiss (1978).

103 This distinction can be better seen in the case of individual morality. It is not wrong for me to insist that you not do what you have no right to do, but unless my right protects a very important or vulnerable interest, it is wrong for me to threaten or hurt you.

104 Mackie (1977b), 187–88.

105 Hart (1968b); Scanlon (1988).

106 With the important and largely deplorable exception of Anglo-American conspiracy law, according to which liability can be incurred at a very early stage of planning.

107 It is worth noting that criminal sentencing is heavily characterological, especially in death penalty proceedings. Punishment is aggravated or mitigated in proportion to the moral worth of the convicted.

108 An account of these goals, and disputes over their importance, can be found in Coleman (1992); Calabresi (1970); and Schuck (1987).

109 The attraction of nonrelational, retributive models of accountability may be due to the seduction of moral philosophers by a purely juridical conception of accountability.

110 Even when the state is apparently the victim, as in tax fraud or treason, we must keep in mind that it has no tax or security interests of its own, but only those of its constituents. This derivative status renders its position, normatively at least, wholly unlike the positions of unmediated victimhood. I am again grateful to Peter Levine for pressing this point.

111 This suggests a modification to Sidgwick's (and Feinberg's) claim, cited in Section 2.2, that punishment is resentment universalized. When punishment is that, as in the case of the death penalty, it is at least unjust punishment. A conception of punishment as universalized indignation is far more appropriate.

## CHAPTER 3: ACTING TOGETHER

1 I will only be discussing in this chapter cases of joint action that are intended by the individual participants. Not all cases of coordination or joint outcomes are so intended by the participants. Sometimes coordination is a result of a third-party planner's intention, as when a city planner coordinates traffic flow among individual drivers. Sometimes jointly achieved outcomes are not intended by anyone, such as invisible hand or tragedy of the commons effects which are brought about by individually oriented economic activity. And some forms of coordination may take place without any intentions at all, as when geese fly in a well-defined pattern, or coughing among a concert audience takes place in blocs. Unintended joint outcomes of intentional activity will be my topic in Chapter 5.

2 John Searle and Margaret Gilbert are tempted by this holistic route, although it is ultimately unclear what each means by reducibility. See Searle (1990); and Gilbert (1989). I discuss these claims in Section 3.5.

3 In these paragraphs, I follow James (1984), ch. 1; and Hillel-Ruben (1985), ch. 1.

4 Three forms of reduction are actually at issue here: (1) ontological, whether collective entities are nothing but sets of individuals; (2) logical/conceptual, whether sentences about collective entities can be replaced by logically equivalent sentences about only individuals; and (3) explanatory: whether a given phenomenon or effect can be better explained by reference only to individuals and their properties.

5 Of course, a thoroughgoing individualist could not identify the appropriate set of individuals as Exxon employees, or the object of trading as Exxon stock.

6 See van Fraasen, "The Pragmatics of Explanation," in van Fraasen (1980); and Kitcher (1989).

7 It is labeled "formal individualism" by Bernard Williams, in Williams (1995c). This weak individualism is also shared with Jon Elster; see Elster (1985), 27–29.

8 See Sober and Wilson (1998) for an argument for the possibility of group selection of altruistic norms.

9 See Hillel-Ruben (1985), ch. 3. There may be nonmereological and nonself-identifying social groups as well, such as social classes defined by their economic interests. Whether such groups can play an explanatory role in social science is a question beyond the scope of this book.

10 See Davidson (1980a) and (1980c).

11 Furthermore, the causal connection between mental states and actions must be reasonably direct, so as to exclude wayward causal chains.

12 Since intentions are intensional, the relation between possible descriptions of events as intentional cannot be simply one of logical equivalence or codenotation. The constraints on appropriate redescription seem to depend on a complex set of psychological and linguistic assumptions. For example, it is probably appropriate to redescribe my making a tuna sandwich as my making a sandwich on rye, or my using up the bread in the refrigerator, if these facts about my sandwich are perceptually salient. But it might be odd to redescribe it as my intentionally eating the first tuna sandwich of the week, even if I know this of my sandwich as well. A theory of salience seems to be doing the work here.

13 This is John Searle's formulation. See Searle (1983), ch. 3.

14 This claim is too strong, because circumstances and consequences also contribute to the characterization of an action. The difference between a killing and attempted murder lies in the fact of death, for example.

15 If he mistakenly pulls out a revolver instead, we would still qualify our description of his action in order to reveal its unintentional aspect.

16 This is an oblique reference to Joel Feinberg's "accordion effect," by means of which "basic actions," or actions I do in order to do something else, may be redescribed in terms of their causal or conceptual consequences. Feinberg (1970d), 134. Feinberg refers to this as a principle of (normative) causal responsibility. I am responsible for what I do and what is caused by what I do. Here, however, I wish to use it as a principle for licensing redescriptions of events, either as causal consequences or as intended consequences. If I intend to do M as a means to E, and M produces E, then my doing M can be redescribed as my doing E. (Unless, that is, E is a very distant causal consequence of M.)

17 See Bratman (1987), 9–11; Block (1980); Grice (1991), 124–25; and D. Lewis (1983).

18 In a general scheme for accounting for mental states, beliefs and desires can be neither inputs nor outputs. But once those states have been functionally specified, they can occur in the definitions of further states, such as intentions.

19 This is Davidson's approach. See Davidson (1984a) and (1984b).

20 The example is Bratman's; the treatment is largely mine. See Bratman (1999a).

21 We must distinguish the more restrictive notion of sharing a goal from having the same goal, which requires only that agents intend the same type of activity or outcome. You and I might have the same goal of going to Chicago by air, and our goals will be satisfied so long as each of us flies to Chicago, though not necessarily on the same flight. By contrast, when we share a goal, the intentions of each are only satisfied by the performance or realization of the same token activity or outcome. We share the goal of going to Chicago when specification of the goal makes reference to the acts of the other, so that we each only achieve our goals when the other comes too.

22 As developed by David Lewis in D. Lewis (1968), 52–60, the claim that some proposition $p$ is an item of comment knowledge among individuals means that each knows $p$, and moreover each knows that each knows that $p$ . . . indefinitely iterated. The weaker idea of mutual openness, or mutually favorable attitudes towards the other's awareness, is also an iterative concept, since each is open to the other's openness to one's own awareness, but nothing in my analysis depends on the logical structure of that iteration. If our intentions do in fact become known to the other, then the cognitively demanding state of common knowledge may obtain. But see Sperber and Wilson (1986), 38–45, for the weaker, and so more pliable, notion of mutual manifestness, which accounts for the shared cognitive background of speakers, a background that need not be the object of explicit beliefs in order to serve its role in assigning determinate content to each other's potentially ambiguous utterances. A fact is mutually manifest to a set of individuals if each individual is capable of representing that fact and accepting it as probably true, and this fact is further manifest to each individual. So, more precisely, mutual openness consists in dispositions favorable to mutual manifestness.

23 Cf. Bratman (1999a), 100.

24 See Hollis and Sugden (1993); Gilbert (1989), 330–36; and Hurley (1988), 145–48. Regan (1980) makes a similar argument in the context of a critique of act utilitarianism, in ch. 2.

25 In game-theory jargon, a pair of choices is a (Nash) equilibrium if and only if each choice is a best reply to the other, that is, if neither player can unilaterally improve his position.

26 There is one other possible solution, actually: We could individually adopt "mixed" strategies, whereby we assign a possibility to the other's possible choice, and randomize our choices in light of the probabilities.

The chief problem with this approach is that its expected value is necessarily lower than that secured by the cooperative solution, because we must on some occasions end up on the train instead of the plane. For discussion, see Regan (1980), 196–98.

27 But it is an addition – it does not follow from the axioms of game theory. See Hollis and Sugden (1993), 11.

28 Again, the competitive context may be the product of cooperation.

29 Postema (1995). As Susan Hurley puts it, they "transform the conceptual unit of agency." Hurley (1988), 145–48. See also Schelling, (1960/1980), ch. 3 and app. C.

30 The last category, being a group of a certain type, might not seem to count as a collective end. But in groups that are defined in part by normatively structured behavior, each member helps to constitute that group (make it the group it is) by acting in conformity with the group's internal standards.

31 One can, of course, be mistaken about the identity of one's coactor, or even about the coactor's nature, as when I discover the person I thought I was playing Internet chess against is in fact a computer. I mean only there is no way two agents can play chess together or dance the tango purely fortuitously, such that it is a discovery to them that they have engaged in a joint activity at all.

32 Problems of overdetermination arise here. I might have worn dark suits anyway, but do in fact wear them as part of fitting into IBM corporate culture. In such cases of overdetermination, we must either expand the domain of the counterfactual's antecedents (i.e., I wouldn't ordinarily wear suits and I don't work at IBM), or avoid the counterfactual altogether and simply rely upon a noncounterfactual, realist claim about the reasons that motivate my action.

33 See Searle (1990), 405.

34 The requirement of counterfactual sensitivity is still met, so long as the workers would slow down if the crisis called for that behavior instead.

35 One problem with what Erving Goffman calls "dramaturgical" sociology, or the explanation of behavior in terms of scripts and roles, is that such approaches presume a scripted role. But any realistic social script is highly underdetermined, leaving agents with the practical problem of determining what content the role demands. A theory of roles must therefore presume also a role-bound model of practical reasoning, and this is what participatory intentions provide. See Goffman (1959).

36 Aristotle likens practical reasoning to solving problems of geometrical construction: One disassembles the given figure into its components until one arrives at a part one can construct from basic elements. Aristotle (1985), bk. III. 3, 1112b15–25. See also Cooper (1985), 10–18.

37 The obligations need not be moral. If I have agreed to do my part in a crime, then I am presumably not under a moral obligation to help with the crime. However, relative to the norms that structure cooperative un-

dertakings, there may be some sense in which I ought to do my part in any collective act in which I have deliberately incurred others' reliance. See Scanlon (1990); see also Bratman, (1999c), 130–41.

38 My reasons for promoting the group act may also not be strict functions of my desire that the group act be realized. I may, for example, do my part in a double play not because I want our double play to be successful (perhaps I have bet against my team), but because I don't want my treachery to be obvious.

39 At least, the issue of free riding on my own act cannot arise without an extremely Parfitian view of personal identity.

40 Bratman (1999a), 96–97. I hope it is clear, despite my disagreements, how much I owe to Bratman's work, as well as to Gilbert, Searle, Tuomela and Miller, and Velleman.

41 Bratman (1999d), 147–48.

42 A similar point can be made about linguistic intentions. An account of communication, like Paul Grice's, can allow for irreducibly linguistic intentions at a later developmental stage so long as there is room at earlier stages for explanation of language use in terms of prelinguistic intentions. See Grice (1957) and (1989b).

43 My distinction is akin to Bratman's between plans and subplans. See Bratman (1987). Since plans represent for him both the contents of intentions and intentional commitments themselves, plans can motivate subplans. However, the notion of executive and subsidiary intentions seems better to accommodate interpersonal relations.

44 Searle (1990).

45 Tuomela and Miller (1991). Tuomela has developed a detailed account of collective action in later work. See, for example, Tuomela (1995). His treatment goes considerably beyond the joint paper under discussion. However, I focus on this earlier paper because of the comparative simplicity of its presentation, and because Tuomela's later work still rejects the minimalist view I argue towards here. I am grateful to Tuomela for discussion of my argument.

46 Searle (1990), 405.

47 If one thinks that acting with knowledge of producing a result is intentionally producing that result, then both groups will jointly intentionally benefit humanity. But only members of the second group intend that result, and that is what distinguishes them from the first set of members.

A similar argument applies to Searle's distinction between a set of individuals independently running to a shelter because of a rainstorm, and a *corps de ballet* making exactly the same moves. Members of the second group, but not the first, make their movements in order to promote the group outcome of the realized dance. The first group's members have no such instrumental intentions. Ibid., 403.

48 J. David Velleman argues that joint action essentially consists in acting

upon such conditional intentions. See Velleman (1997). Below, in Section 2.9, I consider further Velleman's proposal.

49 Gilbert (1989), 357–58.

50 Ibid., 413–14. Gilbert is somewhat hard to read on this point, and so I focus on Bratman and Tuomela and Miller.

51 Bratman (1999a), 105.

52 Tuomela and Miller (1991), 375.

53 In Schelling's terms, I hope grabbing the drinks and heading for the car is salient for you, that is, sufficient to determine your action in the absence of explicit discussion.

54 By contrast, a claim that I intended to hit a difficult basket would smack of empty bragging, as Gilbert Harman points out. See Harman (1986), 90–93.

55 Bratman prefers to distinguish what he calls "pre-packaged cooperation" from fully cooperative action. Bratman (1999a), 106. It is not clear that the distinction is useful in characterizing cooperation as such, since many joint activities provide independence for the participants, although it does isolate what is specially valuable about certain types of cooperation. Beyond that, Bratman's claim seems to have more to do with the ordinary usage of the word *cooperate*.

56 This assumes I realize that ballot stuffing is generally regarded as improper. If I think the prevailing norms do not forbid but perhaps even encourage vote tampering, then I may well regard my act as doing my part of our getting the candidate elected by any means necessary, although I may also accept a norm of circumspection about my stratagem. (And if I am wrong about the norms, this may further be a case in which my participatory intention fails to overlap with others'.) So perhaps there is even a limiting case of collective action in which the ordinary condition of mutual openness is overridden by strategic concerns. But I do not want to rest too much on this example.

57 I am grateful to a referee for *Philosophy and Phenomenological Research* for pointing out this problem.

58 Gilbert (1989), 357–58.This example borrows elements from *United States v. Alvarez*, 610 F.2d 1250 (5th Cir. 1980), *vacated* 610 F.2d 1258, *conv. aff'd* 625 F.2d 1196 (1981). I discuss the *Alvarez* case in Chapter 7.

59 Furthermore, given even a moderate commitment to the indeterminacy of intentional ascriptions, there will be no fully determinate answer to the question of what goal an individual intended, or under what descriptions states of affairs will satisfy an individual's intentions.

60 I don't mean to deny that many claims are both normative and factual, such as "he's a ruthless competitor." I mean, rather, two things. In legal terms, the question is not trivially a "matter of fact," appropriate for a jury's determination, because the answer to the question depends upon the framing of the question. And second, the normative elements of the

question should spur reflection on the values or policy goals being pursued, as should questions about "the cause" of an event.

61  Bruce Vermazen carefully discusses these questions, ultimately to defend intentions with nonindividual act objects. See Vermazen (1993).

62  Bratman (1999a), 98–102. Tuomela and Miller defend their reliance upon we-intentions in similar terms. They claim that we-intentions are necessary to account for characteristic patterns of practical reasoning, such as the inference an individual makes from "We intend to do G" to "I will do P." They also point to the phenomenon of individual-collective weakness of the will, whereby an individual accepts that "We will do G" and then fails to do his part, perhaps because of a contrary individual disposition not to incur those costs. Tuomela and Miller (1991), 367–68.

63  Again, this raises the question of whether participating individuals must be cooperative. Certainly, in any good orchestra, the cellist will be willing to incur extra costs.

64  I am grateful to a referee for *Philosophy and Phenomenological Research* for steering me away from an earlier, mistaken, formulation of these counterfactuals.

65  I am again grateful to the *Philosophy and Phenomenological Research* referee for pressing this point.

66  The notion of collective intention is frequently also raised with respect to statutory and constitutional interpretation. I do not intend to address that issue for two reasons. First, even if there were well-defined semantic collective intentions, it is unclear as a matter of political philosophy why such intentions should control the later application and extension of a statute or constitutional provision. Second, it is unclear whether there are any likely circumstances under which members of a legislative body would satisfy the stringent conditions for assigning a determinate semantic collective intention.

67  Presumably, someone shouting encouragement from the sidelines with the intention of spurring us on will also count as a group member, just as a coxswain counts as a member of a crew. See Tuomela (1993). Wishful thinking alone, however, does not seem like enough for membership, though it may give rise to vicarious identification.

68  Institutional groups may (if they are empowered to do so) formally recognize a member despite that member's failure to meet additional, external criteria.

Alternatively, recognition may not be necessary, as in the case of a cabal of spies jointly stealing state secrets, no one of whom knows the identity of any other. But such institutional cases must be anomalous, since most institutions depend upon easy ways of identifying fellow members.

69  I do not mean to claim that everything predicable of a group is predicable of its members. We, after all, are many, while I am only one. But collective actions are not fully emergent in this way. They are redescriptions of the

actions of each of us, in light of the shared goal that gives those actions their point.

70 The claim that the same action is picked out under different intentional and unintentional descriptions is not undisputed. For a defense, see Davidson (1980a).

71 One can imagine a member of a collective who claims exclusive authorship. "We did not win the championship, I did," says the talented and arrogant quarterback.

72 Meir Dan-Cohen argues that such voluntary identification is sufficient to ground individual authorship of collective acts, whatever the agent's actual role in producing them. While voluntary identification may be sufficient for the kinds of notional "memberships" that ground individual psychological identity – Dan-Cohen's principal concern – it seems to me insufficient to ground third personal attributions of responsibility. Dan-Cohen (1992), 986–87.

73 A qualification: Frequently, in law, a company will be liable for contracts made by its members (and principals for their agents) even if the members exceed their actual authority to make those contracts. (The legal policy is dictated by a concern to protect the reliance interests of third-parties.) Because of the external legal policy, it might be appropriate to say the company does what its rogue agent does, though it might be better yet to say the company is treated as if it did what its rogue agent did.

74 Indeed, collective intentions need not even be embodied. A club, for example, could decide that next year's membership will be selected by computer. The collective intention to invite those particular members, so selected, will then be attributable to the club without being embodied in the mind of any individual. Here the overlap among members' willingness to follow the computer's choices is what grounds the attribution of the collective intention, not any overlap with respect to the list.

75 Each may also have the executive we-intention that the city council enact a street policy. In a large body, however, each member may simply intend to do his or her part, per the whip's instructions.

76 If losing members intended to interfere with the collective decision then, depending upon the context of explanation, different answers might be appropriate to the question "What does the City Council intend to do?" Given certain interests, the correct formal response, that the Council intends to pave downtown streets, might be appropriate. But if a more nuanced answer is sought, the right answer might be to note the vote, and say that the Council, as such, intends no such thing. Some members plan to implement the winning proposal, while others plan to hinder it.

77 Velleman's proposal that shared intentions are generally instances of mutual, conditional intentions may depend upon an erroneous generalization from egalitarian, consensual contexts. See Velleman (1997). Ac-

cording to Velleman, a group's collective intention to do G consists in a shared instance of each individual's intention to do G if others will also. But our group might have formed the collective intention to perform some act, by virtue of a CD all members recognize as authoritative, without all members forming or maintaining any further intention. To take Velleman's example, the Philosophy Department may form the collective intention to endorse candidate A for the open position, and this by virtue of a vote that all recognize as fair. But now, losing members of the department necessarily will not maintain the intention of endorsing A so long as the others do. They simply intend to abide by the results of the collective decision. This latter intention is consistent with fervently hoping the winners change their minds. Velleman's insistence that shared intentions require discretion over the issue only attaches when the shared intentions are executive, group-intentions. There his conditionalization analysis makes sense. When the intentions constitutive of the collective intention are merely subsidiary, participatory intentions, there is no requirement that individuals have discretion over the group outcome.

78  My description of the events largely follows Schama (1989), 399–406; and Cobban (1957), 149–50.

Larry May also discusses the Bastille example in May (1987), 33–41, 58–65. May argues, following Sartre, that mob action can become holistic "group action" through "solidarity relations" among members caused by their recognition of a common interest. Although May's discussion of the phenomenology of mass movement is acute, it remains difficult to understand what solidarity relations are, besides mutual feelings of identification and sympathy. While such feelings may be part of the backdrop of collective action, they are not themselves fully explanatory of the phenomenon. Furthermore, May seems to overemphasize the phenomenology of romantic solidarity incidental to (some) joint action rather than offering an account of how joint action is possible.

## CHAPTER 4: MORAL ACCOUNTABILITY AND COLLECTIVE ACTION

1  The figures and estimates I use are drawn from the following sources: Cross (1987), 159–60; Garrett (1993), 20; Hastings (1979), 340–44; Irving (1971); and Sherry (1987), 260. I am particularly grateful for a private correspondence with Timothy Moy, History Department, University of New Mexico.

A brief note about my use of David Irving's *Destruction of Dresden* is called for, given both the extent to which his research on the Dresden bombing has informed much subsequent scholarship, and given his emergence as a major figure in the Holocaust denial movement. (Now Irving argues both that Hitler was not aware of the murder of the Jews, and that there were no death camps, but only labor camps with high death rates.) It is indeed unsavory to have to use Irving's earlier work, but historians of the period seem generally to concur that his treatment of the sources is scrupulous, even if some of his judgments are prone to exaggeration. See, for example, Gordon A. Craig, "The Devil in the Details," *New York Review of Books*, Sept. 19, 1996 (reviewing *Goebbels: Mastermind of the Third Reich* by David Irving). Moreover, no one disputes the main thesis of the book, that the Dresden bombing was wrong. I am indebted to a correspondence with Peter Caldwell, History Department, Rice University.

2 Quoted in Sherry (1987), 153.

3 Hastings (1979), 342; see also Dyson (1979), 28: "[F]rom our point of view [the Dresden firestorm] was only a fluke. We attacked Berlin sixteen times with the same kind of force that attacked Dresden once. We were trying every time to raise a firestorm. There was nothing special about Dresden except that for once everything worked as we intended."

4 According to Bomber Command Commander-in-Chief Sir Arthur Harris, the decision to begin area bombing had been taken before he assumed command. By 1941 "the principle of attacking morale was at any rate half-admitted, though proposals to concentrate exclusively on this were turned down; the idea was to keep on at small targets for their strategic importance but, to put it crudely, not to mind when we missed them, or at any rate to regard a miss as useful when it disturbed morale." Harris (1947), 77.

A less charitable description of Bomber Command's strategic thinking is found in Hastings and Middlebrook. The American firebombing campaign against Japan presents a similar example (with even higher casualties). The targeting of the civilian population was fully deliberate, the product of extensive earlier planning. According to Sherry, a historian nonetheless deeply critical of the strategic bombing: "The Dresden raids were less the product of conscious callousness than of casual destructiveness." Sherry (1987), 260. See also Schaffer (1985), ch. 6.

5 For sensitive philosophical consideration of these issues see Anscombe (1981); Ford (1970); Rawls (1999); and Walzer (1974). British Air Marshal Sir Robert Saundby's later reflection, in an introduction to David Irving's *The Destruction of Dresden*, is exemplary:

> That the bombing of Dresden was a great tragedy none can deny. That it was really a military necessity few, after reading this book, will believe. It was one of those terrible things that sometimes happen in wartime, brought about by an unfortunate combination of circumstances. Those who approved it were neither wicked nor cruel, although it may well be they were too remote from the harsh realities of war to understand fully the destructive power of air bombardment in the spring of 1945.

Irving (1971), 9–10. For some other historians' assessments, see Garrett (1993), 193; Hastings (1979), 340; Levine (1992), 180; Middlebrook (1980), 347ff; Sherry (1987), 260; see also Markusen (1995). For a more personal account, see Dyson (1979), 29ff.

Although explicit pacifist opposition at the time was present but rare, see for example Ford (1970), the idea of civilian bombing of Europeans (but not Japanese) clearly caused unease among the Americans, who conducted mainly daylight, precision raids. And Churchill quickly repudiated the raids in a memorandum to the chief of the Air Staff, although this may well have been simply an effort at preserving his historical reputation. Garrett (1993), 20.

6 Winston Churchill's quick repudiation of the bombing, in a memo to Air Chief Sir Charles Portal, is telling: "The Foreign Secretary has spoken to me on this subject [targetting civilian centers], and I feel the need for more precise concentration upon military objectives such as oil and communications behind the immediate battle-zone, rather than on mere acts of terror and wanton destruction, however impressive." Garrett (1993), 20. Whether or not Churchill was simply trying to protect his historical reputation, the memo indicates his awareness of the bombing's moral qualities.

Furthermore, Draft Article 24 of the proposed 123 Hague Rules of Aerial Warfare declared that

"[t]he bombardment of cities, towns, villages, dwellings, or buildings not in the immediate neighbourhood of the operation of land forces is prohibited. In cases where [legitimate military] objectives are so situated that they cannot be bombarded without the indiscriminate bombardment of the civilian population, the aircraft must abstain from bombardment."

Garrett (1993), 27. Although the rule was not adopted, as Garrett says, it at least indicates the ethical awareness of the juridical and military leaders who drafted it.

7 To be specific, the first two raids were conducted by British Bomber Command and the third by the United States Eighth Air Force. The first raid began late in the evening of the 13th, and consisted of 244 Lancaster bombers, each with crew of seven; the second raid began early in the morning of the 14th, and consisted of a further 529 Lancasters; and the third, during the following day, involved 316 B-17s, each with crew of ten (some of which appear to have mistakenly bombed Prague).

8 Dyson (1979), 29.

9 See, for example, Browning (1998); Goldhagen (1996); Marrus and Paxton (1981); Gourevitch (1998).

10 There is another feature of the great twentieth century evils that makes them inapt for philosophical treatment: Their enormity stands in the way of generalization to the broad scope of moral life, if only because one always courts trivialization in the process of abstraction. This is not to say that the strategic bombings of German and Japanese cities wholly pale by comparison. The events were, of course, horrors of absolute proportion. But because they were, for the reasons I mention in the text, also products

of still-recognizable motivations and strategies, they lend themselves to generalization with fewer risks.

11 The literature on the social psychology of collaboration in evil finds both obedience and situation as the primary causal factors in explaining individuals' transgressing ordinary moral inhibitions against, for example, the infliction of pain. Milgram (1974) is the *locus classicus*; his findings are treated as robust in the more recent work by Kelman and Hamilton (1989), see 148ff.

12 The Dresden example has its inspiration and analogue in Derek Parfit's ingenious example of the "Harmless Torturers," who collectively electrocute a victim by each turning a dial on a single generator by a tiny increment, the generator aggregates these dial turnings and sends an excruciating pulse of electricity. Parfit (1984), 80. I am greatly indebted to Parfit's article, and to his discussion, which I take up in the following text. Parfit does not treat the cooperative structure of the case in order to consider cases of collective harm by independently acting agents. As a consequentialist, he can reasonably do so, since for consequentialists there is no intrinsically morally relevant difference between purposive and contingent collective action if both forms result in similar harms. I treat the case of independently generated, "unstructured" collective harms separately, in Chapter 5.

13 Garrett (1993), 79.

14 Middlebrook (1980), 348.

15 Ibid., 349. By contrast, the Commander-in-Chief of Bomber Command, Sir Arthur Harris, projects an air of untroubled conformity to superior orders about both Hamburg and Dresden. See Harris (1947), 88–89, 240–42. See also Dyson (1979) and Zinn (1990).

16 McKee (1982), 198–99.

17 Dyson (1984), viii.

18 Middlebrook (1980), 350.

19 Garrett (1993), 77.

20 McKee (1982), 203.

21 Quoted by Walzer (1974), 96.

22 Witness the reflections of one gunner: "For me it was just another target. But once we saw the photographs, some days later, it was another thing altogether. I was sickened. Just nothing there. Just razed." McKee (1982), 144.

23 Samuel Scheffler notes that these restrictions on agent accountability are implicitly supported by the "phenomenology of agency," in which acts dominate omissions, near effects dominate distant effects, and individual effects dominate collective effects. The phenomenology of the present case depends, surely, on how tightly networked are the torturers. For there are contexts of collective action (team sports, e.g.) in which collective effects phenomenologically dominate distant effects. Scheffler (1995), 227.

24 Compare Scheffler's demand for "a set of clear, action-guiding, and psychologically feasible principles which would enable individuals to orient themselves in relation to the larger processes, and general conformity to which would serve to regulate those processes and their effects in a morally satisfactory way." Ibid., 234.

25 Utilitarianism is the best investigated form of consequentialism. According to utilitarianism, states of affairs are ranked by the aggregate well-being of their subjects. It should be noted, however, that utilitarianism need not be a theory of morality so much as a non-moral teleology. That is, utilitarians seek to promote well-being for its own sake, and a system of moral approval is but one way of serving that end. Of course, many utilitarians, and notably Mill, did see themselves as providing the true form of morality.

26 And a necessary and sufficient condition of positive (or laudatory) accountability is that the agent has acted rightly.

27 I follow Derek Parfit's usage here. Allowing for what agents should have believed clearly mixes objective and subjective elements, but this is necessary to save subjective consequentialism from emptiness. Others take subjective consequentialism to be a theory about the propriety of blame, but this seems mistaken. While it is true someone who acts objectively wrongly may not be properly liable to blame, this latter fact need not be explained by the claim that the agent acted subjectively rightly. Peter Railton uses these terms yet again differently, to distinguish between consequentialism as a method of deliberation, and consequentialism as a doctrine of right actions. Railton (1988).

28 Mill's own view seems to have been that we should reserve use of the term *wrong* for acts attracting sanction: "We do not call anything wrong unless we mean to imply that a person ought to be punished in some way or other for doing it – if not by law, by the opinions of his fellow creatures; if not by opinion, by the reproaches of his own conscience." Mill (1979 [1861]), 47.

29 See John Dower for an account of how, in the Pacific war, Japanese and American cruelty on the battlefield fed one another in a spiral of atrocities, including civilian bombings, execution of prisoners, and savage trophy taking. Dower (1986).

30 Of course, if the bombers derive a small but perceptible benefit from participation, then consequentialism dictates the rightness of participation.

31 This is a realistic assumption, since the crucial variable determining survival seems to have been where one took shelter. See generally Irving (1971) and McKee (1982).

32 Differentiating token events by their causal antecedents presumes an independent theory of causal relations. As Bunzl (1979) points out, however, there is often a physical basis for differentiating between causal

chains. Often there is some intermediate event that does distinguish between two rival causal pathways to a type-identical event.

33 Following the same approach, we may say of a firing squad that each member's bullet made a difference to the occurrence of the death-event that occurred, since it was a death-brought-about-by-ten bullets, though no single member's bullet made a difference to there being a death. The trouble with this approach is that by identifying effects by their causes, it solves questions of overdetermination by tautology.

34 Bunzl (1979) makes a similar point, acknowledging there can be normative overdetermination.

35 Even if the difference between events was perceptible, it still might not be ethically significant unless substantial.

36 D. Lewis (1984), 198. Lewis notes that the problem occurs even without the complications of causation by omission. If, for example, the victim had perspired profusely out of terror, thus increasing the severity of the shock, then the event of perspiration would equally be a cause of the shock. But this conclusion, although metaphysically respectable, is of no help in the normative discussion.

37 Here I will use the terms *consequentialism* and *utilitarianism* interchangeably.

38 Strictly speaking, cooperative utilitarians must also indicate their cooperativeness to other potential cooperators. Regan (1980), 164.

39 Smart (1973), 10. See also David Lyons' critique of Rule Utilitarianism, in Lyons (1965).

40 Glover (1975).

41 Glover quotes Solzhenitsyn's Nobel Lecture: "And the simple step of a simple courageous man is not to take part in the lie, not to support deceit. Let the lie come into the world, even dominate the world, but not through me." Ibid., 184.

42 Glover makes this charge against Williams' apparent defense of the Solzhenitsyn principle, under the name of a concern for one's integrity. The difference between admirable and criticizable concern for one's integrity (or "clean hands") depends upon the nature of the acts foregone and the values they would promote, as well as the reflexiveness of the concern.

43 See Mill: "But moral associations which are wholly of artificial creation, when the intellectual culture goes on, yield by degrees to the dissolving force of analysis. . . . " Mill (1979 [1861]), 30.

44 Parfit (1984), 70; (1986), 847.

45 I have been helped by G.A. Cohen's exposition of Parfit in Cohen (1992), 16.

46 I suspect Parfit's principle owes its intuitive force to the rival explanation he offers, namely that it is possible to aggregate dispersed harms, in a context in which there is great suffering. But this presumption also seems mistaken. Affecting large numbers of agents imperceptibly does not "add

up" to great suffering; it adds up only to affecting large numbers of agents imperceptibly. While it may be worse to affect large numbers imperceptibly than to affect only one, it is not the equivalent of causing a single agent great suffering. See the discussion of this point in Section 6.2.

47 These objections are noted in Gruzalski (1986), 777–82; Cohen (1992); Otsuka (1991); and in Parfit (1986).

48 Jackson (1987). Parfit, in unpublished work, has indicated that he now accepts Jackson's position and rejects his collective consequentialist principle. Parfit (1988).

49 Jackson (1987), 103; Parfit (1984), 73, makes a similar schematic claim. While Jackson's topic is objective consequentialism, his conclusions hold so long as the individual agents have reason to appreciate the structure of their situation.

50 If the problem is prospective and strategic – that is, concerning the choices of a set of consequentialist agents trying to decide whether to participate – then Regan's CU would seem to apply. Agents would act individually wrongly if they did not choose the optimific act of not participating, given the presence of other CU agents. But if the other agents are not potential cooperators, then a consequentialist agent has no reason not to participate. This could be the case if agents make their decisions serially, without the possibility of coordination or in ignorance of the motivations of others.

51 Jackson does not clearly indicate whether groups themselves may intelligibly be blamed. I discuss this question in Chapter 6.

52 Gerald Postema makes this point in his reading of Johnson (1991), a book that also argues for a collective interpretation of rule utilitarianism. Postema (1995). Postema explains how the collective perspective from which optimific rules are educed must be in the "first person plural," that is, reflecting individual deliberation about what we should do.

53 Kant (1964 [1785]), 91.

54 For commentary on the categorical imperative procedure for testing maxims, see Herman (1993b); O'Neill (1990); Korsgaard (1996a); and Rawls (1989), 82–86.

55 This interprets the test, in Korsgaard's terms, as a "practical" rather than a "logical contradiction" test. The logical interpretation asks whether the universalized world is logically coherent. The practical interpretation asks whether such a world permits success in acting upon the maxim. Since one reason an agent might not act successfully upon a universalized maxim is its logical impossibility, all cases of logical contradiction are cases as well of practical contradiction.

56 More accurately, there is no universalized world in which agents keep only unsecured, convenient promises.

57 The CW test, like the CC test, does not ask whether the universalized world would be desirable according to a substantive conception of agents' interests, as do forms of RU. Rather, the universalization tests ask

whether willing the universalized world is compatible with fundamental, formal principles of rational agency, such as the requirement that one intend means adequate to one's ends.

58 Kantians would, I think, want to rule out even the case of a limited number of torture victims. Even if I could know that I was not a potential victim, I would be guilty of making an invidious distinction between the agency of the potential victim and myself. According to Barbara Herman, Rawls introduces the device of the veil of ignorance in order to finesse this problem. Herman (1993a), 50 n.1.

59 By saying the connection is one of meaning, I do not mean to imply it is necessarily communicative in the philosophical sense. That is, the agent need not intend to represent the action to another in some way, or otherwise make some recipient aware of the intention behind the action. I mean only that actions are interpretable, in the sense they may be taken to exemplify goals and attitudes of the agent. Actions harmful through their thoughtlessness may simply convey callousness without any wish to do so by the agent. On the self-referential structure of communicative intentions, see Grice (1957) and (1989b).

60 This is not to say the causal connection must be entirely perspicuous, or of very high probability. We routinely ascribe events to agents without any secure knowledge of the underlying causal mechanism, or in contexts in which the event was prospectively highly unlikely to have followed the act. See D. Lewis (1986), 177.

61 I don't want to beg any questions about the applicability of causal language to what Hart and Honoré call "interpersonal transactions." If a causal idiom is ever legitimate in this context, however, it is so when the mediating agent acts nonautonomously. My accountant, in legal terms, would be a mere "innocent instrument." By contrast, if he knew what he was doing, then it would be better to say "We have defrauded the government." I discuss these points more in Chapter 6.

62 See the discussion by Coleman and Ripstein (1995) of the normative, precausal basis of responsibility for harms. They too argue that accountability follows from a conception of agency. See also Ripstein's more extensive discussion in Ripstein (1998), especially ch. 4.

63 As I argue in Chapter 3, this is not strictly true. Agents can intentionally participate in acts they do not, strictly speaking, intend. But the Kantian framework is not well equipped to make this distinction. I discuss this point in the next chapter.

64 McKee (1982), 308.

65 Compare Postema (1995), 64: "For, to say that it a collective responsibility, is just to say that it is *our* responsibility *and hence mine.*"

CHAPTER 5: COMPLICITOUS ACCOUNTABILITY

1 Parfit (1988) suggests a similar point.

2 Middlebrook (1980), 352. Another reported feeling, "*Nun haben wir die Scheisse*," – roughly, "It's payback now." Middlebrook (1980), 352.

3 So Scheffler is right that the phenomenology of agency undermines responsibility – but only (or especially) within the first- and third-personal perspectives. See Scheffler (1995), 227.

4 Thomas Nagel and Christine Korsgaard argue that deontological, or agent-relative, constraints have their greatest force in the personal confrontation of agent and victim, because the attack is viewed by the victim as an attack on his or her "value." See Nagel (1986), 184; Korsgaard (1996d), 48.

5 *Othello*, Act 3, Scene 3, l., 433. Sanford Kadish offers a very valuable discussion, from which I have benefited, of the case in terms of the law of complicity and murder, in Kadish (1985), 385–88. I will return to the legal implications of the example in Chapter 7.

6 Since Iago's deceit is counterfactually necessary for the deaths, it may be metaphysically appropriate to speak of causation here. I return in Chapter 6 to problems of interagent causation.

7 As Bernard Williams suggests we might say of Dr. Caligari, who controls Cesare's actions. Williams (1994), 1671.

8 Shakespeare suggests that the racism of Othello's patrons and father-in-law is also a cause of his suspicion and jealousy.

9 I do not mean that it has never been or is nowhere the case that infidelity can excuse murder. But Venice is painted, at least, by Iago, as a city in which adultery is frequent and accepted so long as it is kept hidden. While Iago has an ulterior motive for casting Venice this way, there is no compelling reason to think him wrong about this.

10 Kant (1949 [1797]), 348.

11 Korsgaard (1996b). I am indebted to this wonderful essay.

12 *Othello*, Act 3, Scene 3, ll., 294–303.

13 Ibid., Act 5, Scene 2, ll., 227–28.

14 I do not mean to place too much weight on the relation of employment in this context, although it is a particularly far-reaching form of involvement in a collective enterprise. Other contractual relations can ground accountability in commercial contexts as well, such as investment or supply of outside resources. Indeed, these other relations may be more significant morally, since they stem from choices that are genuinely freer than those confronting potential or current employees.

15 Of course, the unavailability of information might be informative about the company's moral scruples. One cannot simply insulate oneself from the consequences of one's action by seeking or maintaining ignorance of those consequences.

16 I am grateful to the Cambridge University Press referee for this example.

17 Nagel seems sometimes to identify the force of agent-relative, deontological, constraints with our duties concerning intended consequences, as opposed to our agent-neutral duties to prevent foreseen harms. Nagel

(1986), 179. But it seems a mistake to explain agent-relative constraints entirely in terms of this distinction (the Doctrine of Double Effect). For even the strictest defenders of the Doctrine admit that agents have agent-relative reason to avoid bringing about very bad foreseeable consequences. What I do or bring about intentionally includes the consequences I foresee, not just those consequences I intend. As elements of my prospective or retrospective practical deliberation, they therefore generate moral considerations. In my view, the normative force of agent-relative constraints is better explained by the distinction between Acts and Omissions, at least in the sense that agents have stronger (agent-relative) reason not to cause harm, than to fail to prevent it. In general, one may accept a morality that incorporates agent-relative constraints, accept an analytical distinction between intended and intentionally brought about consequences, and deny any normative significance to the Doctrine of Double Effect, so that agents have equally powerful agent-relative reasons to avoid intended and foreseen harms. Indeed, this seems to me to be consistent with common sense theory of action and ethics.

For discussion of the analytical coherence of this distinction in terms of a theory of action, see Bratman, (1987), ch. 10; Harman (1986), 88–90 and ch. 9; for its normative significance, see Foot (1978); and G. Dworkin (1987).

18 Could the gas pumper make himself an ephemeral member of the robbery gang, simply by rendering aid with the intention of helping them escape the law? Yes, so long as the other members of the collective consider the would-be member to be a participant. This is just the condition of overlapping participatory intentions. As I remarked in Chapter 3, institutional groups often have further well-defined membership criteria.

19 Indeed, if Miriam is the head of the lab, she has had to make a case in her funding application for the relevance of her work to defense purposes.

## CHAPTER 6: PROBLEMATIC ACCOUNTABILITY: FACILITATION, UNSTRUCTURED COLLECTIVE HARM, AND ORGANIZATIONAL DYSFUNCTION

1 On market justification, see Coleman (1988b); Dworkin (1985b); and Rakowski (1991), 199–226. Coleman (1992) justifies the market in terms of the values of political liberalism.

2 At least in an ordinary language sense of *cause*; legal jargon does in fact make use of the term *cause* for such instances, but that usage should make us skeptical about its tendency to displace responsibility, rather than credulous about its implied metaphysics.

3 The trouble is that a causal version of the so-called accordion principle fails to work in interpersonal contexts, though it works in (nonpersonal)

event contexts. The accordion principle says that if person A brings about event a, which causes event b, then A can be said to have brought about b (A's action can be described in terms of b). In the interpersonal context, however, the principle fails: even if A does a which causes B to do b, we do not say that A did b. The term "accordion principle" comes from Feinberg (1970d).

4 Hart and Honoré (1985), 51–61.
5 Mackie (1974), 125.
6 D. Lewis (1986), 184–87.
7 Lewis suggests this is a "compliment" we pay the intervening agent. Kadish similarly argues that our commitment to a noncausal characterization of autonomous actions is too strong to allow the inference to go through. See Kadish (1985); and my discussion in Chapter 7.
8 One possible application of the idea is in dealing with the problem of alternative sufficient causes, only one of which, in fact, is operative. It is plausible causative verbs like *kill* apply only to events and actions that result in normatively significant differences from the antecedent nomic projection of events, while the metaphysical causal relation is indefinitely finely grained and applies to any departure.

Let's look at the famous water-bottle puzzle. A puts poison in V's water bottle before V's desert journey; ignorant of this, B punctures the water bottle and drains it. Both the poisoner (A) and the puncturer (B) perform acts sufficient to cause V's death, but only B in fact does cause the death, since the death is a death by thirst, not poison. But because A's act establishes a nomic projection of the traveler's death, B's puncturing does not cause an ethically significant departure from that projection. So we can say B caused V's death, but did not kill him.

The problem with this approach is that no one kills the dead traveler, since by the time the poison would have worked, en route, the bottle was already drained and V's death was inevitable. So even though A could have killed V, he did not kill him either.

For discussion of this case, see Hart and Honoré (1985), 239–42; Mackie (174), 44–47.

9 A final proposal, albeit one that merely begs the question, is to define *facilitation* as a primitive ethical-causal notion that intrinsically warrants some lesser degree of accountability.
10 In the United States, Arizona, Guam, Kentucky, New York, and North Dakota have criminalized knowing, "substantial" facilitation while denying it as a basis of complicity. See Ariz. Rev. Stat. § 13–1004; Guam Code Ann. § 4.65; Ky. Rev. Stat. § 506.080; New York Penal Law § 115.00; and N. Dak. Cent. Code § 12.1–06–02. In many of the actual convictions under the charge, however, it is evidently a consequence of plea bargaining down from more serious offenses. One recent case in New York does come close to the hypothetical case in the text. A realtor who directed an undercover policeman ostensibly interested in renting a house as a bor-

dello towards a particularly secluded property, and away from another that might have drawn police attention (in the realtor's opinion), was convicted of criminal facilitation. *People v. Mejia Real Estate Inc.*, 672 N.Y.S.2d 645 (N.Y. App. Div. 1998).

11 There are obviously side-effect causal bases of accountability: willing sales may encourage criminal activity, there may not always be alternative sellers, etc. I ignore these considerations again in order to focus upon the principle.

12 Parfit (1984), 80.

13 This supposition makes sense in the harmless torturers and water drops examples that Parfit employs.

14 Even if individual contributions of harm could be conceptually segregated, there would still be the problem of determining the magnitude of that harm. Assuming some diminishing marginal disutility, the average effect of all contributions would be far too great to impute to later contributions. Parfit (1988) discusses, but does not resolve, this problem.

15 So a world with two agents with broken arms is worse than a world with only one agent with one broken arm, and it is also worse than a world with two agents with toothaches.

16 I grant that denying this claim raises the Sorites-like problem of getting from individually imperceptible contributions to perceptible harm. This is a problem that stems from the general fact that the relations "better than" and "worse than" do not display transitivity at all levels of perceptual discrimination. But Parfit does not claim to have solved the Sorites problem. Indeed, as Michael Otsuka has shown, the Sorites problem dogs his own approach. Otsuka (1991).

17 I do not mean to raise the standard objection to utilitarian theories, that there is in fact no agent whose aggregate utility is maximized, and so no point to the maximization. My point is that many individual experiences that are not painful cannot become the ethical equivalent of a very painful experience through imaginative aggregation.

18 CA problems are multiagent Prisoner's Dilemmas (PDs). For the reduction of CA problems to PDs, see Schelling (1978); Hardin (1982), 25–28.

19 These terms are not entirely adequate, given that I will speak of individuals who participate in the collective harm. Participation equals defection or noncompliance, as I am using the terms.

20 This is a constitutive element of minimal economic rationality. In this very restricted context, it is not controversial.

21 The preference schedule underlying CA problems is frequently egoistic, but it need not be. Parfit has shown that commonsense morality, or any normative theory incorporating agent-relative reasons, can lead to CA problems. Parfit (1984), 95–98

22 Roughly, a norm of fairness would hold it impermissible to fail to do one's part of a coordination solution when one prefers general compliance to noncompliance. A number of problems with fairness norms,

albeit in the more demanding context of political obligation, are discussed in Simmons (1979), ch. 5.

23  As Jonathan Glover writes, "It seems a dog-in-the-manger version of justice that objects to one person benefiting because others are left unchanged." Glover (1975), 182.

24  A third problem is more theoretical than motivational: A fairness approach is wholly internal to the cooperative scheme. It does not relate individual agents morally to the potential victims of the scheme's failure, but only to other participants. I seek here a warrant for response to the victims, and to oneself for how one has acted towards the victims.

25  Feinberg (1984), 227–32. More accurately, Feinberg says the "Harm Principle" that legitimates criminal sanctions has no direct application to individuals in these cases. It can at most lend legitimacy to a general legislative effort to reduce the collective harm.

26  Sen (1974).

27  That is, cooperation is rational in iterated CA/PD problems, so long as the number of iterations is unknown (the horizon is functionally infinite). For a discussion of the logic of collective action in iterated, multiplayer games, see M. Taylor (1987); and Binmore (1992), especially ch. 8.

28  The routine example of this is the state's selection of a side of the road for driving. Individuals are indifferent between left and right so long as all drive on the same side.

29  Indeed, a standard justification of the liberal state is its ability to resolve coordination and assurance problems. See Baumol (1965); and Green (1988).

30  There is a middle ground, explored by Robert Cooter in a recent paper: the expressive use of law. Cooter argues individuals who have already internalized norms of law abidingness can use unenforced law to move themselves to a desired state of cooperation. (Cooter calls this a Pareto self-improvement) See Cooter (1998). Expressive uses of law are political solutions, but the antecedent motivational structures must already be robust or extendible enough to support their use, which presupposes a solution to the motivational problem I discuss in the text.

31  By enforcement costs, I mean not just the financial cost of achieving coerced near-universal cooperation in many domains, but the political costs of the requisite, highly intrusive institutions. Actually, the enforcement costs are probably easily bearable in the freon case. Since the state can regulate manufacturers directly, it is only necessary to monitor very few agents for compliance. (Consumers will have no option of buying new, CFC-based systems, nor incentive to replace those systems with older ones.)

32  In the Hobbesian war of all against all, the costs of political failure are high enough that prepolitical cooperation can be explained. But for lower-grade threats, or for the sake of altruistic concerns, the problem of initially establishing a political authority is very great. At the same time, I

do not suggest that political authorities can only be established by collective solutions to CA problems, for authorities are frequently grafted onto or emerge from preexisting authority structures.

33 Furthermore, the prospect of indefinitely repeated Chicken interactions may lead to more compliant dispositions, since the preemptive defection of others can be met or countered at later stages of the game.

A more technical treatment of the prospects for compliance in Chicken is found in M. Taylor (1987), 45–49.

34 Note that I am not offering a general theory of the optimal solution to collective action problems. My account applies poorly to cases of the provision of a public good, where typically something short of universal compliance produces the optimal net benefit. In these cases, the "cooperative surplus," or slack available for some noncompliance, needs to be optimally redistributed. Here I aim only to develop considerations that will lead agents to cooperate in reducing collective harms. I do not claim the situation brought about by these considerations alone is socially optimal.

35 In fact, the greatest consumers of CFC-based refrigerants are industries in the developing world. But realism in the particular example raises too many questions of distributive justice.

36 There is also, of course, the actual robber to blame. But even in cases of individual violent crime, people often look to systemic culprits.

37 In the next section, I will consider the significance of purely collective assignments of accountability, in which obligations of response only make sense at the collective level.

38 I include within the scope of "self-interested" or "egoistic" motivations, motivations spurred by concern for those one cares about especially.

39 Scheffler (1995), 232.

40 Meir Dan-Cohen suggests a similar approach, in Dan-Cohen (1992), 985–89. Dan-Cohen insightfully argues that feelings of vicarious accountability are generated out of a sense of self and identity. Because one thinks of oneself as a member of a group identified with some wrong, one thinks of oneself as accountable for that wrong. Although I also rely here on the notion of identification, my approach differs slightly from his. Rather than taking the collective wrong or harm to be an aspect of the agent's self, I prefer to understand it as a consequence of a shared venture with which one identifies.

41 Williams (1995c).

42 See, for example, Bourdieu (1984), (1990a), (1990b). Though the model of the *habitus* is the Aristotelian *hexis*, or virtue, Bourdieu also draws an analogy to Chomskian grammatical skills. (1990a), 9.

43 As I noted earlier, the very fact that no individual contribution makes a difference to the solution can be incorporated later into the coordination scheme, for example in the form of selective permissions for noncompliance.

44 Martin Putnam, in correspondence, has pointed out an ironic feature of the situation: The more united gun sellers are in their practice of scrutinizing their customers, the harder it is to defend that practice from economic pressure. For if the gun sellers unite in their discretion, then the supply of guns to would-be criminals declines, and the price the criminals would be willing to pay correspondingly increases. The result is ever-greater pressure on current gun sellers to defect from their collective practice, or greater incentive for unscrupulous newcomers to supply those guns. Note that this is not the case in the CFC example, for as more drivers have adopted CFC-free cars, the costs of maintaining older, freon-based systems have actually increased, in part because the economics of scale for freon have disappeared.

Putnam's observation suggest that an internal solution may not be sufficient in gun seller type cases. The gun sellers may need to seek the coercive aid of the state to bar entry to the unscrupulous, or to punish defection. This is in fact the case with regard to restrictions on sales of alcohol and cigarettes to minors. The refusal of large retailers to sell to minors increases the potential rewards for shadier establishments. Accordingly, and unsurprisingly, larger retailers welcome state enforcement efforts. My argument in the text is concerned to show primarily that with appropriate but plausible preference patterns, individual actors can come to see their own compliance as desirable, and will give them reason to seek and endorse ancillary state action. Whether in any particular case these preference patterns are sufficient is another matter.

I am grateful to Putnam for discussion of this and many other points.

45 See Nozick's discussion of "symbolic utility," in Nozick (1993), 26–32 and passim. Nozick in fact suggests that consideration of symbolic utility can lead an agent to cooperate even in a Prisoner's Dilemma (p. 56). This move invites the objection that Nozick's new game is not Prisoner's Dilemma, but an Assurance Game. (Nozick attempts to deflect this criticism by claiming that symbolic utility operates 'above' the utilities within the game matrix, since the symbolism of a given choice depends upon structural features of the matrix. But what is at issue is the game that is played, not the game that is initially represented, and the game that is played is AG, not PD.)

46 Such a motive can be reasonable when agents have information about, or can observe, each other's behavior before making their choices, and when the outcome is sensitive to each individual's choice. I do not mean to invoke the so-called "Twins Fallacy," according to which what any rational agent chooses will be chosen by other similar agents. Nozick flirts with this fallacy in his discussion of the application of Evidentiary Utility Theory to PDs. Nozick (1993), 52.

47 On a revealed preference interpretation of utility it is tautological that the chosen act has greatest utility. But I mean to contrast this motivation with one that calculates the causal consequences of the act.

48 The erroneous assumption that one must deliberate in terms of one's integrity vitiates Kwame Anthony Appiah's discussion of a similar example. Reluctance to sell a potential killer a knife is not necessarily triggered by a concern with what the act means about oneself. It is, rather, generated by the values to which one is committed. Appiah notes the symbolic relevance of a refusal to associate oneself with wrong, but for him any value to the symbolism is essentially pedagogical. See Appiah (1987).

49 See Raz (1986), 196–97.

50 The term *collective accountability* is often used to mean the accountability of an individual for the acts of a set of individuals. I use the term to denote the accountability of a collective subject.

51 See Simon (1976); March and Simon (1993); and Mintzberg (1979).

52 See, for example, French (1984), who argues that corporations are moral persons insofar as they satisfy Davidsonian constraints on intentional action; May (1987); and many of the essays collected in May and Hoffman (1991), as well as the bibliography contained in that volume.

The philosophical question arises in two ways. First, anyone who accepts the Lockean nonidentity of persons and human beings has reason to explore the further extension of *person*. And second, when issues of legal sanction arise, it becomes relevant to wonder what rights or moral protections the collective entity has. My own view is that the latter question is answered in terms of the rights and interests of the constituent members, though the rights of the collective are not simply a bundle of the rights of its members.

53 Many writers on this topic see accountability as an intrinsic, nonrelational, property of an agent. But, as I have argued, such a view is incompatible with the actual nature of our practices, and I will not consider it further.

54 As I argued also in Chapter 3, it is clear that events and intentional actions can be ascribed to groups in a way that is reducible to the causal ascription of events to individuals – indeed, intentional agency need not even be presumed for the former. A swarm of ants can devour a crop, and this makes sense in terms of each individual ant's chewing. And a flock of commuters can cross the Bay Bridge, their crossing being simply the intentional crossing of each individual.

55 See, for example, Dennett (1987). Dennett believes his pragmatic reduction of intentionality will work in the case of individuals as well.

56 Section 3.2 includes additional discussion of the metaphysics and explanatory role of groups and group predicates.

57 A descriptive theory of IBM, for example, will hardly work for a Silicon Valley startup. The essential diversity of organizational theories is emphasized in the valuable book by Fisse and Braithwaite (1993).

58 And, obviously, a legal or regulatory regime can influence a moral culture, both around and within an organization. Antidiscrimination policies began with a legal kick, but have become widely accepted as part of more basic social norms within organizations.

59 This point is emphasized by Susan Wolf, who argues that (some) organizations are analogous to sociopaths, capable of guiding their behavior according to prevailing standards of right and wrong, but lacking in any internal motivation to do so. Wolf (1985). Peter French's proposal for the use of shame-based publicity sanctions for corporate wrongdoing falls prey to this objection. French (1984), 187–202; see also Cooter (1997) for an economic discussion of punitive damages and social norms. To the extent that actual shame, and not loss of goodwill, is effective, it is as a response by individual members of the corporate structure. There is the further psychological problem that an attempt to shame another party tends to foster resentment instead. True shame is a response to a conception of self already held.

60 See the comprehensive *New York Times* series of reports on the disaster, "The Bhopal Disaster: How it Happened," in the 28, 29, and 31 January 1994 issues, all page A1. The Bhopal plant was operated by Union Carbide India, whose shares were owned by Union Carbide Co. (U.S.) (50.9), the government of India (22%), and 23,000 Indian citizens (27.1%).

61 The final settlement by Union Carbide was some $470 million, though the Indian government sought several billions of dollars.

62 There is a similar problem with individual-oriented economic sanctions. In almost all cases, the costs are deflected onto the firm as a whole or third-party insurers. See Kraakman (1984).

63 Increased insurance premiums are financed out of these channels as well. Consumers are only likely to absorb these costs in the absence of competitive alternatives. In order for firms to maintain competitive prices, they must divert the costs anywhere else.

64 For an overview of the different sanctions available to deter and sanction corporate crime, as well as for a plausible, inclusive model, see Fisse and Braithwaite (1993); and for recent caselaw see Note (1999). For a sophisticated economic analysis of the problem, see Arlen and Kraakman (1997).

65 That is, they have a duty (or grounds for a duty) to aid victims that bystanders do not have, even if bystanders have duties of benevolence.

66 By contrast, when a member of a robbery gang kills a guard, each member of the gang is inclusively accountable for the death, and the member who shot the guard is exclusively accountable for it as well.

67 There is a further question whether victims could justly decline the offer of a bystander to render compensation and make a claim upon the agents. This is a general question about corrective justice, individual and collective, and I do not discuss it. Jules Coleman does, in Coleman (1992).

68 French makes a similar point, namely that collective liability schemes do not entail the absence of internal, individual liability schemes. French (1984), 118.

69 Again, the situation is complicated by the fact that much environmental degradation occurs in the third world, and is at least sometimes a consequence of unjust development policies by the first world. In these cases, it

is dubious that the agents owe victims any response, though clearly it would be better for all if they ceased. I will ignore these complications by retreating into the obscurity of prima facie claims by victims.

70 Mill's harm principle, whatever its defects, surely covers enough uncontroversial ground to occupy the attention of any liberal legal regime.

## CHAPTER 7: COMPLICITY, CONSPIRACY, AND SHAREHOLDER LIABILITY

1 See Hart (1968); and Fuller (1977).

2 See *Sandoval v. People,* 117 Colo. 558, 192 P. 2d 423 (1948) ("it matters not how short the interval between the determination to kill and infliction of the mortal wound, if the time was sufficient for one thought to follow another"). See also Lafave and Scott (1986), 642–46.

3 Even if someone does come forward to testify at trial, a great number of studies have cast great doubt on the reliability of eyewitness testimony. See, for example, Lind and Tyler (1988).

4 See, for example, *Brinegar v. United States,* 338 U.S. 160 (1949) ("[M]uch evidence of real and substantial probative value goes out on considerations irrelevant to its probative weight but relevant to possible misunderstanding or misuse by the jury"). Note that evidence of a defendant's criminal history is often brought in after conviction, at the sentencing stage, as an aggravating factor.

5 See Kant (1964 [1785]), ch. 2, 407: "We are pleased to flatter ourselves with the false claim to a nobler motive, but in fact we can never, even by the most strenuous self-examination, get to the bottom of our secret impulsions; for when moral value is in question, we are concerned, not with the actions which we see, but with their inner principles, which we cannot see." That said, Kant's mechanism of evaluating potential maxims does seem to presuppose a large amount of self-knowledge.

6 For Thomas Nagel and Barbara Herman, see the discussion in Section 4.5; Brandt (1979); Harsanyi (1977).

7 As Bernard Williams has emphasized, the idealizations of moral theory, and specifically the demand to eliminate the role of luck, may reflect not so much a vice of theory per se, as an inheritance of a Christian tradition of transcendental grace. Williams (1981a). I also recognize that many theorists do acknowledge the epistemic limitations inherent in the practice of moral judgment. Hardin (1988), for example, argues for rule utilitarianism as a solution to the problem of imperfect information.

8 Granted, a very serious misunderstanding could cause irreparable damage to our relationship. In such a case, however, there were likely other bases of mistrust.

9 One can, of course, take on a new identity as a result of imprisonment, just or unjust. My point is that one cannot return naively to the normal

positions of an equal citizen. One becomes either an antisocial rebel or a sentimental citizen.

10 Douglas Husak is an example of a legal theorist who appears to distinguish too sharply between the two. He argues that questions of the difficulty of proving *mens rea* do not bear upon the justice of a *mens rea* requirement. Husak (1987), 59–60. Although I agree with Husak that intentionality requirements should not easily be compromised for the sake of easing the burden of proof, I do not think the position generalizes to the autonomy of liability rules from epistemic questions.

11 There is a traditional common law distinction between principals in the first degree (direct actors) and principals in the second degree (accomplices present, in fact or legal construction, at the scene of the crime), and between these principals and accessories before the fact, who render aid or encouragement but are not factually or constructively present at the crime's commission. Now virtually all jurisdictions have abrogated these distinctions: Anyone aiding or encouraging a crime's commission is punished as a principal. See Lafave and Scott (1986), 568–72.

The separate category of accessories after the fact is, however, frequently maintained, sometimes as the crime of misprision of felony. Accessories after the fact offer assistance with the objective of impeding law enforcement. Their liability is less than that of principals. Ibid., 596–98.

French criminal law also does not distinguish in punishment between direct actors and accomplices. *Code Pénal*, Art. 121–6 (1994). French law, however, departs from Anglo-American law in restricting complicity to aiders and abettors and to *provocateurs* who, in Anglo-American terms, instigate another's wrongdoing. Simple encouragement of another's crimes is not enough. *Code Pénal*, Art. 121–7.

12 Fletcher (1978), 634–49; Kadish (1985), 337–42. It should be obvious from my discussion and notes how indebted I am to Kadish's article.

13 A majority of U.S. state jurisdictions reject the *Pinkerton* doctrine. But since most conspiracy cases are federal, it is fair to say the *Pinkerton* doctrine governs criminal doctrine in the United States. See Lafave and Scott (1986), 589.

14 See Federal Sentencing Guidelines, 18 U.S.C.S. App. §1B1.3, (a)(1)(B).

15 *Pinkerton v. United States,* 328 U.S. 640 (1946). The *Pinkerton* Rule actually stands for two claims: one, that co-conspirators are subject to liability as accomplices, whether or not they intentionally aided the commission of the particular crime; and two, that as accomplices, they are liable for all acts committed by co-conspirators.

16 *Anderson v. Superior Court,* 78 Cal. App. 2d 22, 177 P.2d 315 (1947) (denying a writ of prohibition barring defendant's prosecution on a grand jury indictment). It was suggested that Anderson should have known that others were likely to be involved in the abortion ring.

17 See, for example, Hart (1968b).

So, for example, in a notorious English rape case, it was held that a defendant's unreasonable but sincere belief that a woman had consented to intercourse could be a complete defense to the rape charge. Now, it is often held that the defendant's belief about consent must be reasonable. *Regina v. Morgan*, [1976] A.C. 182. (The defendants in question were supposedly persuaded by Morgan to believe that his wife enjoyed intercourse under duress.) California requires the belief be reasonable; see *People v. Mayberry*, 15 Cal. 3d 143, 542 P.2d 1337 (1975).

18 The Model Penal Code uses the term *culpability* to refer to the actor's state of mind with respect to the criminal act. M.P.C. § 2.02. This use of culpability seems to me to be too conclusory. As I will use it, the culpability of an agent is the justified liability of that agent to a given legal sanction.

19 Moore (1993) is a powerful and comprehensive attempt to unite criminal doctrine with a volitional account of action.

20 This is not strictly true, since the introduction of certain justifications and excuses requires going outside the bounds of the basic liability package. The justification of self-defense, or the excuse of duress, frequently require an inquiry into the reasonableness of the actor's fear.

21 I disfavor the term *derivative liability* in this context because the source of the liability lies in the accomplice's own wrongful act of aiding or encouraging. Vicarious civil liability, for example *respondeat superior* doctrine, seems genuinely derivative. The employer's conduct may be in no way negligent, while liability will be derived from the employee's negligence.

22 The prima facie qualification arises from cases where P has an "extrinsic" excuse, for example, P is feigning participation as part of law-enforcement activity. See *State v. Hayes*, 16 S.W. 514 (Mo. 1891), *overruled on other grounds by State v. Burton*, 44 S.W. 239 (Mo. 1898). See Kadish (1985), 339.

23 Lafave and Scott (1986), 579–80; Kadish, (1985), 346–439.

24 *United States v. Falcone*, 109 F.2d 579, 581 (2d Cir. 1940) (holding that knowing aid is insufficient for complicity).

25 Kadish (1985), 349.

26 *State v. Lucas*, 7 N.W. 583 (Iowa 1880).

27 This example actually suggests two complications. First, since it seems that V's death was premeditated by S though not by P, S would seem liable for first-degree murder though P is only liable for murder in the second degree. Second, imagine that V has started the fight and escalated it to the point that P has the justification of self-defense. Though S would in fact be helping P perform a justified act, S's murderous intent would seem to provide a basis for liability.

28 *Regina v. Bainbridge*, [1959] 3 W.L.R. 656. The case turned not on the interest Bainbridge had in the resulting crime, but on his awareness of its gist. Still, the facts of the case make clear his interest in the crime ended with his purchase of the torch for the burglars.

29 319 U.S. 703, 713 (1942).

30 59 Cal. Rptr. 628 (1967). Though both *Direct Sales* and *Lauria* were conspiracy cases, the question in both was whether knowing facilitation
amounted to intentional assistance. So they are equivalent to complicity
cases. Accomplice liability could have followed from a conviction in
either case.

31 See *State v. Gladstone*, 464 P.2d 274 (Wash. 1970), in which the court did not
hold S liable as an accomplice for P's sale of 8 ounces of marijuana, when
S only provided a potential buyer with P's address. S's aid here was
clearly substantial, and the crime was a felony. Here the basis seems to lie
in the fact that S in no way profited from P's sale. But this would be an
anomalous basis of exculpation. But see *United States v. Fountain*, 768 F.2d
790 (7th Cir. 1985) (holding S liable for P's act of murder, when S had
knowingly but unpurposefully provided P with the murder weapon).
As I mentioned in Chapter 6, Arizona, Guam, Kentucky, New York,
and North Dakota. See Ariz. Rev. Stat. § 13–1004; Guam Code Ann. §
4.65; Ky. Rev. Stat. § 506.080; New York Penal Law § 115.00; and N. Dak.
Cent. Code § 12.1–06–02.

32 See, e.g., the U.S. Sentencing Guidelines and Commentary, 18 U.S.C.S.
Appx. § 1B1.3 (a)(1)(B). More strictly, P's act must be in furtherance of an
act jointly undertaken with S. It is unclear whether the foreseeable-
consequence rule requires that P be aware of S' intention to assist.
Though the Sentencing Guidelines speak only of liability in the context of
"jointly undertaken criminal activity," there is no apparent reason not to
extend the rule to unilateral assistance. That is, if complicitous liability in
these contexts is justified at all, it is so on the basis of S's intentional
promotion of a related crime. This basis is present in joint and unilateral
cases alike.

33 Note that under this rule, *Lucas* might well have gone the other way. S
might reasonably have foreseen P's robbing V, although not intending the
robbery.

34 Kadish (1985) notes this problem with the foreseeable-consequence rule.
Kadish (1997) focuses on the issue of recklessness as a basis of complicitous liability, arguing it is a permissible basis so long, and only so
long, as P's crime is also one of recklessness.

35 Lawyers typically insist the causal relation between act and event be
"proximate," that is, closely connected in time and space, and relatively
independent of intervening coincidence. Obviously, there are many potential and actual problems with wayward causal chains. In general,
criminal law does no better than philosophy of action in treating deviant
causal chains on a principled basis. Still the best introduction to the
literature of proximate cause is Hart and Honoré (1985).

36 See Lafave and Scott (1986), 576–77.

37 15 So. 722, 738–39 (Ala. 1894).

38 [1951] 1 All E.R. 464.

39 The decision is actually a mess. Lord Goddard, C.J., claims, *inter alia*, that Wilcox' liability is predicated upon his (a) having failed to protest the performance at the time; and (b) having profited from it by writing it up afterwards. But, under common law principles, Wilcox' failure to intervene or protest could not be reckoned a ground for complicity unless he had a prior legal duty to intervene, which he did not have. (To be fair, Goddard later weakens this claim into an evidentiary claim. Protest would have been evidence of Wilcox' disavowal.) And, profiting from the writeup could at most make Wilcox an accessory after the fact, since there is no criminal liability as a principal for retrospective ratification. Such liability for a journalist also raises grave concerns of freedom of expression, though such concerns have far less force in England. It is hard, though, to feel too sorry for Wilcox. Undoubtedly the publicity for the journal was worth far more than £50.

40 The court may have assumed tacitly that this was so. But doctrine reflects only the opinion they wrote, and not the opinion they should have written.

41 See G. Williams (1961), 382–83. Williams suggests weakly that "[d]ifficulties in proving causation may well lead to preference for the authorisation theory." He cites the notorious case of *Bentley,* in which a mildly retarded man cried out in the course of a burglary to his accomplice, Chris Craig, "Let him have it, Chris" as a policeman approached and demanded Craig's gun. As Williams notes, the court made no attempt to determine whether Bentley's exclamation had any effect on Craig's decision to shoot. (And Williams does not note that there was reason to think that Bentley's exclamation meant Craig should hand over the gun, not use it.)

In the United States, Bentley would have been convicted as well, but on felony-murder grounds, a rule already abrogated in England.

42 Kadish (1985), 359.

43 Ibid.

44 Kadish supports his position by citing a line of cases that relieve S of liability when S's aid arrives after P's apprehension. Kadish (1985), 359, citing *Commonwealth v. Haines,* 24 A.2d 85, 87 (Penn. 1942); and *West v. Commonwealth,* 157 S.E. 538, 539–40 (Vir. 1931). While this line of cases can be interpreted to support Kadish's possibility condition, they may also be interpreted in terms of the values served by not finding liability when the public threat posed by the criminal actor has already been defused. There is also the further problem of the consistency of Kadish's possibility condition with the universal acceptance of attempt liability despite the factual impossibility of a successful attempt in the circumstances, for example, *Kunkle v. State,* 32 Ind. 220 (1869) (finding liability for attempted murder though intended victim was too far away to be killed by the weapon in question).

This is in fact the position of the (admittedly revisionary) Model Penal Code, § 2.06 (3)(a)(ii), which holds that unsuccessful attempts to aid are sufficient for liability. See also the M.P.C. Comment at 314.

45  It is unclear whether P must be aware that S is the source of encouragement, or even that he has been encouraged at all. An even more subtle Iago-like S might, for example, discreetly lay out information (say about P's spouse's lover) that has the intended effect of strengthening P's resolve to harm the lover. Here S would seem an accomplice in P's act, though P is no innocent instrument of S's will.

46  S is, of course, also liable for the separate crime of conspiring to commit G.

47  This is not the "overt act" requirement of conspiracy doctrine, which requires merely that some member of the conspiracy perform some act, often legal in itself, that shows the conspiracy is somehow "afoot" and not merely an idle plan. Lafave and Scott (1986), 547–49.

Strictly speaking, S cannot be shown to be a member of a conspiracy by hearsay evidence from another conspirator, since hearsay is only permitted against those already shown to be members of the conspiracy. See *Krulewitch v. United States*, 336 U.S. 440 (1949) and Justice Jackson's eloquent concurrence. But this rule is apparently routinely violated in the procedural chaos and complexity of conspiracy prosecutions. In effect, S may be fingered by one member of a conspiracy and thus liable for the criminal acts of a second member P, though S and P are unaware of each other's existence.

A particularly egregious example of conspiracy prosecution (though not for the underlying offenses) is that of *United States v. Alvarez*, 625 F.2d 1196 (5th Cir. 1980), in which Alvarez was convicted of conspiring to import marijuana. The evidence supporting the conviction was that Alvarez was loading appliances onto an airplane in Miami while in the company of Cruz, who was was making a drug deal with federal agents posing as dealers. Alvarez did not participate in the discussion until one of the agents asked him if he would be at the unloading site (where the marijuana was scheduled to be delivered.) Alvarez nodded yes, and asked the agent if he was going on the plane. Then the agents arrested Alvarez and Cruz. As the dissent in the judgment said, "Alvarez nodded his head and smiled. For this he will go to the penitentiary." 625 F.2d at 1199.

48  See Model Penal Code § 2.04, Lafave and Scott (1986), 587–90; Johnson (1961), 1146–52.

49  I do not mean to minimize the problems in defining sufficient overlap in these contexts – of what constitutes agreement to the essentials of a plan, or knowledge of the other's participation. Given the descriptive-relativity of statements of intention, as I discussed in Chapter 3, these problems are primarily normative and pragmatic rather than theoretical. As such, analytical philosophy of mind or action can provide little guid-

ance here. I will take up the normative considerations in the following text.

50 I do not mean to suggest criminal law is tightly wedded to causing harm, since there are many offenses in which causation, of harm or otherwise, is not at issue. (For example, the inchoate offenses of solicitation, attempt, and unconsummated conspiracies; possession of unregistered weapons or of illegal drugs; theft; and fraud.) Causation gets its attention from its role in violent crimes, which receive the bulk of public and philosophical attention, and which do require the existence of a harmful "result." Even here it is unclear how reliant the criminal law is on causation, since individual liability will often apply despite overdetermination, or in virtue of a culpable omission to perform a duty in law. So, in many respects, the devotion of effort aimed at showing the consistency of causation and complicity doctrine is puzzling.

Although even in standard, primary party liability for so-called result crimes, causal responsibility is not necessary to criminal liability, as in cases of overdetermination – for example, two or more agents stab a victim, any one of whose actions would have sufficed to cause death. Each will be guilty of murder. There is also the possibly noncausal category of culpable omissions and possessory offenses. See the discussion in Husak (1987), 166–71.

51 Sayre (1930), 706. For a modern attempt at a critical reconstruction of complicity doctrine on the basis of causation, see Dressler (1985).

52 139 S.E. 77 (Ga. 1927).

53 Sayre (1930), 707.

54 See Note (1979), 998–99. The writers do not endorse the argument. Justice Frankfurter, in *Callanan v. United States* 364 U.S. 587, 593–94 (1960), advances similar considerations in order to justify the imposition of consecutive sentences for conspiracy and the underlying object offenses.

55 Johnson would solve this problem by stipulating that Anderson and the doctor were the only parties to that particular conspiratorial agreement, and that he may have entered into separate agreements with the other procurers. Johnson (1961), 1148–49. But this does not answer the normative problem of justifying criminal liability in the absence of causation, since even if a common agreement could be shown, there would be no reason to infer a causal relationship among the parties.

56 Kadish (1985), 334–36, 359–61, and passim. Kadish indicates that he agrees with Hart and Honoré's opinion that a special conception of causation explains liability in interagent cases. Ibid., 334. It is only his interpretation of doctrine that proceeds on the assumption that causal analysis per se is inappropriately applied to complicity cases. See my discussion of the problems of interagent causation in Section 6.2.

57 That is, it is consistent to say that P chose to perform C, causing proscribed result E, on the basis of full consideration of the desirability of doing C, and that P's act followed necessarily from P's prior motivational

state and beliefs, including those arising from the encouragement given by S. Since P chose autonomously and caused E, P is liable for E; and we could choose to rely upon S's causal role as grounds for holding S liable for the same act.

58 *Pinkerton*, 328 U.S., 646.

59 The law of partnerships is a division of agency law: each partner is principal and agent of the other. See generally Seavey (1964). Although partners are individually fully liable, plaintiffs cannot collect full damages from more than one partner.

60 The classic case for this principle is *Sir John Heydon's Case*, [1613] 77 Eng. Rep. 1150; see also Prosser and Keeton (1984), ch. 8, § 52.

A related tort doctrine is *respondeat superior*, according to which employers are fully liable for the torts and contracts of their employees, so long as the deal or harm could be said to be a typical product of the enterprise in question. *Respondeat superior* doctrine used to make much of the notion of "scope of employment," and the distinction between an employee's frolic and detour. Employers were liable for any event that could be said to arise from the authority or tasks granted to the employee, even if the employee's actual conduct was expressly disapproved. Today, the scope of employment is very wide indeed, covering even the assorted accidents and imbecilities of drunken seamen. See *Ira S. Bushey & Sons, Inc. v. United States*, 398 F.2d 167 (2d Cir. 1968) (holding government liable for accident of drunken sailor); *Taber v. Maine*, 67 F.3d 1029 (2d Cir. 1995) (same).

61 See Seavey (1949a), 93–97; (1949b) 147–48. On cost minimization, see Calabresi (1961).

62 The unfairness is somewhat offset by partners' ability to sue each other for contribution in most jurisdictions. See Prosser and Keeton (1984), ch. 8, § 50. And it should be noted that requiring plaintiffs to sue all potential defendants would escalate legal fees, which – under the American system that does not permit fee recovery – could substantially reduce the recovery in meritorious suits. Any increased fairness under such a scheme would come out of the pocket of plaintiffs.

63 Victim compensation is sometimes ordered as part of a criminal sentence, but this practice is still exceptional. Crime victims have recourse to civil courts to sue for tort damages. In any event, criminal defendants rarely have (or can acquire in prison) the financial resources to make compensation practicable.

64 328 U.S. at 651.

65 Kadish (1985), 354–55. Kadish does not endorse this justification. Rather, he attempts to explain the law's resort to consent in these cases as a result of its libertarian conception of rational agency.

66 See Thomson (1986), 188–91; Coleman (1988a); and Scanlon (1988).

67 Thomson (1990), 188. Thomson explicitly applies the term only to hypothetical consent, but her argument concerns the lack of force of even the

actual consent of someone discombobulated by an accident. See also Scanlon (1988), 203–04.

68 On a consequentialist view of punishment, any punishment greater than that calculated to deter efficiently would be unjustifiable, regardless of actual or implied consent.

69 I do not mean to suppose that business partners cannot be criminal partners!

70 Though a tongue-in-cheek Chief Judge Goddard does suggest that Hawkins is taking bread out of the mouths of English musicians. 1 All E.R., 466.

71 If violation of a duly enacted law is stipulated to be immoral, then of course any complicitous participation in an illegal act will incur moral accountability. But few modern philosophers of law would go so far with regulatory offenses. I will assume that if criminal acts are also immoral acts, then that is in virtue of the nonlegal properties of those acts. It is then a further question whether one has a moral obligation not to perform acts that are illegal but not immoral.

72 In constitutional jargon, punishment is justified when, and only when, it is the most narrowly tailored means of serving the compelling state interest of the protection of citizen autonomy and interests.

73 With the exception of statutory rape of a young minor, there are no serious criminal offenses of strict liability – that is, without regard to the intentions or beliefs of the agent. Strict liability offenses are typically regulatory, and involve small fines that are often shifted through insurance or indemnification, overtly or otherwise. There are serious penalties for criminal negligence and recklessness, and this category of crime has been the subject of an extended debate. See, for example, Hart (1968c). But these bases of liability typically involve either a gross departure from ordinary standards of conduct, or a conscious disregard for the risks to others attendant upon the activity. Lafave and Scott (1986), 231–42.

74 Hart (1968b); Scanlon, (1988).

75 Scanlon (1988), 202.

76 It is certainly possible that the answer to this question is *yes*. For if all and only principals were punished, deterrence of principals would remain at a very high level, and there would be no one left for undeterred accomplices to assist.

77 See my discussion of the responsive position of the state in Section 2.10.

78 This point is strongest in the case of result crimes such as murder or assault, where actual causation of harm is an essential part of the offense. In these cases, S fails to meet two of the law's criteria of culpability: act and result.

79 *Regina v. Hyde* [1991] 1 Q.B. 134.

80 1 Q.B. 134, 139. The court gets bogged down in the evidentiary question of whether foresight of the possibility of another's intention to kill, plus concerted action with the other, is legally sufficient evidence from which

a jury might infer an intention to participate in the killing. The court's decision was further grounded in the English rule that an assault with the intention to cause serious harm that in fact results in death shall be presumed murder. But this ground was directly relevant only to Collins' guilt. Hyde and Sussex were convicted on the ground that it was foreseeable Collins would murder, not that he necessarily did.

81 Lafave and Scott (1986), 668–69.

82 See also the discussion of the Iago hypothetical in Kadish (1985), 385–88.

83 The Model Penal Code's treatment of extenuating factors for death sentences is exemplary. M.P.C. § 210.6.

84 Indeed, Iago nearly (and treacherously) kills Cassio. Act V, Sc. 1.

85 For this reason, Fletcher's preferred German analysis in terms of "hegemony over the act" (*Täterrschaft*) will not help here. Othello is in control, in every relevant sense, of the decision to kill. Fletcher (1978), 654–57.

86 I refer here, albeit obliquely, to the Gricean literature on communicative intentions, and the problem of insincerity and deceit. See Grice's discussion in (1989b) and Schiffer (1972). The "transparency" of the communicative intention is said to be an object of common knowledge.

87 This is, in fact, the Chinese approach to complicity, at least as of 1987; see *The Criminal Law and Criminal Procedure Law of The People's Republic of China* (Beijing: Foreign Languages Press, 1987), Arts. 24–26. German and Italian law provide for the aggravated punishment of instigators; *Strafgesetzbuch* § 25–27 (1987); *Codice Penale*, Art. 112. See also Fletcher (1978), 654–57.

88 Smith (1991). This seems to me plausible, given that the law (and morality) distinguishes between the wrongfulness of murder and of causing death.

89 *Regina v. Moloney*, [1985] A.C. 905, 1 All E.R. 1025.

90 *Sandstrom v. Montana*, 442 U.S. 510 (1979).

91 See Johnson (1961), 1147 n.40.

92 See Horwitz (1992), ch. 3; Friedman (1985), 188–201, 511–25; Chandler (1977), ch. 1.

93 See Williamson (1981), 1537–68; Roe (1994).

94 The limitation of shareholder liability is a product of the laws of the state in which the corporation is chartered, but the limited liability rule is codified in the proposed standard Revised Model Business Corporation Act § 6.22.

   The agents of the corporation (its managers, directors, and employees) may be personally liable for corporate misdeeds if their own conduct satisfies the requirement of the underlying theory of liability. (For example, a plant manager makes a blunder, releasing toxic chemicals.) But their liability will then be direct, rather than derivative. In any event, it would be highly unusual for any agent to have assets substantially greater than those of the enterprise.

95 So shareholders are (indirectly) liable for all claims against their companies, since any drain on company assets diminishes the value of their equity.
96 This is just to say that plaintiffs may take their choice of defendants among the members of a partnership. Losing defendant partners are then generally allowed to recoup a portion of their liability from the others.
97 Blumberg (1985), 583–97; See also Horwitz (1992), 94.
98 See *Walkovszky v. Carlton*, 223 N.E.2d 6 (1966) (refusing to allow veil piercing on the grounds that capitalization and insurance minimums are matters of state regulation rather than corporate law).
99 Courts have held that incorporation for the express purpose of limiting liability is not sufficient basis for veil piercing. See, for example, *Walkovszky*, and the discussion in Clark (1986), 71–85.
100 18 N.Y.2d at 417.
101 Coleman and Ripstein (1995) refer to the claim that "each person should bear the costs of his or her own activities" as the Principle of Fairness, 95.
102 Prosser and Keeton (1984), § 46. In the words of *Sir John Heydon's Case*, [1613], 77 Eng. Rep. 1150, "All coming to do an unlawful act, and of one party, the act of one is the act of all of the same party being present." Note that "tortious act" in this context refers to any act that results in a tort, including lawful activities that result in liability by strict or negligent liability rules. See, for example, *Resolution Trust Corp. v. Heiserman*, 898 P.2d 1049 (Colo. 1995); see generally Restatement (Second) of Torts (1977) § 876; and Restatement (Third) of Torts (Proposed Final Draft No. 1 [March 31, 1998]), § 24.
103 I am indebted in this paragraph to Hansmann and Kraakman (1992), and to discussion with Andrew Guzmán and Jeannie Sears. See also Leebron (1991); Leebron is sympathetic to the arguments for unlimited tort liability, but concludes the associated transaction costs would be too high for such a rule to be feasible. And see Booth (1994); Booth argues that the current rule is generally efficient, and the most egregious counterexamples generally involve owner-operators and so can be handled as matters of personal liability. This claim is clearly belied by the hazardous waste, oil shipment, and taxi industries, in which the owners typically do not perform as operators.
104 Another version of the economic counterargument centers on the claims that existing capital markets simply could not absorb the increased risk associated with unlimited liability. See Grundfest (1992). Hansmann and Kraakman dispute this claim by pointing to the fact that companies with widely varying levels of investment risk are already successful in attracting stock buyers. Furthermore, the risk created by the new rule could be accommodated through increased portfolio diversification and the possibility of portfolio personal liability insurance. Hansmann and

Kraakman (1991), 1903–06; and (1992a). Hansmann and Kraakman also argue that the increased marginal monitoring costs for investors are unlikely to overdeter investment in the first place, and second, are simply the costs of socially desirable investor control.

Another serious objection to the proposal is that the rule could be easily evaded through transforming vulnerable equity investment into protected bondholder debt, through recruiting risk-happy investors with sufficient money to capitalize the firm but insufficient assets to cover its liabilities, or through jurisdictional maneuvers. See Alexander (1992); and Hansmann and Kraakman (1992b).

105 And in an age of multinational production, declining product demand or employment might hurt most third-world workers who are worse off unemployed than even uncompensated first-world tort victims.

106 Often, of course, the two sets will not overlap, as in the Union Carbide – Bhopal case.

107 The classical origin of this (normative) view of tort rules as maximizing social welfare is found in Calabresi (1970); and Calabresi and Hirschoff (1972), "Toward a Test for Strict Liability in Torts." See also Posner (1972).

108 This description of corrective justice reflects, but is not the same as, that offered by Coleman (1992), especially 303–28. Coleman's conception of corrective justice is shaped by his desire to map actual tort doctrine. I am willing to depart quite far from actual practice. For reasons well elaborated by Coleman, it is unlikely that any univocal account of corrective justice could fit the disparate needs of our social world. Other valuable conceptions of corrective justice include Perry (1999); and Honoré (1995b). See also Eric Rakowski and Arthur Ripstein's important arguments for equality-based theories of corrective justice, in, respectively, Rakowski (1991), Part II; and Ripstein (1998).

109 Even for those who take a strongly economic view of tort law, liability cannot simply be imposed upon any third party. Some morally relevant relation to the harm must be shown. As with theories of criminal punishment, corrective justice provides the global principle of justification of liability, if not the principle of distribution.

110 See, for example, *Escola v. Coca Cola Bottling*, 150 P.2d 436 (Cal. 1944) (holding bottler strictly liable for injury caused by exploding bottle). It should be noted that Justice Traynor's famous concurrence in the case argues for strict (causal) liability on economic grounds. 150 P.2d 440. Richard Epstein has argued for strict liability on noneconomic grounds in Epstein (1973), as a matter of protecting natural property and liberty rights.

111 Background for this example comes from Brodeur (1985), 102–14; Elizabeth Ginsburg, "Court Decisions to Speed Up Thousands of Asbestos Claims" *New York Times*, Feb. 19, 1995, 13NJ 1; Note (1983); and Roe (1984).

112 The workers may have a general claim in political justice for relief of their suffering. Shareholders would face this claim on the same basis as everyone else in the political community.

113 Most employees of a corporation likewise have little control or authority. Yet, if the corporation goes bankrupt, they will by losing their jobs pay an even more substantial price than a shareholder, since their risks are undiversified.

114 See Roe (1994). Note that this claim implicitly concedes that the Control Principle does not block liability in the case of closely held corporations, nor for controlling shareholders.

115 See Coleman (1992), 402–04.

116 For discussion, see Hansmann and Kraakman (1991), 1896–99. They favor an "information-based rule," which would impose liability on all those who hold shares "at the earliest of the following moments: (1) when the tort claims in question were filed; (2) when the corporation's management first became aware that, with high probability, such claims would be filed; or (3) when the corporation dissolved without leaving a contractual successor."

117 The recent emergence of a breed of Internet day traders accentuates this point on the one hand, for many investors now buy and sell in extremely short intervals; and in another way undermines it, for many also see themselves as participants in an exciting entrepreneurial endeavor. I do not want to rest anything on armchair sociology or psychology.

118 For example, investors who buy stock at an Initial Public Offering and sell a day later. I am grateful to the referee for insisting upon the similarity of short-term and long-term investors.

119 Granted, courts and the SEC do not make it easy for individual shareholders to exercise much voice about the ethical quality of their companies' activities. Rather, when shareholders submit proxy statement proposals for distribution by management before the general shareholders meeting, the proposals typically must not raise social and political issues entirely unrelated to the profitability of the firm's activities. See *Medical Comm. for Human Rights v. SEC,* 432 F.2d 659 (D.C. Cir. 1970) (challenging SEC decision not to require inclusion of proposal banning Dow Chemical's manufacture of napalm, on ground that a financial issue was partially involved), *vacated as moot* 404 U.S. 403 (1972). Courts have been even stricter on the rights of shareholders to examine corporate records that give the names and addresses of all other shareholders, in order to solicit those shareholders' support for social or political policy changes. See *State* ex rel. *Pillsbury v. Honeywell, Inc.,* 191 N.W. 2d 406 (Minn. 1971). Judicial reluctance stems in part from a proper concern about the burden upon corporations (and purely profit-seeking investors) that could arise from unfettered pursuit of social goals by small shareholders. But there is clearly a middle ground through which at

least long-term shareholders of even modest stakes may attempt to generate support for basically ethical constraints on corporate business.

120 *Fischer v. Johns-Manville Corp.*, 512 A.2d. 466 (N.J. 1986).

121 See Prosser and Keeton (1984), § 2; for economic analyses, see Polinsky and Shavell (1998) and Cooter (1997). There is a growing legislative trend towards limiting punitive damages, and towards barring plaintiffs from recovering such damages from vicariously liable defenders. There is also a growing judicial trend of blocking these legislative efforts on constitutional grounds. See, for example, *Best v. Taylor Machine Works*, 689 N.E.2d 1057 (Ill. 1997).

122 One good reason to question the legitimacy of the current system of punitive damages is the low level of proof – often, preponderance of evidence – needed to justify the stigma and costs. A further problem for corrective justice is that punitive damages may exceed any compensatory need of the victim, even if moral harm is somehow monetized, thus becoming an unwarranted windfall for the victim plaintiff.

If the worry is deterring corporate wrongdoing, criminal prosecutions of responsible managers and of the company as a whole seem much to be preferred.

123 Punitive damages, like criminal fines, can be tailored so as to mitigate their effects upon nonculpable employees, but usually only by shifting their full brunt onto shareholders, for example by demanding that the corporation make payment in the form of a new stock issue to the plaintiffs. See Coffee (1981), 413–24. Such methods may, as Coffee argues, work well to increase shareholder pressure upon managers, whatever their injustice.

124 I am grateful to Andrew Guzmán for discussion of this point.

125 As I mentioned previously, this point holds of both long- and short-term investors.

126 This claim is argued by Blumberg (1985), 576.

## CHAPTER 8: CONCLUSION: ACCOUNTABILITY AND THE POSSIBILITY OF COMMUNITY

1 Aristotle, *Politics*, Bk. I, ch. 2, 1253a6.

# Bibliography

Adams, Robert M. 1985. "Involuntary Sins." *Philosophical Review* 94: 3–31.

Alexander, Janet Cooper. 1992. "Unlimited Shareholder Liability through a Procedural Lens." *Harvard Law Review* 106: 387–445.

Anscombe, G.E.M. 1981. "Mr. Truman's Degree." In *Ethics, Religion, and Politics*. Minneapolis: University of Minnesota.

Appiah, K. Anthony. 1987. "Racism and Moral Pollution." In *Collective Responsibility*. Edited by May and Hoffman.

Aristotle. 1941a. *Nicomachean Ethics*. Translated by W.D. Ross. In *The Basic Works of Aristotle*. Edited by Richard McKeon. New York: Random House.

———. 1941b. *Politics*. Translated by Benjamin Jowett. In *The Basic Works of Aristotle*. New York: Random House.

———. 1985. *Nicomachean Ethics*. Translated by Terence Irwin. Indianapolis: Hackett Publishing.

Arlen, Jennifer and Reinier Kraakman. 1997. "Controlling Corporate Misconduct: A Comparative Analysis of Corporate Incentive Regimes." *N.Y.U. Law Review* 72: 687–777.

Atiyah, P.S. 1967. *Vicarious Liability in the Law of Torts*. London: Butterworths.

Austen, Jane. 1996 (1816). *Emma*. New York: Penguin Books.

Bates, Stanley. 1987. "The Responsibility of 'Random Collections.' Reply to Held." In *Collective Responsibility*. Edited by May and Hoffman.

Baumol, William. 1965. *Welfare Economics and the Theory of the State*. 2nd ed. Cambridge, MA: Harvard University Press.

Bennett, Jonathan. 1980. "Accountability." In *Philosophical Subjects*. Edited by Zak van Straaten. New York: Oxford University Press.

Binmore, Ken. 1992. *Fun and Games*. Lexington: D.C. Heath & Co.

Bittner, Rüdiger. 1992. "Is it Reasonable to Regret Things One Did?" *Journal of Philosophy* 89: 262–73.

———. 1994. *Ressentiment*. In *Nietzsche, Genealogy, Morality: Essays on Nietzsche's Genealogy of Morals*. Edited by Richard Schacht. Berkeley: University of California.

Block, Ned. 1980. "What is Functionalism?" In *Readings in Philosophy of Psychology*. Edited by Ned Block. Cambridge, MA: Harvard University Press.

Blumberg, Phillip I. 1985. "Limited Liability and Corporate Groups." *Journal of Corporation Law* 11: 573–631.

Booth, Richard A. 1994. "Limited Liability and the Efficient Allocation of Resources." *Northwestern University Law Review* 89: 140–65.

Bourdieu, Pierre. 1984. *Distinction: A Social Critique of the Judgement of Taste.* Translated by Richard Nice. Cambridge, MA: Harvard University Press.

———. 1990a. *In Other Words: Essays towards a Reflexive Sociology.* Translated by Matthew Lawson. Cambridge: Polity Press.

———. 1990b, *The Logic of Practice.* Translated by Richard Nice. Cambridge, MA: Polity Press.

Brandt, Richard. 1979. *A Theory of the Good and the Right.* New York: Oxford University Press.

Bratman, Michael. 1987. *Intentions, Plans, and Practical Reason.* Cambridge, MA: Harvard University Press.

———. 1999a. "Shared Cooperative Activity." In *Faces of Intention: Selected Essays on Intention and Agency.* Cambridge: Cambridge University Press.

———. 1999b. "Shared Intention." In *Faces of Intention: Selected Essays on Intention and Agency.* Cambridge: Cambridge University Press.

———. 1999c. "Shared Intention and Mutual Obligation." In *Faces of Intention: Selected Essays on Intention and Agency.* Cambridge: Cambridge University Press.

———. 1999d. "I Intend that We J." In *Faces of Intention: Selected Essays on Intention and Agency.* Cambridge: Cambridge University Press.

Broadie, Sarah Waterlow. 1991. *Ethics with Aristotle.* New York: Oxford University Press.

Browning, Christopher R. 1998. *Ordinary Men: Reserve Police Battalion 101 and the Final Solution in Poland.* New York: Harper Collins.

Bunzl, Martin. 1979. "Causal Overdetermination." *Journal of Philosophy* 76: 134–50.

Calabresi, Guido. 1961. "Some Thoughts on Risk Distribution and the Law of Torts." *Yale Law Journal* 70: 499–555.

———. 1970. *The Costs of Accidents.* New Haven: Yale University Press.

Calabresi, Guido and Jon Hirschoff. 1972. "Toward a Test for Strict Liability in Torts." *Yale Law Journal* 71: 1055–85.

Calabresi, Guido and Douglas Melamed. 1972. "Property Rules, Liability Rules, and Inalienability: One View of the Cathedral." *Harvard Law Review* 85: 1089–1128.

Chandler, Alfred D. 1977. *The Visible Hand.* Cambridge, MA: Harvard University Press.

Clark, Robert. 1986. *Corporate Law.* Boston: Little, Brown.

Cobban, Alfred. 1957. *A History of Modern France, Volume 1: 1715–1799.* New York: Penguin Books.

Coffee, John C. Jr. 1981. " 'No Soul to Damn No Body to Kick': An Unscandalized Inquiry into the Problem of Corporate Punishment." *Michigan Law Review* 79: 386–459.

# Bibliography

Cohen, G.A. 1992. "The Collective Action Problem." Photocopy. Oxford University.

Coleman, Jules. 1988a. "Efficiency, Utility, and Wealth Maximization." In *Markets, Morals and the Law*. Cambridge: Cambridge University Press.

———. 1988b. "Crimes, Kickers, and Transaction Structures." In *Markets, Morals, and the Law*. Cambridge University Press.

———. 1992. *Risks and Wrongs*. Cambridge: Cambridge University Press.

Coleman, Jules and Arthur Ripstein. 1995. "Mischief and Misfortune." *McGill Law Journal* 41: 91–130.

Cooper, John. 1985. *Reason and Human Good in Aristotle*. Indianapolis: Hackett Publishing.

Cooter, Robert. 1997. "Punitive Damages, Social Norms, and Economic Analysis." *Law and Contemporary Problems* 60: 73–92.

———. 1998. "Expressive Law and Economics." *Journal of Legal Studies* 27: 585–608.

Cover, Robert. 1975. *Justice Accused: Antislavery and the Judicial Process*. New Haven: Yale University Press.

Cross, Robin. 1987. *The Bombers: The Illustrated Story of Offensive Strategy and Tactics in the Twentieth Century*. New York: MacMillan.

Dan-Cohen, Meir. 1992. "Responsibility and the Boundaries of the Self." *Harvard Law Review* 105: 959–1003.

Davidson, Donald. 1980a. "Actions, Reasons, and Causes." In *Essays on Actions and Events*. New York: Oxford University Press.

———. 1980b. "Agency." In *Essays on Actions and Events*. New York: Oxford Universtiy Press.

———. 1980c. "Intending." In *Essays on Actions and Events*. New York: Oxford University Press.

———. 1984a. "Radical Interpretation." In *Inquiries into Truth and Interpretation*. New York: Oxford University Press.

———. 1984b. "Thought and Talk." In *Inquires into Truth and Interpretation*. New York: Oxford University Press.

Dennett, Daniel. 1987. "True Believers." In *The Intentional Stance*. Cambridge, MA: MIT Press.

Dower, John W. 1986. *War without Mercy: Race and Power in the Pacific War*. New York: Pantheon Books.

Dressler, Joshua. 1985. "Reassessing the Theoretical Underpinnings of Accomplice Liability: New Solutions to an Old Problem." *Hastings Law Review* 37: 91–140.

Dworkin, Gerald. 1987. "Intention, Foreseeability, and Responsibility." In Schoeman (1987).

Dworkin, Ronald. 1985a. "What Justice Isn't." In *A Matter of Principle*. Cambridge, MA: Harvard University Press.

———. 1985b. "Is Wealth a Value?" In *A Matter of Principle*. Cambridge, MA: Harvard University Press.

———. 1986. *Law's Empire*. Cambridge, MA: Harvard University Press.

Dyson, Freeman. 1979. *Disturbing the Universe.* New York: Basic Books.
———. 1984. *Weapons and Hope.* New York: Harper & Row.
Elster, Jon. 1985. *Making Sense of Marx.* Cambridge: Cambridge University Press.
———. 1989. *Nuts and Bolts for the Social Sciences.* Cambridge: Cambridge University Press.
Emerson, Ralph Waldo. 1983. "Self-Reliance." In *Emerson: Essays and Lectures.* New York: Library of America.
Epstein, Richard. 1973. "A Theory of Strict Liability." *Journal of Legal Studies* 2: 151–204.
Feinberg, Joel. 1970a. "Problematic Responsibility in Law and Morals." In *Doing and Deserving.* Princeton: Princeton University Press.
———. 1970b. "Justice and Personal Desert." In *Doing and Deserving.* Princeton: Princeton University Press.
———. 1970c. "Collective Responsibility." In *Doing and Deserving.* Princeton: Princeton University Press.
———. 1970d. "Action and Responsibility." In *Doing and Deserving.* Princeton: Princeton University Press.
———. 1984. *Harm to Others.* New York: Oxford University Press.
Fiss, Owen M. 1978. "The Supreme Court 1978 Term – Forward: The Forms of Justice." *Harvard Law Review* 93: 1–58.
Fisse, Brent and John Braithwaite. 1993. *Corporations, Crime, and Accountability.* Cambridge: Cambridge University Press.
Fletcher, George. 1978. *Rethinking Criminal Law.* Boston: Little, Brown.
Foot, Philippa. 1978. "The Problem of Abortion and the Doctrine of Double Effect." In *Virtues and Vices and Other Essays.* Berkeley: University of California Press.
Ford, John C. S.J. 1970. "The Morality of Obliteration Bombing." In *War and Morality.* Edited by R. A. Wasserstrom. Belmont, CA: Wadsworth Publishing Co.
Foucault, Michel. 1979. *Discipline and Punish.* Translated by Alan Sheridan. New York: Vintage Books.
French, Peter. 1984. *Collective and Corporate Responsibility.* New York: Columbia University Press.
Friedman, Lawrence M. 1985. *A History of American Law.* 2nd. ed. New York: Simon and Schuster.
Fuller, Lon. 1977. *The Morality of Law.* Rev. ed. New Haven: Yale University Press.
Garrett, Stephen A. 1993. *Ethics and Airpower in World War II: The British Bombing of German Cities.* New York: St. Martin's Press.
Gauthier, David. 1975. "Coordination." *Dialogue* 14: 195–221.
———. 1986. *Morals by Agreement.* New York: Oxford University Press.
Gibbard, Allan. 1990. *Wise Choices, Apt Feelings.* Cambridge, MA: Harvard University Press.
Gilbert, Margaret. 1989. *On Social Facts.* Princeton: Princeton University Press.

Gilligan, Carol. 1982. *In a Different Voice.* Cambridge Mass.: Harvard University Press.

Glover, Jonathan. 1975. "It Makes No Difference Whether or Not I Do It." *Proceedings of the Aristotelian Society* 49: 171–90.

Goffman, Erving. 1959. *The Presentation of Self in Everyday Life.* New York: Anchor Books.

Goldhagen, Daniel Jonah. 1996. *Hitler's Willing Executioners: Ordinary Germans and the Holocaust.* New York: Knopf.

Gourevitch, Philip. 1998. *We wish to inform you that tomorrow we will be killed with our families: Stories from Rwanda.* New York: Farrar, Straus & Giroux.

Grass, Gunter. 1990. *The Tin Drum.* Translated by Ralph Manheim. New York: Vintage International.

Green, Leslie. 1988. *The Authority of the State.* New York: Oxford University Press.

Grice, H.P. 1957. "Meaning." *Philosophical Review* 66: 377–88.

———. 1989a. *Studies in the Ways of Words.* Cambridge, MA: Harvard University Press.

———. 1989b. "Utterer's Meaning and Intentions." In *Studies in the Ways of Words.* Cambridge, MA: Harvard University Press.

———. 1991. "Method in Philosophical Psychology." In *The Conception of Value.* New York: Oxford University Press.

Grundfest, Joseph A. 1992. "The Limited Future of Unlimited Liability: A Capital Markets Perspective." *Yale Law Journal* 102: 387–425.

Gruzalski, Bart. 1986. "Parfit's Impact on Utilitarianism." *Ethics* 96: 760–83.

Hansmann, Henry and Reinier Kraakman. 1991. "Toward Unlimited Shareholder Liability for Corporate Torts." *Yale Law Journal* 100: 1879–1934.

———. 1992a. "Do the Capital Markets Compel Limited Liability? A Response to Professor Grundfest." *Yale Law Journal* 102: 427–36.

———. 1992b. "A Procedural Focus on Unlimited Shareholder Liability Rules." *Harvard Law Review* 106: 446–58.

Hardin, Russell. 1982. *Collective Action.* Baltimore: Johns Hopkins University Press.

———. 1988. *Morality within the Limits of Reason.* Chicago: University of Chicago Press.

Harman, Gilbert. 1986. *Change in View.* Cambridge, MA: MIT Press.

Harris, Sir Arthur. 1947. *Bomber Offensive.* London: Collins.

Harsanyi, John. 1977. "Rule Utilitarianism and Decision Theory." *Erkenntnis* 11: 25–53.

Hart, H.L.A. 1968a. "Postscript: Responsibility and Punishment." In *Punishment and Responsibility.* New York: Oxford University Press.

———. 1968b. "Legal Responsibility and Excuses." In *Punishment and Responsibility.* New York: Oxford University Press.

———. 1968c. "Negligence, *Mens Rea,* and Criminal Responsibility." In *Punishment and Responsibility.* New York: Oxford University Press.

———. 1997. *The Concept of Law.* 2nd ed. New York: Oxford University Press.

Hart, H.L.A. and Tony Honoré. 1985. *Causation in the Law.* Rev. 2nd ed. New York: Oxford University Press.

Hastings, Max. 1979. *Bomber Command.* New York: The Dial Press.

Hegel, Georg W.F. 1952 (1821). *Philosophy of Right.* Translated by T.M. Knox. New York: Oxford University Press.

Held, Virginia. "Can a Random Collection of Individuals be Morally Responsible?" In May and Hoffman (1991).

Herman, Barbara. 1993a. "Mutual Aid and Respect for Persons." In *The Practice of Moral Judgment.* Cambridge, MA: Harvard University Press.

―――. 1993b. "Moral Deliberation and the Derivation of Duties." In *The Practice of Moral Judgment.* Cambridge, MA: Harvard University Press.

Hillel-Ruben, David. 1985. *The Metaphysics of the Social World.* London: Routledge & Kegan Paul.

Hollis, Martin and Robert Sugden. 1993. "Rationality in Action." *Mind* 102: 1–35.

Holmes, Oliver Wendell, Jr. 1963 (1881). *The Common Law.* Edited by Mark D. Howe. Cambridge, MA: Harvard University Press.

Honoré, Tony. 1995a. "The Morality of Tort Law – Questions and Answers." In Owen (1995).

―――. 1995b. "Necessary and Sufficient Conditions in Tort Law." In Owen (1995).

Horwitz, Morton. 1977. *The Transformation of American Law: 1780–1860.* Cambridge, MA: Harvard University Press.

―――. 1992. *The Transformation of American Law: 1870–1960.* New York: Oxford University Press.

Hume, David. 1978 (1739–40). *A Treatise of Human Nature.* Edited by P.H. Nidditch. 2nd ed. New York: Oxford University Press.

―――. 1983 (1777). *An Enquiry concerning the Principles of Morals.* Edited by J.B. Schneewind. Indianapolis: Hackett Publishing.

Hurley, Susan. 1988. *Natural Reasons.* New York: Oxford University Press.

Husak, Douglas. 1987. *Philosophy of Criminal Law.* Totowa, NJ: Rowman & Littlefields.

Irving, David. 1971. *The Destruction of Dresden.* Rev. ed. London: Corgi Books.

Jackson, Frank. 1987. "Group Morality." In *Metaphysics and Morality: Essays in Honour of J.J.C. Smart.* Edited by Philip Pettit, et al. London: Oxford University Press.

James, Susan. 1984. *The Content of Social Explanation.* Cambridge: Cambridge University Press.

Jaspers, Karl. 1947. *The Question of German Guilt.* Translated by E.B. Ashton. New York: The Dial Press.

Johnson, Phillip. 1961. "The Unnecessary Crime of Conspiracy." *California Law Review* 61: 1137–88.

Kadish, Sanford H. 1985. "Complicity, Cause, and Blame: A Study in Doctrine." *California Law Review* 73: 323–410.

———. 1997. "Reckless Complicity." Journal of Criminal Law and Criminology 87: 369–94.

Kadish, Sanford H. and Schulhofer, Stephen. 1989. *Criminal Law and its Processes.* 5th ed. Boston: Little, Brown.

Kant, Immanuel. 1949 (1797). "On a Supposed Right to Lie From Altruistic Motives." In *Critique of Practical Reason and Other Writings in Moral Philosophy.* Edited by L. W. Beck. Chicago: University of Chicago Press.

———. 1964 (1785). *Groundwork of the Metaphysic of Morals.* Translated by H.J. Paton. New York: Harper Torchbacks.

Kelman, Herbert C. and V. Lee Hamilton. 1989. *Crimes of Obedience: Toward a Social Psychology of Authority and Responsibility.* New Haven: Yale University Press.

Kitcher, Philip. 1989. "Explanatory Unification and the Causal Structure of the World." In *Scientific Explanation.* Edited by Philip Kitcher and Wesley Salmon. Minneapolis: University of Minnesota Press.

Korsgaard, Christine. 1996a. *The Sources of Normativity.* Cambridge: Cambridge University Press.

———. 1996b. "Kant's Formula of Universal Law." In *Creating the Kingdom of Ends.* Cambridge: Cambridge University Press.

———. 1996c. "The Right to Lie: Kant on Dealing with Evil." In *Creating the Kingdom of Ends.*

———. 1996d. "Creating the Kingdom of Ends: Reciprocity and Responsibility in Personal Relations." In *Creating the Kingdom of Ends.*

———. 1996e. "The Reasons We Can Share: An Attack on the Distinction between Agent-Relative and Agent-Neutral Values." In *Creating the Kingdom of Ends.*

Kraakman, Reinier H. 1984. "Corporate Liability Strategies and the Costs of Legal Controls." *Yale Law Journal* 93: 857–98.

Kutz, Christopher L. 1994. Note, "Just Disagreement: Indeterminacy and Rationality in the Rule of Law." *Yale Law Journal* 103: 997–1030.

Lael, Richard L. 1982. *The Yamashita Precedent: War Crimes and Command Responsibility.* Wilmington: Scholarly Resources.

Lafave, Wayne R. and Austin W. Scott, Jr. 1986. *Criminal Law.* 2nd. ed. Minneapolis: West Publishing.

Lear, Jonathan. 1990. *Love and Its Place in Nature.* New York: Farrar, Straus & Giroux.

Leebron, David W. 1991. "Limited Liability, Tort Victims, and Creditors." *Columbia Law Review* 91: 1565–1650.

Levi, Primo. 1988. *The Drowned and the Saved.* Translated by Raymond Rosenthal. New York: Simon and Schuster.

Levine, Alan J. 1992. *The Strategic Bombing of Germany, 1940–1945.* Westport, CT.: Praeger.

Lewis, David. 1968. *Convention.* Cambridge, MA: Harvard University Press.

———. 1983. "An Argument for the Identity Theory." In *Philosophical Papers: Volume I.* New York: Oxford University Press.

————. 1986. Causation and Appendix. In *Philosophical Papers: Volume II.* New York: Oxford University Press.

Lewis, H.D. 1991. "Collective Responsibility A Critique." In May and Hoffman (1991).

Lind, E. Allan and Tom R. Tyler. 1988. *The Social Psychology of Procedural Justice.* New York: Plenum Press.

Lyons, David. 1965. *Forms and Limits of Utilitarianism.* New York: Oxford University Press.

Mackie, J.L. 1974. *The Cement of the Universe.* New York: Oxford University Press.

————. 1977a. *Ethics: Inventing Right and Wrong.* London: Penguin Books.

————. 1977b. "The Grounds of Responsibility." In *Law, Morality, and Society.* Edited by P.M.S. Hacker and J. Raz. Oxford: Oxford University Press.

March, James G. and Herbert A. Simon. 1993. *Organizations.* With the collaboration of Howard Guetzkow. Cambridge, MA: Blackwell.

Markusen, Eric and David Kopf. 1995. *The Holocaust and Strategic Bombing: Genocide and Total War in the Twentieth Century.* Boulder: Westview Press.

Marrus, Michael R. and Robert O. Paxton. 1981. *Vichy France and the Jews.* New York: Basic Books.

Marx, Karl and Friedrich Engels. 1978. "On the Jewish Question." In *A Marx-Engels Reader.* Edited and translated by Robert C. Tucker. New York: Norton.

May, Larry. 1987. *The Morality of Groups.* Notre Dame: University of Notre Dame Press.

May, Larry and Stacey Hoffman, eds. 1991. *Collective Responsibility.* Savage, MD: Rowman and Littlefield.

McKee, Alexander. 1982. *Dresden 1945: The Devil's Tinderbox.* London: Souvenir Press.

Melville, Herman. 1969 (1924). *Billy Budd, Sailor.* In *Great Short Works of Herman Melville.* Edited by Warner Berthoff. New York: Harper & Row.

Middlebrook, Martin. 1980. *The Battle of Hamburg.* New York: Charles Scribner's Sons.

Milgram, Stanley. 1974. *Obedience to Authority.* New York: Harper & Row.

Mill, John Stuart. 1979 (1861). *Utilitarianism.* Edited by George Sher. Indianapolis: Hackett Publishing.

Mintzberg, Henry. 1979. *The Structuring of Organizations.* Englewood Cliffs, NJ: Prentice-Hall.

Moore, Michael S. 1993. *Act and Crime: The Philosophy of Action and its Implications for Criminal Law.* New York: Oxford University Press.

————. 1994. "The Independent Moral Significance of Wrongdoing." *Journal of Contemporary Legal Issues:* 237–81.

Morris, Herbert. 1987. "Nonmoral Guilt." In Schoeman (1987).

————. 1976. "Persons and Punishment." In *On Guilt and Innocence.* Berkeley: University of California Press.

# Bibliography

Murphy, Jeffrie and Jean Hampton. 1988. *Forgiveness and Mercy.* Cambridge: Cambridge University Press.

Nagel, Thomas. 1979. "Moral Luck." In *Mortal Questions.* Cambridge: Cambridge University Press.

———. 1986. *The View from Nowhere.* New York: Oxford University Press.

Nietzsche, Friedrich. 1967 (1887). *On the Genealogy of Morals.* Translated by Walter Kaufmann and R.J. Hollingdale. In *On the Genealogy of Morals* and *Ecce Homo.* Edited by Kaufmann. New York: Vintage Books.

Noddings, Nell. 1984. *Caring.* Berkeley: University of California Press.

Note. 1979. "Developments in the Law – Criminal Conspiracy." *Harvard Law Review* 72: 920–1008.

Note. 1999. "Corporate Criminal Law." *American Criminal Law Review* 36: 445–76.

Nozick, Robert. 1974. *Anarchy, State, and Utopia.* New York: Basic Books.

———. 1981. *Philosophical Explanations.* Cambridge, MA: Harvard University Press.

———. 1993. *The Nature of Rationality.* Princeton: Princeton University Press.

O'Brien, Tim. 1994. *In the Lake of the Woods.* New York: Houghton Mifflin.

Olson, Mancur, Jr. 1965. *The Logic of Collective Action.* Cambridge, MA: Harvard University Press.

O'Neill (Nell), Onora. 1975. *Acting on Principle.* New York: Columbia University Press.

O'Neill, Onora. 1990. "Consistency in Action." In *Constructions of Reason.* New York: Cambridge University Press.

Otsuka, Michael. 1991. "The Paradox of Group Beneficence." *Philosophy and Public Affairs* 20: 132–49.

Owen, David G., ed. 1995. *Philosophical Foundations of Tort Law.* New York: Oxford University Press.

Parfit, Derek. 1984. *Reasons and Persons.* New York: Oxford University Press.

———. 1986. "Comments." *Ethics* 96: 832–72.

———. 1988. "What We Together Do." Photocopy. Oxford University.

Pennock, J. Roland and John W. Chapman, eds. 1985. *Nomos 27: Criminal Justice.* New York: New York University Press.

Perry, Stephen. Forthcoming 2000. "Responsibility for Outcomes, Risk, and the Law of Torts." In *Philosophy and U.S. Tort Law.* Edited by G. Postema. Cambridge: Cambridge University Press.

Polinsky, A. Mitchell and Steven Shavell. 1998. "Punitive Damages: An Economic Analysis." *Harvard Law Review* 111: 869–962.

Posner, Richard. 1972. "A Theory of Negligence." *Journal of Legal Studies* 1: 29–96.

———. 1987. "From Billy Budd to Buchenwald." *Yale Law Journal* 96: 1173–89.

Postema, Gerald. 1995. "Morality in the First Person Plural." *Law and Philosophy* 14: 35–64.

# Bibliography

Prosser, William and W. Page Keeton. 1984. *The Law of Torts.* 6th ed. St. Paul: West Publishing.

Railton, Peter. 1988. "Alienation, Consequentialism, and the Demands of Morality." In Scheffler (1988).

Rakowski, Eric. 1991. *Equal Justice.* New York: Oxford University Press.

Rawls, John. 1989. "Themes in Kant's Moral Philosophy." In *Kant's Transcendental Deductions.* Edited by Eckart Förster. Stanford: Stanford University Press.

Rawls, John. 1999. "Fifty Years after Hiroshima." In *Collected Papers.* Edited by S. Freeman. Cambridge, MA: Harvard University Press.

Raz, Joseph. 1986. *The Morality of Freedom.* New York: Oxford University Press.

Regan, Donald. 1980. *Utilitarianism and Cooperation.* New York: Oxford University Press.

Ripstein, Arthur. 1998. *Equality, Responsibility, and the Law.* Cambridge: Cambridge University Press.

Riskin, Carl. 1973. "Maoism and Motivation: Work Incentives in China." In *China's Uninterrupted Revolution from 1840 to the Present.* Edited by V.N.J. Peck. New York: Pantheon.

Roe, Mark. 1984. "Bankruptcy and Mass Tort." *Columbia Law Journal* 84: 846–922.

———. 1994. *Strong Managers, Weak Owners.* Princeton: Princeton University Press.

Sayre, Francis B. 1930. "Criminal Responsibility for the Acts of Another." *Harvard Law Review* 43: 689–723.

Scanlon, T.M. 1982. "Contractualism and Utilitarianism." In *Utilitarianism and Beyond.* Edited by Bernard Williams and Amartya Sen. New York: Cambridge University Press.

———. 1988. "The Significance of Choice." In *The Tanner Lectures in Human Values.* Cambridge: Cambridge University Press.

———. 1990. "Promises and Practices." *Philosophy and Public Affairs* 19: 199–226.

Schama, Simon. 1989. *Citizens: A Chronicle of the French Revolution.* New York: Knopf.

Scheffler, Samuel, ed. 1988. *Consequentialism and its Critics.* New York: Oxford University Press.

———. 1992. *Human Morality.* New York: Oxford University Press.

———. 1995. "Individual Responsibility in a Global Age." *Social Philosophy and Policy* 12: 219–36.

———. 1997. "Relationships and Responsibilities." *Philosophy and Public Affairs* 26: 189–220.

Schelling, Thomas C. 1978. "Hockey Helmets, Daylight Savings, and Other Binary Choices." In *Micromotives and Macrobehavior.* New York: W.W. Norton.

———. 1960/1980. *The Strategy of Conflict.* Cambridge, MA: Harvard University Press.

Schiffer, Stephen. 1972. *Meaning.* New York: Oxford University Press.

Schlink, Bernhard. 1999. *The Reader.* Translated by Carol Brown Janeway. New York: Random House.

Schoeman, Ferndinand, ed. 1987. *Responsibility, Character, and the Emotions.* Cambridge: Cambridge University Press.

Schuck, Peter H. 1987. *Agent Orange on Trial.* Rev. ed. Cambridge, MA: Harvard University Press.

Searle, John. 1983. *Intentionality.* Cambridge: Cambridge University Press.

———. 1990. "Collective Intentions and Actions." In *Intentions in Communication.* Edited by Philip R. Cohen, Jerry Morgan, and Martha E. Pollack. Cambridge, MA: MIT Press.

Seavey, Warren. 1949a. "The Rationale of the Law of Agency." In *Studies in Agency.* St. Paul; West Publishing.

———. 1949b. "Speculations as to 'Respondeat Superior.'" In *Studies in Agency.*

———. 1964. *Handbook of the Law of Agency.* St. Paul: West Publishing.

Sen, Amartya K. 1974. "Choice, Orderings, and Morality." In *Practical Reason.* Edited by Stephan Körner. New Haven: Yale University Press.

———. 1978. "Rational Fools: A Critique of the Behavioral Foundations of Economic Theory." *Philosophy and Public Affairs* 7: 317–44.

———. 1988. "Rights and Agency." In Scheffler (1988).

Shakespeare, William. 1984 (1622). *Othello.* Cambridge: Cambridge University Press.

Sher, George. 1987. *Desert.* Princeton: Princeton University Press.

Sherry, Michael. 1987. *The Rise of American Air Power: The Creation of Armageddon.* New Haven: Yale University Press.

Sidgwick, Henry. 1981 (1874). *Methods of Ethics.* Indianapolis: Hackett Publishing.

Simon, Herbert. 1976. *Administrative Behavior.* 3rd ed. New York: The Free Press.

Simmons, A. John. 1979. *Moral Principles and Political Obligations.* Princeton: Princeton University Press.

Smart, J.J.C. 1973. "An Outline of a System of Utilitarian Ethics." In *Utilitarianism For and Against.* Edited by J.J.C. Smart and Bernard Williams. Cambridge: Cambridge University Press.

Smith, J.C. 1991. "Comment." *Criminal Law Review:* 134–35.

Smith, J.C. and Brian Hogan. 1988. *Criminal Law.* 6th ed. London: Butterworths.

Sober, Elliott and David Sloan Wilson. 1998. *Unto Others: The Evolution and Psychology of Unselfish Behavior.* Cambridge, MA: Harvard University Press.

Sperber, Dan and Dierdre Wilson. 1986. *Relevance.* Cambridge, MA: Harvard University Press.

# Bibliography

Spinoza, Baruch. 1982. *The Ethics and Selected Letters.* Translated by Seymour Feldman and edited by Samuel Shirley. Indianapolis: Hackett Publishing.

Sreenivasan, Gopal. 1998. "Interpretation and Reason." *Philosophy & Public Affairs* 27: 142–71.

Stephen, Sir James Fitzjames. 1883. *A History of the Criminal Law of England.* London: MacMillan and Co.

Stone, Christopher D. "A Comment on Criminal Responsibility in Government." In Pennock and Chapman (1985).

Strawson, Peter. 1982. "Freedom and Resentment." In *Free Will.* Edited by Gary Watson. New York: Oxford University Press.

Sugden, Robert. 1993. "Thinking as a Team: Towards an Explanation of Non-Selfish Behavior." *Social Philosophy & Policy* 10: 69–89.

Taylor, Charles. 1982. "Responsibility for Self." In *Free Will.* Edited by Watson.

———. 1989. *Sources of the Self.* Cambridge, MA: Harvard University Press.

Taylor, Gabriele. 1985. *Pride, Shame, and Guilt.* New York: Oxford University Press.

Taylor, Michael. 1987. *The Possibility of Cooperation.* Cambridge: Cambridge University Press.

Thompson, Dennis. "Criminal Responsibility in Government." In Pennock and Chapman (1985).

Thomson, Judith Jarvis. 1986. "Imposing Risks." In *Rights, Restitution, and Risk : Essays in Moral Theory.* Edited by William Parent. Cambridge, MA: Harvard University Press.

———. 1990. *The Realm of Rights.* Cambridge, MA: Harvard University Press.

Tuomela, Raimo. 1984. *A Theory of Social Action.* Dordrecht: D. Reidel Publishers.

———. 1993. "What is Cooperation?" *Erkenntnis* 38: 87–101.

———. *The Importance of Us.* Stanford: Stanford Unviversity Press, 1995.

Tuomela, Raimo and Kaarlo Miller. 1991. "We-Intentions." *Philosophical Studies* 53: 115–37.

van Fraassen, Bas. 1980. *The Scientific Image.* New York: Oxford University Press.

Velleman, J. David. 1997. "How to Share an Intention." *Philosophy and Phenomenological Research* 57: 29–52.

Vermazen, Bruce. 1993. "Objects of Intention." *Philosophical Studies* 71: 223–65.

Waldron, Jeremy. 1992. "Aggregative harms." Photocopy. University of California at Berkeley, CA.

———. 1995. "Moments of Carelessness and Massive Loss." In Owen (1995).

Walzer, Michael. 1974. "World War II: Why Was This War Different?" In *War and Moral Responsibility.* Edited by M. Cohen, et al. Princeton, NJ: Princeton University Press.

———. 1993. *Interpretation and Social Criticism.* Cambridge, MA: Harvard University Press.

Watson, Gary, ed. 1982. *Free Will.* New York: Oxford University Press.

Weisberg, Richard. 1984. *The Failure of the Word.* New Haven: Yale University Press.

Wiggins, David. 1991. "Truth, and Truth as Predicated of Moral Judgments." In *Needs, Values, Truth.* Rev. ed. Cambridge, MA: Basil Blackwell.

Williams, Bernard. 1973. "Critique of Utiltiarianism." In *Utilitarianism For and Against.* Edited by J.J.C. Smart and Bernard Williams. Cambridge: Cambridge University Press.

———. 1981a. "Moral Luck." In *Moral Luck.* Cambridge: Cambridge University Press.

———. 1981b. "Utilitarianism and Moral Self-Indulgence." In *Moral Luck.*

———. 1981c. "The Truth in Relativism." In *Moral Luck.*

———. 1993. *Shame and Necessity.* Berkeley: University of California Press.

———. 1994. "The *Actus Reus* of Dr. Caligari." *University of Pennsylvania Law Review* 142: 1661–673.

———. 1995a. "Nietzsche's Minimalist Moral Psychology." In *Making Sense of Humanity.* Cambridge: Cambridge University Press.

———. 1995b. "Formal Structures and Social Reality." In *Making Sense of Humanity.*

———. 1995c. "Formal and Substantial Individualism." In *Making Sense of Humanity.*

Williams, Glanville. 1961. *Criminal Law: The General Part.* 2nd ed. London: Stevens and Sons.

Williamson, Oliver. 1981. "The Modern Corporation: Origins, Evolutions, Attributes." *Journal of Economic Literature* 19: 1537–68.

Winch, Peter. 1965. "The Universalizability of Moral Judgment." *Monist* 49: 196–214.

Wolf, Susan. 1985. "The Legal and Moral Responsibility of Organizations." In Pennock and Chapman (1985).

Wolgast, Elizabeth. 1992. *Ethics of an Artificial Person.* Stanford: Stanford University Press.

Zinn, Howard. 1990. "Hiroshima and Royan." In *The Politics of History.* 2nd ed. Chicago: University of Illinois.

# Index

325